Rise, Fall, and Revitalization of Corporate America

Rise, Fall, and Revitalization of Corporate America

EMIGDIO J. **SALMON**

Printed in New York by:

OMNIBOOK CO.
99 Wall Street, Suite 118
New York, NY 10005
USA
+1-866-216-9965
www.omnibookcompany.com

First Edition

For e-book purchase: Kindle on Amazon, Barnes and Noble
Book purchase: Amazon.com, Barnes & Noble, and
www.omnibookcompany.com

Omnibook titles may be purchased in bulk for educational, business, fund-raising, or sales promotional use. For more information please e-mail
info@omnibookcompany.com

Cover design by: Gian Carlo Tan

To my wife Mayda; Jeanette, her husband Wes,
and granddaughters Jessica, Bridget, and Whitney;
and Elaine, husband Ernie, grandson Elijah
and granddaughter Emmie.

TABLE OF CONTENTS

PREFACE

I migrated to the United States from Cuba in 1961, shortly after Fidel Castro's communist regime confiscated all of my parents' properties. My sister and I travelled together, and my parents remained in Cuba. Both of us were teenagers at the time we came to this country, and neither one of us was able to speak, write, or communicate in the English language. We had relatives in Connecticut, and we went to live with them a couple of days after our arrival in Miami, Florida. We both soon discovered that we had to learn a new language. That was an essential first step in order to communicate and continue our high-school education. We arrived here in this country without a penny in our pockets, but with a great deal of motivation to succeed.

The road to success was a long and, at times, arduous and frustrating journey. Nevertheless, we persisted on our journey and struggled to overcome many difficulties that appeared as obstacles thrown in our path to cause discouragement. But, we would not be discouraged. We knew that overcoming those obstacles would make us stronger. We would be better equipped to deal with many more obstacles that destiny would throw on our path. We both faced adversity and overcame it in spite of strong odds against us. We both realized, at that point, that if we were able to reach our goals, then anyone else would also be able to follow the same path in their journey to attainment of their individual goals.

We both knew that our parents placed a great deal of importance on education. My father used to tell both of us: "Money comes and goes, but the knowledge you have in your brains stays with you forever; nobody will be able to take that from you. And, that knowledge will be the means you will use to earn a living anyplace in the world."

That was great advice, for I was able to earn a living in many parts of the world using my engineering background. In fact, I recalled my father's advice many times while working and living in the Middle East. I realized then that my father had been correct all along.

I gave the same advice to young engineers I was mentoring, but I would paraphrase my father's advice to make it even more relevant and meaningful to them. I would urge them to look at the way Bedouins navigated their way through the desert, knowing exactly where they were going and where to find drinking water along the way. Would the young engineers be able to do the same without the assistance of a Global Positioning System (GPS)? I would remind them that, regardless of their riches, they would get lost and die of thirst unless they were able to navigate their way in the desert and find water. Money would not buy them a bottle of water, but knowledge and a sense of direction would guide them to a source of water. That was how Bedouins survived in the desert. Similarly, knowledge that the engineers acquired and stored in their minds would enable them to earn an honest living and keep them alive no matter what.

Sense of direction is something Bedouins develop early in their lives and continue to improve the longer they use it. It is an internal compass that is fixed in their minds and no one can take away from them. That sense of direction enables Bedouins to navigate their way through the desert without the aid of a high power GPS device. It allows them to find water to survive in much the same way their ancestors did centuries ago. It is impossible to buy a bottle of water in the desert regardless of the amount of money in your pockets or in your savings account. A sense of direction and knowledge, however, can take you to an oasis where there is plenty of clean cool water to drink. My father's advice has become relevant not only to me but also to my younger professional associates.

My parents' advice to my sister and me proved valuable to both of us. We, in turn, gave the same advice to our children hoping that they would see fit to pass it on to their children. Our children, too, heeded the wisdom behind my father's advice on the importance of getting an education. They went on to college to pursue careers in medical fields, engineering, and business. We are happy to say that our parents' advice proved as successful for our children as it had for us. Based on that positive experience, I would recommend that parents give the same advice to their children.

I came to the US and overcame many disadvantages. The most important one was the inability to express myself in the English language. I knew that I needed to learn English to be able to graduate from high school and attend a university in order to pursue a major in chemical engineering. I did not have access to scholarships, because, at the time, most scholarships were given to US nationals, and I was not a US citizen. Later in my professional career, I decided to get a law degree to broaden and complement my engineering background. My situation had changed by that time. I had a family and could not afford to quit my job and enroll full time in law school. Therefore, I attended law school after work, four nights a week, for four and a half years in order to get my law degree. There were many obstacles along the way, but I achieved my goals.

We were born in a town located in the farthest province from Havana. There were public and private schools available in the town of our birth, but our parents decided that we should attend boarding schools in Havana to get a better education. This, they believed, was essential to prepare us for our life journeys. This demonstrated our parents' commitment to and reliance on education as the proper means to earn a living. That decision meant that we would have to learn to survive without our parents' daily guidance, and that skill served us well after our migration to this country. Each of the obstacles we overcame taught us a valuable lesson and made us stronger in order to surpass the next barrier.

My sister and I had many options available to us, but we both made our choices based on strong moral principles taught to us by both of our parents from a very early age. We had the choice of

3

selecting the easy path, but we stood firm on our goals of getting an education. Along the way, we both met many dedicated teachers who helped us a great deal because they realized that we both were swimming against the current and needed encouragement and help to continue. We both graduated from high school, and both continued to further our educational objectives. My sister became a nurse, and I realized my dream of becoming an engineer.

I knew adversity and how to defeat it. I overcame many problems in learning a completely new language, adapting to a new culture, making new friends, and financing my own educational expenses. I had to pay for my college education from my own limited financial resources. Based on immigration status as a "Cuban Political Refugee," I was ineligible to apply or get many scholarships. I could prove financial need and limited financial resources, but I could not do anything about my immigration status. Not all doors were closed, for I was able to get an educational loan, which I promptly repaid after graduation.

If I had overcome all of those obstacles, then anyone born in this country should be able to do the same and do it easier. All that was required was hard work and strong moral principles to do the right thing regardless of outcome. I was able to achieve my goals, and I knew then that I was not the only one capable of doing that. I knew others would also be able to do the same, particularly in this great nation, which offered so many opportunities to make your dreams reality.

I had migrated from a communist country, where freedoms were limited, to a country where freedom was of paramount importance. The system of government was also different. Under communism, people were unable to show initiative; the government told you what you could and could not do. In this country, initiative was valued as the engine driving change and development and providing the means to financial success.

I witnessed political corruption and abuse of power under a dictatorship. I also experienced the detrimental consequences of political corruption leading to the overthrow of a dictatorship and imposition of a communist regime. The ultimate consequence of that level of corruption was the establishment in my home country—Cuba—of the first communist country in the western hemisphere and the confiscation, without payment, of my parents' property. I detested corruption and politics because all they did was to cause harm. In my native country, very few politicians were honest; most of them were corrupt. In this country, however, there were cases of political corruption, but the level of corruption was much lower than in my native country. Corruption ended up in disastrous consequences for all Cubans, and now I am concerned about corruption doing the same here in the US.

I admired the electoral process in this country for it seemed to function in a very orderly and legal fashion; however, that did not mean there was no political corruption in the United States. Corruption in this country was at a much lower level than it was in my own country where most politicians were openly stealing from the national treasure. Here I could see a new president elected and the orderly transfer of power from the incumbent over to the newly elected president. There was no fear of a coup d'état; the US never experienced a situation where an elected president was deposed. We had experienced that in Cuba many times, and that always led to the suspension of individual liberties.

I also was able to compare the system of government prevailing in this country against two very different types of government that I had lived under in Cuba: a corrupt dictatorship and a communist government. The corrupt government regime allowed ownership of private property and allowed you to function in a semi-free atmosphere so long as you did not disagree with the government. The communist regime, on the other hand, confiscated your property and threw you in jail if it thought you were against it or dislike you. Both of these governments were bad. Based on those comparisons and what I experienced in the US, I concluded that there was not better government system than the one in the United States. I embraced that system completely, and I have never regretted that decision.

INTRODUCTION

I have, since leaving Cuba, been able to visit many communist countries and to view how communist systems operate. I visited Russia shortly after Boris Yeltsin took power; my observations at the time verified the correctness of my initial opinion of communism: it is an unworkable ideology.

Communist regimes, regardless of location, are based on envy, class division, hatred, and false promises. It is their primary strategy to cause division among the citizenry on the basis of wealth. The government promises to take from the rich and give to the poor; that is a very good sounding slogan to attract people who are basically worthless and envious of those who have worked hard to amass a fortune. Once the communist regime gets the support of those worthless individuals, it goes ahead and takes from the rich and gives nothing to the poor. In fact, in many cases it forces the poor into slavery, and if they prove to be unproductive, then they are promptly sent to prison to be re-educated.

When I hear US politicians advocating the same ideas that I have seen fail in Cuba, I become very concerned about the future of our country for several reasons. Number one, I have never seen a government give anything without attaching strings except, perhaps, in the recent bailout of financial institutions. I am not aware of any case where a government has created a new industry to create jobs. And, I have not seen the government reduce dependence on welfare to break the cycle of poverty. Politicians advocating class hatred and taking from the rich are the ones who are destroying the ideals articulated by our founding fathers. The rich are an essential part of our society and economic system. They invest their money to create jobs to benefit the rest of society. If you take from the rich, who among the poor is going to invest in new enterprises to generate new job opportunities? This political rhetoric attracts voters and gets politicians elected instead of sending them into retirement. That same rhetoric destroys nations.

During many business trips to communist countries, I have been able to observe communist systems at work. The population in all of those countries was always living under miserable living conditions and lacking basic necessities for their daily living. Those are the things that we take for granted here in the US. The communist system in those countries did not work and failed. So, what makes us think political rhetoric along communist lines would work here in the US? I was able to see how a system deprived its citizens of all incentives. Citizens in those countries could not show initiative. Private initiative was tantamount to risking individual freedom and the loss of life. Consequently, people were unable to make their dreams come true, which was unlike what we have practiced in our capitalist system in the US.

I had many opportunities to discuss with many scientists and engineers the scientific environment in the Soviet Union and, in particular technological developments. Without exception, I learned that these scientists and engineers were brilliant and had been able to develop many technologies similar to those available in the United States or Europe. The difference, however, was they were unable to commercialize the use of those newly developed technologies to manufacture new products to benefit society. The reluctance to implement ideas was based on the fear of failure. Failure was not tolerated and was punished severely. Communist regimes did not realize that failure in many cases normally results in doubling efforts to succeed.

In the United States, everyone has the incentive to take risks and develop anything, even if the result may lead to failure. This condition has prevailed in the United States for many years, including the early years of our nation's history. That motivation to take risks and solve problems has led this nation to new achievements, including several exploratory manned trips to the moon.

This willingness to tolerate initial failure has been illustrated by countless examples, including the case of Henry Ford's persistence that led to the founding of Ford Motor Company. Henry Ford failed many times, but he succeeded in establishing an automobile manufacturing company bearing his last name. That is the system that prevails in the United States. And, it is a system that we should encourage.

The freedom to take risk and succeed is the fundamental reason many immigrants come to our shores. They migrate to our shores to try things they are unable to do in their own countries. That freedom to take risks encourages individuals from these ethnic groups to develop and implement their ideas without reprisal. Many of these ideas deal with problems that, in the eyes of these individual entrepreneurs, could become the basis for success; in many cases, these ideas are indeed successful. That desire to develop new things and to make dreams reality is the fuel that keeps the US ahead of every other country in the world. That is the key to US success, and it should be cherished.

The motivation to succeed drives our nation to develop new technologies, new products, and new manufacturing processes, which in turn create employment opportunities and enhance our living standards. In other words, the US government, unlike communist governments, does not tell anyone what to do or how to do it; the government relies on individual initiative to take risks and either succeed or fail without repercussions. That is a very important concept to keep in mind because it is the key to the success of the United States.

There is nothing more powerful than the human mind and its power to dream. The mind is a complex supercomputer controlling all emotions and providing reasoning power to define and establish the methodology necessary to make dreams come true. But, the mind needs to be educated in order to challenge existing concepts and to develop new ideas and reasons to replace or expand prior knowledge. It is for that reason that the US cannot afford to neglect the educational system. As demonstrated in my own case, teachers have been extremely important in ensuring a supply of well-educated citizens to continue the development of our nation and to enhance our standard of living. This does not mean, however, that the entire burden of educating our children should be placed on teachers. Parents have a primary responsibility for overall education and reinforcing the concepts taught in schools to their children.

During my lifetime, I have witnessed many changes that have not always been beneficial. Some of these changes have been in the political arena and some in industrial settings. The impact of my observations on my personal development has become the primary motivation for writing this book. I have experienced transformations in the industrial world. I have seen attempts on the part of government and politicians to control industrial operations and corporate behavior. Many of those attempts have involved issuing unrealistic norms and mandates that tended to direct or take control away from industry. Some government regulatory control is necessary, but unnecessary and excessive control is detrimental. Politicians in communist countries have been unable to make the economies of their countries prosperous. How can we expect our politicians to obtain different results following similar policies?

I have learned that, in most cases, government bureaucrats are incapable of enhancing productivity and industrial development. Many people in the Soviet Union and other communist countries have told me that in their countries the government told them how to do everything and pretended to pay them for doing so. They, in turn, pretended to do it and got paid for doing nothing. That attitude leads to complete failure. That degree of government control was the leading cause of the collapse of most communist regimes.

The United States, on the other hand, has been successful by having the government play a role to facilitate economic development rather than being a controlling force. This has been clearly demonstrated by the successes achieved by our nation when the US government, industry, and people work together. Recently, however, the US government has begun to intervene excessively in economic matters, thus raising a red flag for all of us to worry about. If the system is not broken, why fix it? The US government has played very important roles in achieving our high degree of industrialization. The first role focuses on encouraging new developments leading to new products and new employment opportunities; government plays that role by funding research and development activities. The other function is that of a large consumer of goods and services that enables economic development. Those are proper and worthy functions of government. The government, however, should not dictate how industry addresses problems; that is probably the root cause leading to the collapse of communist regimes.

Bureaucrats and lawmakers in the US government have begun to abuse their power by telling industry how to address problems. Bear in mind that most of these bureaucrats are unable to solve any of these problems. A case in point is Secretary Ken Salazar threatening to take over from BP the efforts to control the Gulf Oil spill; this forced Admiral Allen to remind the secretary that the government does not know-how to solve the problem. Secretary Salazar needed to realize that the private sector knows how to solve problems and should not be impeded from doing that. Nevertheless, bureaucrats have not gotten the message. They continue to impose mandates penalizing industry and killing all incentive to improve operations.

An example of unnecessary and worthless bureaucratic activity is the mandate that petroleum refiners mix a certain amount of ethanol into gasoline. The government also forces refiners to use ethanol produced from corn even though this is not economical; the government has to subsidize this production. The government does that to reward special interests contributing to politicians through their lobbying efforts. It is a bad idea because it is not an economically sound decision; it reduces the amount of corn causing a general increase in the price of corn destined for human and animal food consumption. Furthermore, this increases the price of meat products including pork, poultry, and beef. On top of that, it forces refiners to reduce capacity leading to potential job losses. The government loses tax revenues. Who wins?

There are other examples leading to the conclusion that elected officials are abusing their power by mandating these worthless activities to satisfy their own financial interest. They do that by accepting bribes from special interest groups such as the corn lobbying group even though they are doing that at the expense of the interest of the majority of constituents.

I have also witnessed abuse of corporate and political power leading to the destruction of the American dream of many of our citizens. Citizens lose their jobs and homes while executives enjoy huge bonuses. There is nothing wrong with executives getting a bonus if it is well deserved. What is wrong is to use taxpayers' funds to bail out failed financial institutions and then reward those inept executives with bonuses at taxpayers' expense. These are the actions on the part of executives and political officials leading to the destruction of our economic system, our nation, and our American dreams.

I decided to undertake a historical analysis to learn the factors leading to the establishment of Corporate America and its influence on the economic growth of the nation. This includes determining the process credited for transforming the US economy from its agricultural roots to an industrial basis unequaled in history. That transformation has elevated the United States to preeminence among the industrial nations in the world. In doing so, that transformation has achieved the highest standard of living in the world for our population.

Obviously, this industrial development is the result of bringing together many factors. These include the roles played by labor, entrepreneurs, and managers in the establishment of individual companies that in the aggregate become Corporate America. This also includes the effect of industry and people on the US government. Labor, industry, and government play individual roles that are the foundation for the development and growth of Corporate America. The private industrial sector is the result of cooperative efforts by all of these parties. However, the action of a single party can have profound impacts on the continuing viability of our entire corporate sector. In fact, these actions may lead to the destruction of an enterprise within the realm of Corporate America as we know it today. For instance, take a look at the case of General Motors filing bankruptcy as a result of poor management decisions. That is a detrimental result not only for its employees, but also for the communities where they live and for the entire nation.

This historical analysis starts with a detailed investigation tracing the sources of entrepreneurs and managers as well as workers for our industrial sector. Immigration is the main source of manpower. The United States initially focused on agriculture. The emphasis on agriculture continued from the settlement of the thirteen original colonies up to the mid-1800s. Then, there was a fundamental shift in the pattern that was followed by further development of the country from that point on. The Industrial Revolution began to gain ground in England and in other Europeans countries. Europeans migrated to this country, bringing with them ideas for developing new industries similar to those flourishing in Europe at the time. These are the original entrepreneurs who took advantage of opportunities in the US to make their dreams come true. That same motivation is still present in the minds of modern-day immigrants.

The size of the US presented many challenges to new immigrants. These were opportunities waiting to be exploited. It was a brand-new country located far from what, at that time, was civilization. It was a country with a small population, living under very rugged conditions. It was a country where people had to be nearly self-sufficient as possible. But, all of those obstacles were nothing more than opportunities waiting to be satisfied. In other words, the foundation was there for developing a thriving economy. And, so it was to be. That was a clear demonstration that immigrants saw the glass half full and did their best to fill it with their successes.

The large land mass presented the opportunity to grow many

different crops for food, clothing, and shelter. It also provided the means to cultivate and produce these crops not only to satisfy the needs of an immediate nuclear family, but potentially to sell or exchange with others, thus establishing a primitive market economy. The next step was the expansion of the market from the local arena to one crossing international boundaries. But, to be able to achieve that, it became necessary to develop more efficient and productive means of cultivating and harvesting crops.

Yes, indeed.

The land was there and so were the markets for agricultural products. Necessity became the mother of invention, prompting Americans to develop new implements and tools. These new tools made farming more efficient and enabled cultivation of larger land areas to produce larger quantities to supply growing markets. The larger land mass was both a blessing and a curse. It was a blessing in providing sufficient arable land to not only satisfy local demand but to export to other countries. It was a curse in that long distances were a fact of life in transporting these crops. Those new obstacles were opportunities waiting for new solutions.

Machinery had to be designed specifically to solve problems faced by farmers. Once these mechanical devices became available, then another door opened to address other recurring problems that, once again, were opportunities in disguise. New agricultural equipment made farming easier and more productive, and it had a snowball effect on other activities. For instance, larger quantities of cotton could be cultivated and made available for conversion to fabrics; this, in turn required new machinery to sew the fabrics into clothing. The US became a gold mine attracting entrepreneurs from all over the world. These entrepreneurs were attracted by the opportunity to solve problems faced by the majority of the population. They solved those problems, and they marketed those practical solutions, thus planting the seeds for additional consumer demand. This was the basis for starting an industrial revolution in the United States. It was also the foundation for the creation of wealth by entrepreneurs. The side effect of that was creation of job opportunities for many citizens.

As new industries were established by European and native-born Americans entrepreneurs, new opportunities were identified that led to further industrial growth. These new opportunities become the fuel for increasing the standard of living of the general population. Automobile production is an example depicting the snowball effect manufacturing of one product has on other sectors. These workers were not only able to purchase automobiles creating a demand for better roads, hotels, restaurants, gasoline stations; they were also able to buy many other things to make their lives more comfortable. In short, manufacturing bloomed and positively impacted other sectors of the economy to create additional jobs. As manufacturing grew so did the demand for workers, and that demand could only be satisfied by allowing more immigrants to come to our shores. Fortunately, the US had an open immigration policy that welcomed immigrants from many southern and eastern European countries.

The US government's policy at the time was not to interfere with business. That was not surprising in view of the fact our founding fathers had a desire to create a country in which government would have minimum intervention into the business activity of the population. The founding fathers saw the role of the central government as one essentially to provide solutions to common problems such as defense, intrastate as well as international commerce, and protection of individual liberty and property. These were principles our founding fathers truly believed in and embodied in the US Constitution. In other words, our founding fathers did not want the government involved in their daily business activities, but rather they wanted the government to focus on activities required to protect the orderly conduct of business.

The wisdom of our founding fathers has created a nation that values personal business initiate and freedom to make their dreams come true. This system of government has served us well for over two hundred years and has made our nation the best place in the world to establish a business enterprise. That is so because citizens are in the best position to determine what to do, when to do it, and how to do it. That does not mean, however, that we have the right to harm others or the environment we live in. Our forefathers believe the proper role of government is to ensure all citizens are able to exercise their freedoms without interference or injury.

Compare the government role envisioned in our constitution to that practiced in communist countries. In our country, the government has a hands-off attitude, thus allowing individual citizens to do their thing so long as the rights of others are not interfered with. In communist countries, however, the government tells the citizens how to do everything, thus depriving citizens of the right to exercise individual initiative and undertake risks to make their dreams reality. Denial of individual initiative destroys individual motive to come up with solutions to problems to existing problems and to establish industries based on the implementation of those individual ideas. In many cases, manufacturing is the tool needed to achieve full implementation of the initial idea. Private individual initiative is the secret and driving force making the US the great economic success and preeminent industrial powerhouse it is. Communist regimes, on the other hand, have fallen like houses of cards by failing to cherish individual initiative.

A personal story might be useful in conveying the meaning of what I'm trying to say. I have travelled to make communist countries before and after the fall of the Iron Curtain. In my capacity as an engineer selling chemical manufacturing and oil processing technologies, I have witnessed situations where the technology I'm trying to sell is inferior or very similar to existing technologies. And, so the question I ask, why are you looking at my technology as opposed to your technology. The answer is always the same. Your technology works and it is proven and ours is not commercially proven. I continue to question what prevents them from proving their technology. The answer I get is that the process they follow to prove their technology accepts no failure meaning that if the technology does not work then the ones pushing for commercialization are sent to Siberia. They definitely do not want to go to Siberia. In short the story tells a very important thing and that is that you are not rewarded for taking personal initiative or risks. Contrary to that, in the US we believe in getting rewarded for positive personal initiative results and failures is merely a way of saying try again and do better next time. The story reinforces the reason why the US is the economic powerhouse it is. It is concerning to hear inept politicians encouraging adapting communist to the US economic system. It is also surprising to hear many politicians opine that there is no room for manufacturing activities in the US. How wrong can these individuals, who have never done anything, be?

The US system of government holds my admiration because I have witnessed the devastation resulting from implementation of communist ideology in all the communist countries I have visited, including in my own country of birth – Cuba. I have seen people in these communist countries reach out for the liberty that we hold so dear in the US only to be incarcerated because they are deemed threats to the state. I have seen and felt the disdain citizens of communist countries have for their government. A case in point is the situation I witnessed in Moscow when I saw a convoy of soviet army trucks carrying young soldiers and I noticed a Red Star painted on the door of one of the trucks covered with a "Marlboro Country" sticker. Given the adverse health impact of smoking, I have interpreted the message from that act to mean those young soldiers would prefer to die for a Marlboro rather than the Red Star oppressing them. Unfortunately, they would be unable to convey that message directly to their superiors because they would be promptly sent to Siberia. In the US, the Second Amendment to our Constitution would be a deterrent preventing government from depriving us of Freedom of Expression.

Developments in the early formative period of our American Industrial Revolution completely transformed our country. It was a time when mass manufacturing began to develop from its infancy. It progressed through the 1920s and culminated in a period of great prosperity for the population. It was then followed by one of the largest economic crisis of all times spreading throughout the world and causing unimaginable suffering. That economic crisis ended the period of prosperity, and it was followed by a period of austerity and misery known as the Great Depression.

The fundamental causes of that economic crisis were corruption and uncontrolled greed. It was a difficult period, resulting in the loss of jobs, and yet no government, business entity or person was able to provide a workable solution. Many businesses failed or were forced to go into bankruptcy. Consequently, the rate of unemployment reached a maximum level of approximately 25 percent. The government became concerned with this situation because of the potential for civil unrest and overtones of political and social upheaval. It was a situation that had no end in sight. The US government started spending on infrastructure projects with the dual expectations of creating jobs and improving the country's infrastructure. That program was partly successful in reducing unemployment to approximately 15 percent, but it was not sufficient to get the country back on the road to prosperity.

Another part of the federal involvement in addressing this crisis was passage of major legislation regulating financial practices that had led to the collapse of banks and other industrial concerns. This began a period of governmental involvement in regulating the activities of Corporate America that culminated in overregulation. In other words, our government overreacted to the situation and instituted many measures driving control over economic activity from one extreme to the other, i.e., no regulation to over regulation.

The regulatory regime started in the 1930s reached a peak in the number regulations enacted causing the private sector to be choked with uncertainty. Uncertainty in the regulatory arena led to economic paralysis and burdened the private sector with unnecessary cost. The recent oil spill in the Gulf of Mexico is good example of what happened in an unpredictable regulatory environment out of Washington, DC. The Environmental Protection Agency (EPA) allowed BP to use a type of oil dispersant that supposedly was approved and considered safe from the environmental perspective. Then, EPA reversed itself and admitted it did not know the real impact of that dispersant on the environment. EPA then ordered BP to switch to a different dispersant. In light of these confusing and contradictory mandates from EPA, BP questioned that new mandate. In response, EPA admitted it did not know the real impact of that second dispersant on the environment, either. Why was EPA recommending something as safe when it did not know anything about the true effect on the environment? There were and are many other examples of this nonsense reflecting a lack of common sense by regulatory agencies personnel. This situation would lead to confusion and inaction on the part of Corporate America.

The Great Depression finally came to an end. It did that not by government expenditure on infrastructure projects but rather by government spending on manufacturing activities required for the war effort. Spending on the acquisition of products destined for military use ended the depression and started a period of prosperity unequaled in prior history. In short, it would be desirable to recognize that the Great Depression ended as a result of the domino effect provided to all economic sectors by war effort manufacturing activities. That would be an extremely important lesson to learn and keep in mind from that sad period in our history. Unfortunately, our present government experts learned nothing from that period that could had been used to combat the Great Recession of 2009. Consequently, our citizens lost their jobs, homes, and savings. Banks deemed too large to fail and ineptly managed corporations such as GM were the beneficiaries the only beneficiaries of government action to deal with disastrous 2009 Recession.

Contrary to what seemed to be lessons learned from ending the Great Depression, our government chose to address the 2009 economic crisis by bailing out failed financial institutions. It would have been preferable to let those institutions go under once and for all. The United States donated taxpayers' money to banks and their unethical and corrupt executives instead of pumping money into manufacturing. The results of these efforts were obvious: banks' executives enriched themselves by awarding themselves huge bonuses for driving the economy to the ground and showed no mercy while foreclosing home loans of unemployed workers causing these taxpayers to lose their homes. We all prayed that God would save this country from all the corruption and abuse of power present in the political and corporate arenas.

The period after World War II was a period of great concern for at least two reasons. One was the fact demand for armaments was significantly reduced, threatening the loss of many jobs in many sectors of the economy. This potentially could have led to a period of uncertainty causing consumers to reduce their spending. Second, in order to keep the manufacturing engine going, it was necessary to develop export markets. Exports markets were devastated but these markets were unable to purchase manufactured and agricultural goods from the United State. The US government came to the rescue and devised a plan to assist with reconstruction efforts by all of our World War II adversaries.

The Cold War was a period that provided growth and economic development based on an expanded reliance on science and engineering; this was necessary to keep us safe from our enemies. It was a period of great scientific discoveries leading to another period of prosperity. Unfortunately, the Cold War ended putting a stop to our motivation to continue excelling. The private industrial sector failed to improve manufacturing efficiency and reduced its R&D expenditures thus leading to fewer new products and less manufacturing. In fact, there was a movement of manufacturing activities from the United States over to China that decimated our manufacturing sector. This movement was supported by our own politicians and corporate leaders without taking into consideration the impact it would have on our nation and its citizens as well as on our national. As a result of this misguided effort, China was transformed into a major manufacturing power house, and the United States became highly indebted to China. The lack of high-paying manufacturing jobs translated into a reduction in the standard of living that could not be overcome by the creation of minimum-wage service jobs. Politicians reacted to this phenomenon by proposing increases in the minimum wage, but all that did was to eliminate minimum wage jobs. This confirmed, once again, the wisdom of our founding fathers in creating a country that encouraged individual initiative rather than government interference in economic matters.

My purpose in writing this book is to shed light on the impact American industry has had on the realization of the American Dream for individuals in this country. This is a country that was established by the hard work and efforts of immigrants. These are people considered undesirables in their own country because of their political or religious views or their desire to improve their economic status. In other words, this country represents the best efforts of citizens from throughout the world, who have come to prove their capabilities and to regain some degree of human dignity. These citizens have labored long and hard to make this country a better place and to leave it in a better shape than they found it. The country is, therefore, the product of sweat and tears shed toward the creation of a shining place where the dreams of individuals can become reality.

Finally, I look at the causes leading to economic crisis and the impact these elements have had on the overall economy. Once these causes are identified, it becomes relatively easy to propose solutions to address present-day problems. This is done in a factual manner without bringing political correctness and nonsense into the picture. Political correctness and lack of common sense are driving this country into third-world status, and we as citizens of this great nation need to rescue our country from the hands of corrupt politicians and unethical, incompetent, and overpaid corporate executives. We want our country back, and we must do our best to regain it from the hands of corrupt politicians and corporate executives.

Our forefathers in the Declaration of Independence from England warned us about abuse of power in these words:

But when a long train of abuses and usurpations, pursuing invariably the same object evinces a design to reduce them under absolute despotism, it is their right, it is their duty, to throw off such government, and to provide new guards for their future security. --Such has been the patient sufferance of these colonies; and such is now the necessity which constrains them to alter their former systems of government.

Those words are as relevant today as they were in 1776. Our

elected and corporate leaders need to know that common citizens have the power to get rid of them by the power of our votes and our consumer dollars. Those are the weapons that we need to use to get our country back from these corrupt and uncaring officials. Let's do that to save our country and make it a shining beacon of hope, justice, and prosperity for all of us.

CHAPTER 1

SETTING THE STAGE

It is essential to start this historical analysis by understanding where Corporate America is at the present time and determining how it got there. That position reflects the culmination of a sequence of steps leading to its establishment, development, and growth to its present status. Once that picture is framed and understood, the next step becomes one of isolating elements that have proven beneficial from those found to be detrimental, thus defining a point of reference for future comparison. When that preliminary overview is completed, it will become possible to compare the present situation with that reference point for the purpose of drawing suggestions to chart a future course of action to follow. Hopefully, the impact of that new direction would be beneficial in raising the standard of living in the United States. It is expected that the result of that effort would be to keep United States' preeminence intact in the technological, industrial, and military arenas.

It is undisputed that the corporate sector has played a central role in the emergence of the United States of America as a major world super power. But, sustaining that economic and military status is contingent on maintaining a strong and viable manufacturing base capable of satisfying all the needs of the United States independently of foreign sources. Consequently, the American way of life as we know it today depends on being able to create a strong manufacturing base that generates high-paying job opportunities to keep up with the growing population base.

Anything that threatens the industrial sector also threatens our standard of living and the status of the US as the most powerful industrial and military nation in the world. The industrial sector has to become stronger and more efficient to not only compete on an intrastate basis but also in the international arena against very formidable competitors.

This book focuses on tracing the roots of the corporate world from its humble beginning, and it does that by exploring its historical origin and subsequent growth from its inception to the present time. That historical perspective becomes the basis for understanding the contributions made by corporations to our society and, more importantly, for deciphering how past problems have been successfully solved. That provides a set of tools to use in solving the problems our society presently faces as a result of adverse economic conditions being experienced by many leading and, at one time extremely powerful, US corporations. These conditions have led many of these pillars of corporate power to declare bankruptcy and, in many cases, go out of business. That situation is of great concern to all of us because it leads to permanent job losses at a time when many American families are struggling to survive economically. It is also concerning from the point of view of not being able to create new jobs for the growing population.

The term "Corporate America" refers to an agglomeration of corporations, partnerships, and other types of commercial entities operating as individual businesses. Those entities are created by state law and granted the legal right to conduct business in a predetermined format.

A corporation, being a legal creation, is granted a very important legal status analogous to that of juridical "person." This means that a corporate entity can act legally in more or less the same fashion as a human being. In many cases, this position leads to some confusion because corporations do not act directly but through its officers. Those individuals are granted immunity when they perform their duties in conformance with their corporate authority for the corporate entity. That immunity, however, does not relieve officers from liability resulting from their acts outside the scope of their corporate authority. In other words, corporate officers are shielded from liability if they act within the scope of their authority and consistent with their corporate charter and for the benefit of their corporation.

Officers can be held accountable when, for example, they seize a corporate opportunity for their own financial benefit. For example, an officer can be held liable for appropriating a corporate opportunity such as diverting customers to a competitor. In most cases, however, corporate officers are protected from financial ruin by insurance carried by the corporation.

The most relevant feature distinguishing corporations from human beings is that, unlike human beings, corporations do not have a life of their own but act through and reflect the actions of corporate officers. In a sense, corporations are similar to a governmental unit. A corporation acts in accordance with its corporate charter, which is analogous to its constitution. Government units follow the state and/or federal constitutions in performing duties delegated to that particular governmental unit.

Corporations have officers, including a president and a board of directors. In a manner mimicking state and federal government, the president of the corporation is responsible for enforcing the rules and policies directed by the board of directors, which is analogous to the legislature or congress. The board of directors is charged with the duty of developing and setting policies to be implemented by corporate officers in the performance of daily activities; this is analogous to congressional or legislative functions. Edicts mandated by the board are designed to achieve goals described in the corporate charter, thereby satisfying the conditions for which the corporation was founded.

Some corporations have larger operating budgets than the governments of many countries; this is the case of ExxonMobil. It is possible that the growing power and influence of a given corporation may transform it into an "empire" capable of influencing the national wellbeing of any nation in a positive or negative manner. When that happens, corporate leaders may ignore or simply overlook the national interest in favor of their selfish goals and desires, which is what has happened in the US. Given that corporate owners are immune from legal liability for the corporation and that officers are also immunized from actions taken in accordance with the corporate charter, one can imagine the immense power corporate officers and executives exert on our lives and our status as a nation.

There is no question that corporations such as ExxonMobil, General Motors, and many others are or were very powerful at one time or another during our history and have influenced governmental action either in a positive or in a negative fashion. These corporations have made many significant positive contributions to our American Way of Life, including providing employment opportunities. That has enabled many Americans to realize their American Dream. Lately, however, many corporate officials and executives have acted in ways that undermine previous contributions; these are the results of greed, ineptness, and corruption. That course of action is having a detrimental impact on our society and causing the American Dream of many of our citizens to be shattered.

It would be worthwhile to define the meaning of the term "greed" as used in the context of this book. Greed is defined in the dictionary as "excessive or rapacious desire for wealth." Greed is defined as the motivation to accomplish a task or tasks creating or resulting in wealth. In other words, we all know that greed is what drives entrepreneurs to achieve goals. Greed in that sense of a motivational drive to achieve personal goals is good. If, in the achievement of that goal, wealth is created, then it is an even better result. In that sense, greed is a motivator and a good thing; that is what I would refer as constructive greed.

At the other end of the spectrum is the desire for more wealth regardless of how that wealth is achieved. That is a very destructive kind of greed; it is avarice plain and simple. Avarice is malicious and destructive. Avarice drives a person to place greater importance on wealth than on anything else, regardless of the destructive impacts it may have on other human beings, corporate entities, society as a whole, or even on the person himself. Avarice, unlike greed, is not a motivator to achieve goals but rather a driver to acquire wealth regardless of the means used to get that.

Corporations exert power by pressuring politicians and government officials through their lobbying efforts, which is the politically correct term for the act of bribing politicians. In many instances, these corporate lobbying campaigns cause politicians to act in the most advantageous way to the corporation regardless of impact on voters or society as a whole. In effect, these actions on the part of our national and local governments reflect a malicious kind of greed, which is different from the role contemplated by our founding fathers. The ideal set forth by our country's founding fathers is the creation of a government of the people, by the people, and for the people. Instead, corporate lobbyists have replaced that fundamental ideal with their own principles—government is for the benefit of corporations, run by corporations, and owned by corporations. That is the result of corporate lobbying, and it is simply corporate avarice.

Corporations, like historical empires, have grown and become powerful; this has led to the beginning of a complacency period causing the status quo to remain stagnant and unchallenged. That attitude ultimately leads to decadence and an eventual downfall. That's where Corporate America is today.

The corporate sector needs to return to its roots and renew its commitment to the same pursuit of excellence that, in the past, has led to success and to our once enjoyed prestigious status. Corporate decadence is the result when corporations are driven by inept executives who focus only on the short-term to satisfy their avarice. Current executives prefer the short-term over a broader, long-term outlook that would ensure growth and prosperity in the future; they do that to ensure getting a good bonus regardless of impact on the corporation. Executives are great believers in manpower reductions and political correctness as the only feasible means to solve problems faced by their corporations and to improve the so called "bottom line." These executives fail to consider other more valuable and less destructive alternatives to improve the long-term outlook for their companies.

These executives focus on personnel reductions because they lead to immediate cost reductions that translate into a momentary spike in profit margin. That does not last long, but it may last long enough to result in the award of performance bonuses to executives. But, that manpower-reduction solution leaves the corporation in a weak position to address future growth in demand for their products, or it causes other detrimental results, including poor employee morale and loss of employee loyalty. Corporate executives could care less about the long-term viability of the corporation; they are concerned only about themselves and prefer having the company deposit bonus money in their bank accounts now so that they can spend it playing golf immediately rather than at a future date. That attitude is an example of what I have termed malicious greed or avarice.

The survival of the private industrial sector is a long-term goal rather than a short-term objective. It is essential that cost reductions achieved by Corporate America improve manufacturing technology or a reduce raw materials and utilities usage. This ensures long-term survival. Labor cost is only a small part of the entire cost picture and not the total answer. Labor cuts usually result in imaginary cost reductions. In fact, personnel reductions last only for a short period of time and usually result in additional cost increases. These cost increases are manifest in terms of additional training costs, worker frustration, reduced productivity, and liability from accidents.

These cost increases are best illustrated by the cost of accidents that are a direct result of overworked and fatigued workers. Fatigue leads workers to act unsafely, thus raising the potential risk for industrial accidents with many fatalities and adverse impacts on the environment. Another adverse impact to the corporation is when those workers who remain on the job become frustrated by being overworked and quit for jobs with other employers. That leads to an increase in training costs and reduced productivity. In short, labor is the most valuable asset a corporation has, but employers fail to understand that. We say employers, but keep in mind that corporations are not human beings; these entities reflect the actions of executives.

In the event Corporate America fails to improve its efficiency and cost structure, it will be unable to compete against foreign competitors thus paving the way for its demise. That, definitely, would be a tragedy. It would be a national calamity that would drag the entire nation to the edge of an economic precipice that could result in an economic downfall severe enough to end the American Way of Life as we know it.

The present economic crisis is the result of lobbying efforts, avarice of corporate officers, and lack of regulatory enforcement against corporate abuses. It is a fact of life that there are no enforcement actions to prevent political abuses of power; lawmakers steal with impunity. When they get caught, the only thing that happens to them is to get their hands slapped softly; they get to keep the fruits of their transgressions and perhaps get a retirement package. These corrupt lawmakers should be sent to prison as common criminals for they have violated the sacred trust of constituents. These acts boil down to corruption not only in Corporate America but also at all levels of government. This is criminal activity at its worst.

Empires throughout recorded history have risen and prospered. Some of these have lasted longer than others, but without exception, all of them have fallen. Recent empires such as the British and Japanese empires have collapsed in the same fashion as earlier empires. Common causes leading to the collapse of empires include malicious greed or avarice, abuse of power, corruption, political correctness, internal enemies, war, and complacency with the status quo. All of these elements are now part of our corporate world and firmly embedded in our political system in the US.

The American industrial sector since its inception has grown and prospered, and in some cases become extremely powerful in a manner analogous to historical empires. In fact, some corporations can be considered present-day empires. The thought-provoking statement by the American philosopher George Santayana to the effect that those who cannot learn from history are doomed to repeat it provides an incentive to learn the causes for the demise of historical empires. Once those lessons are learned, they can be applied to present-day corporations to prevent their collapse and that of our American Way of Life.

Abuse of power, avarice, corruption, political correctness, internal enemies, intercompany warfare, and complacency with the status quo are part of present-day Corporate America and of our political system. If those were the causes leading to the collapse of historical empires then we have to be worried about the very future viability of our corporate entities. That is a very disturbing thought because anything that threatens our corporations also threatens the very existence of the US.

In this context, it is worthwhile recalling the words of Lord Acton relating to power, whether it is corporate or governmental power. Lord Acton was a British historian and moralist who cautioned in a letter to Bishop Mandell Creighton in 1887, that "Power tends to corrupt, and absolute power corrupts absolutely."

Corporate America has substantial power to act and to influence government institutions. The exercise of that corporate power corrupts not only corporate officers but also government officials, thus setting the stage for the collapse of the corporate empire and, in the larger context, the collapse of the nation itself. Isn't that what we are experiencing today in the United States where we see many corporate officials being sent to prison for stealing millions of dollars from unsuspecting consumers? Isn't that exercise of corporate power in the form of bribes to politicians and regulatory agencies officials what prevents the discovery of major fraudulent schemes? Isn't the exercise of corporate influence over regulatory agencies enough to raise conflict-of-interest flags?

Regulatory and governmental agencies should operate independently in a manner analogous to judicial proceedings where parties may ask the judge to disqualify himself in case of a conflict of interest. In many cases, the judge disqualifies himself even before beginning a legal proceeding in order to avoid even the appearance of conflict of interest. Why are potential conflict of interest situations in the regulatory, political, and corporate arenas allowed to continue unimpeded without recusals on the part of regulators or lawmakers? Why don't regulators with private agendas opt for recusal when the appearance of a conflict of interest arises? Why are regulatory officials, who overlook their duties or fail to execute them, not removed from their positions and sent to prison? If that had been done in the past, very few, if any, of the cases of corporate abuse we have seen lately would have been possible. These blatant abuses of corporate and political power are the root causes undermining our nation's industrial might.

One might argue that "war" in the context used to designate military conflicts between nations or factions within a nation are not a factor when it comes to corporate life in the US. Do you really think that's the case? Think again! Why do you think Dow Chemical Company bought Union Carbide Corporation and destroyed anything relating to or associated with established Union Carbide corporate culture?

Corporate acquisitions are a form of warfare between competitors in which, at the end, the victor destroys the vanquished. The fundamental difference between corporate warfare and war among nations is that corporate warfare uses mergers and acquisitions instead of military weapons. Victory, in the corporate sense, eliminates competitors from active participation in markets, which allows the victor to capture a larger market share and enhance profitability.

Does that always happen?

Consider the result of a typical acquisition. In most cases, the acquiring corporation is forced to split the acquired company and sell those parts that do not fit within the core functions of the acquiring company. Proceeds from the sale of unwanted parts or components of the acquired company are used to pay debts arising out of the acquisition. That prevents economic collapse of the acquiring company as a result of unsustainable financial obligations.

Mergers and acquisitions almost always end up dismantling a company that, prior to its acquisition, was attractive on the basis of all its individual parts working together as a profitable unit. That is a contradiction. The term merger tends to imply union

31

or coming and staying together. Unwanted parts of the acquired company that, at one time, have been positive contributors to the acquired company are disposed of to generate cash to pay for the acquisition. The acquired company is broken, which causes one to wonder what the acquiring company found interesting about the acquired company to justify its acquisition? It is very unlikely that only selected parts of the acquired company would have the same beneficial impact on the surviving company. If that had been likely, would it not have made more sense to acquire only those parts of the acquired company considered desirable? The main goal of the acquisition is, therefore, to destroy the acquired company.

Corporate officials tend to look at mergers and acquisitions in terms of capturing synergies. For example, two companies produce the same type of product but market them under different brand names, such as the case of detergents. Executives figure that, if one of these producers were eliminated from the marketplace, then the remaining producer would be in a better position to expand its market share. They figure the acquisition would reduce cost by eliminating duplicate functions such as advertising. That is a valid argument, but it is expressed in very simplistic terms.

The truth is that in many cases these synergies are not captured. If indeed synergies were captured, one would expect corporate officials to announce to shareholders the beneficial impacts capturing those synergies have had on the bottom line of the surviving corporation. In most cases, the acquiring company fails to report to its owners whether the expected synergies and projected profitability enhancements are realized. This leads one to the conclusion that synergies are not captured at all. Executives are too proud to admit their stupidity. If anything at all is said after the acquisition, it is that the acquisition has been a complete success as expected right from the beginning. That is a wonderful outcome!

In many situations, corporate acquirers are disappointed by the results of the acquisition, which in many cases do not confirm projected or anticipated profit enhancements. This perhaps is due to personnel clashes resulting from different corporate cultures. For example, Dow Chemical Company experienced poor financial performance after the Union Carbide acquisition. That indicated that the acquisition was not as successful as originally expected. Poor performance became the main reason Dow Chemical fired its CEO, Mike Parker, who had succeeded the acquiring Dow CEO, William Stavropoulos, who had retired after the acquisition. [1] In other words, Mr. Parker became the sacrificial lamb for Mr. Stravropoulos's acquisition of Union Carbide.

The acquisition of Arco Chemical Company by Lyondell Petrochemicals and subsequently that of Lyondell by Basell are examples of corporate warfare resulting in unrealized goals and demonstrations of the abuse of corporate power. The primary reason for the Arco acquisition by Lyondell was the elimination of one competitor in the propylene-oxide business. The acquisition by Lyondell included processing technology, manufacturing facilities, and marketing. Propylene oxide is a chemical used in the carpet and rug business. [2] Standard & Poor's reacted to this acquisition in 1998 by placing both Lyondell Petrochemicals and Arco Chemical Company on its "CreditWatch" with negative implications. [3]

In order to survive after the acquisition, Lyondell was forced to sell its worldwide Polyols business to Bayer; Bayer became an equity partner in the Lyondell propylene-oxide business and a formidable competitor. [4] Polyols are products made from propylene oxide and are, in turn, the chemical raw materials for production of polyurethanes used in consumer applications such as furniture. As a result of the Arco acquisition, Lyondell never fully realized its acquisition goal and was placed in a very precarious long-term financial position that, in turn, led to it being acquired by Basell, thus becoming LyondellBasell. LyondellBasell, in turn, filed for bankruptcy shortly after the Lyondell acquisition. [5] How can it be possible for a company to undertake an acquisition that forces the resulting merged company into bankruptcy? Is this an example of a successful merger and acquisition exercise or merely an abuse of corporate power?

We have recently seen US automotive companies, airlines, chemical companies, major department store retailers, financial institutions, and other companies enter bankruptcy protection.

We have also seen reductions in US manufacturing activities, which raises several interesting and disturbing questions that point to a malignancy in our economy. That malignancy is a cancer that is growing and threatening our very existence as an industrialized nation.

If one goes to a store to purchase anything a cursory examination of the products for sale makes it evident that most manufactured goods are imported from foreign countries, particularly China. Is that a concern? This continuous reliance on China for manufacturing a significant number of products leads to a movement of money away from the United States and over to China. As a result of the trend in relocating manufacturing activities away from the US, China has become a major holder of US currency in its reserves. China has also benefitted by increasing its manufacturing manpower while the US has been harmed to the extent it has lost manufacturing jobs. China can use these funds to exert unwanted financial pressure on the US economy. In fact, China is the largest creditor of the US today. In simple terms, the US has become a hostage to Chinese manufacturers, which are basically owned by a communist country that fosters an agenda contrary to our ideals.

The United States is, slowly but surely, becoming a poor nation. China continues to increase its manufacturing base and it is becoming a richer nation at the expense of the United States. The Chinese communist regime could not defeat our capitalist system by military means during the Cold War, but it is doing so through the use of economic means. At some point, the Chinese government will exert pressure on the US government that may lead to adverse consequences on our freedoms! There is nothing wrong with China becoming a rich nation, so long as it does not do that at the expense of the United States, which is one of the largest and most desirable consumer markets in the world.

Keep in mind, however, that Chinese manufacturers are not the ones causing the movement in manufacturing away from the US. The real culprits causing the demise of US manufacturing base are none other than our own American corporate officials who are placing their own interests above the interests of our nation. These corporate officials are doing that to maximize short-term profits of their corporations so that their bonuses will be larger than would have been otherwise. And, since these corporate officials are only concerned about the present, they tend to dismiss anything that does not pertain to the situation now. In many instances, the results of these activities do not become obvious until present executives are either retired or replaced. Then their successors have to shoulder the blame for poor corporate performance caused by the actions of their predecessors. At that point, the company suffers, and there are no immediate fixes to restore the company to its former glory.

The government is unable and unwilling to stop manufacturing relocation for several reasons. Politicians are indebted to their corporate masters. These corporate masters spend a significant amount of money on politicians and regulators through lobbying activities. Politicians become indebted to their corporate benefactors and shut their eyes to corporate abuses. Politicians fail to exert pressure to protect the US manufacturing base against the adverse effects of subsidies given by foreign governments to products manufactured in their countries. Those subsidies benefit, in many cases, the manufacturing activities of US manufacturers that have relocated there. For instance, they fail to impose or delay imposition of custom duties on Chinese imports to overcome adverse impact due to an artificially low currency exchange rate benefitting the Chinese. That artificially low exchange rate make Chinese imports cheaper than comparable US made products.

Regulatory agencies pass and enforce regulations that burden our manufacturers while leaving Chinese and other foreign manufacturers unaffected by the same regulations. Why don't these regulatory agencies impose a fee based on the cost of implementing regulations on imported goods from countries that do not meet the same standards? That would be a common-sense approach to level the playing field. Expensive regulatory burdens force many manufacturers to relocate to manufacturing friendly foreign nations to remain competitive. US workers are the losers in that situation.

Foreign corporate entities have a cost advantage equivalent to the cost of implementing regulatory mandates. Despite the relocation of manufacturing, lawmakers and regulators continue to burden our industries with excessive regulation that continues to add unnecessary cost. China is the only beneficiary of all those excesses. It makes you wonder whether China is lobbying lawmakers and rewarding them for their faithful service. It also makes you wonder who is paying the salaries of these regulators and lawmakers. Perhaps, they are thinking their actions will lead the Chinese to abandon their communist ideals and become democratic communists. Let's hope the Chinese do not become democratic communist financiers. Perhaps the better course of action would be to send all of our corporate executives and lawmakers to China to achieve the same end.

Politicians continue to enact more and more restrictive legislation and regulations driving US manufacturers away from our shores. Regulators take over when politicians fail to make the US manufacturing climate more difficult for manufacturers. An example is the recent case aimed at controlling carbon-dioxide emissions to the atmosphere on the pretext of preventing global warming. Congress backed away from enacting legislation on this subject. But, the Environmental Protection Agency (EPA) took the initiative and declared that it will take control over the situation regardless of congressional action. That is an example of usurpation of governmental power from an agency that has not been given statutory authority by Congress to act on this particular matter.

Politicians and regulators react indignantly when an economic crisis becomes imminent. This is particularly true when the United States faces the downfall of an entire industrial sector, leading to mass unemployment. These politicians ignore the fact their actions caused the collapse in the first place. The Gulf oil spill seemed unstoppable and damage to the beaches is inevitable, but regulators failed to bend rules to remedy the situation. The remediation effort could have been started sooner if regulators and the Obama administration had been willing to suspend the Jones Act, thus allowing foreign flagged vessels to skim oil from the water. Then these same regulators appeared before the American people to express their concerns and anger at the oil industry for causing the environmental damage. What hypocrisy! Isn't that an example of an internal enemy trying to destroy our way of life and economic wellbeing?

Continuing on the present path will lead to the collapse of the corporate sector, and this will result in the demise of the United States as a world superpower. The American people need to wake up and examine the harm done by corporate leaders, government officials, and financiers. We, the American people, need to rescue our country from the control of corrupt and inept public and corporate officials before it is too late. We need to take our country back from those whose agendas include their financial benefit without regard for the wellbeing of the rest of the population or the country.

The solution is to refocus corporate and governmental power to benefit our own country rather than foreign nations. We need to deny our votes to incumbents who seek reelection to stay on the gravy train that enriches them with corporate contributions and bribes. Politicians should be voted out. They should be denied reelection and prohibited from taking bribes from corporate lobbyists under severe prison penalties. Corporate officers should be prosecuted for corporate abuses causing economic harm to their corporate entities. Existing regulations have to be enforced against corporate leaders to ensure the survival of the US industrial might. Additionally, these regulations have to be enforced fairly against both domestic and foreign manufacturers.

Corporate America must be prohibited from contributing to the reelection of any politician. In fact, politicians should be prohibited from raising funds for any campaign outside the district or state they represent, and contributions must come exclusively from the voters in the district or state. This is to stop political abuses and corruption. It is worthwhile to paraphrase Lord Acton's admonition in terms of access to somebody else's money as follows: Access to money tends to corrupt, and absolute access to money corrupts absolutely.

Corporate America has exerted and continues to exert significant levels of influence on US economic policy. It does so by encouraging enactment of tax incentives, revising trade policies, and other polices. In most situations, Corporate America's influence in the past has been exerted positively to improve our nation's standing. This indirectly benefited our own individual economic wellbeing. In the last twenty five to thirty years, however, corporate leaders acting on behalf of their corporations have begun to focus greater attention on issues reflecting their own immediate financial greed and avarice rather than the interest of the corporations they lead. They have done that without regard for either the long-term corporate wellbeing or the economic wellbeing of the entire nation; this for sure does not benefit anyone but those corporate leaders. The question that should be asked is whether these actions on the part of corporate leaders reflect the best interest of the company.

Politicians, who are the beneficiaries of corporate lobbying dollars, are willingly assisting corporate officers to enrich themselves and dismantle the economic power of the United States slowly but surely. Politicians are reluctant to oppose anything that threatens the continuing financial support they receive from lobbyists who represent corporate special interests. They know money talks, and that voice gets louder as the amount of the contribution increases. Isn't this political corruption? This is corruption at its best and most expensive level. It has to be stopped because that level of corruption is the stepping stone to the demise of our corporate empire.

The implication of continuing on the present path is not only disastrous for our corporations but also for our individual self-interest. It adversely impacts the economic, military, and financial wellbeing of the entire United States of America. Corporate leaders do not care, because they profit immediately without concern for the long-term wellbeing of the corporations they lead or their country. Timing is of the essence to undertake and implement corrective actions in order to prevent ruinous consequences to American corporations and to the American Way of Life.

Ordinary citizens can and should undertake to, first of all, influence politicians and the private sector through the power of their votes and spending habits, respectively. These are the only actions that will stop corruption and abuse of corporate and political power. Citizens as voters have the power to withhold their votes from incumbents and force legislators to either pay attention to the citizens and represent their interest or face removal from their powerful political positions. Citizens as consumers also have the power to change the direction of corporate policy. This power can be exerted by, among other things, buying products from competitors that manufacture in the United States. Corporate leaders would promptly react to consumer opposition to the purchase of their corporate products. They understand the consequences of ignoring popular outcry against their abuse of corporate power. Corporate officials would dare not risk disastrous financial consequences to corporate bottom lines that would ultimately threaten their own individual bottom lines.

Let's illustrate the type of action envisioned to overcome corporate abuses. Let's assume a company lobbies congressmen for beneficial tax incentives to relocate its manufacturing activities to a foreign country. Let's further assume that the company plans to sell product from that foreign manufacturing activity here in the states. Manufacturers justify their actions and requests to lawmakers on the need to be competitive on a world-wide basis. This, no doubt, has repercussions and causes significant changes in local American communities where the product was made prior to relocating to the foreign location. While politicians cannot prevent or stop such a move, they are empowered to impose heavy import duties on products from that foreign manufacturing facility. Companies that move overseas claim they do that because they want to be competitive on a worldwide basis but so does the manufacturer that remains in the US and is harmed by such relocation acts. That action will force corporate officials to reconsider their moves.

This can be addressed in several ways to minimize adverse impacts on the US economy. First of all, if manufacturers are convinced that the manufacturing costs are lower in the foreign location, then the product will have to be sold in the US at a price reflecting that lower cost. Secondly, the manufacturer will be denied deduction of income taxes paid to foreign governments relating to that manufacturing activity. Furthermore, American manufacturers would be responsible for paying income taxes on all profits generated by the company regardless of location and without deductions for taxes paid on their foreign manufacturing activities. Thirdly, foreign manufacturers relocating their manufacturing activities to the United States would be given tax benefits equal to those provided to all American manufacturers.

It is difficult to understand why some manufacturers choose to move their manufacturing activities from locations close to the markets where those products are sold. It is even harder to comprehend when one takes into consideration worker productivity and taxation issues. It is undisputed that US worker productivity is very high as compared to workers in many foreign locations. The rate of taxation is similar to that in the US. What could be the attraction of foreign manufacturing particularly when very little, if any of the product, is sold in the local markets where manufacturing occurs?

There are many examples of corporations deciding to relocate their manufacturing activities away from the US, such as the cases involving shirt maker C.F Hathaway and shoemakers G.H. Bass, Cole Haan, and others. In many cases, this relocation is justified by corporate leaders on the basis that we live in an interdependent world. But, do you hear them justify the move on the basis that this would lead to selling their products worldwide, including the country where manufacturing occurs?

If that were the case, everyone, including the US would benefit. But, in reality, that does not happen. The fact is that the manufacturing country achieves real short and long-term benefits by: 1. developing a new manufacturing base, 2.enhancing local employment opportunities, 3. improving its balance of trade, and 4. improving its technological base. China is a good example of that. The US, on the other hand, loses its manufacturing base and its technology, and its balance of trade is adversely impacted. Corporate America benefits from moving its manufacturing activities in the short term, but the long-term consequences obviously outweigh the benefits. In view of that, it is necessary to impose import duties to balance the short-term benefits received by the corporation against the long-term harm to local US communities.

Reduction in local manufacturing leads to reliance on foreign manufacturers of goods required for the defense of our nation, unemployment, loss of technology, financial difficulties, and establishment of formidable foreign competitors to threaten the very existence of our corporations. Isn't that what we are witnessing in our relations with China?

A case in point is the manufacturing of solar panels, which is a US development. China is a leader in solar panel manufacturing; the US is a small player. The American people need to wake up and force our corporate and governmental institutions to maintain our world leadership. If we fail to act promptly, we will witness the demise of the United States as a world power and also as a technological and industrial leader.

Shirt maker C.F. Hathaway made high-quality shirts in Maine; in fact, it supplied shirts to the Union Army during the Civil War. Unfortunately, it became the last shirt maker to carry the "Made in the USA" label when it closed its manufacturing facilities in Maine after making shirts continuously for 165 years. Ironically, the demise of this shirt maker was partly attributed to the loss of a contract to supply shirts to the U.S. Air Force as reported by an article published in the New York Times on October 20, 2002.[6] Donald Sappington, president of Hathaway, in the same article stated that "it was hard to compete when products can be made elsewhere at vastly lower cost" but failed to mention that normally those corporations were selling the foreign-made products at the same price as that of locally manufactured product. The result was that corporate profit margins increased at the expense of reducing the purchasing power of displaced American workers.

If there is validity in the statement indicating that C. F. Hathaway was the last shirt maker to carry the "Made in USA" then the implication is that all shirts are made in foreign countries. Does that include shirts for our military personnel? What happens in the event the US becomes engaged in a war against the country manufacturing shirts for our soldiers? Does that mean that our troops will be going to the battlefield shirtless?

The result from the C.F. Hathaway situation demonstrates several things. The US government, through its U.S. Air Force procurement office, is complicit in allowing this last shirt maker to shut down production facilities and ignoring the consequences on the local economy and acting without any concern for future national security issues relating to the procurement of clothing for military personnel. Isn't this a case illustrating that the US government is part of the problem rather than the solution? Politicians are complicit in the demise of this and other manufacturing facilities by encouraging the move to foreign locations through enactment of beneficial taxation policies making those moves feasible; this is paid for by lobbyists. Ordinary citizens are also complicit in the demise of this and other manufacturing facilities by continuing to purchase those foreign goods at the same price they were paying when made in the US. The only party benefitting is the corporation and its executives.

Rest assured that the Chinese population does not buy Hathaway shirts—they are unable to afford them. It may also be that corporations are unwilling to sell their products in the local foreign markets at more affordable prices because they want to maximize profits. At the same time, a parallel manufacturing and distribution channel develops for fake products to sell pirated products to tourists and the local citizenry.

Who benefits from this situation?

Corporations benefit in the short run by inflating their profit margins without regard to the wellbeing of the community. Consumers also benefit in the short run by either paying slightly lower prices or ignoring the situation. In reality, all parties involved suffer some injury. The government, corporations, and consumers all suffer economic harm. Government has to pay unemployment compensation; corporations face competition from fake products and newly established foreign competitors using the same technology to make the same product; and consumers are unable to afford the products any longer because they are either unemployed or do not have high-paying jobs to allow them to buy expensive products. Think about this problem and become part of the solution by buying "Made in the USA" products.

What kind of action would prevent similar situations with other products? First of all, the US government should make clear to corporations that their profits will be taxed heavily. In particular, the tax rate will be higher on profits made on foreign goods manufactured by American corporations for exclusive sale in the US. Unless American corporations include a very high percentage of US made components probably in excess of 60 percent, the US government would impose a very high import tax to stop this practice that is so devastating to our country. Secondly, the US government should impose import duties on foreign-made goods to equalize the difference in the manufacturing cost, particularly for those foreign products made exclusively for consumption in the US. Thirdly, the US government should encourage local manufacturing by purchasing goods with the "Made in the USA" label particularly for its military and defense needs and should avoid, at all costs, relying on foreign goods for our defense needs. Fourthly, the US government should mandate that companies engaged in foreign-manufacturing activities be required to sell a portion of their foreign-manufactured products at reduced prices to reflect actual manufacturing cost. Finally, ordinary citizens should buy goods with the "Made in the USA" label, provided these are of comparable quality as foreign-made goods; this is required to prevent corporate abuses in selling inferior quality products.

Make no mistake, the US is one of the largest, if not the largest, market in the world, and most companies want access to such a market. The only thing at issue is how access to this US market will be allowed. It should be made clear that any company that wants to participate in the US market should also plan to manufacture in the US at some point when market demand justifies it, as has been done by most foreign automotive companies. Toyota,

Nissan, KIA, and other automobile manufacturers have chosen to manufacture in this country and have enjoyed the benefits of being a participant in the US market. They have grown, and our own car manufacturers have faced nothing but difficulties and bankruptcy. Something is wrong with the mentality of US manufacturers that leads to failure while foreign manufacturers become successful in the same market and employing American workers.

It is true that some foreign goods are manufactured at a lower cost but usually sold at the same or slightly lower price as that of locally manufactured comparable goods. That is both a blessing and a curse. It is a blessing in the short run because it stretches our families' budgets. In the long run, however, our selfish interest destroys our manufacturing base, which results in loss of employment. The government then has to pay unemployment compensation, causing an increase in our tax burden. The standard of living of unemployed workers declines. The net result is that the overall transaction ends up costing us more in terms of a lower taxable manufacturing base and higher government expenditures to pay unemployment benefits; this requires collecting additional taxes from citizens and increases the national debt to be financed by China.

Let's recognize that ordinary citizens have power to change the course of government and corporate policy as demonstrated in the case where popular outcry and government action forced Stanley Works to reconsider its corporate headquarters move from the US to Bermuda, and the company remained incorporated in the US. Stanley Works' greed in making such a move is very well described in the following opinion piece published in the New York Daily News on May 12, 2002.[7]

Stanley Works has been making tools in New Britain, Conn., since 1843. It likes to stamp "Made in America" on its products. It likes raking in dough from U.S. government contracts. It just doesn't like paying U.S. taxes. Nothing personal. It's only business.

Stanley wants to "move" to Bermuda and make its headquarters a post office box. The company admits it would not do any manufacturing—or even any real business—on the island. What it would do is avoid a $30 million-a-year tax bill on exports. And because Bermuda does not enforce American court judgments against companies headquartered there, Stanley would have immunity from many lawsuits.[7]

Public outcry against Stanley Works is the typical type of action available to ordinary citizens. It should not, however, be misunderstood as encouraging a total ban on purchasing foreign goods because in many instances that is the best option available to both the corporation and consumers. For example, a corporation may choose to manufacture one type of good in a given country and other types in other countries. That practice leads to efficiencies and manufacturing cost reductions benefitting both the corporation and consumers and it does not diminish manufacturing in either the US or the foreign country; there is nothing wrong with this approach. This is the approach followed by many car manufacturers such as Honda Motors, which simultaneously manufactures models of cars for sale in the US and Japanese markets.

What cannot be tolerated is the practice whereby manufacturing is done exclusively in a lower-labor cost country to be exported and sold exclusively in the US at a higher price. This is done for the purpose of enhancing corporate profitability without regard for the destructive impact it has on the manufacturing base of the US. This is detrimental of all parties concerned including American citizens and the US, which is the home country of the corporation.

Let's not fool ourselves into believing that Stanley Works is the only company acting in this manner. All companies are contemplating similar moves. Do you really think that shoe makers such as Cole Haan sell shoes where they are manufactured? The answer is without question—"no." Those shoe makers are definitely making shoes in lower-wage countries to inflate their profit margins without regard for long-term consequences to the wellbeing of the community that purchases their products or to benefit the citizens of the country where they are manufactured. There are indications that these corporate entities shut their eyes and ignore inhumane treatment of workers at those foreign locations.

There is no question present corporate leaders are not concerned about what happens to their corporate sales five or ten years from now. Why? Future sales have no impact on the current financial performance of their companies, which is what determines their present compensation package. If, on the other hand, corporate leaders were convinced that ordinary citizen would not purchase their foreign made but American branded shoes now, then they would be very reluctant to eliminate all manufacturing in the US because that would bring an element of risk to their compensation package. That, without question, would get the attention of corporate leaders.

Think about the following questions: Do we want to be held hostage to foreign manufacturers for our shoes? Do foreign manufacturers make shoes for our armed forces, and does the US government buy shoes from these foreign suppliers? If our troops have to rely on foreign suppliers for shoes, uniforms, and weapons can we really say that US is in control of its destiny. Certainly not, and particularly in view of the contempt many foreign countries have for the US. That is a something to think about and, more importantly, to act on.

Next time you go to a store take a look at some of the creative ways foreign manufacturers use to mislead American consumers. For example, you might find a men suit with a "Made in China" label that indicates the fabric used in its manufacture is imported from the US. Does anyone believe that the label present a true statement? Is the label meant to indicate that the fabric was manufactured in the US? It is more likely than not that the real meaning of that label is that the fabric is made in a country other than the US; it is shipped to the US for storage; and then it is shipped to China? If that is not the case then where in the US is the fabric made?

I do not advocate a complete ban on the importation of foreign-made products. In fact, it should be clearly understood that in many instances selective manufacturing is the most efficient way to achieve an end. For example, Toyota, Honda, and other Japanese car manufacturers partially satisfy the local demand for their all of car by manufacturing some models in the US. Other models are manufactured in other manufacturing sites, including foreign plants. The point is that models manufactured in the US are shipped to foreign markets, including Japan, to satisfy the local demand for those models throughout world markets. Similarly, models that are not locally manufactured in the US because of either low demand or other factors can be made more efficiently in foreign locations and brought to the US. That's acceptable trade. What is unacceptable and should not be tolerated or encouraged are actions discouraging local US manufacturing; imports should be tolerated only to develop the market before beginning local manufacturing activity in the US.

China, for example, is an example of a situation that should not be tolerated. US corporations are encouraging the industrial development of China at the expense of the American consumer and jeopardizing our nation's welfare. Perhaps, the real reason behind all the assistance to China is to encourage and develop "democratic ideals" in Chinese society, but tell that to the person who lost his job because the corporation he worked for moved all of its manufacturing activities to China.

In short, if there is no willingness to manufacture in the US or buy US produced goods in any foreign location then there should be no willingness on our part to purchase from that country regardless of who they are or the human or political conditions existing in that country. The concept of "survival of the fittest" is of paramount importance not only in the animal kingdom but also in the economic arena. We all know the US is held hostage by the Chinese because China finances our huge national debt that results from our lower manufacturing activity. It is time to cut that umbilical cord. It is time to develop our own country and improve economic conditions in this country to benefit our own citizenry.

Another situation, frequently brought on by US regulatory agencies, is to allow foreign manufacturers to produce under less stringent conditions than those permitted for local US manufacturers. For example, environmental restrictions on US manufacturing activities are more stringent than those imposed in many foreign countries such as India and China. The sad thing is that many officials in governmental positions of authority are in favor of granting exemptions to the amounts of pollutants emitted by manufacturing activities in China and India while penalizing the same emissions of pollutants from US industry. Isn't that action by our government officials adversely impacting our national industry? Why? Have these officials been bribed by lobbyists from those foreign manufacturing companies or their associates in US corporations to influence their decision making process?

It is ironic that many corporations take advantage of the US government's misguided policies to the detriment of the entire nation. A case in point is the rescue of Chrysler Corporation--an American corporation--by the US government by means of a loan enabling Chrysler to remain in business; the loan amounts to a total of approximately $12 billion. [8] Chrysler, to show its gratitude to the American taxpayers, announced its plan to manufacture the Fiat 500 Model car at a Chrysler manufacturing facility in Mexico. [9] It shows how much Chrysler appreciates its US workers, the US government and the American taxpayers for saving the company from bankruptcy and liquidation! The point is Chrysler and its corporate officers do not care about anything other than their selfish interests. Why is the US government tolerating this situation?

Toyota Motors--a Japanese corporation—has not been the beneficiary of any loans from the US government to keep it solvent in these economic hard times. It has many auto manufacturing facilities in the US and employs many US workers in those facilities. Toyota Motor Corp decided to expand manufacturing in the US and announced its plans to boost production of four-cylinder engines by adding capacity at its Huntsville, Alabama, plant; this represented a significant manufacturing move from Japan to the US. More importantly, it represents a vote of confidence on US workers and markets. [10] Who is the enemy in this instance? Is it the American corporation or the Japanese corporation?

Indications are that despite the rescue package by the US government, Chrysler's actions decimated its relationships with the US government and American taxpayers. These actions are analogous, therefore, to acts performed by internal enemies destroying industrial empires. Toyota Motors, on the other hand, has shown its confidence in the US economy and continues to invest in manufacturing activities in the US where American workers are employed.

Toyota's action emphasizes the continuing importance of immigrants, including foreign corporations such as Toyota, to US national wellbeing. The US government should investigate and prevent Chrysler from using American taxpayers' money to eliminate jobs in the US. In fact, the US government should reward Toyota, Honda, and other car manufacturers for expanding their manufacturing facilities in the US. If that forces Chrysler to go out business so be it!

Yes, historical empires have risen and fallen, and the case of Corporate America is little different from that of any other collapsing empire. The difference, however, is that the collapse of our corporate sector also will precipitate the demise of the US as a super power. If that were to happen, then Americans citizens and the US as a whole would be the losers. That point is driven home very clearly by paraphrasing the old saying: "As General Motors goes so does the US." We all know where General Motors is today. Do we want the same fate for our country? It is inconceivable to think that the majority or any silent minority of American citizens would answer that question in the affirmative. It is essential, therefore, to stop corruption at all levels in private industry and in our governmental institutions. We as American citizens need to do everything in our power to rebuild this nation and make it the shining star that it was.

In light of the foregoing discussion, it is worthwhile to understand the development of Corporate America and its growth throughout its entire history. In particular, the emergence of new manufacturing concepts leading to the establishment of mass production describes a period of industrial infancy and the growing pains associated with implementation of those ideas. It is a period when Corporate America is growing and creating high-paying job opportunities, leading to prosperity for all workers. It is a period when Corporate America is unable to find enough workers to satisfy its demands and relied on immigration to supply the workers required to do the job. It is also a period when the whole economy became very prosperous. And, it is a period that should be replicated to overcome our current adverse economic conditions. Those conditions need to be studied and understood to dispel present myths and fears causing stress in the minds of many members of our present-day population, such as, for example, the immigration issue that is currently dividing instead of uniting our nation.

The period of prosperity experienced in the 1920s was followed by the Great Depression in the 1930s. Prosperity was followed by misery that was occasioned by the same conditions that have brought us to the financial crisis in 2009. The disastrous economic conditions leading to economic chaos during the Great Depression were basically corruption and avarice. Similarly, corrupt practices leading to the Great Depression brought us to the Great Recession of 2009. History has indeed repeated itself. Finally, government intervention began to turn the era of misery into a period of prosperity as Corporate America came alive to supply military equipment to our allies and to prepare for World War II.

Corporate America became a major contributor to US military and industrial power during World War II. This was the era when Corporate America began to develop and grow to satisfy the US national defense needs. Those conditions formed the foundation for the establishment of our present-day corporate structure. At the urging of the US government, the private sector embarked on a journey that lead to many technological breakthroughs, providing the means to enhance manufacturing practices developed and commercialized at that time. Those technological achievements formed the basis for the emergence of US industry as a leading manufacturing force in the world. Keep in mind that the US government was the major sponsor of the research work and industrial efforts leading to the establishment of that industrial manufacturing might. It is doubtful that the corporate world would have been as vibrant and successful as it was without US government assistance.

Those same conditions and technological attitude need to be emulated to revitalize the creation of new industries to improve our existing manufacturing base and to overcome the advantages of lower wages in competing foreign countries. The war years were a period that should be referred to as the true "American Industrial Revolution" because it was during that period when the US demonstrated its capabilities and the "can do" attitude of the American people to innovate and to overcome obstacles in order to satisfy market and national needs. It was a period when parents encouraged their children to get an education and to work hard to have a brighter future than their parents had. This was the period when people relied on their abilities and intellectual power to make the future, rather than sit around and wait for a government handout. This was also the period when all Americans were united to pursue common goals. It was the period when the American people, Corporate America, and the US government worked together as a team to jointly defeat the Great Depression and to demolish the Nazi and Japanese Empires.

The war years were followed by a period that showed the greatness of the American people. That occurred when the US joined hands with former Europeans and Japanese adversaries to get them back on their feet. This was done without any concern for possible the consequences resulting from helping competitors get into the market. More importantly, this was the period when Corporate America told the whole world that it did not fear competition! This was a period when individuals citizens relied on their ingenuity and resources rather than government welfare and handouts to build a better tomorrow for themselves and their children. Corporate America did not fear competition after World War II and should not fear competition after defeating the Great Recession of 2009.

The American Industrial Revolution was the cradle of many new technological developments. These related to manufacturing processes and also to the commercialization of important technological discoveries pushing the boundary of American science beyond any limit known to man at that time. It was also the engine driving the introduction of many new products. Some of the same factors present during the early pre-World War I period were present during this post-World War II and post-Great Depression period, but the results were completely different. This was a period during which Corporate America had a "yes, we can do" attitude and was willing to show its vibrancy to the entire world. It was an attitude that served us well during many historical periods.

Unfortunately, corporate leaders failed to recognize that reviving European and Japanese industries would lead to the birth and growth of very powerful foreign competitors. Newly revitalized foreign industries incorporated the latest manufacturing technology available at the time. The result, therefore, was that European and Japanese industry had the potential of becoming much more efficient than our own industrial base. But, our corporate leaders figured it would take some time for these foreign competitors to learn, operate, and optimize those technologies. Corporate America, however, still has some lead time to continue improving, modernizing, and commercializing new developments to maintain its leadership position. There was another advantage enjoyed by Corporate America: access to markets while their foreign counterparts had to begin their market-development efforts. Corporate leaders, instead of improving their operations, became complacent, thus setting the stage for defeat.

American corporate leaders were satisfied by the status quo. They failed to modernize existing plants and, instead, kept relying on their past glory. They failed to understand that past arrangements in the supply of US manufactured goods to Europe and Japan did not guarantee similar future arrangements. They continued to think that past arrangements would continue for years and that there would be no change in that situation. In other words, corporate leaders were happy with the status quo and failed to invest in the development of new manufacturing technologies to meet competition from European and Japanese companies head-on using more modern manufacturing facilities and processes. One good example was the failure to improve steel manufacturing or invest in new, larger, and more efficient steel plants, which led to abandonment of steel production to foreign competitors. They also failed to keep up with product quality resulting in the loss of market share. Corporate America taught the Japanese quality control and failed to practice in its own facilities what it had taught Japanese manufacturers.

Corporate America began to show its arrogance after World War II. Corporate America believed it would be able to focus only on highly profitable products product lines to maximize profits. One example was abandoning production of smaller and less profitable cars to foreign competitors to concentrate on production of high-margin cars. Unbeknown to these corporate leaders, foreign competitors had intended all along to capture the lower-margin markets first and then pursue higher-margin markets after gaining consumer acceptance and capturing their loyalty on the basis of product quality and customer service.

As expected, consumers accepted foreign cars based on their initial cost and higher quality compared to the higher price and lower quality of domestic brands. Market share relinquished to foreign competitors was never again recovered. In fact, foreign competitors captured the low margin market and then took over the higher margin markets. The result of this misguided philosophy on the part of US automobile manufacturers was to drive some of our most powerful companies to the ranks of lesser importance, such as in the case of GM. Instead of facing reality and doing something about the problem, companies developed a defeatist attitude preventing them from recovering this market share. Consequently, that attitude led to reductions in manufacturing activities in many sectors of the economy. Corporate executives blamed everything under the sun except their ineptness for the failures.

That defeatist attitude infected other sectors of society and led to a lowering of individual expectations. Lower educational standards became the norm for our students. That prevented them from achieving to their full potential. The results of these lower expectations were apparent in secondary school graduates who are unable to solve simple scientific and mathematical problems.

Eventually, that defeatist attitude infected a significant segment of the population, damaging or destroying its work ethic and thus leading to a greater reliance on government welfare and handouts.

Reliance on government handouts by part of the population condemns them to poverty without any means or hope of ever getting out of that unfortunate state. Government handouts are the keys to poverty and slavery. There is no free lunch. In short, we are beginning to notice signs of a crumbling empire. Is that what we want? The transformation from a nation of people who are capable of doing anything to one in which a portion of the people are totally satisfied and unwilling to do anything or as little as possible is troublesome.

A "developed country" such as the US cannot stop its development efforts. It needs to continue its development journey in the same manner an educated person needs to continuously update his knowledge base. In other words, if we are not keeping up with new developments, then as a result we fall behind. A developed country needs to continue to rely on research and development efforts to improve its technological base and keep up with the rest of the world. It is easier and cheaper to lead rather than follow.

Corporate America had, as of the late 1980s, decided to rely on financial gimmicks rather than scientific and engineering developments to improve its manufacturing base; this will never work! Financial gimmicks create no tangible goods that you can sell for profit. The only thing it does is to create a bubble that is easily busted—as the present financial crisis has clearly demonstrated.

There are two sides to corporate profitability: cost and sales. The cost side can be reduced by making the manufacturing process more efficient, as for example by incorporating technological improvements. These may lead to production rate increases, lesser usage of raw material and utilities, and improve quality and on-stream reliability; these are lasting cost reductions. It is impossible to enhance profitability only by reducing labor costs; this is only a temporary fix that falls by the wayside by adversely impacting quality, on-stream factors, and safety. Financiers concentrate only on labor cost because they do not have a handle on the other cost elements. In addition, labor is very visible.

The other side of the profitability equation depends on increasing sales. Costs can be reduced significantly by new production technologies requiring R&D investment for their development. These new technological development may also lead to new products, thus increasing sales. This is, therefore, the preferred way of increasing profitability by simultaneously reducing production costs and introducing new products to the market to enhance sales. Both cost and sales have to be taken into consideration to improve profitability.

Corporate leaders have taken advantage of favorable tax policies encouraging R&D in order to inflate corporate profitability, but have failed to modernize their production facilities. In some cases, newly developed US technologies have been commercialized in foreign countries to manufacture solar panels and electronic components. This practice frustrates the reasons for the favorable tax treatment granted by the US government to manufacturers of these products. The reasons for tax incentives include creating jobs and manufacturing facilities to enhance income-tax revenues for the government. There are additional examples showing how the US government is allowing US industry to decimate US industrial might. Cases in point are the discovery of light emitting diodes, flat panel displays, and carbon fiber components made for the new Boeing 787 Dreamliner airplane. [11] How can that situation be tolerated and allowed to continue?

Corporate America has become arrogant and very bureaucratic, and its leaders have failed to understand market dynamics and to project future trends. US car companies are but one example of manufacturers that have exhibited these traits. The rising cost of gasoline should have indicated to executives that at some point consumers would demand more fuel-efficient cars. Even though US car manufacturers make and sell fuel-efficient cars in many parts of the world, the decision is made to abandon that market segment to foreign competitors. It is done on the basis that selling gas guzzlers is more profitable in the short-term. They are blinded by their avarice and are only interested in maximizing their yearly bonuses. Gas guzzlers maximize profits and bonuses now. Next year, in their view, is a different story. That corporate avarice has proven to be very destructive to US car makers.

Foreign car manufacturers, armed with the same information as US producers, reached a different conclusion. Foreign car companies saw the growing demand for fuel-efficient cars as an opportunity to get a beachhead in the US, leading to the establishment of manufacturing facilities for their more fuel-efficient and lower-margin cars in the short term. They were temporarily satisfied producing more fuel efficient and lower margin cars until they could convince consumers of the value and quality of their products. At that point, these manufacturers focused on the manufacture of larger and more profitable models. Looking at the long term and understanding market dynamics proved beneficial to foreign car producers to the detriment of their US counterparts.

Foreign automobile producers are selling not only smaller, low-profit-margin cars but also higher-margin luxury cars and pickup trucks. The result is that foreign car manufacturers are able to manufacture products for all market segments while US counterparts are unable to do so. The ability to cover the entire product spectrum enhances the company overall profitability. American car manufacturers, on the other hand, cover a very small fraction of the product range, which limits sales, particularly as consumer preferences and demand change. In other words, foreign-car companies plan products for all market segments instead of limiting their product offering to only one particular segment of the market. Needless to say, the profitability of American producers is such that, with the exception of Ford Motor Company, bankruptcy and government aid is the only means of survival.

US automakers fail to understand that, by ceding market share, they give foreign competitors the opportunity to gain consumer loyalty. That then becomes the stepping stone leading consumers to develop a sense of loyalty and preference for cars produced by foreign automakers over those made by American producers. This becomes even more relevant when cars sold by the foreign-car producers have fewer mechanical problems and are more reliable than those made by US companies. Consumer loyalty results in a move up the profit chain from lower-margins cars to higher-profit-margin models as illustrated by the move from a low-profit margin Toyota model up to a high-profit-margin Lexus. The foreign companies improve profitability by participating in all market segments. The same logic also applies to other products.

Corporate America has developed a sense of arrogance (we are number one) that is detrimental to its profits. Corporations have taken consumer for granted, and consumers have lost faith in them. Instead of blaming workers and rewarding management, Corporate America should blame its poor performance on the incompetence of its managers and replace them with more competent individuals. The preferred ones should be leaders who are interested in improving the long-term profitability of the company rather than immediate financial reward based on short-term returns.

We all have heard automotive leaders blaming poor corporate performance on high labor costs and other problems associated with or blamed on American auto workers. Honda, Toyota, and others foreign-car manufacturers employ American workers to produce cars that are in high demand and sell at a profit to loyal consumers who keep coming back for more. Why? Quality and better understanding of market dynamics are the basis for better performance by these transplanted automobile companies.

Auto workers are blamed for high cost and lack of productivity, and yet those same American workers are employed by Honda, Toyota, and others to make high quality cars that sell well not only in the US but also in Japan. It is obvious then that the problem is not the workers but rather the management of these US automotive companies.

GM CEO Rick Wagoner's total compensation, including salary and bonus, amounted to $9.3 million in 2006, nearly double what he earned in 2005. Toyota's top executive Hiroshi Okuda compensation for 2006 was $903,000. In fact, Toyota's top thirty-seven executives earned a combined $21.6 million in salary and bonuses, according to filings with the Securities and Exchange Commission. At Honda, the top twenty-one executives earned a total of $11.1 million in salary and bonuses, SEC filings showed [12]. Rick Wagoner received a compensation package valued at $14.9 million in 2008, broken down into a salary of approximately $3 million and the balance of $11.9 million in stock and options. [13]

In view of the disparity in compensation, it would be fair to question whether Mr. Wagoner's services were more valuable than the services of all top twenty-one executives at Honda. The results would reveal that Mr. Wagoner was overpaid. That conclusion would be reinforced by taking into account losses amounting to approximately $82 billion during Mr. Wagoner's tenure as GM CEO. Yet, the GM Board of Directors consistently rewarded Mr. Wagoner for his incompetence.

It has been said many times that corporations need to pay high salaries to attract talented managers. Perhaps a less talented manager than Mr. Wagoner would have achieved better results for GM and its shareholders. Adding insult to injury is the multimillion dollars salary pay to Mr. Wagoner for driving GM to bankruptcy.

Wall Street greed, reliance on poor advice from academic and business gurus, and reliance on financial gimmicks to satisfy Wall Street demands and reward management are indicative of internal enemies contributing to the demise of Corporate America.

Wall Street has substantial influence over Corporate America. Unfortunately, the goals of Wall Street and corporations are not always identical in that Wall Street wants immediate gratification of greed while the corporate sector should be focused on long-term growth for its survival. Disastrous long-term consequences are the results for a corporation that attempts to satisfy Wall Street demands. How? Let's illustrate by using a hypothetical example that, in many cases, represents the actual situation in the corporate world.

Let's assume a company produces mechanical equipment that requires a year to be manufactured and delivered to the customer. The salesman sells the equipment and places the order with the shop, and the company starts to manufacture the product. The end of the quarter comes, and the company reports a modest but adequate return on its investment. Wall Street reacts to the report by indicating that it is not enough as compared to what Wall Street is expecting from the company. This causes the company stock to go down in value. Company executives get the message from Wall Street and decide to lower costs, thereby endangering the company's future performance. They decide to terminate the salesman on the basis that the shop is busy, and the company cannot manufacture anything else until it completes the manufacturing of current orders in the shop. Comes time to report the results for the next quarter, and the return is better because it has reduced the labor costs represented by the terminated salesman's salary and benefits.

Now, Wall Street rewards the company and its management for a job well done. The stock goes up, management gets a bigger bonus, and everyone is happy. Fast forward to the time when the ordered equipment is delivered, keeping in mind that it is a year after placement of the original order. Now, what? There are no additional orders in the pipeline because no salesman has been beating the bushes to generate additional business. Management issues its quarterly report and blames poor market conditions for its lack of manufacturing orders; the real reason is that the company has no sales force. In addition, the company details its plan for further cuts in labor costs by eliminating some of manufacturing staff. Management gets rewarded, once again, for saving the company in a very difficult operating environment. Then, the company disappears, and its corporate officers relax in expensive vacation spots, buy lavish homes, or otherwise spend their bonuses. Wall Street, on the other hand, repeats the cycle, as it continues to pursue the destruction of other businesses.

There is no question that management has to be aware of costs involved in manufacturing and has a paramount duty to lower those costs by taking effective action. If management, however, is knowledgeable only about financial matters and is unaware of technological and manufacturing requirements, then how can it lower manufacturing costs?

In fact, most companies have gotten on a path leading to reduction of technical staffs with the justification for such reductions coming on the recommendation of highly regarded and highly paid academic consultants. The problem is that consultants do not really know the answers for a company's problems. One day, consultants tell you one thing and charge you a high fee for that advice, and the next day, they tell you the opposite story and charge you again. The problem continues without solution, and management is unaware it has been taken for a ride.

It seems that there are many ways of reducing manufacturing costs, including introducing technological changes, reducing raw material consumption, reducing manpower, and many others. The point is that manpower reduction is not the only option available, which has been the only solution used by Corporate America since the 1980s. Focus on financial matters to the exclusion of technological improvements is definitely a cause for failure. Technological improvements usually come after expenditure of capital, which is something companies do not want to do when facing tough competition. Unfortunately, financial people neither understand manufacturing nor are capable of doing anything to improve it other than by reducing manpower. That is the only thing financiers can think of to reduce production costs. Long-term reduction in employment, in turn, is a clear signal that the company is on a self-destructive path to failure.

It takes technical knowledge to understand manufacturing and to devise ways to reduce manufacturing costs. The duty of management is to improve profitability by reducing production costs and increasing sales, which are the most important factors influencing profitability. One cannot be done at the exclusion of the other. Instead of blindly following Wall Street desires to cut cost and improved profitability, corporate management should pursue a path ensuring the continuing existence of the company by improving its manufacturing technology, building larger manufacturing facilities, and optimizing its product mix, among other things. Rest assured that, if these things are done, then the company's long-term viability and performance will be enhanced, and profitability will improve significantly. This will, no doubt, eventually bring praises from Wall Street, but technological improvements take time to implement and to show value. However, the value is real as opposed to the illusory results from financial gimmicks. The problem, however, is that corporate officers and Wall Street do not benefit immediately. This causes significant stress in the financial community.

Financial gimmicks are real enemies of Corporate America, but corporate leaders love them. Auditors, for example, commonly refer to principles used in the auditing profession to avoid answering questions on the financial health of a company. What does it mean to follow auditing standards? Does it mean that auditors take a random sample of the contents of a tank in a refinery or petrochemical plant to determine that the tank is full of product instead of air or water? Auditors do not measure sample product quantities randomly but instead take the word of management and certify that everything is okay. Why should ordinary stockholders rely on audited results to detect irregularities or fraud being perpetrated by corporate officers? Why should a public company or corporation pay these auditors high fees for doing absolutely nothing? What is even more insulting is that these auditors get paid huge sums of money for performing a worthless job, which is disguised in terms of fictitious auditing standards. This is an area that contributes nothing other than a false sense of security and deserves further scrutiny, particularly to reduce costs.

Recent scams by supposedly reputable financial people and institutions raise flags about the abuses and corruption levels present in Corporate America. If there is no confidence in auditors, how can there be confidence in Corporate America? The solution is to regulate auditors and enforce existing regulations and/or enact more effective regulations that will lead to long prison terms for those who violate them.

How can it be said that the $50 billion fraud committed by Bernard Madoff and the $7 billion fraud perpetrated by Allen Stanford could not have been detected in time to protect consumers relying on these financiers for their investments? If auditors had looked at the books kept by corporate entities run by these crooks and asked probing questions, then they would have been able to discover the frauds being committed. Auditors never bother to look at the books as they are supposed to do or to demand data to back financial claims; it is easier to take the word of these venerable corporate executives as the truth. In other words, auditors earn their high fees by doing nothing other than to listen to the lies of corrupt and unethical management.

Henry Clay, who was the nation's most important and powerful congressman during most of the first half of the 1800s and secretary of state during the presidency of John Quincy Adams, provided a very insightful and relevant message in the context of this book. He cautioned that: "Every Nation should be able to feed and clothe and defend itself. If it relies upon a foreign supply that may be cut off it cannot be independent."

The US is currently capable of defending itself, but that capability may be at risk. Manufacturing electronic components has become rare in the US, including those for computers. That places a cloud over the ability of the US to secure electronic components needed for its defense, particularly if production is in a hostile region. If there is no local US manufacturing of these components, where will the US get these essential electronic components required for use by our armed forces? Think about the remarks from Mr. Clay.

Let's keep Mr. Clay's valuable advice in mind as we witness the results of abuses perpetrated by corporate bank officers, manufacturing companies, and government officials. Their actions, based on avarice and corruption, are destroying the manufacturing base of the United States, condemning the general population to a lower standard of living, and bankrupting the country. The US relies on China for clothing, housing materials, and perhaps even some hardware for military applications. In view of that, we are risking our own independence. In simple terms, China owns us, and the US is on a path to self-destruction.

CHAPTER 2

IN THE BEGINNING

Immigrants escaping political and religious persecution arrived in the US to settle in a new land. This enabled them to pursue their dreams freely. They no longer had to be concerned about political and religious persecution. Furthermore, they would ultimately ensure that their new national governing body would be prohibited from discriminating its citizens on the basis of religious or political beliefs. Most of these immigrants were farmers, and some were skilled artisans.

The Industrial Revolution transformed England to an industrial society from its agricultural base. This caused a socioeconomic shift that resulted in an increase demand for unskilled workers to man factory jobs. Demand for unskilled workers caused agricultural workers to migrate to cities to work in factories. Gradually, other European countries experienced the same shift that England had undergone.

Industrialization continued, causing further changes in the socioeconomic structure of cities. Agricultural workers were employed in factories to manufacture the same products previously made by skilled artisans in their shops. This caused skilled artisans, who saw their futures threatened, to start thinking about migrating to the US to continue practicing their trades. As factory production spread throughout Europe, more skilled artisans were replaced. Consequently, they began to migrate to the US where they initially continued to practice their trades.

The industrial revolution brought new employment opportunities to unskilled workers. This also introduced the concept of economic cycles in which the demand for workers varied up and down in accordance with prevailing economic conditions. As the economy slowed down, the demand for workers diminished, resulting in unemployed workers. Economic turmoil in Europe and increasing industrialization in the US forced a large number of unemployed European factory workers to migrate to our country. Among those newly arriving immigrants were skilled and unskilled workers. Some of them had entrepreneurial motivations and knowledge of manufacturing technology in use in European factories. Those early entrepreneurs began to establish new factories leading to the birth of Corporate America.

The evolution of Corporate America to its present status is a story bringing together many different elements necessary to establish a manufacturing base. Human resources, capital availability, management structure, manufacturing technology, and sales are essential factors in any type of industrial activity. The importance of government regulations and tax issues cannot be underestimated, but these are beyond the direct control of the manufacturer. In its industrial infancy, Corporate America is free to develop without any direct influence or regulatory control from the government.

Favorable tax and regulatory policies, for example, can benefit industrial activity. Benefits include faster depreciation enabling faster recovery of capital invested in equipment and research and development efforts. The result of favorable industrial government policies is to make more capital available to manufacturers and also to encourage new technological developments aimed at reducing production cost in order to make manufacturers more competitive versus foreign companies.

Manpower, without question, is the most important element. Human beings generate ideas necessary to establish new businesses and to develop know-how for solving recurring problems. Often, these new solutions become the basis for new products satisfying consumer demand, reducing manufacturing costs, or establishing new businesses. The continuing status of the US as a world economic and military superpower depends on having a large manufacturing base producing goods satisfying not only consumer demand but also the demand for products necessary for its own defense. This can only be achieved by a cooperative attitude between labor and corporate leaders together with government support and encouragement, as shall become apparent later on.

Unfortunately, corporate management tends to downplay the importance of human resources. It believes human capital is a replaceable commodity that can be manipulated at will thus the term "employment at will". In reality, the experience and knowledge in the minds of employees cannot be easily replaced; it takes time and money to train replacements. This belief on the part of management leads, at times, to abuses generating labor conflicts. These conflicts lead to unionization drives enabling workers to negotiate labor contracts for all employees rather than for a single employee. Managerial abuses end up adding unnecessary costs, damaging labor relations, and adversely impacting the competitive position of the company.

Manufacturing, in general, is production of goods by performing a series of processes or steps in a methodical and sequential manner. Human beings perform those repetitive steps, either manually or by operation of a mechanical device, to accomplish the production of a single product. For example, manufacturing a metal tray requires cutting the metal sheet to size, shaping the cut-metal piece, preparing the shaped object for painting, inspecting the end product for quality compliance, and packaging it for sale. Some manufacturing steps require operating mechanical equipment such as, for example, machinery to shape the metal piece.

In pre-Industrial Revolution times, a single skilled artisan would perform all activities required to produce a product either alone or with the help of apprentices. The output from an artisan was limited to what could be produced by that single individual in a given period of time; therefore, it tended to be considerably lower than the output from a factory or manufacturing facility employing many unskilled workers performing many individual repetitive tasks required in the production of the final product.

Mechanical equipment aids the manufacturing process and it increases production significantly. Operating such mechanical equipment requires trained operators. It is a fact that unskilled workers can be trained to operate any piece of mechanical equipment, and they become very proficient operating such equipment. The advantage of employing unskilled workers is that they are normally paid lower wages than artisans or skilled workers. Consequently, the resulting production cost in a factory setting is lower. It is lower because of higher output and lower wages paid to workers who produce the item as compared to custom production of the same item in an artisan shop.

The growth of factories in Europe displaced artisans and skilled workers, thus creating social tensions within the community. At the same time, it increased the demand for unskilled workers causing large migrations from rural areas to cities where factories were located. That migration broke the bond existing between the land and its workers, thus contributing to a socioeconomic problem in the cities. As a result of growth in the number of factories, skilled artisans lost their jobs and were forced to migrate to a different location to pursue their skills and faced two choices either to migrate to a different country in order to continue practicing their trades or accept employment in a factory as a supervisor or mentor to unskilled workers. In any event, the numbers of supervisory positions available at any one time were insufficient to provide acceptable employment to all displaced skilled workers. This forced many of them to depart for the US to pursue their dreams in the land of opportunity.

Skilled workers often had the entrepreneurial spirit necessary to establish factories in the US. Furthermore, many of these individuals also had an understanding of the technology practiced in factories in either England or other European countries. That know-how could, in many cases, be adapted to operate or to be implemented in US factories. In any event, these individuals had the motivation and/or financial resources to contribute to the development of their newly adopted country in a manner different from what their predecessors had done in Europe.

Establishing a factory requires access to relatively large amounts of capital as compared to the requirements of an artisan shop. Regardless of whether mechanical equipment is purchased or fabricated on site, large amounts of capital have to be made accessible to acquire or produce the equipment; this is commonly referred to as capital investment. Additional capital has to be spent in building the manufacturing facility and to have cash in reserve to pay workers for their labor.

A management team is required to plan production, to coordinate the performance of all process steps required in any manufacturing sequence, to justify expenditure of capital for new equipment, to allocate resources such as human and capital to each of the required production steps, to control production costs, to sell manufactured products, and to ensure delivery of the product to customers in a timely fashion at the expected cost.

Capital required for manufacturing can be raised in many different ways. Each of these methods has some pros and cons that have to be balanced against each other. In the absence of owners with sufficient capital to fund the business by themselves, it is necessary to borrow capital from financial institutions. Securing a loan from a bank is not an automatic or easy thing to do. Most banks are extremely risk adverse and require business owners to satisfy the bank's lending criteria and agree to repay the loaned amount with interest in an agreed upon timely fashion.

Banks do not assume risks that might jeopardize recovery of the loaned amount. These institutions want to be isolated from business risks that result from fluctuations in sales price, raw material costs, level of demand, production cost, or anything else impacting profitability. Profits are essential to repay bank loans. Fluctuations in profitability are the result of changes in product sales, quality, favorable pricing, and many other factors such as equipment breakage and downtime affecting product output. Banks expect timely reimbursement of the amount loaned plus interest regardless of what happens to the business or to the economy. If that is not acceptable, then other means of raising capital have to be investigated.

Business owners may decide to fund the business by pooling financial resources rather than getting loans from banks. This can be achieved in many different ways following one of several business models that satisfy requirements prescribed by the law of the state where the business or manufacturing site is to be located. The simplest of these models is that of a partnership where two or more individual owners share in the business investment and divide profits generated by the business activities in proportion to the amount invested by each partner. Liability is the main disadvantage of any partnership arrangements. Each partner can be held responsible for the total liability of the partnership. Personal liability can be limited by establishing a limited liability partnership. In that case, a partner can have his liability limited to the extent of his investment.

The corporate model, on the other hand, protects owners from any and all sources of corporate liability. It is the model preferred by large business entities that require large amounts of capital to operate and potentially subject to high liability. Corporate Statutes in each of the fifty states prescribe procedures for incorporating and for dissolution of the corporate entity. Upon incorporating, these entities are granted the status of a legal person. In other words, a corporation is a person in the eyes of the law.

Many attributes render the corporate business model a very attractive to business owners. First of all, individual owners—commonly known as shareholders—are immune from prosecution for the crimes committed by the corporation, such as, for example, fraud or failure to pay taxes. Shareholders or owners are protected from corporate liabilities. The corporation continues to exist even when shareholders die or when individual owners sell their interest in the corporation.

The corporate model, therefore, is the preferred and most useful vehicle to pool capital for the purpose of establishing a business entity. In essence, shareholders exchange their capital for a portion of the business equity valued in accordance with the value of corporate assets and corporate performance. Shares may be sold publicly or there may be restrictions imposed by the corporation on sale of individual shares. Restrictions are always known to the owners. The corporate charter describes the purpose for which the corporation is established and also details how the corporation will perform its functions; this is analogous to the constitution of any country.

A corporation is organized for a business purpose that presumably will result in the generation of profits. A portion of these profits is divided and paid to shareholders as dividends, which is analogous to interest paid to banks for the use of money; the balance is reinvested or use by the corporate entity. Dividends do not have to be paid at any time, which is unlike the duty to pay interest owed to banks. Interest is a fixed amount set at the commencement of the loan and payable regardless of corporate performance. Dividends, on the other hand, are not fixed but depend on the generation of corporate profits and are payable when so declared by the board of directors. Failure to pay dividends by the corporation may be acceptable to shareholders as a means of increasing the equity value of the corporation.

The corporate home state depends on benefits granted to the corporate entity by the state of incorporating. In some cases, the state of incorporation is selected on the basis of a particular reason such as clarity in their corporate statutes or interpretation of those statutes by state courts. Incorporating in one state does not preclude corporations from undertaking corporate activities in other states of the union. In many instances, the only requirement to operate in a state other than the state of incorporation is that the corporation register with the secretary of state where it plans to expand operations in order to become amenable to the laws of that state. Federal law requires all corporations to be treated equally in any given jurisdiction regardless of the state of incorporation. Obviously, the states have power to levy taxes on the amount of income received by the corporation within each state jurisdiction.

IMMIGRATION

Early immigrants brought to our shores their skills and talents as well as the latest European technology developed during the Industrial Revolution. Those individuals were primarily skilled artisans displaced by unskilled workers who had become laborers manning the growing number of factory jobs. Those early artisans coming in the first wave were hoping to continue practicing in this country the trades they had learned in their home countries. The second wave of immigrants, unlike the first, was composed primarily of unskilled workers who had been part of the human capital staffing factories established to take advantage of technological developments and manufacturing concepts developed during the Industrial Revolution.

Unskilled workers arrived on our shores seeking employment opportunities in established US factories. Those unskilled workers, like the skilled artisans arriving before them, were displaced workers coming from northwestern Europe. Unlike skilled immigrants who had lost their jobs as a result of technological advances, unskilled immigrants had lost their jobs as a result of adverse economic conditions. Both skilled and unskilled workers took advantage of an open US immigration policy in effect at the time to escape economic conflict and famine in Europe.

The United States at the time of this influx of immigrants was an underdeveloped country with a very small local population unable to support a growing industrial base. Those early immigrants planted the industrialization seeds in northeastern US cities and were active participants in developing, establishing, and staffing new factories; this marked the start of the American Industrial Revolution. The technical know-how brought by these immigrants expanded the local industrial base and became the foundation for additional technological developments that, in turn, furthered the industrialization effort. Additionally, these immigrants became instrumental in solving problems inherent to US sites and industrial conditions at the time.

Those problems had to be solved and new solutions had to be

developed, tested, and implemented. These new solutions became the foundation to either start a new factory or to improve the existing industrial base of the country. New solutions propelled the expansion of the local technological basis and resulted in the establishment of new factories enhancing employment opportunities for the ever-increasing number of unskilled immigrants arriving on our shores. In short, immigrants came seeking greener pastures in the land of opportunities and created new opportunities to expand the industrial base of their new adopted country and to make the grass greener for other members of the community.

The Industrial Revolution caused significant changes in the way products were manufactured. It introduced the concept of division of labor, which transformed the methodology employed in manufacturing products. Under this new manufacturing regime, unskilled workers would do individual activities in a series of steps required to make a single product as opposed to doing all the activities previously done by skilled artisans. In short, unskilled workers would be employed to perform repetitive single tasks such, as for example, cutting fabric and sewing the fabric to make a suit. Those unskilled workers would become very proficient at performing their assigned tasks thus contributing to enhanced productivity and lowering production cost as compared to a single skilled worker doing all of the activities required to make the same product. Consequently, the production process became very efficient when measured in terms of output from a single factory compared to the output of a single skilled artisan shop. This new concept revolutionized production.

A situation similar to the one prevailing in Europe at the time of the Industrial Revolution developed in the United States. This ended up causing the replacement of higher-paid, skilled artisans by lower-paid, unskilled workers. Needless to say, skilled artisans resented that situation and had to change their mode of operation to survive under new economic realities in the US. The demand for skilled artisans decreased, but increased significantly for unskilled workers as a result of the ever growing number of new factories being established. An increased influx of unskilled immigrants from southern and eastern Europe satisfied the additional demand. Luckily, the US had an open immigration policy at the time that enabled unskilled workers to come as required to satisfy a growing demand for factory workers.

Early skilled immigrants brought to the US their skills with the expectations of continuing to practice those trades in their new adopted country. Among those early skilled immigrants were some technically sophisticated and very capable individuals who sought opportunities using their technological expertise; those individuals were the first engineers to come to the US and to establish new industries. Keep in mind that these early skilled workers were relatively well off financially as compared to other early arrivals, and they could use their accumulated capital to start new businesses in their adopted country.

Early engineers focused on overcoming obstacles peculiar to their new surroundings and made many technological developments that would become the foundation for new products. Production of those new products required establishing new factories in the US, as had been the case in Europe, thus further increasing demand for unskilled workers. The relatively low number of unskilled workers in the population of the US was insufficient to satisfy the demand for unskilled workers from the ever-increasing, new factories, thus creating a snowball effect on the influx of unskilled workers. The additional demand for unskilled workers was made easier to satisfy by the economic turmoil and the potato famine in Europe.

Industrial growth in the US was the result of developing and applying technology. This also had a beneficial effect on other segments of the economy, leading to further growth. Manufacturing always requires experimentation or research and development to solve problems as these appeared. Those efforts resulted in new products and improvements to the technological base, thus advancing the country's development. This suggests that part of the success Corporate America enjoyed was due to the establishment of and reliance on Research & Development (R&D) to address problems leading to design of new products, design and building new machinery needed to make new products, and development of processes to make these new products commercially. Unfortunately, modern-day Corporate America forgot those early lessons and ignored the fact the US depends heavily on new technological developments for its continuing pre-eminence as a world super power. And all of that could only be achieved by investing heavily in R&D and new plants.

Unfortunately, R&D efforts declined significantly during the last twenty to thirty years of the Twentieth Century and Corporate America chose to invest in China and other low labor cost countries to enhance the business bottom line. Who benefits from that? Certainly, American workers who never saw those new manufacturing facilities and jobs would not benefit from this misguided corporate strategy. US Industry would not benefit either because foreign competitors soon would be in a position to learn new technologies and use it to the detriment of all concerned. The US government would end up on the losing end to the extent of the R&D write off deducted from the corporate tax liability of the company owning the technology. In short, the foreign country would be the only beneficiary in this scheme at the expense of workers, corporate entities and US Government. And then, to add insult to injury, the American company would market foreign manufactured product in this country to maximize profits.

As a result of misguided corporate activity, Corporate America lost its competitive edge over foreign competitors. More importantly, reduced R&D investment coupled with movement of process technology to these lower wage countries resulted in the closure of manufacturing facilities in the US. But, at the same time, Corporate America lost control over its proprietary intellectual property to its detriment. Corporate America complained to the US government because on the basis its Intellectual Property was stolen by entities in those lower wage countries. Was that a fact? Or, more realistically, was its proprietary intellectual property but given away by Corporate America to entities in lower wage countries? It was also a fact that many, if not all, of the products developed by corporate R&D efforts in the US were manufactured in plants overseas.

As in the European case, the US began to experience economic turmoil from its early industrialization efforts. Newly arrived unskilled immigrants began to feel the wrath of local population that now included earlier skilled immigrants who had been assimilated within US society. The local population blamed recent arrivals for their economic setbacks and misfortunes without realizing the benefits that those unskilled immigrants were providing or had provided to their new adopted country. Was this opposition to immigration a prelude to what was to come later as the US began to look down on other sources of immigrants contributing in different manners to the continuing development of our nation?

Settled skilled workers and artisans resented the influx of unskilled immigrants because they knew that factories employing those unskilled workers would become competitors that eventually would force them out of business. Their livelihoods depended on continuing to practice their trades, but now that livelihood was threatened by the industrialization effort; this was a repeat of what they had experienced in Europe. In other words, skilled immigrants were concerned about losing their livelihood in the US, and this fear culminated in resentment toward all new unskilled immigrants arriving from Europe. That anger, based on a perceived threat to their economic interest, was aimed at immigrants rather than the factories employing them. There was nothing, however, these artisans could do to stop. They had to adapt to change as it became apparent that the only constant thing in our lives is change.

Immigrants from southern and eastern Europe were considered inferior by well-established, Anglo-Saxon, skilled workers and that added fuel to the anti-immigration fire. That contempt for immigrants continues to be practiced—admittedly to a lesser extent—in our present-day society. That disdain arose to a level of unwarranted prejudice that divided our nation then and continues to divide us today.

Both skilled and unskilled workers brought to this nation their own prejudices against other nationalities. Europeans were divided and, to this day, continue to be divided by historical, ethnic prejudices. Conflicts in the Balkans and other parts of Eastern Europe, based on historical prejudice about race, religious, or cultural beliefs, continue to the present day. Yugoslavia, for example, disintegrated into groups headed by Serbs, Croats, and Muslims. Armed conflict led to civil war and many deaths and untold suffering to the local populations. The situation in Yugoslavia represented one extreme of this ethnic conflict present in Europe from time immemorial to the present. Present-day citizens of Czechoslovakia recognized their irreconcilable differences and decided to peacefully split their nation along lines of their Czech and Slovak heritages.

Obviously, the outcome in Czechoslovakia was preferable to the one in the former Yugoslavia. Those ancient hatreds were brought to the US by immigrants from those countries. The resentment and hatred felt by different ethnic groups were dampened somewhat by the recognition that team effort was essential in the US to overcome difficult problems faced by all immigrants. Nevertheless, some resentment still exists to divide ethnic groups; although diminished, that resentment continued to the present.

It is on that historical basis, inherited from our ancestors, that this nation is built. You still see discrimination based on race and to some extent on national origin. But, we are getting better at becoming one nation of Americans for all Americans rather than a nation where the nationality of our ancestors is used as an adjective to modify or describe the term American. In short, racial or ethnic prejudice continues to be practiced in the US, but we use it to a lesser extent than our forefathers. We need to focus on the good things that our individual cultures provide to our adopted new country and society. That includes learning the culture and language of our ancestors so that we may, in turn, become better adapted at understanding and respecting cultural differences. There is no need to keep practicing the same old prejudices.

IMMIGRANTS' NATIONALITIES

There were immigrants coming to the US from many European nations, as detailed in Table 1. Early settlers from England primarily settled in the northeastern United States. The Industrial Revolution in England expanded eastward into continental Europe causing social distortions throughout Europe and forcing skilled artisans to migrate to the United States. Up until the 1860s, the majority of immigrants were from northwestern European nations including British, Irish, and Germans nationals. The expanding US industrial base after the 1860s demanded more unskilled immigrants as laborers. New immigrants began arriving from northwestern Europe and Scandinavia but were soon complemented by immigrants from southern and eastern European countries.

Immigrants from eastern and southern Europe were different in many respects from Anglo Saxon immigrants who arrived earlier and had been assimilated by US society. Whereas early arrivals were relatively well-off, displaced artisans, later waves of immigrants were mostly unskilled, relatively poor, agricultural workers. Those differences based on skills and educational level became the basis for exclusion and prejudice.

Ethnic prejudices added another dimension to the separation or discrimination issue. Nevertheless, each immigrant group contributed to the development of the new nation. Perhaps, the common problems faced by all immigrants demanded solutions developed in common. This led to the realization that all of them were on the same boat and had to rely on each other's cooperation to solve common problems affecting the entire group. Perhaps, this had a dampening effect on the feeling of ethnic prejudice.

Chinese and Japanese immigrants started arriving on the West Coast of the United States, and they became very controversial due to differentiating facial features that set them apart from European immigrants. There were grounds for distinguishing between immigrants from Asian countries. Chinese unskilled immigrants became the most controversial, because, unlike

Country of Origin	1841-1850	1851-1860	1861-1870	1871-1880	1881-1890
Austria Hungary			7,800	72,969	353,719
Belgium	5,074	4,738			
Canada			153,878	383,640	393,304
China			64,301	123,201	61,711
Denmark	539	3,749	17094	31,771	88,132
France	77,262	76,358	35,986	72,206	50,464
Germany	434,626	951,667	787,468	718,182	1,452,970
England	32,092	247,125	222,277	437,706	644,680
Scotland	3,712	38,331	38,769	87,564	149,869
Unspecified	229,979	132,199			
Ireland	780,719	914,119	435,778	436,871	655,482
Italy			11,725	55,759	307,309
Netherland	8,251	10,789			
Norway / Sweden	13,903	20,931	109,298	211,245	568,362

Table 1. Migration Sources to the US-1841 to 1890 [14]

Japanese immigrants, Chinese males came alone without their spouses, which seemed to indicate to many Americans to be an expression of a desire not to settle in this country. Japanese immigrants migrated with their families, which tended to indicate a desire to settle in this country permanently.

Chinese immigrants were brought to the US to work on the transcontinental railroad. Construction of the railroad was a great achievement for it truly made the US one nation from the east coast to the west coast, thus providing for westward expansion and growth. The railroad expanded the amount of land available for agricultural and industrial activities. It also made it possible to explore and develop the western part of the country. Chinese immigrants provided a service under very difficult conditions leading the Honorable John T. Doolittle of California to acknowledge in a speech given in the US House of Representatives on April 29, 1999 that "without the efforts of Chinese workers our development as a nation would have been delayed by many years." (15)

Common cultural traits and needs became the foundation for establishing individual ethnic communities resulting in a de facto exclusion of members of other ethnic groups. These communities provided the means to maintain their cultural heritage and provide a support base for its members. A subtle impact of these communities was the attraction of additional unskilled immigrants from the home country based on family or other connections. Nevertheless, the exclusionary influence of the emergence of individual ethnic communities segregated immigrant groups. These communities became the driving force to establish businesses geared toward satisfying cultural needs and creating job opportunities for members of each individual ethnic group. They also provided the means of protection against aggressive actions by another immigrant groups or local citizenry. This overall pattern resulted in the creation of ethnic enclaves that continue to the present day in many US cities.

Identification of present-day American citizens with a given ethnic group is very traditional in US Society, not as much as a defense, but rather to uphold traditions passed on by their parents. And, yet very few of these present-day descendants have continued the tradition of learning their parents' native language. These modern-day descendants are unable to communicate in the language of their parents, primarily because of the pressure based on discrimination suffered by their parents as a result of not being fluent in the English language. That is a tragedy.

Learning a foreign language should not only be encouraged by parents but should also be made a requirement to graduate from high schools and universities. Learning and using a foreign language fluently should not be interpreted as a refusal to learn English, which is the language that commonly binds all citizens of the United States. It is merely a call to expand educational boundaries and provide a well-rounded and useful education for all American children, particularly now that communications among all peoples of the world are so important for conducting business and to prevent misunderstanding leading to potential conflicts.

These long-surviving ethnic communities have fostered the development of a nationalistic sentiment and pride among settlers expressing their cultural uniqueness and differences. On one hand some have argued that these individual communities are divisive and prevent assimilation of their members into the larger, single, national American society. It is curious to note that present-day descendants of these early immigrants still tend to align themselves with the country of their individual ancestors as if that were a badge of honor or pride. The descendants still tend to focus on differentiating themselves from the rest of the population rather than on focusing on the similarities that bind us as Americans.

We all are Americans either by birth or naturalization. We all are different, but we all need to recognize our similarities and jointly contribute to the betterment of our beloved nation regardless of race, creed, skin color, or national origin. Our differences are the means to nourish and strengthen our similarities. Our beloved nation becomes stronger on a worldwide basis as we rise above the ethnic and religious differences that once divided our ancestors.

Cultural diversity is a source of power benefiting the whole society. It provides the tools necessary to understand other cultures, to influence foreign policy, to improve international commerce, and to improve foreign relations. Imagine a situation where we, as Americans, are able to communicate in one or more foreign language. Add to that idealistic vision the power to understand cultural behavior. If that were the case, would our nation not be more influential to have our foreign policies accepted and our communications better understood by our trading partners and adversaries? Would it not be more persuasive on a personal and business level to communicate in the language of our client?

Anyone who has been involved in international commerce would agree that it is extremely important to be able to communicate with clients in their native languages. If we were able to express ourselves in those languages, then transactions would go much smoother and the benefit to our business sectors would be substantial; the net result would be to place US corporations on the same level as their European or Japanese competitors. A side benefit might be world peace rather than conflicts resulting from lack of understanding or failures to communicate.

Notably absent from Table 1 were immigrants from African countries. These immigrants were excluded from any official government statistics on the basis that they were considered property rather than human beings. This was a great injustice that would lead to repercussions on the behavior of many segments of our present society and lead to divisions splitting US society as a whole. As a matter of fact, these African immigrants made contributions in the agricultural sector. They, like present-day illegal immigrants from South America, made and continue to make contributions in the agricultural production that was and is so essential to survival as a nation.

Considering the fact African immigrants were brought into the country as property rather than human beings, implied many different things. First, it meant these immigrants could be bought and sold in an open market. Secondly, if considered personal property then they were totally dependent on the owner for all of their needs including shelter, food, and medical care. Finally, the implication of the property concept was that they did not need to be educated. If that were still the case in our society today, which had become so dependent on technology, our society would lose this segment of our population and be unable to take advantage of their abilities. They would be excluded from the manpower pool required to staff our production facilities, and our society would end up depending on immigration to supply those technically savvy workers. What a waste of human talent! It was, and continues, to be an economic waste.

It is a waste in several respects. First of all, the concept of property implies dependency. That dependency continues to be manifested in terms of government handouts and/or welfare payments that continue to drain government funds without providing a means of ever replenishing those funds. More importantly, this government paternalism continues to hold this group in dependency which is another term for economic slavery. Secondly, that dependency is something our government wants to continue by denying adequate educational opportunities to members of these minorities and thereby denying the country benefits that can be derived from the ideas generated in the minds of members of this group; it is a shameful political and economic situation that needs to be eradicated from our society. That dependency leads to further dependency on taxpayer funds and becomes a breeding ground for crime due to desperation and hypocrisies. Crime leads to incarceration and further expenditure of taxpayer funds. That dependency is the modern-day version of slavery.

The alternative is simple. Allocate sufficient funds to educate everyone, and those educated people will then repay the expenditures many times over through payment of income taxes. They would then regain their dignity and, in the process, would get themselves out of poverty. And, our nation will benefit significantly.

It is fair to say that our present-day society has progressed significantly, but we have not progressed to the extent necessary to grant African immigrants the recognition that their status as human beings requires. Our present-day society continues to hold the majority of Americans of African descent hostage to a welfare system and in bondage to a political party that only cares about them on election time. Nothing should stop this group from achieving their God given potential so that they, too, can contribute their talents to the betterment of our society.

Furthermore, these African Americans are condemned by our society to a poor education simply because the schools in their neighborhoods are of the lowest quality possible and unable to attract the funding necessary to improve their lot. These are the conditions that politicians, the business sector, and the population as a whole should eliminate from our society, for it results in a very costly waste of talents. Politicians continue to hope that dependency on their generosity will enhance their political power, leading to job security for these officeholders. The American people should realize the damage these politicians are doing to our nation and send them home.

Bear in mind that Anglo Saxon politicians will always question the capabilities of any African American in the same fashion they have questioned the qualifications of any member of any other ethnic group save Anglo Saxons. They questioned the qualifications of Sonia Sotomayor as a nominee to become a Justice of the US Supreme Court. They questioned her qualifications merely on the basis of race, national origin, sex, and economic status. In the case of Justice Sotomayor, her detractors questioned her qualifications merely on the basis of being a Hispanic woman. In that same fashion, these politicians have questioned the capabilities of President Obama on the basis of the color of his skin. Both of these individuals are capable individuals as compared to their detractors.

Corporate America, like Anglo Saxon politicians, failed to understand the benefits of cultural diversity. It expected to conduct business transactions exclusively in the English language because it was the only game in town. That situation changed when it became apparent to customers and trading partners that there were viable alternatives available that were willing to be more customer friendly than American and British companies that were so prominent and powerful on the international scene. That situation changed resulting in American and British companies being relegated to international competitors for business and not as the only game in town. The result was the realization that our companies had to change their business practices or accept the loss of business.

Now, our foreign international competitors provide an alternative. Employees of those foreign companies, unlike employees of our corporations, are fluent in many languages and are able to conduct business in many foreign languages. Foreign competitors can negotiate commercial deals in the language of the host country, which is a legal requirement in many foreign countries nowadays. That gives our competitors an advantage to the detriment of our own corporate sector and our nation. Many foreign countries require that contracts with their companies be drafted and negotiated in the native language of the host country rather than in English. This is an issue that gives American corporate lawyers a bad case of heartburn and indigestion.

The cultures of Japan and that of other foreign competitors are very homogenous. Those countries do not have access to the cultural diversity present in the US. Japan and other foreign competitors do not have access to the multicultural pool of talent available in the US; however, our competitors overcome that disadvantage by learning foreign languages and familiarizing themselves with the cultures of their clients. American companies, on the other hand, are very distrustful of anyone who is not an Anglo Saxon and fail to access the diverse pool of talented people available in the US to its detriment.

Why doesn't corporate America use the diversity of talent available in the US to its benefit? In essence, the corporate sector simply does not understand benefits provided by such cultural diversity. It is a failure not to realize that US cultural diversity represents an advantage over anything available to our foreign competitors.

Companies continue to rely on the erroneous belief that Anglo Saxons are superior. Our foreign competitors have clearly shown that concept to be erroneous. Foreign competitors are presently beating our corporate entities in the market place, and they are doing that in our country as is so evident in the automobile business. If Corporate America continues to stick to that nonsense then the consequences will be devastating. The consequences are significant and will adversely impact our future wellbeing and the economic standing of our industrial sector, if it has not already done so. This, in turn, will adversely impact our wellbeing as we witness our individual American Dreams shattered.

Corporate America and its officers tend to be suspicious of those whose cultural backgrounds are different from their own Anglo Saxon heritage. Corporate leaders fear multilingual employees would advance in the corporate ranks at the expense of Anglo Saxons, who are generally unable to communicate in a language other than English and are well entrenched in the management ranks of many corporations. Is that a valid reason for continuing doing business in the same old-fashioned way? American corporations and their officers should reconsider this policy in order to avoid losing further market share in international markets. In short, our corporations must change their attitudes toward diversity to hold on to their present status.

In the event Corporate America fails to change, there will be severe consequences on corporate profits as well as a weakening in the US status as a major world super-power. Our corporate sector faces a simple dilemma: either change attitudes toward ethnic diversity or suffer the consequences, including loss in their markets that could undermine their sustainability. That would be a step that could potentially culminate in their demise.

Skilled immigrants and artisans arriving from northern European countries primarily Great Britain, Germany and Ireland (See Table 1) were early contributors to the development of the US. Immigrants from other countries also contributed to the development of the US. But, as in the European case, skilled artisans began to face an untenable situation when US industries demanded more unskilled workers to staff factories. Social problems similar to those experienced in Europe began to appear as the US industrialized; these problems became particularly acute during times of economic turmoil. These problems resulted in divisions and discrimination by one group against others. That discrimination was very similar in nature to the prejudice experienced by Irish unskilled immigrants, primarily farmers, looking for employment in English factories during the Industrial Revolution. Discrimination was, therefore, the result of fear, insecurity, and lack of self-esteem. It was a feeling developed as a result of being unwilling to prove self-worth.

That bias was based on a superiority concept developed by nineteenth-century intellectuals who believed in the idea that human evolution culminated in the development of a superior Anglo Saxon race. That concept was brought to the US and was popularized by local intellectuals. John Fiske, who was an American philosopher and historian, was one of those early intellectuals and follower of this myth. Supporters argued that all progress and developments made in the US were the result of efforts made by skilled Anglo Saxons workers who had been assimilated in the new country and were relatively well off financially. This argument ignored the contributions made by other groups such as the Irish who together with the Chinese were instrumental in making the transcontinental railroad a reality. The Anglo Saxon superiority myth, however, became a discrimination tool to be used against anybody who was unable to trace his heritage directly to England.

The Irish were Anglo Saxons from a northern European country. Unfortunately, they were considered inferior and discriminated against in the northeastern United States by the English-Americans in much the same way as they were discriminated against in England merely because they were farmers. Irish immigrants who moved to California used the same Anglo Saxon superiority concept to discriminate against Mexicans and Spaniards; it is indeed curious to note the drastic change in status as these Irish immigrants moved from inferior to superior merely by a cross-country move. That showed the nonsensical nature of such superiority myth.

Racial superiority myths continued to very dangerous and divisive discrimination based on fiction and erroneous beliefs. The extermination of 6 million Jews by Nazis in Germany was prejudice under the "Arian Race" superiority concept.

Figure 1. Annual Immigration to the US [16]

Figure 1 shows the number of immigrants arriving in the US on a yearly basis from 1820 to 2008. It clearly shows an increasing trend in the number of immigrants arriving around the 1860s. This growing trend in arrivals corresponds to commencement of the American Industrial Revolution and the establishment of new factories. Staffing these new factories is done by employing an ever-increasing number of unskilled workers arriving from Europe and other places. The other side of the coin is that, in the absence of jobs, immigration is significantly reduced. This also happens when there is a recession or a slowdown in economic activity that forces reductions in labor requirements.

In the absence of job opportunities, there is a reduction in the influx of immigrants. Notice the drastic reductions occurring in the years 1883, 1911, 1924, and in the 1930s corresponding to periods of economic turmoil, including the Great Depression. On the other hand, notice the sharp increase in immigrants starting around 1897. Figure 1 only shows the number of legal immigrants coming into the country and excludes slaves brought in to be sold. In short, immigration is an indicator of labor shortage. When there is a labor shortage, immigration increases to satisfy that need. Conversely, if there is a lack of employment opportunities, then immigration diminishes and becomes insignificant.

It is during those times when manufacturing facilities began to flourish in the US that a massive influx of unskilled workers started. Obviously, those unskilled workers satisfied the needs of emerging industries. But those production facilities, in turn, impacted the growth of cities where those industries were located and changed the demographics pattern to resemble somewhat the character of the incoming immigrants' countries.

The influx of immigrants depends on the state of economic conditions prevailing in both the immigrants' countries and also in the US. For example, if economic conditions in the foreign country are recessionary and the economy in the United States is booming, then that disparity will be sufficient to attract foreigners from that foreign country to our shores. If the reverse situation were true then that will deter foreigners from migrating to our country. This is clearly the situation shown in Figure 1 where there are several periods when the number of legal immigrants arriving drops significantly even though, prior to 1920, there was no limitation on the number of immigrants allowed.

There are periods showing reductions at times when restrictions are imposed that limited the number of immigrants allowed into the country such as, for example, by the use of quotas. As economic conditions in the United States deteriorated in the early 1910s there was a popular movement in favor of restricting immigration. That movement culminated in the enactment of legislation restricting the number of immigrants allowed into the country. Quotas significantly restricted the number of immigrants as shown in the early 1920s.

Immigration patterns have changed throughout our nation's history. There have been immigrants coming from different parts of Europe at different times and possessing different skill levels. Skilled workers migrated to find refuge from the growth of factories in Europe threatening their economic wellbeing. This migration occurred before the 1860s when Europe was undergoing economic turmoil and the US was enjoying unprecedented economic prosperity. It lasted until the 1920s, when the era of open immigration ended. The enactment of the Emergency Quota Act of 1921 was the result of two factors: economic turmoil and fear on the part of the local population of immigrants who potentially could present threats to their continued employment. The quotas set by this legislation are listed in Table 2. Notice the bias in terms of percentage of immigrants allowed to be admitted from countries in Northwest Europe and Scandinavia as compared to immigrants from Eastern and Southern European countries. Notice the low numbers of non-Europeans immigrants allowed.

The Emergency Quota Act allowing 165,000 immigrants reflects prejudice against immigrants from eastern and southern Europe and China. Notice that quotas for eastern and southern Europeans represent a very low number as compared to the actual number of immigrants from the same countries shown in Table 1. For example, the number of Italians immigrants during the 1881 to 1890 decade was 307,000 or approximately 30,000 per year. The quota, however, allowed only 3,845 Italians per year to come in after 1921. The annual number of German immigrants allowed was approximately 51,000 versus the average annual of 145,000 during the 1881 to 1890 decade. The disparity in the quotas for immigrants from northwest European countries over those from eastern and southern European countries showed a clear preference for immigrants from a given part of Europe, namely those considered Anglo Saxons.

There were unskilled immigrants coming from China to the US West Coast during the 1860s and peaking in the 1870s. But, then the number of Chinese immigrants reaching our shores declined considerably as a result of being totally barred by the Chinese Exclusion Act of 1882. [18] The reason for that exclusion was blatant discrimination based on the desire to maintain "white racial purity." At that time, Chinese immigrants allowed into the country were mainly males because of the rule excluding females on the assumption they were prostitutes.[19] Fear of interracial marriages between Chinese males and local women became the

Northwest Europe and Scandinavia		Eastern and Southern Europe		Other Countries	
Country	*Quota*	*Country*	*Quota*	*Country*	*Quota*
Germany	51,227	Poland	5,982	Africa other than Egypt	1.100
Great Britain and Northern Ireland	34.007	Italy	3,845	Armenia	124
Ireland	28,567	Czechoslovakia	3,073	Australia	121
Sweden	9,561	Russia	2,248	Palestine	100
Norway	6,453	Yugoslavia	671	Syria	100
France	3,954	Romania	603	Turkey	100
Denmark	2,789	Portugal	503	Egypt	100
Switzerland	2,081	Hungary	473	New Zealand & Pacific Islands	100
Netherlands	1,648	Lithuania	344	All others	1,900
Austria	785	Latvia	142		
Belgium	512	Spain	131		
Finland	471	Estonia	124		
Free City of Danzig	228	Albania	100		
Iceland	100	Bulgaria	100		
Luxembourg	100	Greece	100		
Totals	142,483		18,439		3,745
Total (%)	86.5		11.2		2.3

Table 2. Immigrant Quota (17)

root cause of very vocal opposition to new Chinese immigrants. As a result, constituents petitioned their elected officials to exclude Chinese, which was exactly what they did in passing the Chinese Exclusion Act.

The Chinese Exclusion Act, passed by the Forty-Seventh Congress, suspended Chinese immigration for a period of ten years starting on May 6, 1882. It prohibited the naturalization of Chinese immigrants. The ban on Chinese immigration provided by the 1882 Act was extended by the Act to Prohibit the Coming of Chinese Persons into the United States of May 1892 [20] that was even more restrictive than the 1882 Act. President Franklin D. Roosevelt signed an *"Act to Repeal the Chinese Exclusion Acts* [21] *to lift , that, to Establish Quotas, and for Other Purposes"* lifted restrictions on naturalization, but others restrictions remained in place against Chinese immigrants until the Immigration Act of October 1965. [22]

Unlike Chinese women, Japanese females were allowed to immigrate on account of being "picture brides." [23] Japanese immigrants arrived in the United States West Coast with their families, which seemed to indicate a desire to remain in the country indefinitely. The San Francisco School Board segregated the city's Japanese students in schools where Chinese students had already been segregated. This caused diplomatic tensions between the United States and Japan that resulted in a diplomatic "understanding" negotiated by President Theodore Roosevelt and the Japanese Government restricting immigration from Japan. This agreement became known as the Gentlemen's Agreement of 1907. [24] This agreement was never ratified by Congress, but Japan agreed to stop issuing passports to its citizens in order to implement the negotiated understanding between Japan and the US.

Discrimination is still a fact of life not only in Corporate America but also in all of our nation's institutions. This is clearly demonstrated by the opposition of many US Republican Senators against the confirmation of Judge Sonia Sotomayor to become an Associate Justice of the US Supreme Court. Instead of basing their opposition on her educational background, or her public professional record of more than 4,000 published legal opinions on a variety of subjects that demonstrate her legal experience and legal reasoning as an experienced judge in the US District and Appellate Courts, or on her answers to the Senate Committee, Republicans politicians centered their objection to her confirmation on a silly statement uttered by Judge Sotomayor. The offensive comment was something to the effect that a "wise Latina" would be incapable of making more logical and better legal decisions than Anglo Saxon males. That off the record comment became the rallying point for Republican opposition. This opposition reflected their sentiment that perhaps Justice Sotomayor was better qualified than her tormentors.

There was no question Judge Sotomayor was extremely well qualified and her legal opinions were well received by the legal community. This demonstrated that she was a very capable legal professional. It was also beyond question that she was a very intelligent and wise human being, but that offended those were envious and incapable of accepting the fact that Latinos and Latinas could also be intelligent and wise. But, in the perspective of Republican politicians she had two things working against her. She was a female who happened to be a very qualified Hispanic candidate for the US Supreme Court.

There had been another well-qualified Latino justice in the US Supreme Court, who was believed to have been one of the best legal minds to ever serve in the highest court of the land. That US Supreme Court justice was Benjamin Cardozo, who happened to be of Portuguese ancestry and, therefore, a Latino under the more inclusive definition of being part of a nation where the native language was derived from the Latin language and therefore, Latino.

The majority of Republicans could not find anything wrong with Judge Sotomayor's qualifications except for the fact she was not an Anglo Saxon! That was a tragedy when one witnessed a group of supposedly educated and intelligent legislators acting the way they did and, in doing so, show their lack of common sense!

Our country is in trouble when we, as ordinary citizens, entrust our national institutions to individuals of the caliber represented by these legislators. They lack common sense and rely on nonsense to prevent well-qualified individuals from serving our nation. The case of Justice Sotomayor is not the only instance where US senators have shown a lack of common sense. President Obama has been the recipient of similar nonsense by none other than the Democratic Senate Majority Leader Senator Reid who opined that candidate Barack Obama could possibly be an acceptable black candidate for president based on the lighter color of his black skin.

Does that nonsense comment from Senator Reid mean that President Obama's intellect is of no concern? Does a darker skin color indicate a person unable to think or lead this nation? Senators and politicians, in general, are not the only ones to lack common sense, and their contemptuous attitude should be offensive to all Americans. Undoubtedly, many corporate officers are of the same caliber as those politicians. Ordinary citizens as individuals and collectively as a nation deserve better. If the actions of these legislators reflect their intellect, then it must be said that the country is in trouble. It is in trouble when we elect lawmakers of that caliber to rule the country. We need to remove them and replace them with better qualified individuals to prevent the demise of our American Way of Life.

OCCUPATIONS OF IMMIGRANTS

Table 3 presents a simplified profile of the occupations of immigrants arriving in the United States from 1630 to 1998. The first settlers came to the United States at a time when an open immigration policy was in effect. At that time, there was no need to list occupations on their arrival forms. It would be conceivable that among those early immigrants there were some who had had skills; however, most were unskilled workers and farmers. Those failing to list an occupation probably did not have one.

Starting in the 1820s, the United States began to collect data on occupations of arriving immigrants. Approximately 40 percent of those arriving listed an occupation on the arrival forms. The occupations ranged from professionals all the way to laborers, farmers, and servants. The term "professional" as used then should not be confused with the same term as we use it today. It was possible that some of the people listing their occupations as professionals were writers and others were technical experts who had lost their industrial positions as a result of an economic downturn in Europe. The important thing to keep in mind was that the term had a different connotation to that attached by present-day usage. The same can be said about the term commercial which would include many types of occupations including salesmen and business owners.

The important thing to capture from data in Table 3 is that the majority of those reporting an occupation had some commercial expertise or background qualifying for employment as traders, bankers, etc. The unskilled workers category shows significant increases from 1820 to the early 1910s, corresponding to an accelerating trend in US industrial activity requiring unskilled manpower. There is also a subtle increase in the number of professional immigrants arriving in the United States during the same period. These early professional immigrants migrating from Europe might be considered engineers or tradesmen to assist in the effort to convert local manufacturing activity from factories assembling products all the way to mass production.

Year	Yearly Ave	Total Reporting Occup'n	Number of Immigrants				
			Profesional	Comercial	Other Skills	Total Skilled	Total Unskilled
1630-1700	2,200						
1700-1780	4,325						
1780-1819	9,900						
1820-1831	14,538	5,670	170	1,588	1,701	3,459	11,079
1832-1846	71,916	31,643	316	3,797	8,544	12,657	59,259
1847-1854	334,506	153,873	0	9,232	27,697	36,929	297,577
1855-1864	160,427	75,401	754	9,048	17,342	27,144	133,283
1865-1873	327,464	150,633	1,506	9,038	36,152	46,696	280,768
1874-1880	260,754	138,200	2,764	5,528	33,168	41,460	219,294
1881-1893	525,102	267,802	2,678	8,034	53,560	64,272	460,830
1894-1899	276,547	171,459	1,715	6,858	42,865	51,438	225,109
1900-1914	891,806	659.946	6,599	13,199	19,798	39,506	852,210
1915-1919	234,536	147,758	7,388	5,910	7,388	20,686	213,850
1920-1930	412,474	251,609	10,064	12,580	10064	32,709	379,765
1931-1946	50,507	20,708	3,934	828	3,106	7,869	42,638
1947-1960	252,210	118,539	18,966	5,927	5,927	30,820	221,290
1961-1970	332,168	146,154	33,615	2,923	7,308	43,846	288,322
1971-1980	449,331	184,226	46,056	(a)	14,738	60,794	388,537
1981-1990	733,806	322,875	45,202	(a)	25,830	71,032	662,774
1991-1998	950,634	399,266	63,883	(a)	27,949	91,831	858,803
(a) Included in separate category							

Table 3. Occupations of Immigrants [25]

There are several things worth noticing from these data on immigrant occupations and trends shown in Table 3 for skilled and unskilled immigrants. The number of unskilled workers has always been significantly larger than that of skilled workers. The number of unskilled immigrants increased over the time period covered by data in the table, but, the number of skilled workers remained a small fraction of the total yearly number, particularly, as compared to the total number of unskilled workers. The level of skilled immigrants appears to be fairly constant over the entire period of time, but there appears to be an upward trend in the number of skilled workers arriving on our shores after World War II that has continued to the present time.

Notice the number of professionals becomes a substantially higher fraction of the total number of skilled immigrants after World War II. Given that many professionals are displaced by the destruction caused by war in Europe, it is not unexpected to see many of these displaced European professionals migrating to the US at the end of World War II. As a result of immigration laws, the number of professionals and those who have skills in short supply entering the country increases. This immigration policy no doubt tilts the balance toward professionals. During the same period, there is a steady decline in the number of those with commercial expertise. Finally, political conditions in foreign countries also have an impact on the number of professionals coming into the US. It is possible that the level or type of skills represented by these skilled immigrants may have changed during the time periods covered in the table.

The number of professional immigrants has increased since World War II. These professionals come from countries other than those coming immediately after the end of World War II. The first wave of professionals is composed of Europeans. They are professionals unable to find work because of the industrial devastation caused by aerial bombardments of their countries. As conditions in Europe improve, most of those scientists and engineers find satisfying work in their home countries and lose all interest in migrating to the US.

The second wave of professionals comes primarily from Asian countries, particularly India and Taiwan, due to modifications of the immigration laws in 1965. It is conceivable that, as in the case of European scientists and engineers, these professionals would also have preferred to remain in their native countries as opposed to migrating to the US. Presumably, these scientists and engineers are coming to the US because shortage of these professional people in our country. This raises a very important question in regards to the future supply of engineers and scientists for our own industrial base. Will there be sufficient home grown and educated engineering and scientific talent to satisfy the needs of our industrial base and take us to the next level of technical development?

Are primary and secondary schools providing a strong enough foundation in math and science to enable students to continue on to technical careers? Is industry providing the leadership required to attract the best students to scientific and engineering careers? Unfortunately, the answer to these questions is clearly no. Our primary and secondary students rank very low in science and math as compared to foreign students. The number of students continuing on to a technical education is diminishing, primarily because industry does not place a high value on these people.

Scientists and engineers are the first to go when the economy turns south. Corporate America needs to reconsider this self-defeating policy. Unlike financiers who create nothing but a map for self-destruction, scientists and engineers develop the manufacturing processes necessary to mass produce new products being invented in R&D laboratories. These are the activities that add value to the corporation and not financial gimmickry.

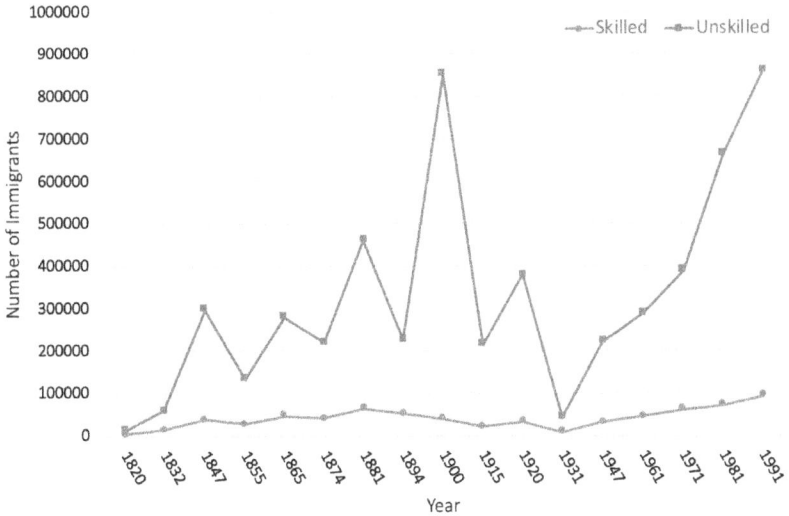

Figure 2. Skills Distribution.

Figure 2 shows the number of unskilled immigrants entering the US increasing from the 1930s on. This trend appears to accelerate to a very significant rate, particularly after World War II. These are primarily laborers and agricultural workers coming from Latin American countries. One might ask what causes such high demand for these unskilled workers. The answer is a simple but controversial one in view of the current debate relating to "illegal immigration." On one side of the argument is the impact of this migration of unskilled workers on social issues such as healthcare, unemployment, educational opportunities, and other factors that supposedly increase social costs and burden citizens with additional taxes. The other side of the argument is the benefit provided by unskilled workers in many sectors of the economy such as agriculture and home construction.

The simple reason these unskilled immigrants are coming is the availability of unfilled jobs in the US. These are jobs that are unfilled by local workers who are either unavailable or unwilling to accept those positions at the low wages being paid by employers. The other side of the coin is that those unskilled immigrants are unable to secure jobs in their home countries either because suitable jobs are unavailable or there are an excess number of workers for every available job. That's the reality that we face in the US. It is something that needs to be addressed by immigration reform and fair government action.

The number of professional immigrants increased steadily up until the 1900s, which is when industry began to switch from factory assembly over to mass production. There was a spike in the number of professionals arriving in the United Sates prior to and immediately after World War I (World War I), which may reflect difficult economic conditions in Europe during that period and favorable conditions in the US. As expected, the Great Depression caused economic turmoil both in Europe and the US, resulting in lower demand for employees and thus a lesser need for immigrants. Consequently, the total number of immigrants regardless of skills arriving in the US during the depression years is lower than in the previous twenty years when industrial activity was at full speed ahead. World War II also had a similar adverse impact on immigration, but prevailing economic conditions were on the upswing due to the need for armaments to fight the war. This improved economic situation attracted immigrants to work in industries engaged in war-related production.

The distribution of skills among skilled immigrants varied as shown in Figure 3. There are three subcategories included in the "Skilled Immigrant" classification: professional, commercial and miscellaneous or other skills. It is certain that the skills levels associated with each of these categories may have changed with time. For example, immigrants included in the "commercial skills" category initially may have been included in the "professional" category but at a later date may have been excluded from such classification due to a lack of proper training, education, or other factors. That may be a plausible explanation for the decline seen in the "commercial" category from the 1940s on.

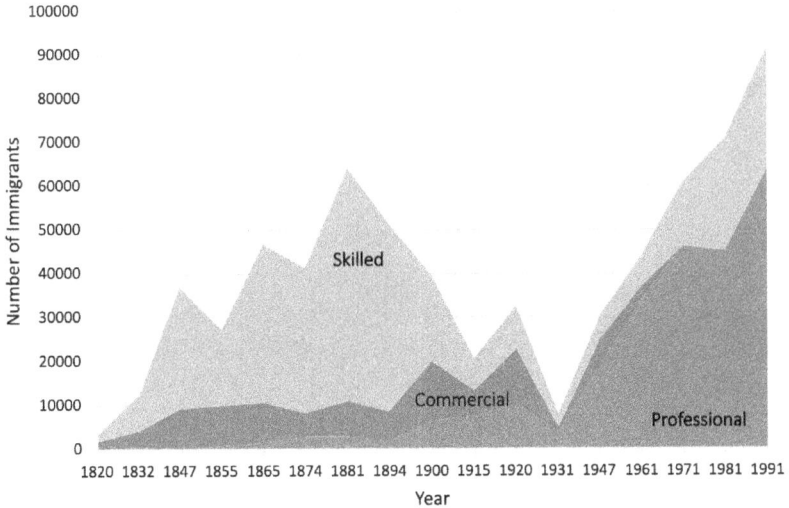

Figure 3. Immigrant Distribution

The figure shows a very substantial increase in the number of professional immigrants arriving in the United States after the end of World War II. Reasons for this large migration of professionals may include poor or lack of adequate industrial activity in Europe after the war and excellent economic opportunities available in the United States at the same time. Keep in mind that European industry was devastated during the war while that of the US was intact and vibrantly growing to satisfy the demands of the entire world. As Europe recovered from the devastation caused by World War II fewer European professionals migrated to the US, preferring to stay in their home countries and partake of the opportunities presented by the economic recovery of their own countries. This would imply, therefore, that the source of immigrants after the late 1960s and early 1970s changed from European countries to countries in the Western Hemisphere and Asia.

There is no question that the US, as is well known, is a country built by immigrants. It is a country that attracts those who have been rejected by their own countries because of their economic status, political, or religious beliefs. The US is a country with a vibrant economy because of the efforts of newly arrived immigrants. The American people are very generous people who understand the suffering of others and extend their hand to help those who are down. It is inconceivable, therefore, to think that the American people would reject those in need and those who come to our shores.

Lately, however, we have seen some effort to exclude illegal immigrants from Mexico and other Western Hemisphere countries. The anger against those immigrants does not represent the American character but rather represents the hatred preached by some members of our society who stand to gain economic benefits or political power. The silent majority of Americans expects the government to enforce immigration laws and, at the same time, provide the means for an orderly process to attract the required number of agricultural workers on a yearly basis. In fact, that anger may be misplaced, because employers keep hiring these immigrants. Why not place the anger on the shoulders of employers who want to hire people at less than minimum wages? Why not place the blame on lawmakers who fail to address the immigration problem?

It is not enough to blame poor, unskilled, illegal immigrants for all that ails our society. After all, these illegal immigrants are performing a valuable service and making a positive contribution to our society. It is difficult to imagine that only legal Mexican immigrants work on road construction, build houses and hospitals, and work in restaurants in the Houston, Texas area. Additionally, there are many more Mexican immigrants working the agricultural fields and performing a valuable service for our society. Are the services performed by these individuals necessary? If you don't believe so then consider how the US would be able to provide the required number of farm workers at harvest time to pick crops before spoilage? There is no question that the selling prices of fruits and vegetables would be much higher if these immigrants were not allowed to work in the fields.

In summary, immigrants and their descendants have not only provided the laborers but also the management and professional personnel required for industrial development. It is fair to say that immigrants have made the US an industrial power house unequaled anywhere in the world. The most important contribution made by these immigrants and their descendants is their brain power. That is what differentiates the US from the rest of the world, and it is the root benefit of the ethnic diversity present in the United States and available to US industry.

Working people have always been exposed to exploitation by the corporate world in its search for higher profits. This has forced laborers to join together to repel those abuses. A labor movement emerged as a result of abuse against labor that culminated in the formation of what is known today as labor unions. Many examples of these abuses have been recorded throughout our industrial history. In response, the government passed legislation to protect workers and, in parallel to that, many lawsuits were filed and decided by courts addressing these issues. For example, in the case of Oklahoma v. Coyle[26] the Oklahoma Court of Criminal Appeals wrestled with the idea of extending legal protection to workers in a price-fixing conspiracy in the cotton trade. Judge Henry Furman found the antitrust statute to be a legitimate protection against labor exploitation. The judge reasoned that labor was the most important element and focal point of any industrial activity. He chose to express his findings on this matter in these very eloquent words:

Labor was made by God; capital is made by man. Labor is not only blood and bone, but it also has a mind and soul, and is animated by sympathy, hope, and love; capital is inanimate, soulless matter. Labor is the creator; capital is the creature. If all the capital in the world was destroyed, a great injury would thereby be inflicted upon the entire human race; but the bright minds, the brave hearts, and the strong arms of labor would in time create new capital, and thus the injury would be ultimately cured… Labor is always a matter of necessity. Capital is largely a matter of luxury. Labor has been dignified by the example of God. The savior of mankind was the "carpenter's son."

CHAPTER 3
THE BIRTH OF AN
INDUSTRIAL GIANT

In the late eighteenth century, the United States was a relatively new country focusing on agriculture and facing many challenges. Cotton was a major agricultural staple providing raw material for clothing and for international trade. The fibrous lint and seeds had to be manually separated using slave labor to produce fibers necessary for spinning and weaving into cloth and useful for making garments. Eli Whitney, an American, saw an opportunity to improve the separation of cotton seeds from the fibrous lint. He designed and built a simple machine to achieve that goal, but with the added advantage that he was able to increase production and reduce labor costs as a result. His invention revolutionized cotton production. Mr. Whitney's invention was granted US Patent number 72X dated March 14, 1794 [27] and he became a pioneer in the US textile industry.

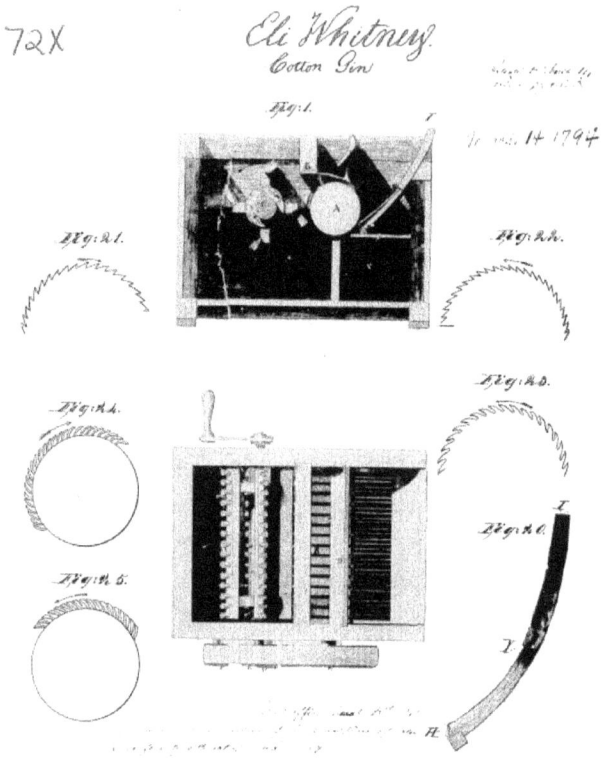

72X

Eli Whitney.
Cotton Gin

Figure 4. Eli Whitney's Cotton Gin – Patent Number 72X

A drawing of Mr. Whitney's cotton gin is shown in Figure 4. It is obvious, looking at the bottom half of the figure, that there is a crank enabling the manual rotation of a couple of cylinders connected to one another via an arrangement of belt and pulleys. These internal cylinders are fitted with spikes to grab and pull cotton fibers through slotted openings to separate seeds from lint.

It is interesting to note that this machine is manually driven, but it could be modified to be driven by an electric motor, thus making it even more useful and efficient. That conversion from manual operation to motor driven becomes possible by either replacing the crank with a pulley that, in turn, is connected to a motor or connecting the motor directly to the shaft holding the crank. Replacement of the crank by a pulley also makes it possible to drive multiple machines simultaneously from a central shaft. This modification, therefore, makes it possible to have parallel production lines in a factory. Generation and transmission of electrical power did not become reality until the late 1880s to mid-1890s, when Thomas Edison, a descendant of Dutch immigrants, set up the first centrally electric generating power plant.

Mr. Whitney did not stop his pioneering effort after the cotton gin invention. He faced many legal problems enforcing his patent against those who copied his cotton gin design and, as a result, failed to profit from this invention. In 1807 after many lawsuits, the 1794 Cotton Gin Patent was finally found to be valid by the courts, but the remaining term of patent validity was relatively short (approximately four years). In 1798, he made another very significant contribution by developing and implementing the concept of interchangeability of standard mechanical parts in the manufacture of muskets. This became a very important development revolutionizing the assembly process and, more importantly, it became the basis for making spare parts available to quickly repair industrial machinery used in manufacturing processes. Mr. Whitney's persistence paid off in the end.

In 1793, Samuel Slater [28], an English Immigrant, built the first successful water-powered cotton-spinning mill in Rhode Island. Mr. Slater had been an apprentice at a textile mill in England. He decided to migrate to the US at the end of his apprenticeship. At the time, England had a policy restricting or preventing the export of technology outside of its border. In view of that, Mr. Slater decided to memorize the technology used in textile mills and replicated in a Rhode Island textile mill. He had ambitions of becoming an entrepreneur, and he made his dream come true by migrating to the US. His story became part of the pattern followed by subsequent immigrants arriving in the US.

In 1810, Francis C. Lowell [29] visited textile mills in Lancashire, England, and became convinced that English textile mills employed manufacturing technology superior to that currently accessible to US textile mills, including the one practiced in Mr. Slater's mill. Lowell sought to bring such technology to the US, but he discovered that England prohibited the transfer of mill technology to other countries. This forced Mr. Lowell to memorize what he had witnessed and to try to recreate the technology from memory for use in mills in the US.

He was able to improve the technology with the assistance of Paul Moody, who was a skillful machinist and mechanic who could be considered an early mechanical engineer. Mr. Moody was able to design machines that not improved cloth quality but made it feasible to perform all operations required for converting raw cotton into cloth under a single roof. The Boston Manufacturing Company was established in 1813 to practice this new textile technology. The actions of Mr. Lowell were an early attempt to compete with Mr. Slater and at gaining an advantage by using more efficient process manufacturing technology. This would become very relevant as the country industrialized further.

Mr. Lowell started his Boston Manufacturing Company by raising capital using the novel idea of selling company shares to investors. These investors pooled their financial resources to form a joint-stock company. That novel concept was analogous to that of a present-day corporation. The advantages of this business model were many. In particular, this business arrangement made it feasible to raise large amounts of capital to build, operate, and expand the business by simply offering additional shares of the business to other investors and by making those shares transferable. The ability to issue more shares provided access to a larger investor pool for the purpose of raising needed capital. The corporate model enabled the business entity to continue operating even in the event of death of a shareholder. This was a very significant advantage provided by the joint-stock company over the single proprietorship or partnership arrangements common at the time.

There were other contributions made by Mr. Lowell in his pioneering effort to establish the textile industry in the United States. These efforts focused on manufacturing the right product for the market at the lowest possible cost, minimizing marketing risks, and providing a reliable labor force. These actions were essential to the success of the venture. In other words, Mr. Lowell had a global view of the business and devised a business plan to achieve his goal of becoming a major player in the textile industry of the young country.

The invention of the sewing machine was another development in the evolution of the textile industry; it focused on using cloth or fabric produced in textile mills to produce garments. In 1830, French tailor Barthelemy Thimonnier patented a sewing machine that sewed straight seams. This sewing machine was used to make uniforms for the French army in a factory. His factory was burned by tailors who were afraid of losing their livelihood; this was a typical reaction by skilled artisans who felt threatened by factories being established during the industrial revolution.

There were other inventors who contributed to the development of the sewing machine, particularly in the stitching operation. Among them was Elias Howe [30] who in 1846 was granted US Patent No. 4750 for the sewing machine shown in Figure 5. Howe's machine included improvements made to the lockstitch sewing machine invented by Walter Hunt in 1833; Mr. Hunt had failed to patent his lockstitch mechanism. While Mr. Howe was in England trying to sell his invention, Isaac Singer and others were designing their own sewing machines using the lockstitch mechanism invented by Mr. Howe.

Figure 5. Elias Howe Lockstitch Sewing Machine

Patent litigation over the invention of the sewing machine between Elias Howe and Isaac Singer was a very interesting outcome resulting from motivation to do better than the original inventor. The issue of the litigation boiled down to an attempt to determine who invented the lockstitch mechanism employed in the sewing machine. If Walter Hunt had decided to patent the lockstitch mechanism he invented in 1833, then Elias Howe would not have been granted a patent on that mechanism. Mr. Singer would have won the litigation in 1854. That end would have been simply on account the original invention had occurred twenty-one years earlier which would have exceeded the seventeen year statutory life of any patent at that time. Since Howe's Patent was granted in 1846, it was still valid in 1854 and therefore subject to infringement by Mr. Singer's unauthorized or unlicensed use without royalty payment. Mr. Howe's sewing machine was capable of making 250 stitches per minute, which exceeded the output of five hand sewers with a reputation for speed.

Elias Howe continued making contributions to the textile industry and, in particular, to the clothing industry. One of those contributions was an invention of what he called an "automatic continuous clothing closure" which was very similar in concept to a modern zipper prototype; he was granted US Patent No. 8540 issued on November 25, 1851, for this invention. Mr. Howe failed to market his invention. Whitcomb Judson marketed what he called a Clasp Locker, which was very similar to the device described in Howe's patent forty-four years earlier. Gideon Sundbac was issued US Patent No. 1219881 on March 20, 1917, for his design of the modern zipper shown in Figure 6. The name zipper came from the BF Goodrich Co., which used this type of fastener in rubber boots.

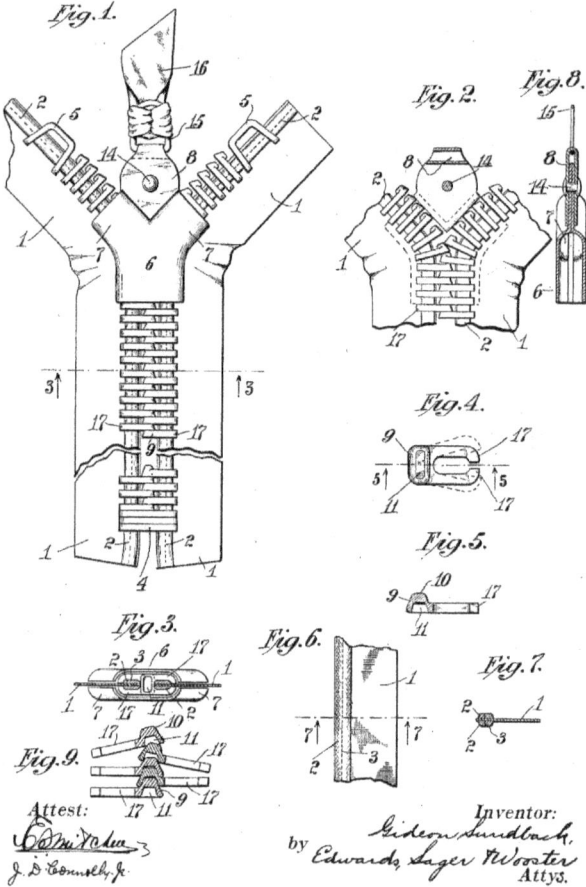

G. SUNDBACK.
SEPARABLE FASTENER.
APPLICATION FILED AUG. 27, 1914.

1,219,881.

Patented Mar. 20, 1917.

Figure 6. Gideon Sunback's Zipper in US Patent 1,219,881

There were subsequent inventions and US patents granted on improvements to the zipper as originally envisioned by Mr. Howe. Efforts at improving either the technology or the product of that technology have continued to the present time. Initially, the discovery was revolutionary, but it became an evolutionary process after a continuing effort at improving the existing process made it possible for other inventors to contribute a better solution either as individuals or groups of people.

One such example is the closure used in plastic bags for food storage. This demonstrates that industrial progress is a continuing process; it cannot be stopped, otherwise the existing manufacturing process falls behind others who improve on the original idea or invent and produce a better product at a lower cost. This is the reason engineering has become and continues to be so important to industry. Unfortunately, industry has alienated engineers in their recent cost cutting efforts, thus setting the stage for falling behind technologically. These exercises have decimated the number of engineers employed by industry, and the industry has not achieved the cost-cutting goals set by management. Industry has gone the wrong path by allowing financiers to reduce cost by simply reducing employment, which is a temporary fix. Unlike financiers, most engineers focus their on improving manufacturing processes to achieve lasting cost reductions.

Several lessons can be derived from this brief narrative on the early days of the textile industry in the US. The ingredients of any successful industrial development are: technology, availability of engineering talent, access to capital, access to operating personnel, a capable and motivated sales force, management flexibility, and continuing R&D efforts. Nowhere is the government involved in these efforts except in protecting inventions by the issuance of patents. In other words, the early industrial successes in this nation are the direct result of individual effort by entrepreneurs at developing and using technology to satisfy a market need or make life easier. The motivation of these entrepreneurs is to succeed. But the road to success sometimes has many detours which lead to failures. The important thing to keep in mind is not the number of times one fails but, rather, how many times one gets up and tries again.

Both Mr. Samuel Slater and Mr. Francis Lowell recognized that technology was an essential ingredient in starting the textile industry in the US. Neither one of them was able to get access to technology because of export restrictions imposed by the government of England on licensing technology for use outside its borders. They resorted to copying the technology and using it without a license. Obviously, both of these textile pioneers reversed engineer technologies for their own use and benefit.

Copying technology does not amount to taking physical possession of an object but rather understanding the intellectual concepts embodied in such operating process or product. The result is the same, i.e., expropriation to the detriment of the lawful owner. It can be argued that copying technology is analogous to stealing technology. Technology copying or reverse engineering achieves the same results in depriving the lawful owner of the benefits of his invention. The difference is that, in many cases, reversed engineering eliminates many problems inherent in the original technology. It is for this reason companies are very strict in restricting visits to their facilities and prohibiting visitors from touring certain areas of the manufacturing facility or from taking photographs of areas the companies deem important.

Both Slater and Lowell recognized the importance of investment capital. Mr. Slater became a partner in a Rhode Island textile mill by investing his intellectual capital in exchange for an ownership share in the mill. Mr. Lowell, on the other hand, chose to raise capital by selling equity shares in the mill to investors, which is analogous to the concept of stocks in the present-day corporate model. Lowell knew that selling the product was extremely important to cover production costs and to generate profits to grow the business and to pay dividends to investors. Lowell relied on agents selling the output of his mill to third parties. Commissions provided the incentive those agents needed to market product.

The importance of technology and the value of engineers in making dreams come true were recognized by Mr. Slater and Mr.

Lowell. Mr. Slater was an engineer by training. Mr. Lowell, on the other hand, depended on Paul Moody for engineering support. Immigrants provided manpower as laborers and managers to operate textile mills. It was also obvious that these entrepreneurs continued to improve their manufacturing facilities by inventing new tools, developing new operating procedures, and reducing costs; all of these things were done to stay competitive and satisfy market demand.

Technology can either be developed as done by Eli Howe in designing the sewing machine, or it can be licensed in exchange for payment of royalties as done by Isaac Singer at the conclusion of the litigation on the infringement of Mr. Howe's sewing machine patent. Companies realize that their technologies can be copied or stolen, and for that reason rely on different mechanisms to protect their technologies. None of these mechanisms, however, is perfect in ensuring total protection. Each of these mechanisms has advantages and disadvantages, and it is for those reasons that companies may choose one method over the other or they may rely on a combination of methods.

Patenting, for example, is one example of a technology-protection mechanism. The US government grants the inventor an absolute monopoly right over the invention disclosed by the patent. The main disadvantage, however, is that, at the end of the current twenty-year statutory period, the technology becomes part of the public domain and anybody can use it legally. Maintaining the technology as a secret is an alternate mechanism preferred by many companies. The disadvantage of secrecy is that trade secrets can become public and, once that happens, there is no means to prevent third parties from using such technology or keep the technology secret any longer.

Regardless of the method used in protecting technological developments, there are many situations in which technology is copied by companies in developing nations and practiced in those nations to the detriment of technology owners. Typically a developing nation licenses technology from companies in developed nations to use at a given defined location, which is acceptable.

But, then that technology is duplicated at other locations without additional payments to the technology owner. In many cases, the technology user develops improvements to the original technology and then claims the whole technology is its own.

The other situation is when the technology is stolen outright without compensating the owner. The US government has a fundamental interest in preventing the stealing of technology by developing countries. It has the means to see that this practice of stealing or copying technology stops either by restricting imports from an offending country, confiscating product, or by imposing huge import duties on all products from that country. Unfortunately, US companies have chosen to transfer manufacturing to foreign countries, which has led to very high risks of losing all US technological developments to those countries. That practice destroys US technological leadership.

A case in point is the manufacture of cell phones and TV sets. Technology used in manufacturing cell phones has been transferred to China by US inventors and corporations. China produces basically all cell phones based on that technology. What happens in the event the Chinese cell phone manufacturers want to produce a cell-phone design based on its know-how? It is very likely the Chinese manufacturer will consider US technology as part of its knowhow and will use it to achieve his goal. Who paid for the development of the technology? Who loses on that deal?

All machinery used in manufacturing facilities up until the late 1880s was driven by steam, which required access to a large source of fuel to vaporize water into steam for industrial use. Wood and coal were the preferred fuels for such purpose, and these had to be easily accessible in large quantities to generate vast amounts of steam required for driving manufacturing machinery. This, therefore, limited location of factories to areas near abundant sources of these fuels. Electricity was an alternate means of driving such machinery, but that alternative would not become available until Thomas Edison demonstrated its practical use by lighting his Menlo Park Laboratory in 1879.

Once Mr. Edison realized the importance of his lightning

demonstration, he focused his efforts on developing a system to generate electricity in a central location so that it could be transmitted to users located at different locations. He achieved that goal in 1882, resulting in the establishment of predecessor companies to the General Electric Co. and Consolidated Edison Power Co. of New York as we know them today. Edison's idea was based on using 110 volts direct current (DC). DC electrical power transmission was limited to a distance of approximately one mile radius, which limited the concept as far as the location of users was concerned. By the end of 1880s, there were many small, central, electrical-power generating stations providing electricity to many US cities for use in lighting the streets and also for manufacturing activities.

Edison did not invent the light bulb as popularly believed. He improved light bulbs by using carbonized filaments and improving the level of vacuum inside the glass globe. Vacuum prevented oxygen access to the carbonized filament preventing its decomposition; this breakthrough extended the practical life of the light bulb. Edison, however, demonstrated the feasibility of a complete lightning system at his Menlo Park Research Park and undertook the development of an electrical generating and transmission system to enable its industrial use.

Electricity has many advantages over steam. Steam generation required large amounts of coal or wood for fuel to produce sufficient quantities of steam for the purpose of either driving machinery used in manufacturing activities or for driving turbines to generate electricity. Electricity is easier to transmit over long distances as compared to steam. This means that electricity consumers or users can be located far from the central generating station. That is so because steam tends to condense over the transmission route, thus lowering its energy content and limiting the distance over which it can be transmitted. Condensate has to be returned to the boilers in the central generating station to vaporize once again into steam, and long return lines add to the cost of the system. This cycle minimizes the amount of water consumed. For that reason steam is used to drive turbines generating electricity and the condensate is returned to the boilers located relatively close to the turbine. In this fashion, water usage and the cost of returning condensate by pumping it to the boilers is minimized. In short, electricity is a more versatile form of energy than steam, and it is easier to transmit over longer distances.

Thomas Edison [31] was not an engineer by education but shared all the attributes of a typical engineer: curiosity, willingness to solve problems, hunger for learning how things work, eagerness to experiment, and persistence to make things work better and more efficiently. Edison was a prolific inventor who was granted more than a thousand US patents for all his inventions, including improvements to the incandescent light bulb, phonograph, and many others items related to the telegraph. Over the years, many factories were established around the original Menlo Park located southwest of New York City. This was a production center employing more than 10,000 people by the late 1910s.

There are many similarities in the stories of Francis Lowell and that of Thomas Edison. Both of these individuals were industrial pioneers driven by a desire to establish an industry to manufacture useful products for society and to improve the standards of living of the general population. Both of these men know that success in their ventures would translate into personal wealth. Consequently, both focused on making their ventures successful and worked hard to achieve success. Both recognized the importance of technology to the success of their ventures, but they acquired technology by different means. Edison foresaw a need and invented a product to satisfy that need. Mr. Lowell, on the other hand, chose to become acquainted with the technology, recognized its shortcomings, and then improved it.

Both Lowell and Edison were aware of the large sums of capital required to make their dreams reality. Lowell established a stock company, and Edison relied on investment bankers such as J.P. Morgan to invest in his ventures. Neither one relied on the government for handouts or entitlements as is customary to do nowadays. It is also worth noticing that no taxes were imposed by the United States government or any state government during this period in US history. This enabled companies to reinvest profits to expand the business.

Although there were sales taxes imposed on distilled spirits and other things, there was no income tax in the United States until 1862. In that year, Congress enacted the first income-tax law to raise funds for the Civil War effort. In 1872, Congress eliminated the income tax and focused its taxation efforts on tobacco and distilled spirits to generate revenues. In 1913, the Sixteenth Amendment to the US Constitution made the income tax permanent. The result of not having an income tax was that people like Edison, who were establishing the industrial base of the US, could keep more of the profits from their ventures for further industrial investment.

George Westinghouse [32] had an interest in electricity and decided to investigate Edison's scheme for transmittal of electricity, which was based on low-voltage DC current. That meant that large electrical currents would be necessary and would result in large power losses. There was a competing scheme, based on transmitting alternating current (AC) at high voltages being worked on by Nikola Tesla. The AC system required the use of transformers to increase the voltage of the current at the generating stations and another transformer to reduce voltage at the consumption points. Transmitting electricity at higher voltage resulted in fewer electrical losses, so the AC system became the preferred system for transmitting electrical power over long distances. Westinghouse demonstrated the transmission of AC electrical power by transmitting hydroelectric power generated at Niagara Falls to consumptions centers in Buffalo, New York.

Westinghouse made additional contributions to the transportation industry, particularly railroads. He invented the railway air brake that enabled all rail cars to stop simultaneously rather than requiring the application of brakes to each individual car manually. He was also instrumental in devising a signal system to guide and control railroad traffic. All of these inventions resulted in the creation of many employment opportunities to staff the growing number of manufacturing facilities being established to manufacture products of the inventions.

The result of the efforts by Edison, Westinghouse, Lowell, and others was the establishment of a very dynamic and strong manufacturing base in the United States. These manufacturing facilities became the beneficiaries of an ever-increasing number of immigrants attracted to this country by the vitality of its industrial base.

The expanding US industrial base depended on technology and the engineers to develop such technology. Consequently, demand for skilled workers increased as previously noted in Figure 3, particularly around the 1870s. This shift in the skills level required for the manufacturing facilities had a direct impact on the wages paid to skilled workers and, undoubtedly, had a positive influence on the wages of unskilled workers. High-paying manufacturing jobs were the result of commercializing the products of R&D discoveries. Instead of government entitlements to discourage citizens from seeking employment, workers developed a strong work ethic to earn and maintain their livelihoods. Furthermore, the government played a key role in not taxing manufacturing activities, thereby providing the incentive for more investment in such industrial activities to continue creating job opportunities.

There were other inventors who contributed significantly to the development of the US industrial base. Among these were Charles Goodyear, Cyrus McCormick, George Eastman, Herbert H. Dow, Andrew Carnegie, and many others. For example, Charles Goodyear invented the rubber vulcanization process and started a brand-new industry enabling the use of rubber is such things as shoe soles, automobile tires, and etc. His was a very compelling story in persistence and goal-oriented focus. His company, The Goodyear Tire and Rubber Co as we know it today, had approximately 60,000 employees manufacturing products derived from his inventions back in 1860 when he died.

This illustrious group of inventors set the foundation for establishing the following companies bearing their founders' names in some cases: rubber and tire (Goodyear Tire and Rubber Co.), farm machinery and trucks (McCormick - International Harvester), photography (Eastman Kodak), chemicals (Dow

Chemical), steel (Carnegie – predecessor to US Steel). They demonstrated what is meant by "Yankee ingenuity" which was nothing more than the willingness to solve problems. Solving daily problems became the foundation for creating manufacturing jobs. Those were manufacturing jobs making new products for daily use.

Nothing was unreachable! All that was needed was a dream and hard work to make the dream reality. In many cases, these industrial pioneers faced obstacles such as bankruptcy as in the case of Mr. Goodyear. That merely was an obstacle that he had to overcome on the way to success, and that obstacle did not stop him from continuing his work. Perhaps, he realized that when one is down on the floor there is no other place to look at but the stars.

What is the moral of the story thus far? US Industry depended heavily on technology and R&D. The products invented by these R&D efforts become the basis for creating manufacturing jobs that paid higher wages than service jobs. These are the jobs that Corporate America must create in order to maintain the standard of living Americans have become accustomed to. Anything that impedes or frustrates R&D and manufacturing efforts has a detrimental impact and grave consequences on our standard of living.

Nowadays, the trend is for business entities to relocate manufacturing facilities away from the US. That definitely has a detrimental impact on our standard of living in the US and diminishes the global influence of US power. Something has to be done to reverse this destructive trend. The American people have the power to stop the trend by casting their votes and by the spending their consumer dollars on US made products.

As Corporate America becomes more and more dependent on technology, the requirement for highly skilled engineers becomes extremely important. But is the educational system up to par to provide the scientists and engineers required to maintain and continue our industrial development? The answer is clearly no. The public educational system is broken and in need of immediate repairs. Politicians recognize that the educational system needs to be revamped, but nothing is done to improve the quality of education or to make equal educational opportunities available to all Americans. Political leaders talk about improving the existing educational system but send their children to private schools; their actions speak louder than their words. In many instances, the product from our educational system is on par with those from less-developed countries. How can these graduates go on to lead Corporate America?

MASS PRODUCTION

The trend started during the Industrial Revolution in England toward production away from artisan shops and into factories was replicated in the US but along a different path. Artisans made a high-quality, custom-made product, but the result was relatively expensive. Factories, on the other hand, made acceptable-quality products at lower cost; factory made product was not custom made, but price overcame objections. The quality of factory-made product was not on par with custom-made product, but it would improve significantly with time. The benefit of factories was making acceptable-quality product at affordable prices. Factories relied on unskilled workers for labor; these unskilled workers became very proficient doing the same task repetitively, but were paid lower wages than paid to artisans.

Making product in a factory was a team effort undertaken by a group of unskilled workers, each performing a single task in the manufacturing sequence. Consequently, the production rate in a factory was much higher than that of a single artisan, and the cost of production was lower. These unskilled individuals, no doubt, developed skills necessary to perform the assigned single task very proficiently, but individually were unable to perform all of the steps required to manufacture the product. In short, an unskilled worker could cut the fabric for a suit, but could not make the suit.

Unskilled workers in this manufacturing scheme would perform menial jobs, but it was the skilled workers or displaced artisans who supervised and inspected the final product to ensure that it was done properly. In the US, skilled workers were in short supply as compared to Europe. As a result, it became necessary in the US to follow a different path in the progression toward full industrialization. US industrialists had to rely more on machinery to do more of the steps required in the manufacturing process. Consequently, products made in US factories were not of the quality of comparable European products, but the US had the advantage of producing acceptable-quality products at lower production cost than those produced in European factories.

US industrialists, unlike their European counterparts, thought all along that product selling price would be extremely important to consumers who would prefer to purchase the lowest cost products. Obviously, European products were of higher quality but were sold at higher prices. Production of acceptable-quality goods at the lowest possible cost became the driver for industrialization in the US.

In a typical factory, groups of workers perform a single task; after that task is completed, the output from that group is manually transported to the next station so that the next step may be performed in the manufacturing sequence; this continues until the final product is assembled or completed. The next evolutionary step in the factory process is the introduction of the assembly line concept. This concept involves transporting the output product from each assembly group at the completion of each task to the next station via a mechanical moving belt that brings work to the workers on a continuous basis. If there are problems in the assembly line, it becomes obvious where the problem is because work accumulates at that given station.

The mass production concept can best be understood using a simple example. A tailor performs all the steps required to manufacture a suit. In a factory setting, however, one unskilled worker cuts fabric to a given dimension or pattern, another worker sews it, another takes care of buttons, and others continue the sequence of steps until the suit is made. In the case of mass production, however, all steps are performed in a continuous sequence without interruptions. A machine, for example, cuts the fabric following a prescribed pattern and drops the fabric onto a moving belt to be transported to the next station where another machine or worker sews it in a prescribed manner. The machines are equipped with jigs and gauge blocks ensuring all dimensions and sewing patterns are done correctly and done in a preset fashion. Additionally, all tools required to perform each task are available to the worker at every work station; this reduces the time required for completing the task.

Obviously, mass production relies more on machines to do the work of skilled workers. These machines are operated by unskilled, lower-paid workers, who are used sparingly to ensure that the machines are performing as designed or to feed raw material to it. It is a concept that relies on performing the same steps repeatedly. Any change to the product requires alterations to the assembly sequence, resulting in assembly line stoppages. Changes introduce significant delays or result in total line stoppage. Production stoppages stop the assembly line and reduce production rate. In other words, changes result in delays, lower production rates, and adversely impact production cost and profitability.

Mass production tended to incorporate more of the knowledge required for running the process into the logic used in controlling the operation of manufacturing machinery. The process depended heavily on organization structure to ensure unskilled workers performed the assigned task in the proper sequence. Reliance on machinery had the advantage of reducing the number of skilled workers required thus, reducing labor costs and expediting output. The greater use of machinery and control placed a greater emphasis on engineering and on trained engineers to design and improve the machines and processes required to make mass production workable. The main disadvantages of the scheme were the high amount of capital required to purchase equipment and the lack of flexibility to make product changes. In other words, mass production was a capital intensive rather than a labor intensive activity. The greater use of machinery became necessary in the United States because the US, unlike Europe, had a shortage of skilled workers to do the work. Obviously, the goods made by such machinery were simpler and rougher than the goods produced in European facilities because of the greater reliance on skilled workers.

The advantage was that US manufacturing made available a broader range of products to the population at lower cost than comparable goods made in Europe. Perhaps, this gave rise to the idea that European goods are of higher quality and cost than comparable US made products. Prior to the assembly line, cars were crafted individually by teams of skilled workers; this was a very expensive and slow procedure. Henry Ford would change automobile manufacturing to make the process more efficient and the product more affordable to the general population.

Henry Ford was a pioneer in adapting and expanding mass production to manufacture automobiles, in particular the Model N in 1905.[33] Ford built a capital-intensive plant that incorporated the concepts developed by his engineers, who focused on continuously moving work to workers. The line moved partially assembled product from one station to another until the product was completely assembled. The line did not stop unless there were mechanical problems preventing its motion. Large amounts of capital were invested in the scheme. This increased business risk and forced management to keep the line moving to continuously produce product in order to generate a continuous stream of revenue to recover the initial investment. Anything threatening continuous production was potentially extremely risky because it would directly impact the income stream and reduce profits. That included labor strife.

Consequently, Henry Ford tried by all means to increase job satisfaction among his employees. His main concern was to prevent labor unrest leading to unionization drives. Similarly, excessive worker turnover was another threat to mass production. Excessive worker turnover would increase production cost by the additional training requirements. He recognized that the work required to be done at his assembly line was very hard work that not every worker was willing to do for low wages. Workers would leave for less strenuous jobs. Ford correctly concluded that labor turnover presented significant threats to his business and decided to increase wages from the normal $2.00 per day up to $5.00 per day. This was a great strategy implemented to pacify labor unrest and to minimize production stoppages. This action placated the assembly line workers and made Henry Ford a celebrity. Raising wages for assembly line workers moved Ford's workers into the ranks of the middle class. Now, Ford had assured that his workers would be working at Ford Motor Co. for the long term. It also had the added benefit of reducing training expenses.

Ford was very successful in implementing the moving assembly line concept in 1913. His main focus at the time was on ensuring that nothing would interrupt production or stop the assembly line at Ford Motor Co. Any interruption on the assembly line translated into lower production, higher production cost, and lower profitability. The assembly line as implemented at Ford was very successful for manufacturing a single model car, but it was a very inflexible concept. It was not possible to change the line to produce different car models sequentially. Consequently, Ford rejected any and all changes that would potentially cause production interruptions. He is quoted as saying: "Any customer can have a car painted any color he wants so long as it is black". Japan Black was the preferred paint used because of its ability to cure within forty-eight hours or less. There were other colors of paints available, but they would take in the range of fourteen days to cure, thus rendering their use impractical in automobile mass production.

Ford had a brilliant idea in increasing the wages of his workers in 1914. This action by Henry Ford illustrated Yankee ingenuity at its best in solving a problem that stood in the way of making his dream reality. The higher wages secured, or better yet purchased, the loyalty of workers at Ford Motor Co., who knew their wages were the highest among all workers. Those workers realized that their job was a personal asset that had to be protected. They knew that unless they performed their jobs well they would lose those valuable assembly line jobs, and not one of them wanted to face that possibility. Secondly, workers did not have to join together to organize a labor union and resort to strikes to secure higher wages; Ford was already paying them higher wages than anybody else. Assembly line jobs were brutal but Ford Motor Co was paying approximately three times the going rate. As a result, assembly line workers were willing to tolerate those grueling jobs because of the higher wages Ford was paying. This brought labor peace to Ford Motor Co. and ensured that the assembly line would continue to produce cars without interruptions, thus making Henry Ford a very wealthy individual. Finally, higher wages ensured that a larger pool of workers would be available for business expansion.

Custom-automobile manufacturers were able to produce cars painted in different colors using the slower curing paints. Those custom producers could provide variety to satisfy consumer tastes but could not do that in large volumes or at relatively low cost to consumer. In other words, custom-car manufacturers were selling higher-price cars that were not directly competing with mass-produced automobiles; these were manufacturers focusing on luxury models.

Olds Motor Works, established in 1899, was the first US factory to produce automobiles. In fact, Oldsmobile branded cars manufactured by the Olds Motor Works were the first high-volume, gasoline-powered automobiles made in the US; this company produced 425 cars in 1901. Ford Motor Co. production of the Model T in 1908 surpassed the output from all other car manufacturers and became the No.1 automobile producer in the US. Cadillacs were initially manufactured by the Henry Ford Co, which was founded by Henry Ford in 1901. Oldsmobile, Buick, and Cadillac were brands of automobiles that would be later absorbed by the General Motors Corp.

Mass production was also adapted to the manufacture of washing machines, refrigerators, and other domestic appliances. The standard of living of the general population improved as a result of these technological advances; mass production resulted in the creation of a large number of high-paying jobs. Workers holding one of those high-paying manufacturing jobs were able to purchase a broader range of products, including cars and home appliances. As the level of manufacturing activities increased, purchases led to mass consumption and market saturation. But mass consumption resulted in a need to differentiate products to satisfy consumer tastes.

Ford was only willing to manufacture and sell automobiles painted black, but consumers wanted a broader range of colors available to satisfy their own desires and tastes. Those consumers were willing to pay premiums to have a car different from those owned by neighbors. Henry Ford faced a dilemma caused by consumers wanting to express their tastes and uniqueness. Manufacturing cars painted in different colors other than black paint would slow production and increase production cost, thus defeating the purpose of mass production.

Black paint was preferred by Ford because of its curing and hardening characteristics as compared to other paints, but if Ford failed to satisfy market demands for additional colors, then he would be alienating consumers who had demanded the change and, as a result, would lose market share. That action would attract competitors willing to satisfy that market need. Ford was facing a difficult dilemma: if he used different color paints then a reduction in production would result that would adversely impact profitability at his company. And, if he failed to provide different to his customers, the customers would look for a suitable replacement. Either way, this was a major problem that had to be solved without adversely impacting profitability.

Mass production had made automobiles very affordable, and consequently, the market grew significantly. The chemical company DuPont realized the importance of this market and attempted to solve the paint problem by developing a paint formulation capable of drying quickly. This would enable manufacturers to satisfy consumer tastes and, at the same time, make it feasible for use in mass production. Obviously, the new paint formulation had to be supplied in different colors to satisfy consumer demand. The problem was solved in 1920 when DuPont [34] chemists working with films were able to produce a thick pyroxylin lacquer, which was quick drying, durable, and capable of being colored. DuPont marketed it under the name Viscolac® in 1921. Assisted by General Motors engineers, DuPont refined the product further and renamed it Duco. The success of Duco led to further experimentation with finishes, and late in the 1920s, DuPont developed Dulux, an even more effective alkyd finish. Duco retained a niche market, however, and DuPont continued to produce it at Parlin until the late 1960s; Parlin is a manufacturing site located in New Jersey. The technical cooperation between GM and DuPont engineers and scientists was valuable evidence showing that a single manufacturer could not address all problems but had to rely on suppliers to help provide solutions.

Henry Ford's reluctance to change was very costly to Ford Motor Co. and, perhaps, played a significant role in causing the departure of some of his best engineers for jobs at General Motors. Those same engineers, who perhaps felt frustrated by Ford's intransigence, had played a pivotal part in developing and implementing the mass production concept at Ford Motor Co. They had made Ford Motor Co. the No. 1 automobile producer, and, no doubt, had other plans to make it even better. Now, they were forced to abandon Ford and join General Motors. The result of that intransigence on the part of Henry Ford was the establishment of General Motors as a very able competitor to Ford Motor Co. Ford Motor Co. would lose a significant share of the automobile market. More importantly, Ford would now have to address market and consumer needs as well as to match new developments and improvements made by GM to lower manufacturing cost or improve the performance of its cars.

General Motors was established by bringing together manufacturers producing their own brands in their own factories; these were Buick, Oldsmobile, Pontiac, and Cadillac. Chevrolet was the last manufacturer and brand to join the GM family. Chevrolet focused on competing directly with the Ford Motel T. GM now had under its umbrella many brands, providing the means to differentiate products and to sell to a broader segment of the population. This marketing mantra across all of the GM brands was described by GM legendary chief executive Alfred P. Sloan as "a car for every purse and purpose." GM's marketing strategy was solidified by the establishment of GM Acceptance Corp for the purpose of financing car purchases. Once again, Henry Ford missed the boat by his opposition to the extension of credit to consumers. As a result of GM's ability to supply brand differentiation and credit to consumers, its market share surpassed that of Ford in the late 1920s and remained so for many years thereafter.

GM was more open minded than Ford as far as making improvements to production facilities and its products was concerned. Some of those improvements were the direct result of a willingness to work on issues of concern to consumers such as painting cars different colors. Granted the selection of paint had a direct impact on production speed and thus product cost. Nevertheless, GM showed a willingness to address that issue and worked with DuPont to develop acceptable paints enabling production of a variety of colors capable of being cured within a reasonable time frame and eliminating interruptions or delays in the assembly line. As a result of this technical cooperation, DuPont became a major GM shareholder favoring GM over Ford.

GM established the General Motors Research Corporation to improve its products and manufacturing processes and operations. Henry Ford, on the other hand, was opposed to any change to either his company's manufacturing facilities or products. As a result of this reluctance to change, Ford market share dropped significantly. GM continued to grow and gain market share. Chrysler, which had been the No. 3 automaker, became the No. 2 automaker behind GM for four consecutive years from 1938 to 1941 as a result of its innovative automobile stylish designs. It was not until 1950 that Ford overtook Chrysler and became the No. 2 automaker once again. It was ironic that the No.1 automaker had to lose its leadership position because of an unwillingness to change. This, no doubt, ended costing Ford a lot in profitability, which was the reason Ford was so adverse to change. In other words, Ford had to learn that the only thing that was constant was change, but that was a very costly lesson.

US automobile manufacturers failed to learn the lesson taught to Henry Ford by his refusal to implement manufacturing changes to satisfy consumer demands. Ford Motor Co. lost market share as a result of Henry Ford unwillingness to satisfy consumer demands regarding the color of their cars. GM and Chrysler gained market share at the expenses of Ford Motor Co. The result was the same when US manufacturers failed to satisfy consumer demand for more fuel-efficient and higher quality cars in the latter part of the Twentieth Century, and Japanese car makers gained market share at the expense of US manufacturers.

Mass production brought many successes not only to manufacturing companies but also to the American people. Those achievements resulted in higher wages paid to workers. Higher-income levels enhanced the standard of living of workers and of the general population. Obviously, the net effect was an expansion of the US middle class and attainment of the highest standard of living any place in the world. Furthermore, higher wages and accessibility to credit increased consumer spending and provided the means for a more leisurely living. Additionally, these factors contributed to mass consumption that, in turn, provided the impetus for expanding industrial activity. Mass consumption also enhanced corporate profitability as shown in Table 4.

Notice the sudden drop in corporate profitability after 1919 for both manufacturing and trade corporations; this is an indication of a down cycle or possibly a recession. In fact, data in Figure 2 would tend to support the idea of a recession by the sharp drop in immigrants coming into the country looking for greener pastures. It is also apparent that industrial activity picks up around 1922 and continues to show improvements up until the Great Depression, which starts in 1929.

Year	Manufacturing, %		Trade, %	
	Before Tax	After Tax	Before Tax	After Tax
1919	18.3	13.1	24.2	17.1
1920	12.3	9.6	11.4	8.6
1921	2.9	1.9	6.6	4.9
1922	10.2	9.1	14.9	13.3
1923	11.2	10.0	15.4	13.7
1924	10.0	8.9	13.4	11.8
1925	12.1	10.7	14.0	12.2
1926	12.4	11.0	13.6	11.8
1927	9.5	8.4	13.1	11.4
1928	11.0	9.8	12.3	10.9

Table 4. Corporate Net Income to Capitalization [35]

Corporate America has been very successful improving living conditions in the US. It establishes a manufacturing base that creates thousands of high-paying jobs. It has sufficient funds for investment, but the market is now saturated. It becomes necessary, therefore, to look at other markets for expansion. Europe and Japan become ideal locations for expansion due to population level and the after effects of World War I. Many US corporations acquire or establish manufacturing facilities in those countries and undertake manufacturing in those locations with the same vigor as has been pursued in the US. Bear in mind that the profit motive is driving these corporations, and that both the local population and corporation would benefit from these activities as has been the case in the US. That initial manufacturing activity in foreign countries would have some impacts on US manufacturing later on.

The US government contributes to this industrial expansion and improvement in living standards by keeping taxes at relatively low rates as shown in Figure 7; corporate tax rates at that time are relatively low in comparison to present corporate tax rates in the range of 35 percent.

Figure 7. Tax Rates on Corporate Net Income [36]

Income taxes are imposed by the US government upon ratification by the states of the Sixteenth Amendment to the US Constitution. At times during our national history, it becomes necessary to raise revenue to pay for government activities relating to national defense and welfare. This happens several times particularly when the country is involved in a war as is the case during World War I in the late 1910s. But, even then, the tax rates are low, allowing corporations to retain more of their profits for reinvestment and business expansion. Low tax rates are essential to fuel further industrialization, but these low rates would not automatically or necessarily reduce government revenues.

Notwithstanding the low rates of taxation, the amount of revenues that are raised by the US government during the period from 1910 to 1928 increases yearly as shown in Figure 8.

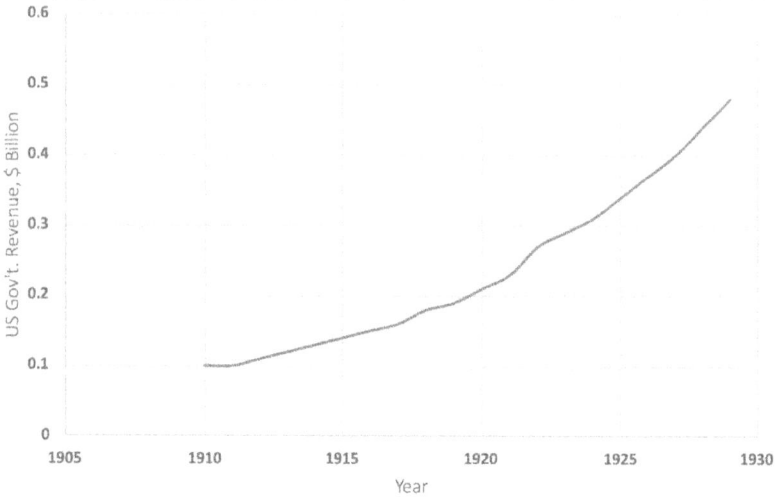

Figure 8. Annual Tax Revenues [37]

This is not a surprising conclusion; the same result has been demonstrated more recently when federal income taxes have been reduced significantly. [38] For example, in 1968 a proposal by President Kennedy reduces the top tax rate from 90 percent to 70 percent causing revenues to climb from $94 billion up to $153 billion. There is also a similar result achieved under President Reagan sweeping tax reforms in the 1980s causing tax revenues to increase by more than 99 percent. This conclusion is contrary to the belief held by many politicians who advocate tax increase for everything. These politicians are just trying to exert power to get into our pockets.

In reality, politicians are always looking at new sources of income to fund their pet projects. Politicians always want to spend our money rather than their money. They want to risk our money rather than theirs, and that benefits them. They benefit to the extent of bribes received from those doing their pet projects; this is corruption at the highest level of government. In particular, politicians are interested in continuing funding welfare programs to keep those individuals totally dependent on their largesse and preventing them from ever pulling themselves and their children out of poverty. The unfortunate thing is that these citizens like receiving free things and fail to realize that, in doing so, they become completely dependent on politicians, and after that dependency comes slavery from which they cannot liberate themselves. In reality, many welfare recipients become property owned by politicians. The result is best stated by paraphrasing a famous Chinese proverb:"Give a man a fish and he will eat for a day, but if you teach him how to fish he will eat for a lifetime". It is for that reason I'm a great believer in the power of education.

Instead of spending money on welfare, welfare funds would be better spent on educating welfare recipients so that they, too, can become productive, wealthy citizens. It is only in this manner that their children can have the bright future others in this country have achieved. Politicians just like to spend other people's money without concern for the value derived from such expenditures; politicians like to have people depend on them so that they can get their votes and keep their jobs.

Why would one expect revenues to increase as a result of lower tax rates? There are several reasons for that. This is best stated by the observation made by former US Representative Jack Kemp (R-NY), who was one of the chief architects of President Reagan tax cut. He opined:

"At some point, additional taxes so discourage the activity being taxed, such as working or investing, that they yield less revenues rather than more. There are, after all, two rates that yield the same amount of revenue: high tax rates on low production or low taxes on high production".

The growing annual Gross Domestic Product (GDP) results shown in Figure 9 reinforce the conclusion that lower taxes do, in fact, improve the economic wellbeing of the individual and of the nation as a whole. GDP is a measure of the annual value of all goods and services produced in the country. The term Gross National Product (GNP) represents GDP plus capital gains from overseas investment minus income earned by foreign nationals in the US. In the context of this book, GDP and GNP are used interchangeably. The growing levels of GDP can only mean more products being produced supporting what US Representative Kemp alluded to as a reason for advocating lower taxes; Figure 7 shows Tax Rates.

US GDP, Billions $

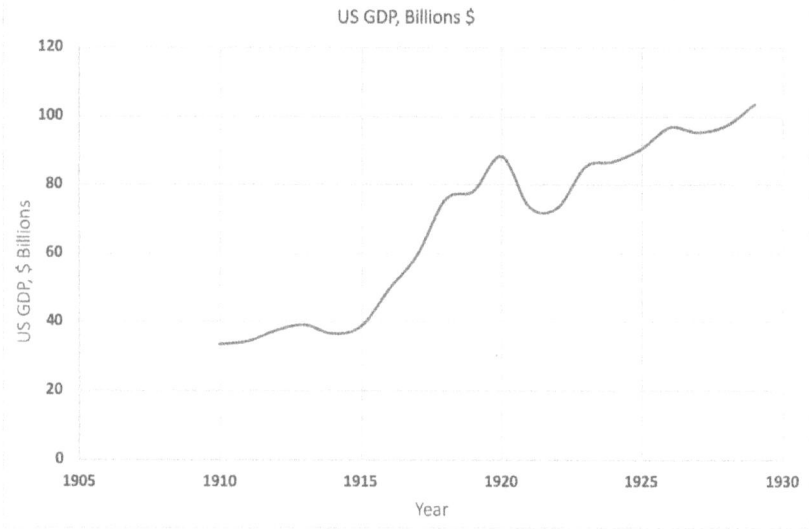

Figure 9. Annual US Gross Domestic Product [39]

It is also worth taking issue with the popular belief held by most politicians who advocate raising tax rates. Those politicians always mention that the impact of the higher tax rates will be only on the rich, but in reality everyone is affected. This is a misguided belief based on class warfare and envy, which are based on Karl Marx's vision of society. It is worth noticing that the rich are the ones who invest and take risk with their money to create jobs for the rest of the population. If the rich do not invest the rest of us do not have jobs. In other words, if the rich are heavily taxed, then their investment funds are depleted to some extent, and we suffer to the extent that no new jobs are created.

Opposition to high taxes was the primary cause leading our nation to break away from Great Britain to become the independent sovereign nation it is today. Let's not repeat the same mistakes of the early colonial powers. It is also worth mentioning that communists believe in doing away with the "rich" who are supposed to be evil simply because of their economic status. That is wrong, and it is done to divide the population and cause class warfare. Keep in mind that politicians create nothing by raising taxes, and that rich folks create jobs by investing the money in their pockets.

Members of the Communist Party in the former Soviet Union were part of an elite class oppressing the majority composed of simple working people. Under the communist system, everyone was supposed to be equal, but in reality some were more equal than others. Communist leaders instigated class warfare and frustrated the free enterprise system, causing the former Soviet Union to collapse. Those communist politicians were the only ones who benefitted from the communist system in the former Soviet Union, and the rest of the people suffered. After the collapse of the Soviet Union, there were no communists to be found anywhere in any of those socialist countries, including those holding the highest rank in the communist party. Why? The answer was that their system was based on nonsense and would never work. Workers in any communist country would say that the government pretended to pay them fair wages for their work, and they pretended to work. Our politicians learned nothing from the collapse of the communist empire.

Let's not allow our politicians to destroy our country in much the same way communists destroyed the Soviet Union. Let's tell these politicians to either change or face defeat at the polls because we Americans do not want our American Dream shattered.

CHAPTER 4
FROM MISERY TO RECOVERY
THE GREAT DEPRESSION

The Great Depression was undoubtedly the most dramatic decline in business activity in US history. This phenomenon impacted not only the United States but also the whole world. It caused major economic upheaval, forcing nations to rethink some of their economic policies and to develop and implement drastic changes to counteract the crisis. This extreme economic catastrophe was, by no means, the only recession experienced in the US up to that time; however, it was the most damaging of all previous crises. There had been several recessions during the 1920s such as the ones in 1920, 1923, and 1926; each of those recessions lasted approximately one year. In comparison, the Great Depression started in late 1929 and lasted for approximately ten years. Many factors came together at the right time causing all economic activity to collapse. Speculation, credit availability, excess manufacturing capacity, government action or inaction, corruption, and economic imbalances each played a part in bringing about this economic tragedy.

In the period leading to the 1920s, Corporate America had progressed to the point where it was able to make the US a major world industrial power. This raised the standard of living in the US beyond those in any other country in the world. Wages paid to workers in many sectors of the economy rose as shown in Table 5 in terms of "real earnings" based on the 1929 Consumer Price Index (CPI) equaling 100. Worker weekly earnings declined slightly during the recessions occurring in the periods between 1920–1921 and 1924–1925; this was particularly true for unskilled and female workers. Farm workers also saw their earnings declined during the same periods.

A larger drop in weekly earnings occurred in the period from 1929 to 1930, which was caused by the impact the Great Depression had on all sectors of the economy; this reduction in weekly earnings amounted to approximately 17 percent for skilled males as compared to about 7 to 8 percent for unskilled workers and females.

In the period preceding the Great Depression, manufacturing worker productivity increased approximately 32 percent from 1923 to 1929 but wages increased only 8 percent. The higher productivity resulted in an increase in corporate profitability averaging 62 percent. The higher profitability enabled corporate entities to increase dividends approximately 65 percent during the same period. [40] Corporate entities, however, did not share their good fortunes with their workers.

| Year | Real Average Weekly Earnings (1929=100) | | | | |
| | 25 Manufacturing Industries | | | Mining | Daily Real Farm Wage Rate |
	Skilled Males	Unskilled Males	Female	Bituminous Coal and Lignite	
1920	29.16	22.28	15.14		2.82
1921	26.19	19.41	14.96		1.96
1922	28.73	20.74	16.19		2.04
1923	30.93	22.37	17.31	25.51	2.36
1924	30.61	22.45	16.78	23.47	2.40
1925	30.57	22.41	16.78	25.64	2.30
1926	30.60	22.47	16.72	27.51	2.32
1927	31.09	23.22	17.14	23.85	2.32
1928	31.94	23.89	17.15	24.46	2.30
1929	32.60	24.30	17.61	25.11	2.30
1930	26.93	22.47	16.40	22.61	2.21

Table 5. Typical Real Average Earnings. [41]

Given rising earnings and accessibility to installment credit, it became possible for consumers to finance purchases of mass-produced cars, household appliances, and other consumer goods. The increasing demand for automobiles and other mass-manufactured goods became the catalyst for growth in other industries, particularly those supplying steel, chemicals, and electrical devices. Additionally, widespread use of automobiles had a very significant effect on the construction and housing industries as consumers moved to new homes in the suburbs resulting in additional road construction to accommodate such migration.

There were many signs reflecting the level of prosperity brought about by manufacturing industries. Those signs included availability of consumer credit to purchase home appliances and many other high-ticket items to make life easier at home. The booming economy and the mobility provided by the automobile impacted construction of hotels, restaurants, etc. Consumers demanded more and better things from manufacturers reflecting the high level of prosperity. Consumers also demanded more and more from personal investments. Financial institutions fueled the speculation fire, leading to risky investments inflating an insecurity bubble of that would, eventually, burst and clouded the otherwise clear horizon. That bubble exploded and that led to misery.

At some point, the US market became saturated, and manufacturing entities could not expand any further. It became necessary to look for additional markets to expand production. An alternative would have been to introduce new products; that would require an expansion in manufacturing to make those products. Corporate America chose to focus on developing export markets. That move ensured long-term growth, thus keeping manufacturing plants producing at full capacity and, in some cases, expanding existing capacity; this had the effect of reducing production costs and increasing corporate profitability.

Europe was recovering from damage suffered by its industrial sector during World War I. The US, on the other hand, was experiencing unimaginable prosperity in the 1920s. The US had suffered no war damage and, in fact, had become a reliable food supplier, banker, and manufacturer for the entire world. Corporate America was producing at a level sufficient to not only satisfy the needs of the US market but also the needs of the export markets. Consequently, there was an excess in manufacturing capacity. Europe, therefore, became a logical outlet market for US manufactured goods.

Corporate America continued to rely on exports to maintain its manufacturing sector at nearly full capacity. Credit was extended to European countries to enable those countries to purchase US manufactured goods. But, the US government imposed a 50 percent tariff on all imported goods from those same European countries. The imposition of high tariffs resulted from passage and implementation of the Smoot-Hawley Tariff Act of 1930. This was an attempt to protect Corporate America from foreign producers.

European imports to the US became more expensive due to the high tariffs imposed by the US government and were not competite with comparable locally made products selling at lower prices. This attempt at protecting Corporate America backfired as Europeans were unable to generate sufficient funds to pay the war debt owed to the US. Furthermore, Europeans were unable to purchase US made goods, causing US manufacturers to reduce production, which resulted in the layoff of thousands of workers. The downturn in the economic environment exacerbated the unemployment rate in the US when companies reduced employment and attempted to balance production with demand. The unemployment rate increased significantly starting in 1929 as shown in Figure 10. This was an example of good intentions having bad consequences.

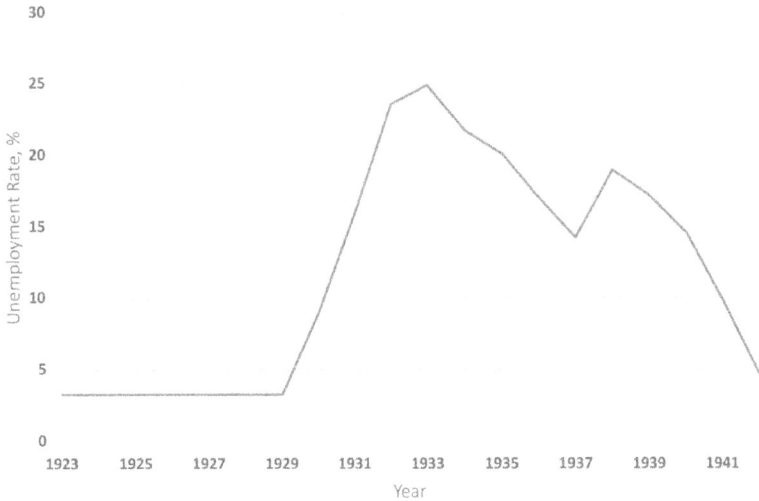

Figure 10. Unemployment Rate [42]

US consumers became intoxicated with prosperity. This caused unrealistic expectations that resulted in unsustainable market conditions. A bubble was created based on speculation in the financial markets that sooner or later had to burst. Greed in the form of avarice was the motivation inflating this bubble and culminating in the stock market crash in October 1929. It was avarice because nothing was being created other than imaginary wealth.

The Dow Jones Industrial Average doubled from a level of 191 in early 1928 to 381 in September reflecting the level of speculation. [43] The market crash and the rising unemployment rate had a grave effect on the behavior of the general population that culminated in a panic atmosphere and eventually led to the failure of financial institutions; by the end of 1932, more than 1,493 banks had either failed or suspended operations. [44] The bubble had busted! More banks would fail in subsequent years, causing massive losses for consumers.

There was another complicating factor coming into play. That factor was reliance on the gold standard, which was a mechanism used by countries to peg the value of a country's currency to the value of its gold reserves. This had the effect of limiting the amount of currency that could be printed and in circulation at any one time. Reliance on the gold standard prevented relaxation of national monetary policies to restrict consumption. Lower consumption, in turn, forced cuts in manufacturing activities. The situation was particularly harmful to European countries because of the magnitude of their national debts to the US. Those countries were unable to pay their US debts, because printing more money would reduce their gold reserves to such an extent that the country would be unable to support the amount of currency in circulation. That situation ended up affecting credit by making it less accessible to many countries unable to pay their debts. A downward economic cycle had begun. Eventually, the situation would snowball into a worldwide economic crisis. US industry was, therefore, unable to sustain production.

There was no question that the Great Depression brought misery to many families over a period lasting more than ten years and that without government intervention that misery would have lasted for many more years. The US government acted decisively in enacting many significant pieces of legislation addressing just about every facet of the economy. Among those pieces of legislation were those legislative acts listed in Table 6. These legislative acts were enacted to counteract abuses leading to the economic collapse and to start an economic recovery from the Great Depression. The US government established many programs aimed at reducing unemployment and, at the same time, society's most pressing needs. It created the Public Works Administration that became instrumental in creating many jobs in many sectors of the economy.

Year	Legislation Title	Effect
1933	Agricultural Adjustment Act	Authorizes farmers not to grow crops
	Federal Securities Act	Regulates offer and sale of securities
	Glass Steagall Act	Established Federal Deposit Insurance Corporation (FDIC) including banking reforms
1934	Gold Reserve Act	Title to gold and gold certificates transferred from Federal Reserve Bank to the Federal Government
	Civil Works Emergency Relief Act	Funded local projects to create employment.
	Reciprocal Trade Agreements Act	Reduced tariff levels and promoted trade liberalization
1935	National Labor Relations Act	Grants right to workers to organize labor unions for the purpose of collective bargaining.
	Social Security Act	Provided social welfare and benefits programs for workers.
	Banking Act	US Monetary system reorganized centralizing power in the Board of Governors.

Table 6. Legislation Enacted to Kick-Start Recovery.

US Gross Domestic Product (GDP) had grown steadily until 1929 and declined thereafter until it reached a minimum in 1933 as shown in Figure 11.

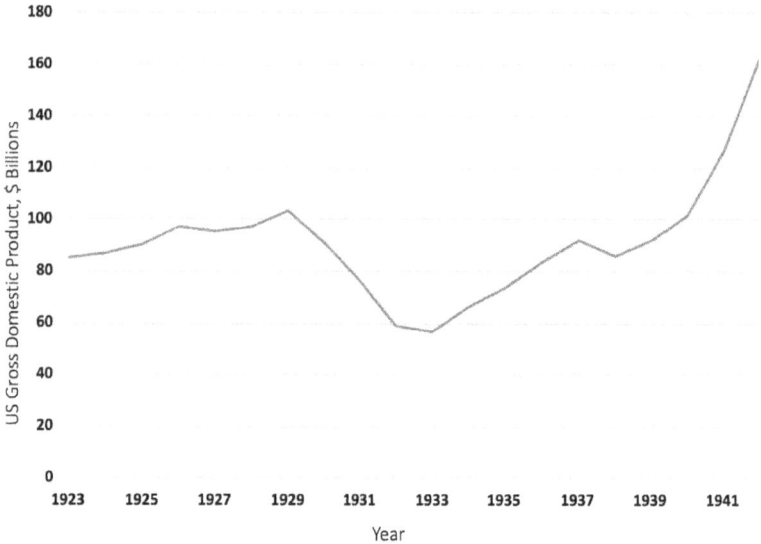

Figure 11. Annual GDP – 1923 to 1942[45]

Government revenues showed a pattern similar to that of GDP as shown in Figure 12. President Franklin Delano Roosevelt began to implement a very bold program aimed at reversing the pessimism that was fueling the poor economic climate prevailing at the time. Included in this government effort was a jobs-creation program that apparently succeeded in reversing the decline in GNP started in 1929. The jobs-creation program was a success leading to a reduction in unemployment rate as shown in Figure 10. As more jobs were created, consumer confidence began to increase and to be reflected in a higher level of consumption as shown by the rise in GNP.

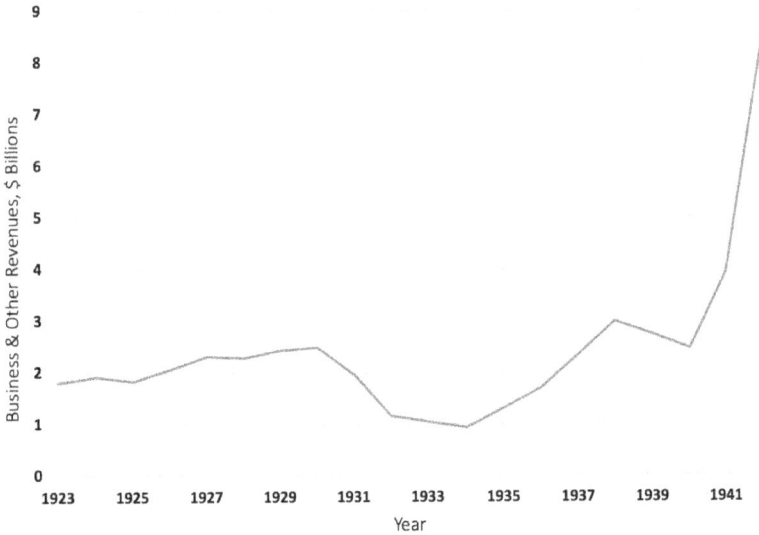

Figure 12. Annual Revenues – 1923 to 1942[46]

This early phase of economic recovery snowballed across other sectors of the economy, and people were able to return to work and earn wages. Consumers began to regain confidence and began to increase spending. Consumer confidence was increased consumer demand and economic activity. As a result, people and corporations began to pay income taxes from their earnings. Consequently, government revenues increased without the need to raise income tax rates. In short, these federal programs had a positive impact on job creation and became a signal to manufacturers to ramp up production in order to satisfy growing demand from consumers.

The growth in government revenues shown in Figure 12 was the result of improving economic conditions as shown by the rising level of GNP (Figure 11). The government wisely chose to hold income-tax rates essentially constant as shown in Figure 13. This allowed manufacturer to retain a larger portion of their earnings for investment in expanding facilities increase employment and increase employment opportunities. That represented a win – win situation for both parties and a step in the right direction towards reovery from the depression.

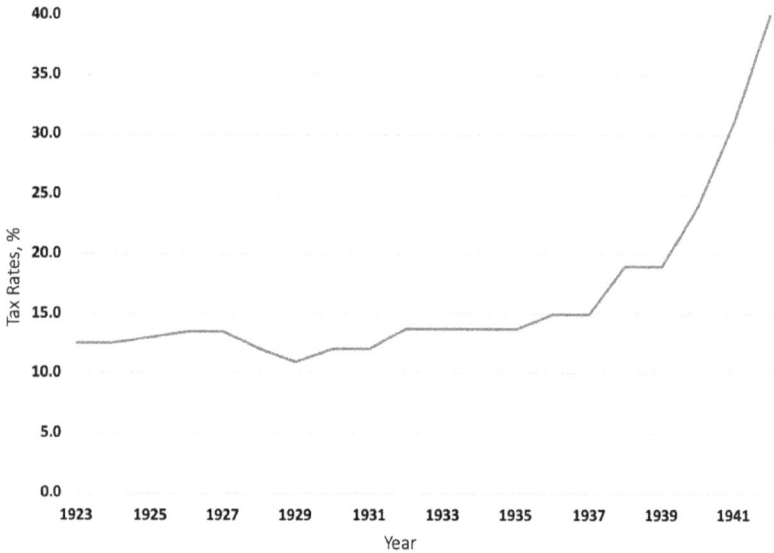

Figure 13. Corporate Tax Rates. [47]

The government realized the economy had to be stimulated further. The government itself was the only party capable of doing that by financing and undertaking infrastructure or public projects that the private sector would neither do nor fund. Those projects were eventually successful in creating employment and in positively impacting other sectors of the economy. Roads, bridges, and ports were funded and constructed during this period. These projects were beneficial in providing incentives for future economic activity. For example, new roads opened up new areas for economic development particularly by providing the new locations and the means for transporting manufactured goods.

In addition, the government established some very creative agencies such as the Tennessee Valley Authority (TVA) which, as described by President Roosevelt, would be "a corporation empowered to be clothed with the power of government but possessed of the flexibility and initiative of a private enterprise."

TVA, in turn, undertook construction of projects pertaining to irrigation, power generation, navigation, flood control, and many other activities. TVA, as a governmental corporate entity, from the start had a problem-solving attitude that was atypical of other governmental agencies. This attitude contributed significantly to local development and creation of many job opportunities. TVA achieved the goal set out by President Roosevelt for this type of agency.

The program implemented by President Roosevelt starting on or about 1933 was very effective in generating employment opportunities and in reversing the downward trend in GNP started in 1929 and continuing up to 1934. The government recognized that jobs creation was essential to start the economic recovery because it would enhance consumer demand and stimulate manufacturing thus creating additional jobs. The government knew that job creation was the key to get the economy going and to generate revenues through taxes to enable it to fund the projects it had undertaken. Government revenues, shown in Figure 12, increased as expected. More importantly, these projects also had a beneficial psychological impact on the population because people began to witness an improving economic situation. The improving economic situation began to turn the general population away from the pessimism that had been part of their lives for so long.

Public projects required expenditure of massive amounts of funds the government did not have. Where was the money coming from? These government expenditures had to be paid by revenues generated by either by raising taxes or incurring a public debt. Raising taxes would have a negative impact on the fragile economic recovery starting to take root because it would reduce consumer spending, which was the vehicle stimulating other sectors of the economy. Tax rates remained unchanged. Consequently, the only alternative left for funding these projects was by borrowing. As a result, the national debt began to increase as shown in Figure 14.

The debate on funding governmental expenditures has always revolved around balancing dual options available to the US Government: taxation or borrowing. External financing is another term for deficit spending. Which method is preferable? The answer depends, to some extent, on existing economic conditions and

economic climate at the time of the expenditures. Many factors
are considered to arrive at a common-sense solution addressing
a very complex issue. This is particularly so at a time when the
country is battling an economic crisis causing high unemployment
levels and shortage of funds.

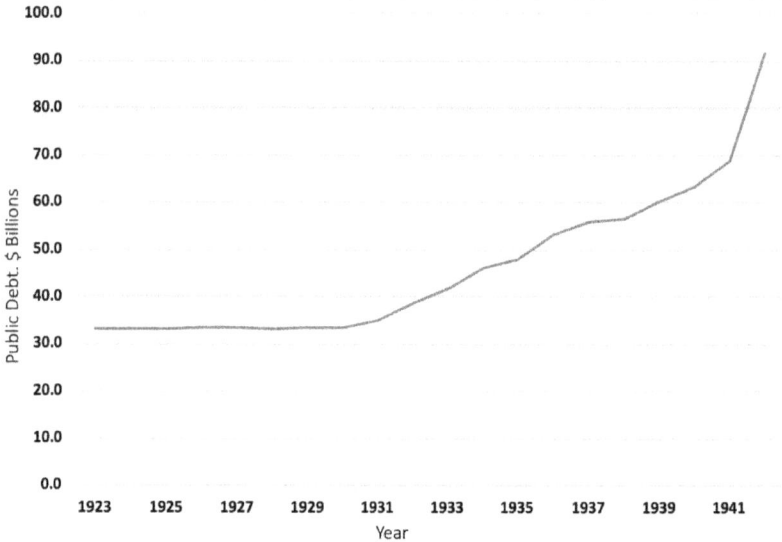

Figure 14. US Public Debt. [48]

Given an economic crisis of the magnitude of the Great
Depression, it must be recognized increasing income tax burden
on individuals or business would not solve the problem. High
unemployment levels preclude people from getting jobs to earn
an income and pay income taxes; raising taxes on companies
generating little income or bankrupt would be a futile exercise.
On the other hand, the debate would have to proceed beyond an
impasse resulting in paralysis. The government had to take the
initiative to create jobs by all alternatives open to it. It had to
undertake and finance public projects to create jobs that would
eventually create jobs to get people back to work. It also had to
undertake major purchasing programs to achieve the same end.
Those actions on the part of government improved the economic

climate and made it possible to collect taxes and repay the debt incurred as a result of undertaking such job creating activities.

In a situation like that of the Great Depression, consumers could not spend because they did not have jobs or income. The corporate sector could not undertake production and hiring expansions because there was no demand from consumers. Therefore, the government was the only body capable of intervening and addressing the situation to make a positive impact to get the economy going. In view of that, there is no question that some level of government intervention and spending was necessary to improve economic conditions.

Government expenditures had to be financed, thus adding to the national debt. That was the only logical and reasonable alternative available to solve the problem. It had to be recognized that incurring a debt to overcome an economic crisis was as important as repaying the debt as soon as possible when economic conditions permitted. Lawmakers would have to create a scheme and discipline to spend only on necessary activities rather than for the sake of spending. Unfortunately, that turned out to be a losing battle that had kept the national debt increasing on a yearly basis. In other words, the government had to save for rainy days. It could not continue to spend indefinitely. Ideally, that discipline would exercise control over the national debt. It would also provide a means to react to an economic emergency..

Conservatives are always opposed to deficit spending because the impact it has on creating a burden for future generations. The reality, however, is that deficit spending in some cases is necessary in order to make the present generation able to earn a living and to sustain future generations. If consumers are unable to increase spending because of unemployment or pessimism, then how is the economy going to recover from a deep recession or depression? The government cannot ignore that situation, pretend there is no problem, or allow it to continue. If it does that, it risks social unrest. The only common sense approach is for the government to spend money regardless of the impact on the national debt.

If the government takes action by going ahead with projects to stimulate t it undertakes, then it begins to create a more favorable economic climate that ultimately influences consumer confidence and spending. Additional consumer spending has an immediate influence on manufacturing and on job creation, thus leading to GDP growth. The better economic climate leads to higher revenues for the government through taxation. The government incurs a debt to be paid when economic conditions improve, but that debt should not be looked at as a real debt. Instead the debt so incurred should be viewed as an investment for the common good. There is nothing wrong with that. What is wrong is to continue to add to the national debt to pay for worthless projects that end up benefitting no one except politicians and their lobbyists' supporters.

There were many similarities and differences between the Great Depression of the 1930s and the Great Recession of 2009. Speculation was a major contributor to the collapse of the stock market in both cases. Many financial institutions and corporations failed and had to seek bankruptcy protection from creditors in both situations. Massive layoff of employees led to unacceptably high levels of unemployment among all sectors of the economy.

Banks failed in the 1930s but the government did not rescue those failed banks. In the 2009 recession, the government came to the rescue of failed banks even though those banks and their executives caused the crisis. The excuse given by government officials for bailing out these failed banks was that those institutions were too large to fail. If the truth were known, the bailed out banks were saved because politicians were forced, indebted to, or owned by those banks and lobbyists and these politicians had to act. Politicians knew that if the banks were not rescued then they would suffer in terms of reduced political contributions and financial gifts from those sources. That would have been a disastrous outcome for politicians and their bank accounts. Consequently, those failed banks had to be saved.

Prior to the 1930s, the US was a creditor to the rest of the world, but by 2009 this situation had changed. The US had become a debtor to the rest of the world. In other words, the US status changed from rich to poor. The transition from rich to poor probably started in the decade of the 1990s and continued to the present day. The change in national economic status had a very important implication on the status of American in that we were becoming poorer.

In the 1930s, the government very quickly recognized that creating jobs was essential to reverse the impact of the economic crisis. In the 2009 recession, lawmakers in the government focused on saving financial institutions that should had been allowed to go out of business to deter similar abuses from ever occurring again. The failures of financial institutions were the results of using financial gimmicks to inflate an artificial bubble that sooner or later had to burst, and when it did in 2009, the government rushed to the assistance of the perpetrators instead of aiding the victims of financial scams perpetrated by those failed financial institutions.

Financial institutions executives risked their institutions survival and wellbeing on a bet. Those executives should have been allowed to enjoy the results of their gambles and not rewarded with bonuses for poor performance. Instead, they should have been given a long vacation in jail and all of their assets confiscated to repay victims of their scam. That would have taught those institutions a lesson and prevented future occurrences of the same scam.. If one of us were to risk the entire amount of a paycheck gambling in a casino and were to lose it, the government for sure would not come to our rescue. That would have the end of the story. Why should government come to the rescue of those perpetrating? The only plausible reason would be that lawmakers would never risk biting the hand that feeds them via lobbyists.

Massive amounts of money were given to failed financial institutions without attaching any conditions on the use of taxpayers' money. In other words, the government in 2009 funded the banks that caused the economic collapse of the nation. Why was that done? It was done on the pretext that those banks were too big to fail. Perhaps the better explanation would have been be that those banks were big contributors to corrupt politicians in the US Congress responsible for enacting legislation to bail out their masters. That legislation used taxpayer funds to perpetuate inept management in power and to make future unchecked risk taking an operating standard. As a result, banks lost nothing and taxpayers whose money had been used to bail the banks out of their misery lost their homes and their retirement savings. There was no effort made to help homeowners for their losses. Politicians helped their financial masters but did not do a thing for those who provide votes to keep corrupt employed and misusing taxpayers' funds. It would be ideal for voters to demand accountability from these corrupt politicians. And, we can do that by withholding votes from those who misallocate taxpayers' funds.

Funds given to failed financial institutions were provided free of any conditions. Where was Senator Dodd when these massive amounts of money were given to banks? Perhaps, he and other politicians were lining up to collect their share of the proceeds from bank lobbyists. Failed financial institutions used taxpayers' money to reward financial and corporate executives for their ineptitude. In many cases, financial institutions and corporations had no recourse but to face ruin and bankruptcy. Lawmakers, on the other hand, showed their ineptitude and lack of concern for taxpayers' funds by making those loans free of any condition for repayment. Would it not be nice for constituents to get the same kind of treatment from financial institutions? Constituents can only get a similar loan if, and only if, you are a lawmaker like Senator Dodd. Otherwise, you would be out of luck.

Those failed financial institutions used taxpayer funds to grant their inept executives huge bonuses for meritorious service in driving their businesses into bankruptcy. The banks would not even consider lending those taxpayers dollars given to them to desperate consumers facing foreclosures to keep their homes. A better solution would have been to force banks to fire all of those worthless and inept executives and to confiscate all assets owned by them to repay losses caused by their ineptitude and risk taking.

There was no question politicians and government officials were complicit in shattering the dreams of many Americans. Wasn't that a shame that the same inept executives who caused these financial institutions and corporations to fail were allowed to continue employment while the victims of their ineptitude lost their jobs, homes, and had their share of the American Dream shattered?

In the 1930s, the government recognized the nature of the economic crisis and reacted rather quickly to pass massive amounts of legislation as shown in Table 6. President Franklin D. Roosevelt was a leader unconcerned about polls or political correctness. He acted quickly on a broad front because he knew the economic crisis was not going to be resolved by just one single fix; it had to be attacked using a multipronged approach. This multipronged approach was provided by all the legislation enacted. In fact, many individual pieces of legislation were challenged in court and found to be "unconstitutional," but benefits had already been achieved. In the meantime, people were back working and paying taxes to further stimulate the economic recovery.

After much discussion during the 2009 crisis, legislation was passed and signed into law primarily to bail out financial institutions. There was nothing on the jobs creation front until well into the crisis, and that was a very limited discussion that resulted in nothing. The banks received their loans but failed to lend any money to consumers or businesses to start the job creation engine, and congress said okay. The president kept on telling a good story and patting himself and members of his cabinet in the back. The American people instead of getting a pat in the back for donating money to failed banks ended up losing their homes, life savings, and their jobs. That was the meaning of change you could believe in!

Another essential difference between the Great Depression and the Great Recession was the amount of preparatory work required prior to undertaking a project. In President Roosevelt's time, there was no need to do environmental studies or to waste time in satisfying competitive bidding requirements leading to unnecessary delays in executing projects. Today, it would be almost impossible to start a public project without competitive bidding, an exhaustive environmental impact statement completed, and ultimately the whole package would be challenged in court because it failed to ensure all minorities got a piece of the action and included protections or a newly discovered insect. This change reflected the nonsense coming out of Washington, DC and contributing nothing to reduce unemployment. In fact, it would likely increase unemployment.

If time were of the essence as much now as it was back in the 1930s, the government would have suspended all of these politically correct procedural requirements. It would award projects with the understanding that tight controls would be enforced ensuring accountability for taxpayer's funds; long prison terms would be the reward to those who tried to take advantage of the situation by stealing taxpayers' funds. On top of that, the government would suspend all environmental requirements imposed on projects that delayed or make it difficult, if not impossible, to satisfy within a reasonable amount of time. Politicians managed to kill common sense by the massive amount of procedural requirements included in all applicable legislation in force nowadays. Now would be the time to eliminate all of that nonsense coming out of Washington, DC, and restore accountability and common sense.

Politicians have even managed to kill jobs. Highly paid executives of failed financial institutions have been rewarded with undeserved bonuses paid by taxpayers' money. Politicians do not seem to be concerned or care about the impact these actions have on taxpayers. They fail to protect unemployed taxpayers from foreclosures by the failed banks but reward those who created the crisis. A much better result would have been achieved by distributing funds equally among all American families instead of disbursing those funds to inept executives and failed financial institutions. The American people would have spent those funds wisely, repaying their mortgages and stimulating consumption through the purchase of cars and other goods. More importantly, the American taxpayer would continue to pay their fair share of taxes instead of deducting the losses generated by those failed institutions as a result of excessive risk taken with other people's money. The US government should prevent deductions of those losses from banks' income tax liability; let the banks recover the losses in the old fashion way through hard work and honest dealings. Banks should also be compelled to pay for consumer losses arising out of this crisis.

The unfortunate side of bailing out these failed financial institutions is that the American people do not benefit in any way. In fact, failed financial institutions have or will deduct their losses from their income tax liability, and the American taxpayers will pay again. Congress should act to prohibit banks from deducting these losses arising out of these excessive risk taking activities. The American people and the entire nation would have benefitted much more if the government had rushed to the side of manufacturers. The government should have purchased products for the military or any other governmental institution to increase demand for manufacture product and cause a surge in demand for new employees.

There was no question politicians acted in a manner consistent with improving their financial wellbeing at all times, regardless of what happens to the people they supposedly represented. A case in point was the situation leading Senator Chris Dodd of Connecticut to propose legislation addressing reform for banks and financial institutions. Keeping in mind the senator was the beneficiary of a very favorable mortgage package from a bank, it is almost impossible to believe any other American would be able to get the same deal from Senator Dodd's bank. The legislation he proposed was approximately 2,000 pages long, so you can imagine how many loopholes were available to bankers to continue doing business as usual. Opposition to Dodd's legislation stemmed from the fact it would expand the federal government's ability to bail out not only banks, but any large politically connected company. It was unquestionable that Senator Dodd's action was tantamount to having a fox guard the hen house! Luckily, the Senator chose to retire because he could not see himself being voted out of office. Perhaps, the banks he saved would show their gratitude to the senator by rewarding him with a job at one those failed banks.

Who would benefit from this action by Senator Dodd? Certainly, the American people would not benefit. Senator Dodd and the banks who contributed to his political campaigns would be the only beneficiaries of the 2,000 plus pages of nonsense in the proposed legislation. This is typical of the corruption in our government, and it exemplifies one of the most important contributing factors to the destruction of the American dream. This type of activity on the part of elected officials certainly is leading to the collapse of the US as a major superpower.

Another example of government action leading to the elimination of jobs is the so-called cap on greenhouse gases, which is a misnomer for something that is neither green nor found in a house. It is essential to recognize that the US depends on hydrocarbons to sustain the American Dream. It does not mean that the level of exhaust gases cannot be minimized by using appropriate technology that is either available or in need development. If that technology were available it could be used to reduce carbon-dioxide emissions. If not available, then it could be developed by an R&D effort funded by the US government in much the same way the government funded technology development during World War II. Carbon-dioxide production is an indication that the economy is functioning. The level of economic activity in the US is unattainable without burning hydrocarbons to generate electricity and steam for the purpose of driving industrial machinery.

Carbon-dioxide emissions and containment are not a national problem and not just a problem caused by the petroleum industry. It is an international problem that cannot be solved unilaterally by the US. It is a problem that all nations in the world have to address as a group. That means every country in the world has to do its part to solve the problem if, in reality, a problem exist. Scientific data purporting to show evidence carbon-dioxide emissions present a problem have been shown to be flawed at best.

If it is shown to be a problem, then carbon-dioxide emissions should be addressed by funding R&D work by the US government to develop technology to solve the problem. In any case, the best solution is not a total ban but rather to create a blueprint for better utilization of this byproduct of combustion. The government would then in a position to charge a license fee for the use of such technology by operating companies and other industrial concerns on a worldwide basis. That would allow the government to recover its initial investment in the development of this type of technology.

Instead of using a simple and common-sense approach, politicians opted to float the idea of capping carbon-dioxide emissions. Then, they realized that the solution was worse than the problem it intended in that it eliminated thousands of jobs by preventing any type of activity requiring hydrocarbon combustion. The common-sense approach would require backing away from that position to develop alternatives capable of dealing with the problem, if one exists, and creating jobs at the same time. Notwithstanding, the refusal by congress to act in this area, the Environmental Protection Agency (EPA) declared carbon dioxide a toxic gas and proceeded to announce proposals to cap these emissions. The refusal by congress was an indication to EPA that it does not have power to act because it had not been granted that authority by congress. The EPA, however, did not appear inclined to get that message from congress.

EPA's logic in declaring carbon dioxide a toxic gas shows the lack of scientific knowledge in the agency. In fact, it shows that this agency is pushing the private agendas of its administrator or that of former Vice-President Al Gore, who claimed at one time to have been the inventor of the Internet. Carbon dioxide is essential for plant growth. If the EPA were to ban all carbon-dioxide emissions, then it would essentially be banning the growth of vegetation. If that were to happen, then the so-called global warming problem would be compounded. Our planet would be a desert! That's the fallacy behind blind mandates from people who are scientifically illiterate. I think EPA would be better off concentrating on exploring beneficial effects of controlling carbon dioxide emissions without eliminating jobs or killing all vegetation.

It is obvious that EPA's action lacks credibility. Carbon dioxide is used in soft drinks such as Coca Cola. Has anybody heard of people being killed as a result of drinking a Coke? Will the label of toxic gas imposed by EPA on carbon dioxide lead to the banning of soft drinks? What about the use of carbon dioxide as a refrigerant in the form of dry ice to enable shipment of perishable meats? Would the use of carbon dioxide contaminate the meat it is protecting during shipment? This is the kind of nonsense passed by Washington bureaucrats who are totally scientifically illiterate. Would the Food and Drug Administration (FDA) be forced to declare meats exposed to carbon dioxide poisonous? How about eating vegetables and salads containing all kinds of leaves? Something is wrong with EPA's logic!

Labeling carbon dioxide a toxic gas and mandating drastic reductions in emissions to the atmosphere is an action favoring manufacturing in China. How? Our manufacturing sector depends on energy to drive machinery. Burning hydrocarbons either from petroleum, natural gas, or coal is essential to generate steam and produce electricity for the purpose of driving industrial machinery. The combustion process generates carbon dioxide as a byproduct. Manufacturing is impossible without steam or electricity. Will China ban carbon-dioxide emissions? No, China will very likely have to increase carbon-dioxide emissions to compensate for the loss of manufacturing activity in the US resulting from the nonsense coming out of a misguided EPA mandate. Furthermore, carbon dioxide emissions generated in China would end up being transported by normal air currents over to the US. EPA would then require US industry to clean up those emissions too. In short, EPA's mandates favor manufacturing in China and will end up costing taxpayers lots of money to subsidize the cleanup of Chinese carbon-dioxide emissions from US airspace. That's how the present administration creates jobs. EPA, instead of carbon dioxide, should be banned to prevent further harm to our nation's economy.

There are many different ways of generating electricity such as nuclear power, geothermal, wind, etc. The point is that these so called green sources of energy are insufficient to satisfy the US requirement for energy; therefore hydrocarbons are and will continue to be the primary source of power generation in the US for the foreseeable future. Do you think the Chinese or Indian government would comply or care about EPA toxic designation or attempt to control carbon-dioxide emissions? The Chinese will continue to burn coal and petroleum products and emit large amounts of carbon dioxide to the atmosphere to keep their manufacturing on line, producing and shipping goods to the US. In essence, then, the EPA action amounts to a license for the Chinese to continue emitting more carbon dioxide and other pollutants.

What is the net effect of carbon-dioxide emissions from China? Carbon-dioxide emissions generated in China or India are dumped directly into the atmosphere and are dispersed throughout the world. Some of those emissions undoubtedly reach US airspace, and the next step is a mandate from EPA to reduce atmospheric levels of carbon dioxide present over our country. That would be the ultimate best deal for China and India because it would the US to pay for cleaning up emissions generated outside the continental US. Unless politicians and EPA formulate sensible policies to achieve environmental cleanup and job creation, American citizens can expect to have their American Dream shattered and our nation relegated to third-world status. The American people need to wake up, take a more active part in government, and remove all politicians and regulators who are actively contributing to shatter our American Dream and taxing us to poverty. We did it once before when we got rid of the British. Now is time to get rid of all those politicians and regulators in Washington, DC. We can also get rid of inept corporate officials by boycotting products made by their corporate entity in foreign plants.

THE LABOR MOVEMENT

There were very few successful efforts at organizing labor prior to the mid-1930s. Henry Ford recognized that labor strife could paralyze production at Ford Motor Co. He devised a solution meant to prevent labor from organizing and causing interruptions to his production line. He became very proactive in preventing labor unrest by addressing causes of workers dissatisfaction. He recognized the main cause of dissatisfaction among the workers was the grueling work at the assembly line and the low wages paid for such hard work. Henry Ford's solution was to significantly increase wages paid to his workers beyond the going rate; that solved the problem he feared most—production stoppages.

Henry Ford increased wages beyond those of comparable occupations. He, in effect, bought the loyalty of his workers because they knew there was no other place where they could get paid the same wages, and for that privilege the workers were willing to do the grueling work at Ford Motor Co. The trend started by Henry Ford in setting high wages for manufacturing workers in the decade of the 1920s was not continued during subsequent decades. Even when workers productivity improved significantly influenced profitability of their corporations, workers' wages failed to keep pace with productivity improvement. In the period from 1923 to 1929 the average output per manufacturing worker rose 32 percent but manufacturing worker wages increased only by 8 percent! [49]

Corporate America became extremely greedy and opposed any and all efforts to organize workers, and used all tools at its disposal to prevent unionization drives. Consequently, the labor movement was not a very effective tool in protecting workers' rights. Corporations, unlike Ford Motor Co. under the leadership of Henry Ford, failed to recognize that employees were the most valuable assets a company could have. Instead of treating their workers fairly, corporations chose to fire anybody who tried to organize a labor union for the purpose of gaining strength in negotiating better employment conditions. Government was also complicit in preventing workers from organizing unions.

Comparing manufacturing workers weekly wages (See Table 5) to wages of union workers (See Table 7), it becomes obvious union workers are better paid. In fact, union workers earn at approximately twice the level paid to manufacturing workers. For example, in 1920 a manufacturing skilled worker earns about thirty dollars per week while a typical bricklayer or painter earns about fifty-five dollars thanks to the union. The situation is similar in 1925 and continues thereafter. There is an undeniable impact on earning power of a typical worker resulting from organizing and negotiating working conditions by unions.

Occupation	1913		1920		1925	
	Hours per week	Earnings per hour	Hours per week	Earnings per hour	Hours per week	Earnings per hour
Bricklayer	44	$0.75	44	$1.25	44	$1.50
Painter	44	$0.65	44	$1.25	44	$1.50
Plumber	44	$0.75	44	$1.25	44	$1.205
Stonecutter	44	$0.625	44	$1.25	44	$1.375
Newspaper Typesetter	48	$0.50	48	$0.988	44	$1.191
Bricklayer	44	$0.75	44	$1.25	44	$1.50

Table 7. Union Wages [50] and Hours in Chicago

Unions are unsuccessful in organizing manufacturing workers until the mid-1930s. Unionization become easier after passage of the Davis Bacon Act in 1931, which require payment of prevailing union workers on federal contracts on construction projects and the National Labor Relations Act.

In the early years of the Great Depression, employers lay off workers in large numbers. As a result, many workers are available to replace those who have dared to even attempt to engage in union organizing activities. This deprives employees of their ability to either challenge employers' abuses individually for fear of losing their jobs or collectively in the form of a union organizing drive. The courts and government favor employers during this period. Therefore, workers have no option but to overlook abuses or lose their jobs!

Our legal system and government institutions never act proactively. They always react to a situation after some damage has occurred. That is as true today as it was back in the 1930s. This concept also applies to politicians who prefer to overlook corporate abuses while corporate contributions continue to fill their coffers. It is only when the government and politicians realize that popular unrest is imminent that they act to deflate the situation in order to remain in power.

Politicians felt threatened in the decade of the 1930s on account of several things. First, the large number of unemployed workers could provide fertile ground for social and civilian unrest, including the potential for overthrowing the government. Secondly, the Communist Party presented an ideology contrary to the one framed by our founding fathers forming the basis of our national heritage. But, communist activists were getting a friendly ear for their message among unemployed workers. Thirdly, the government was not assisting workers in any manner. Fourthly, membership in the Communist Party was growing as unemployed workers joined the party and started to identify with the "class-struggle" ideology of Karl Marx. Finally, the Communist Party became very active in unionization drives, therefore alarming the same politicians who had overlooked corporate abuses against workers. Workers' reaction, at the time, was desperation, but it was effective in preventing the shattering of the workers' American Dream. Politicians got the message and reacted to communists' overtures to workers.

Continued deterioration in economic conditions in the late 1920s and early 1930s led to massive layoffs and very high levels of unemployment. This led to further dissatisfaction for workers and growth in Communist Party membership, which became very active organizing workers, thus improving chances for unionization.

Facing this growing influence on the part of the Communist Party, politicians became concerned about their reelection prospects. That level of concern caused politicians to look at and address some of these corporate abuses. It was then that politicians acted after feeling threatened by successes of the Communist Party.

The government began to scrutinize working conditions and started enacting legislation that tilted the balance of power toward labor in an effort to overcome corporate abuses. The enactment of the Child Labor Act of 1926, for example, set the minimum age at fourteen years old for workers engaged in industries shipping their goods either intrastate or overseas. In 1935, Congress passed the National Labor Relations Act (NLRA) to protect the rights of employees and employers. It specifically recognized in Section 1 that:

> *"The denial by some employers of the right of employees to organize and the refusal by some employers to accept the procedure of collective bargaining lead to strikes and other forms of industrial strife or unrest, which have the intent or the necessary effect of burdening or obstructing commerce by (a) impairing the efficiency, safety, or operation of the instrumentalities of commerce; (b) occurring in the current of commerce; (c) materially affecting, restraining, or controlling the flow of raw materials or manufactured or processed goods from or into the channels of commerce, or the prices of such materials or goods in commerce; or (d) causing diminution of employment and wages in such volume as substantially to impair or disrupt the market for goods flowing from or into the channels of commerce.*
>
> *It is declared to be the policy of the United States to eliminate the causes of certain substantial obstructions to the free flow of commerce and to mitigate and eliminate these obstructions when they have occurred by encouraging the practice and procedure of collective bargaining and by protecting the exercise by workers of full freedom of association, self- organization, and designation of representatives of their own choosing, for the purpose of negotiating the terms and conditions of their employment or other mutual aid or protection."*

The **NLRA** recognized the importance of labor to not only Corporate America but also to the entire United States and its economy. It granted labor the power to negotiate labor agreements with employers thus leveling the playing field between labor and the corporate sector. This action on the part of government was, without question, very significant and definitely a proper exercise of government authority in promoting the general welfare and preventing abuses by Corporate America against its workers.

There was an important parallel in the unionization movement among workers and in the creation of ethnic communities by immigrants. Both of these groups recognized that there is strength in unity. Based on that, labor unions organized workers to gain strength in negotiating labor agreements that provided better working conditions for all workers. Immigrants in a similar fashion recognized that sticking together brought them protection against other ethnic groups and provided the means to satisfy their own needs for protection of their national heritage.

The values of both ethnic communities and labor unions are better protected as a group rather than as individual members. Ethnic communities protect their common values and heritage. Labor unions protect their rights to decent working conditions and fair wages. Immigrants fear abuses from other ethnic groups and come together to protect themselves against such abuses committed against them. In the case of labor unions, all workers identify themselves as members of that union regardless of ethnicity. That ought to teach all of us to focus on our similarities as Americans rather than our ethnic differences, which are fewer, to form a more perfect union as foreseen by our founding fathers. We all are Americans regardless of our ancestry, and our allegiance should be to the US first and foremost. We, as Americans, ought to recognize that things we hold in common surpass those things that keep us apart.

Communists, unlike those of us who believe in unity, tend to create a very divisive environment to strengthen their power base. Politicians, like communists, focus on class warfare to split society and achieve their goals. For example, whenever politicians talk about increasing taxes they always refer to the "rich" as those who are going to be affected the most. They mention the rich as if the poor and homeless were able to pay any amount of taxes no matter how low. At the same time, they refer to the poor as if they are going to benefit the most by paying less tax or getting more money from the government. In fact, the poor gets no breaks from the government. The rich cannot invest as much, thus creating fewer job opportunities for the poor. Who is going to invest to create new jobs? For sure the poor would be unable to invest. Why be so anti-wealth?

Political rhetoric tends to make the poor think they are going to benefit when, in reality, politicians are really intending to keep oppressing the poor. They do that by forcing them to depend heavily on money and handouts from the government. Those politicians who are so anti-rich should focus their energies on providing educational opportunities to get the poor out of their unfortunate economic status and able to become well off so that they may also realize the American dream.

Have you ever heard any politician talk about improving the school system in Washington, DC? Politicians in Washington, DC, send their children to private schools while poor local children are unable to get an adequate education. That action reflects very strongly their opinion that local public schools in the Washington, DC, area are not good. At the same time, you hear these politicians tell us about their concern for the poor. If they are so concerned about the poor, why don't they improve the quality of public school education for local children in Washington, D.C., and other parts of the nation?

If they were to do that, then they would be able to send their children to the same public schools as the poor. Furthermore, their actions would speak louder than their words in showing their concern for the poor, for they would be taking a very important first step to breaking the cycle of poverty. An alternate solution would be to subsidize attendance by poor children to the same private schools attended by politicians' children. Would they do that? No, that has never happened and will never happen, because politicians will continue to send their children to private schools, including religious schools, while opposing attendance at those same parochial schools by the poor. In view of that, are these do good politicians really concerned about the poor? What hypocrisy!

Why do politicians fail to provide funds to build first-rate educational facilities to enable the poor to improve their lot? That's the only way to break the addiction and dependency on government welfare. The answer is simple. Politicians want this dependency to continue so that they keep getting the vote from the poor and perpetuate themselves in office. They do that in exchange for a promise to do something about the poor's situation, which they never do. They do not want the poor to have a chance of making their American Dream reality. This allows politicians to control and enslave the poor by forcing them to depend on politicians' kindness and generosity in disbursing our hard-earned tax dollars. Is that fair? The reality is that no politician is concerned about the poor or anybody else. They are only concerned about themselves.

The American people need to reject this divisive philosophy and be united as Americans, regardless of ethnicity, social, or financial status. We all need to educate ourselves to convert our dreams into reality and, in so doing, prevent our American Dream from being shattered by corrupt politicians. This will only be achieved by voting against incumbents seeking reelection regardless of race, age, ethnicity, social status, or political affiliation. Politicians should focus on uniting all Americans and on making the poor wealthier rather than on making the richer poorer, which will never happen. Improving educational opportunities for the poor is the key to overcome poverty.

ON THE WAY TO RECOVERY

President Franklin Roosevelt encouraged unionization under the National Labor Relations Act. This opened the door for them to engage in collective bargaining with employers to improve working conditions and wages. The government knew that labor unions would negotiate higher wages for workers, and it did not oppose such increases because of beneficial impacts higher wages would have on purchasing power, income tax revenues, consumer spending, and the economy.

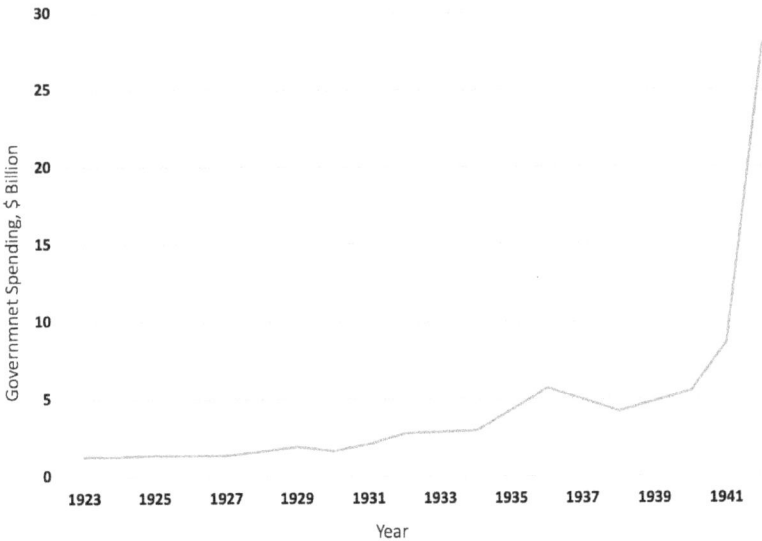

Figure 15. Federal Spending [51]

Higher wages would definitely result in additional consumer demand and would favorably impact manufacturing activity. That was a necessary first step to stimulate industry and create additional jobs. It was expected that additional manufacturing activity would have a snowball effect on suppliers, who would also have to hire workers to increase production. Economic stimulation reduced the unemployment rate significantly. The government was also expecting to reduce public spending by shifting the job-creation burden away from the public sector over to the private sector. Armed with this logic, it began to reduce spending around 1936 (Figure 15), but that resulted in a mini-recession that started in 1937 and continued through 1938. It became apparent that, in the absence of further government spending, industry would not to commit to additional speculative manufacturing.

The Obama Administration, like the Roosevelt Administration in 1937, signals cuts in spending at a time when the economy is beginning to recover from the Great Recession of 2009. It has does so by cancelling some military procurement programs and by trimming spending by NASA. It also announces its intention to increase taxes by not extending all tax cuts enacted under President Bush. Again, their basis for doing that is to penalize the rich. Here we go again with that nonsensical communist ideology about class warfare. There is nothing mentioned about creating jobs. The president should instead focus his energy on improving public schools in Washington, DC, so that both his daughters and poor local kids can benefit. In other words, why not change from the view focusing on making people poorer over to making people wealthier.

The Roosevelt Administration cuts spending and increases taxation in an attempt to balance the federal budget. Tax rates increase from 15 percent to approximately 20 percent in 1937 (Figure 13). Federal expenditures aimed at creating jobs are reduced from about $6 billion to around $5 billion. These actions result in lower GDP (Figure 11), lower revenues (Figure 12), higher unemployment rate (Figure 10), and a slight increase in the national debt (Figure 14). The results are contrary to the government's expectations at the time these measures are taken. President Obama's economic policies lead to the same results under similar policies under President Roosevelt.

Actions taken by the federal government during the Great Depression demonstrate the importance of government spending in reestablishing economic health to the country. It is not enough for government to spend funds just to kick start the economic recovery and expect the private sector to continue fueling the job-creation engine going without further government assistance. It is conclusively shown that, without the initial spark government spending on infrastructure projects creates, the jobs-creation engine would never have started. Moreover, it is also shown that government expenditures are not only necessary to start the recovery but also to keep it going.

As shown by the impact on GDP and unemployment rate, government expenditures have conclusively proven to be beneficial. When the government decides to reverse its course and cut spending in 1937, the unemployment rate rises again, (Figure 10) and government revenues begin to show a declining trend (Figure 12). The government once again reverses course and increases spending, starting in 1938. As a result of that decision, GDP (Figure 12) begins to rise and the unemployment rate (Figure 10) starts to show a decreasing tendency. The unemployment rate falls slightly after the government begins to increase spending in 1938, but the decline is insufficient to indicate the Great Depression has ended. In fact, unemployment is still at a very high level (18 percent) indicating the depression is still alive and doing well.

The first signs of potential conflict begin to appear in Europe as Germany begins to expand its territory outside its borders by first forming a union with Austria and then going ahead with annexation of Czechoslovakia in 1938. France and Great Britain initially permit these actions, but those actions fail to appease Hitler. Emboldened by his success in Czechoslovakia, Hitler decides to grab the rest of Europe by force with the intention of making all European territory part of the new Germany under a superior race. Those early signs of potential conflict brewing in Europe signal a red flag to many European countries as well as the US. It indicate the time has come to rearm and prepare their economies for war. In 1939, Germany invades Poland provoking a declaration of war from France and Great Britain. .

The United States realizes it would not, initially, be militarily involved in the European conflict, but it would have to play a role in this conflict. Instead of engaging in military activity, the US would become a major armament and food supplier to basically all European Allies as done during the early phases of World War I. In order to be able to do that, the federal government has to get its house and develop a plan detailing a reorganization of Corporate America to ensure available manufacturing facilities would be able to supply goods needed for war.

The private sector would be responsible for production of armaments and other goods not only to satisfy our own national needs but also the needs of Great Britain. Food production is also part of this picture. This obviously increases government spending significantly as shown in Figure 15 starting around 1940 and accelerate after the December 1941 Japanese attack on Pearl Harbor. Federal government spending approximately doubles from 1940 to 1941 and quadruples from 1941 to 1942. This unprecedented level of government spending drops the unemployment rate from approximately 15 percent down to 5 percent during the 1940 to 1942 period. Then and only, it is possible to claim the Great Depression has finally ended.

The question that frequently arises is whether government spending is required to maintain a healthy economic environment? The answer is clearly "yes" as shown by the impact government expenditures had on job creation during the depression and to get the economy going. The facts clearly demonstrate that the economic crisis is overcome after massive government spending. Those data also indicate that spending on public projects is not enough to cause a recovery. But, spending on the acquisition of manufactured products ended the Great Depression. Manufacturing, therefore, is the engine driving the recovery. That's a lesson the Obama Administration fails to learn from data on the recovery from the Great Depression. In other words, manufacturing is essential to the economy of the US. Anything that hinders manufacturing causes a detrimental impact on our nation's economic health.

A better question, however, would be to address how much government spending is really necessary to maintain and keep the economy on an even keel and productive manner. That's a harder question to answer but suffice it to say that some government spending over and above the level required to maintain essential services and ensure national security is mandatory for several reasons. The government is the only institution capable of tackling major R&D efforts that end up providing beneficial effects on the whole economy. An example is spending on the space program. Technologies developed from the space program have been transferred to the private sector and have resulted in many new products benefiting the common good of our entire nation.

A similar situation is the case relating to defense spending on programs focusing on development of new weapons. These programs or systems required for national defense often become stepping stones to benefit some segment of the civilian population, the whole country, or even the entire world. The internet is the best example of the type of result contemplated by this last statement. The internet is a development that owes its existence to the US Department of Defense, and now the whole world depends on this development to communicate.

Many people tend to oppose government spending no matter what. The problem with that opposition is that they do not understand the real reason for such spending or see the end products or benefits derived from those programs. There is no question that there is wasteful government spending generating no benefits, and that should be avoided. Examples of these expenditures are situations where congress appropriates funds to build projects to benefit only a very small segment of the population in a particular congressional district; these are typical projects done every year. This wasteful spending is focused on satisfying politicians' egos so that the beneficiaries of those expenditures can continue bribing their political benefactors with abundant sources of funds for their political campaigns. The only way to stop wasteful spending is to prohibit expenditures unless justified by a requesting agency or department and subject to strict scrutiny by a federal board charged with the duty of eliminating wasteful spending.

It is essential to understand differences between government and private-sector spending. Corporations base their capital expenditures on getting a return on the money invested.

Government expenditures, on the other hand, do not depend on getting a return on such investment; the government is looking for and getting a social return on its investment. For example, the government goes ahead and spends money on building a bridge that ultimately benefits not only the local communities where the bridges are built but also corporations using federal and state highways to ship their manufactured goods to customers. The government, in many cases, does not charge any fees to users of those things government has funded. It, however, gets a return on the taxes it collects based on enhanced economic activity.

Corporations would never spend any money to build public bridges or roads, even though those corporations need those roads and bridges. That's understandable because these are considered infrastructure projects benefiting not only the corporation but the entire community. Why should corporations spend money for the benefit of the entire community including competitors? These are types of expenditures more appropriately done by the government as representative of the entire community?

There is precedent for government spending to develop new sources of energy and commercialization of such sources. This is illustrated by building dams to generate electricity such as done by the Tennessee Valley Authority. There are also cases where government expenditures focus on developing new technologies with ramifications for the industrial sector, such as nuclear power. These developments have benefitted the entire nation, which indicates that not all government expenditures are bad per se. In many cases, government spending is essential to undertake beneficial projects such as spending on NASA programs.

What would have happened if government had not spent money to undertake public works projects starting in the early in 1930s? The Great Depression would not have ended because the private sector would never have decided to start projects or engage in manufacturing merely to create jobs. The private sector would have evaluated the situation and decided that no investment could be justified on account of poor market conditions. Think about that, and decide whether government spending was necessary at that time to overcome the economic crisis. Certainly, that was the only alternative available. Huge expenditures by the government were required to overcome the crisis. Those huge expenditures undoubtedly added to the national debt, but it was preferable s compared to other possible scenarios including civil unrest and starvation. The better way to categorize government spending in time of crisis is to look at the expenditure as an investment for the common good. That investment returns benefits as the economy gets back on track and government revenues increase to pay off the debt.

There are times when government has to develop technology and that technology becomes useful in the private sector. In those circumstances, the government should insist that any company getting access to those technological developments pay a royalty to the government so that taxpayers recover part of the cost of developing that technology; companies would certainly charge a royalty to users of its proprietary intellectual property. Additionally, the government should insist that any company utilizing taxpayer-developed technology should do so in manufacturing facilities located in the United States. In many cases, taxpayer-funded developments are taken over by corporations who fail to compensate the government for such use and, to add insult to injury, manufacture products from such development in countries other than the US. This is particularly true in the case of electronic devices and components.

There are several lessons to be learned from the Great Depression. Number one, all government spending is not bad per se. In fact, in many cases it is an essential weapon to be used in overcoming economic crises as demonstrated during the Great Depression. Number two, spending on infrastructure projects, while beneficial to some extent, is not the magic bullet required to overcome economic crises. The reason is that it takes time to get infrastructure projects to the point where they begin to exert some influence on other sectors of the economy, and by that time consumer pessimism sets in. Number three is that government expenditures on manufacturing have a greater beneficial impact on reducing unemployment than spending on infrastructure projects. In fact, increasing manufacturing increases government revenues by the income taxes it collects. Number four, government expenditures have to come quickly to be effective in solving the problem. Finally, government expenditures have to continue for as long as needed to overcome the crisis.

The government did not address the 2009 economic crisis properly, because it focused on infrastructure projects that failed to have any influence on reducing unemployment; the recovery period from that recession was very long indeed confirming what had been said. In many cases, meeting regulatory requirements such as preparation of environmental impact statements delayed projects significantly, thus preventing any benefit from such government spending; regulatory requirements would have to be suspended during times of crises. Handling funds to banks was not the answer either for all it did was to enrich bankers. Bankers used taxpayers' funds to reward themselves with huge bonuses for doing a great job of driving their financial institutions to bankruptcy.

"I FEAR ALL WE HAVE DONE IS TO AWAKEN A SLEEPING GIANT
AND FILL HIM WITH A TERRIBLE RESOLVE."

JAPANESE ADMIRAL ISOROKU YAMAMOTO
AFTER PEARL HARBOR

CHAPTER 5.
THE GIANT AWAKES
WORLD WAR II YEARS

Government spending on the private sector is a very important means of influencing economic activity. There is, however, no simple formula to calculate the amount of money that should be spent to end a recession or depression such as the Great Depression of the 1930s and to initiate a recovery. Government spending by itself is not sufficient to end the depression but it is a necessary step to seed the recovery process. It is insufficient if dedicated to infrastructure projects such as the construction of highways and bridges, which normally take a long time to get started. Those projects do not normally influence other sectors of the economy initially because it takes a while to get those projects going. A significant amount of time is spent doing preparatory work before supplies such as steel and cement are required to be onsite. Nevertheless, these infrastructure projects impact other sectors of the economy when construction starts. In other words, infrastructure projects impact employment but that impact is not immediately felt but rather delayed until actual construction starts.

The annual amounts spent by the government from 1933 to 1940 are shown in Figure 15; these expenditures amounted to approximately $5 billion per year. As a result, unemployment declined during that same period, but that reduction was not to end the depression. In fact, the unemployment rate dropped from 25 percent in 1933 to 15 percent in 1937. Unemployment increased to about 20 percent in 1938 when the government became concerned about deficit spending and reduced its level of spending. In any case, the unemployment rate was still unacceptably high at around 15 percent in 1940 as shown in Figure 10 despite significantly higher government expenditures as compared to the amounts spent prior to 1933.

When war preparations began in 1938, the emphasis shifted from spending on infrastructure projects to spending on armaments, which provided a major boost to the manufacturing sector. That spending, unlike spending on infrastructure, had a very quick impact on many sectors of the economy. For example, airplane production impacted raw-material suppliers, engine manufacturers, fuel suppliers, and so on. More importantly, those activities also impacted other such as the development of intellectual property as a result of a significant increase in R&D efforts; those efforts influenced development, testing, and implementation of new ideas and scientific concepts. R&D results led to the establishment of additional manufacturing facilities to produce new products coming out of the development part of the R&D work.

R&D discoveries provided fertile ground for new manufacturing opportunities creating new employment opportunities. These jobs were in facilities producing electronic and mechanical components required to produce superior airplanes and armaments as compared to those of our enemies. Clearly, those government expenditures had a greater and more immediate visible impact on unemployment than had been the case with infrastructure projects. Notice that the unemployment rate dropped steadily from 15 percent in 1940 down to 5 percent in 1942 (Figure 10) indicating a very significant and rapid positive impact on unemployment rate.. Furthermore, scientific discoveries resulting from government-sponsored R&D efforts provided many new products including synthetic rubber that became the basis for future growth in job opportunities. New manufacturing facilities had to be built to produce those new products, thus creating new jobs in the construction sector. These new products had a snowball effect on production of derived products. For example, production of synthetic rubber enabled production of gaskets, shoe soles, adhesives, tires, etc.

In 1939, Germany invaded Poland, forcing England and France to declare war on Germany. After a few months of inactivity, the powerful German army swept through Belgium and defeated France in a matter of weeks. The small British army was evacuated in the nick of time across the British Canal, and the war shifted to a battle in the air, which the Germans saw as preparation for an invasion of Great Britain.

President Roosevelt was determined to aid the British, and the US government undertook the role of supplier of war materiel and food, while at the same time, remaining neutral. This economic assistance caused a substantial increase in government expenditures to purchase and transport products manufactured in the US overseas. This program enabled Great Britain to survive the first two years of the war after defeating attacks by the German air force and stalling a planned German invasion.

The US industrial sector had to retool its manufacturing facilities from private-sector production to producing goods for military purposes. The unemployment rate declined from a double-digit rate down to approximately 5 percent in 1942 after the US entered the war on two fronts. Following the Japanese attack on Pearl Harbor and the American declaration of war against Japan, government expenditures took off, and the wartime demand for workers dropped the unemployment rate even further—to approximately 1 percent by 1944-1945.

Economic activity increased significantly as a result of the war effort and government expenditures. Manufacturing activity coupled with government spending were the key contributing factors ending the Great Depression and re-establishing economic vitality. Government expenditures on infrastructure projects did not end the Great Depression but served as the initial spark for recovery. Spending on wartime manufacturing, on the other hand, did end the Great Depression.

The giant had indeed awakened, as feared by Japanese Admiral Yamamoto. The attack on Pearl Harbor jolted the United States strengthening not only the United States government but also Corporate America. The United States would become the most powerful military and industrial nation on the face of the earth as a consequence of creating a very powerful and effective team uniting labor, government, and the private-industrial sector.

Furthermore, the US had also managed to become a scientific and engineering powerhouse. And, by the end of the war, US industry had survived the war intact as compared to the industrial base of our foreign competitors such as that of Germany, Japan, and other European nations, all of which had suffered tremendously. The industrial base in those nations had been badly damaged or totally destroyed. Corporate America had gained an advantage over its foreign competitors that had to be protected. That advantage could only be protected by investing to modernize existing US manufacturing facilities. Although severely damaged by devastation caused by war, manufacturing plants and industries in Japan and Europe would be rebuilt and re-emerge with the latest in terms of buildings, manufacturing plants employing the latest technology and production processes. Only vigorous investment and new technology would make it possible for older US facilities to compete effectively against newer Europeans and Japanese companies. It would take a while for these modern foreign manufacturing facilities to get on stream, but they would be extremely efficient in terms of production capacity, quality, and production cost.

The emergence of the United States as an industrial powerhouse was the result of many factors coming together. The first was the role played by the US government focusing expenditures on building manufacturing facilities and purchasing goods required for the war effort. The second was a well-trained labor force experienced in manufacturing activities. That labor expertise resulted in production increases, operating cost reductions, and manufacturing quality control. It was also the cooperative effort among labor, management, and the government that ensured no breakdown in the production effort. Finally, Corporate America provided the management expertise to ensure that the country would be capable of defeating our nations' enemies.

The R&D effort going on in parallel with manufacturing also

contributed substantially to the outcome of the war. It did that by developing new products to shorten the war and to ensure that our armed forces were provided the best weapons, tools, and equipment to wage war effectively against our enemies. All of these factors contributed to the creation of new manufacturing facilities that, in turn, increased demand for workers; manufacturing jobs were and continue to be the present time relatively high-paying job opportunities.

Industry reluctantly rose to the initial challenge presented by the government war preparation efforts around 1939. It did so for several reasons. It was reluctant first of all to shift production from the private sector over to the war effort because it was concerned of the adverse impact that move would have on market share. This was a very real concern in an improving economic environment when unemployment rate was trending downwards and consumer spending was on the upswing. Secondly, new investment would be necessary to change facilities to war production from production of civilian goods. Would the companies be able to recover the new investments? Finally, this shift would call for training and learning new tasks and would add to the corporate cost base. For example, automobile producers would have to shift their manufacturing facilities from production of automobiles over to manufacturing airplanes, tanks, and other military vehicles that required different processing steps or schemes. That learning process would be costly for Corporate America to undertake with assurances that it would ever recover such investment.

Those concerns called for some major arm twisting by governmental agencies to convince corporations that every industry would be required to participate in view of the national crisis the US was facing. In addition, the government played a very active major role in planning and focusing manufacturing activities to provide goods required for the war effort. Unbeknown to Corporate America, this seemingly intrusive action on the part of the US government would strengthen US industry and significantly reduce unemployment. It would also plant the seeds for future profitability.

Automotive manufacturing facilities ceased production of cars and trucks for the private sector and retooled their facilities to manufacturing military vehicles and aircrafts. Obviously, this switch required additional capital investment, which stimulated the activities of mechanical equipment and raw material suppliers. A secondary effect was the construction of new facilities at decentralized locations throughout the country to minimize risks of damage from military attacks. These facilities were built and owned by the US government; the government leased the facilities to industry. Fortunately, none of these facilities were ever attacked by the enemy.

Spreading the location of military manufacturing facilities around the nation benefitted the entire country. It forced the industrialization effort on a nationwide basis. In 1940, the majorities (about 87 percent) of airframes manufactured were located in five states, but by 1944, airframe manufacturers were located in twelve states, thereby reducing the risk of having these facilities damaged by enemy air raids. The same thing happened in the case of other manufacturers that focused on critical aircraft components such as engines, propellers, etc. Most of the expansion occurred at inland locations rather than at existing coastal facilities. These major shifts in manufacturing also provided additional benefits in creating infrastructure projects throughout the nation.

Year	Reference [41]	Reference [42]
1937	3100	
1938		
1939		2141
1940		6086
1941	1941 to 1945 Yearly Average Aircraft Production was 59440	19433
1942		47836
1943		85898
1944		96318
1945		46001
TOTAL 1941 to 1945 Aircraft Production	297,199	295486

Table 8. Total annual aircraft Production

The annual number of aircraft produced during the 1937 to 1945 is shown in Table 8. Comparing the number produced in 1937 to the annual average number produced from 1941 to 1945 reveals the awesome increase in manufacturing output that occurred.

Yes, Mr. Yamamoto, the giant is awakened as shown by the number of airplanes manufactured for the war.

The types of aircraft produced during this period included those listed in Table 9. These aircraft were not only used by our armed forces but also by the armed forces of our allies. This became a means of providing recognition throughout the world for the high quality and reliability of US produced airplanes. This reputation would be beneficial to continue selling both civilian and military airplanes for many years after the war. In other words, the world had an opportunity to evaluate the products of Corporate America during the war years, and that experience was the driver for opening markets for American produced goods during peace time. The world had a very good impression of American produced goods after World War II. That reputation was earned on the basis of performance and quality. It was a time when "Made in the USA" really meant a great deal.

Aircraft types	Fighter	Attack	Bomber	Transport	Training
Number	99,950		97,810	23,929	57,623

Table 9. Types of Aircraft Produced [52]

President Roosevelt in 1940 urged the US aircraft industry to produce at least 50,000 planes a year. This was a significant increase considering that production had been in the range of 2,000 to 3,000 per year before war had broken out in Europe. The goal set by President Roosevelt would require production of approximately 4,000 aircraft per month. Huge amounts of capital were required to build new manufacturing facilities to produce the number and types of aircraft demanded. Considering that Corporate America had been through a very long recession, it was doubtful Corporate America would be able to handle this feat. The US government recognized this dilemma and stepped up to the plate, causing development and implementation of programs to expand production capacity.

The Emergency Plant Facilities program and the Defense Plant Corporation (DPC) were established to address this issue. The DPC, established in August 1940, built, equipped, and held title to several aircraft assembly plants, which then were leased to the manufacturers. [53] The industry became very efficient manufacturing aircraft. Production of a B-17 in 1941 required 55,000 individual work hours. By 1944, this number of work hours had been reduced to about 19,000 hours, which was a very significant improvement enhancing efficiency and productivity. The same production line concepts developed by Henry Ford and others were adapted to produce airplanes.

Shipbuilding was another essential activity undertaken by the private sector under the auspices of the US government for several reasons. The US Navy had to have warships to conduct the war both in the Atlantic and Pacific theaters of operation. Additionally, the US had to produce merchant ships to transport goods necessary to supply our own armed forces as well as those of our allies in the European and Pacific war theaters. As in the case of aircraft production, industry rose to the occasion and became very successful at building both naval and merchant ships.

The US government, once again, undertook a program to construct shipyards in coastal areas of many states. Again, the goal was to reduce risk of damage to shipyards from military attacks on these facilities. Any attack on those shipyards would cause significant damage to the war effort by delaying delivery of both naval and merchant ships. Assembly line concepts first employed in the auto industry were adapted for mass production of not only ships but also airplanes and other war materiel. Table 10 shows the number and types of naval as well as merchant ships built during the war period. Note that the number of merchant cargo ships is expressed in terms of tonnage. Based on total tonnage and the fact a typical "Liberty Class" ship had an approximate tonnage of 10,000 tons, it would be possible to estimate the number of cargo ships that could be built to be in the range of 3,400. This was a significant achievement of tonnage built before the war.

Aircraft Carrier	Battle-ship	Cruiser	Destroyer	Convoy Escort	Submarine	Merchant Ships (a)
22	8	48	349	420	203	3400

Table 10. Naval and Merchant Ships built during WW II [54]

It is worth keeping in mind that most of these cargo ships were built toward the end of the war, which would indicate that the average production exceeded 800 cargo ships per year. The construction of this large number of cargo ships was required to overcome the losses caused by German submarines attacks. This represented a significant increase from the approximate 45 merchant cargo ships built in 1940 with total tonnage of 445,000.

Table 11 lists the number of vehicles and ground weapons production manufactured during the war.

Tanks and Self Propelled Guns	Artillery	Mortars	Machine Guns	Military Trucks
88,410	257,390	105,055	2,679,840	2,382,311

Table 11. Vehicles and Ground Weapons Production [55]

Results by manufacturers in terms of airplanes, ships, military vehicles of all types produced represented a great success. This was an awesome achievement considering the US military had entered the conflict on December 1941 short of all sorts of weaponry and ended the war in September 1945 with the best-equipped armed forces on the planet.

There was no doubt that the response to Japanese Admiral Yamamoto expressed concern about awakening a sleeping giant had come true. Furthermore, the resolve of that giant was to exceed all expectations and to show what could be done by close cooperation among Corporate America, the American worker, and the US government. Did our response show Admiral Yamamoto what Corporate America, American Labor and the US government working together could do?

During the war, workers were in great demand to staff jobs available in manufacturing production facilities involved in production of weapons and other war necessities. This situation raised some concerns about creating ideal conditions for runaway inflation based on shortages of raw materials and labor. Based on a labor shortage, it was believed wages would increase under the threat of labor unrest, therefore potentially resulting in work stoppages and paralyzing production during this critical period of national crisis. This presented the perfect justification for increasing wages, but the government had imposed a ceiling on annual wage increases. Workers were able to receive compensation in other forms such as subsidized health insurance and other benefits not considered wages by government regulations.

It would be worth recalling that during the 1920s and 1930s workers were unable to effectively organize labor unions because of fear of losing their high-paying manufacturing jobs. In the late 1920s and 1930s, economic conditions became very difficult and resulted in high unemployment rates and a deep depression. That sort of economic conditions favored employers at the expense of employees. In 1935, the National Labor Relations Act (NLRA) was enacted to encourage employer-employee negotiations and better labor conditions thus encouraging unionization. Furthermore, the US government began requiring employers used unionized labor to work on projects it was financing during the 1930s. This action by the government leveled the labor-relations playing field and empowered workers to pursue union organizing activities in order to negotiate labor agreements resulting in higher wages and better working conditions for workers.

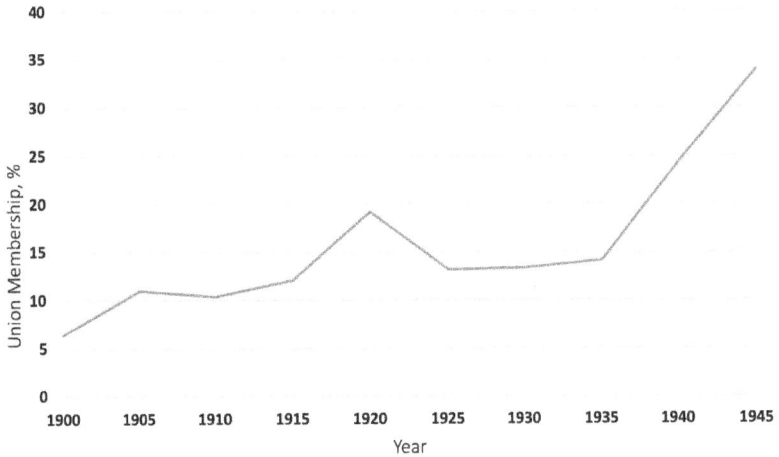

Figure 16. Percentage of Unionized Labor Force [56]

Unionization activity from 1900 to 1945 is shown in Figure 16. Notice the low percentage levels of union membership in the early 1900s as compared to the mid-1940s. There is a slight increase from 1915 on that peaks in 1920, which is about the time Henry Ford started his its mass production facility of automobiles. It is also the time when Ford intentionally more than doubled the wages of manufacturing workers in order to ensure labor peace and prevent labor stoppages in his manufacturing facilities; either one of those would have been extremely expensive for Ford Motor Co. From 1920 on, there is a tendency on the part of workers to avoid labor disputes and unionization for fear of losing their jobs; Henry Ford, for example, would not have hesitated to fire any worker who even thought about joining a union. During that period, employers had the upper hand with workers.

The Great Depression and the resulting high unemployment rates were the economic reality of the 1930s, causing workers to lose all negotiating power. But, after passage of the NLRA in 1935, the balance of power shifted back to workers, and union membership began to increase and continued its upward trend during the war years. In particular, this increase in union membership could be attributed to two factors. Number one was the increase in manufacturing activity resulting from the war effort. And, secondly, the increase in manufacturing activity resulted in an increasing demand for workers to man unionized manufacturing facilities; this had the effect of forcing workers to become union members.

Labor shortages during the war became fertile ground for union organizing activities. The labor shortage coupled with the legal right to engage in open organizing activities under the NLRA increased union membership from approximately 9 million in 1940 to 14 million in 1945 as shown in Figure 17. That was a very significant increase in union membership.

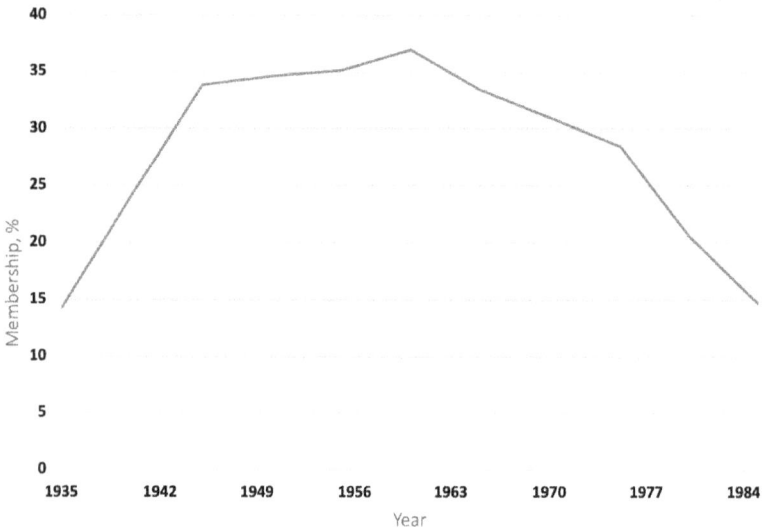

Figure 17. Union Membership [57]

Manufacturing workers wages more than doubled from 1940 to 1949 with the largest increases being realized during the 1940 to 1944 period. [58] The average weekly hours worked increased from 38.1 to 45.2 in 1945; overtime was paid for the number of hours exceeding forty hours per week thus enhancing the take home pay of the workers. After the war, the average number of hours per week declined slightly to 39.1 in 1949.

The earning power of manufacturing workers increased substantially, but these workers were unable to spend that money because of the shortage of consumer goods. This created inflationary pressures on the economy as a whole and caused the government to create several agencies to impose controls on wages, prices, labor strikes, and production. The Consumer Price Index (CPI) reported by the Bureau of Labor Statistics (BLS) increased by more than 35 percent reflecting this inflationary tendency during the war period. This showed the degree of preparation the US government had undertaken; the government was prepared for every contingency unlike the situation in 2009. That degree of preparation back in 1940s showed real leadership on the part of government officials as opposed to what happened in 2009.

In light of wage restrictions, employers began to offer valuable benefits to attract new employees. These new benefits were in lieu of wage increases and included retirement pensions, medical insurance, paid holidays, and vacations. The improvements in fringe benefits were considered non-inflationary as there was no cash transferred to employees to enable them to spend on consumer goods. Nevertheless, these fringe benefits had a monetary value, and more importantly, they provided a means for taking care of future problems such as a sickness or retirement. Since the value of fringe benefits were excluded from the calculation of wages their worth were outside wage-control mechanisms set up at the time.

The National War Labor Board (NWLB) was created by an executive order signed by President Roosevelt in 1942 and was charged with the duty of settling labor disputes and approving all wage increases in which the annual remuneration was below $5,000. This was an effort to control inflation. The NWLB had the power to offer mediation, voluntary arbitration, and compulsory arbitration to resolve labor controversies and prevent production interruptions but had no authority to enforce its decisions. The US government, under the War Labor Disputes Act of 1943, had authority to take over plants needed for the war effort where production had stopped due to labor disputes. The government, however, found out that it was easier to enforce decisions against

Corporate America than it was to enforce those against labor particularly at a time where labor was in short supply. As a result, there were significant numbers of labor strikes as shown in Figure 18.

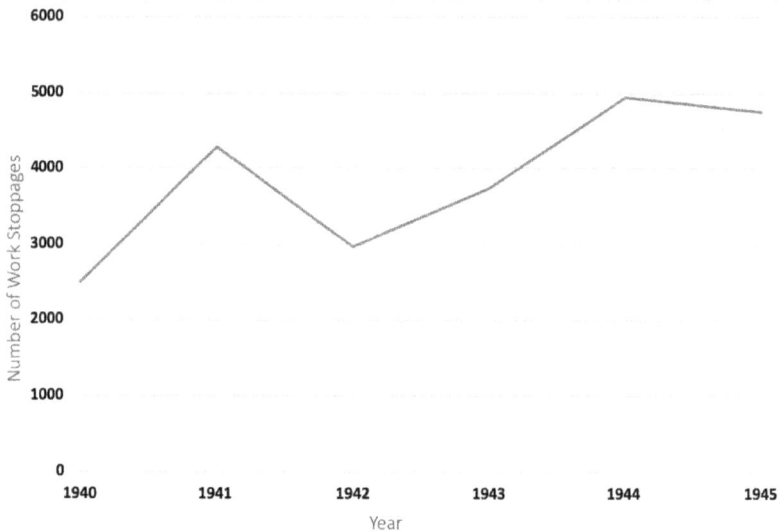

Figure 18. Labor Work Stoppages. [59]

In summary, the war years provided the foundation for great achievements by combining the capabilities of Corporate America, labor, and the US government; they became a winning team capable of great accomplishments. This, undoubtedly, turned the US into the greatest economic and military nation on the planet. It was not the achievement of a single party but rather a team effort. This was the recipe for future success. This triumph was due to the cooperation of the three parties involved that resulted in prosperity for all and made the American Dream a reality for many people. This, therefore, provided a model to be emulated by future generations.

If one were asked to identify the catalyst or magic ingredient making all of this possible, then the human factor would outshine all others. Human beings provided brain and physical power to overcome untold obstacles and develop the ideas that resulted in a complete transformation not only of industry but also of the entire nation. This recognition, therefore, provided an excellent basis for continuing the development and improvement of our nation's economic wellbeing as well as that of its citizens, regardless of national origin, race, or religious belief as truly anticipated by the following text in our Declaration of Independence from Great Britain: "We hold these truths to be self-evident, that all men are created equal, that they are endowed by their Creator with certain unalienable rights that among these are life, liberty and the pursuit of happiness."

SCIENTIFIC AND ENGINEERING ROLE

Given the demands of the war effort, it became necessary to increase production capacity for armaments, military vehicles, medical supplies, food, and so on. This increase in production had a snowball effect on production and supply of raw materials and other components required for assembly and operation of those weapon systems. This forced greater reliance on engineering and scientific disciplines to convert existing manufacturing facilities from one type of production to another, to scale up production from laboratory or development stage up to commercial quantities, to develop manufacturing processes, and to ensure achievements of quality and production goals.

Automobile manufacturing plants, for example, were converted to produce airplanes. This conversion was not an easy undertaking considering that, while an automobile was composed of hundreds of mechanical parts, an airplane had many thousands of parts that had to work correctly at all times. In addition, it was apparent that scientific and engineering discoveries would be essential to not only produce required weapons but would also have to produce better weapons than those used by our adversaries to ensure success in the battlefield.

Reliance on science and engineering was the best means of developing the capabilities of the nation. This reliance reinforced what was learned in early days of US industrialization. Science and engineering had provided and continues to provide the tools required by any country on the road to development. No country ever achieved complete development without relying on science for development and on a continuous improvement process that never ends. If it were to end, then that would be a sign that the country was on a path of self-destruction.

During the war years, Corporate America was producing, on the average, in excess of 50,000 aircraft per year. This represented a very substantial increase over the 3,000 or so aircraft manufactured annually prior to the war. Obviously, sophisticated metal alloys, electrical, and electronic components in large quantities were required to assemble this large number of aircraft on a continuous annual basis. On top of that, the amount of aviation fuel required to operate these aircrafts as well as the quality of the fuel presented additional obstacles that could only be overcome by developing new manufacturing alternatives based on solid scientific and engineering concepts.

When Germany invaded Poland in 1939, England and France declared war on Germany. Germany retaliated by attacking France and overcoming its defenses shortly thereafter, and this set the stage for the Battle of Britain in the summer and autumn of 1940. The German Luftwaffe (Air Force) had as a primary objective to gain air superiority over Britain by defeating the Royal Air Force. The Luftwaffe relied on heavy aircraft for this campaign while the British Air Force depended on fighter aircraft. This was a critical point in the war because it undoubtedly demonstrated that the outcome of the war depended on the quality of aviation gasoline to power high- performance fighter aircraft flown by the British. But to defeat the German Luftwaffe, Britain had to have large quantities of high-quality aviation fuel. The result of a US R&D effort made the manufacturing of such fuel possible thus saving

Britain and defeating the Germans.

The quality of aviation gasoline depended on octane rating, defined as a measure of resistance to auto ignition in internal combustion engines. In 1939, the octane rating of gasoline was 75, indicating that a significant improvement had to be made to reach the 100-octane rated aviation gasoline required to fuel high-performance engines of fighter and bomber aircrafts. Lower octane ratings would have resulted in premature ignition and adversely affect engine performance and reducing engine power and efficiency.

Aviation gasoline, like automobile gasoline, is a liquid mixture of many chemical compounds separated from petroleum crudes during the refining step. Typically, this is a liquid mixture composed of many chemical compounds including aromatic compounds such as benzene and toluene that greatly enhance octane rating and other chemical components such as butane that control vapor pressure. The vapor pressure is a measure of the fuel vaporization rate that is necessary to control the amount of fuel vaporizing and mixing with air prior to combustion. Too little fuel in the fuel-air mixture results in insufficient power, thus poorer engine performance. Benzene and toluene, however, were also the raw materials for other products that were in great demand during the war years. Benzene was a precursor to styrene, which was a raw material for synthetic rubber used to manufacture tires for airplanes and automobiles. Toluene was a raw material for production of explosive TNT.

Supplying aviation gasoline in sufficient quantity and of the right quality presented several issues that had to be quickly addressed by the engineering and scientific community. Refining capacity had to increase significantly to supply the required quantity. Consequently, several steps were taken to solve this problem. First, the immediate step to follow was to divert the required chemical components from uses in the private sector over to the military, which enabled a small increase in the supply. But, restricting supply to the private sector was not the final solution. The best solution was to expand refining capacity to increase supply, but that took time; it could not be done overnight. The engineering community working with the industrial sector, and the US government had to undertake a massive amount of design work to build additional refineries very quickly. It also had to address the shortage of octane enhancers such as benzene and toluene.

It proved to be quite a challenge as the scientific and engineering communities worked diligently to develop chemical manufacturing processes in the laboratory and then to scale those laboratory results to commercial processes to produce required quantities; this was done. The next step was to design, construct, and operate these new commercial facilities. Refining processes developed at that time included alkylation, catalytic reforming, and catalytic cracking and proved very successful. These refining processes continue to be use in present-day petroleum refineries to produce aviation and automobile gasoline as well as diesel fuel.

As the name implies, catalytic reforming is a reaction wherein molecules of one type are converted or "reformed" into a different type of molecules. This process is important not only because it produces valuable chemicals for use as raw materials for chemical synthesis but also because of its impact on production of chemicals useful for improving octane rating of gasoline.

The catalytic cracking process is a refining operation that takes heavy organic molecules present in heavy oils and cracks them into smaller molecules. Heavy oils are obtained as products from the distillation of petroleum crudes. The lighter molecular fraction can be used as a blend component in the production of gasoline.

The product from alkylation units provided a high-octane blending stock, known as alkylate, that increased not only the amount of aviation gasoline available but also enhanced its octane rating. More importantly, alkylate provided a means of diverting benzene and toluene from the aviation gasoline pool over to the manufacture of styrene and TNT. The reforming process also was instrumental in enhancing the production of aromatic compounds including benzene and toluene for not only aviation gasoline pool but also for other chemical uses.

Contributions made by the engineering and scientific

communities enabled Corporate America to supply aviation gasoline in an ever increasing amount, as shown in Figure 19, to satisfy the war demands; satisfying this demand would have been impossible for Corporate America acting alone. In view of that, it can be concluded that the bonding between the corporate and the engineering and scientific communities was very effective. That bonding occurred during the war and was indicative of better things to come. That reliance and mutual dependence resulted from the ability to solve problems enriching our lives and making the American Dream a reality for all of us as citizens of this great nation.

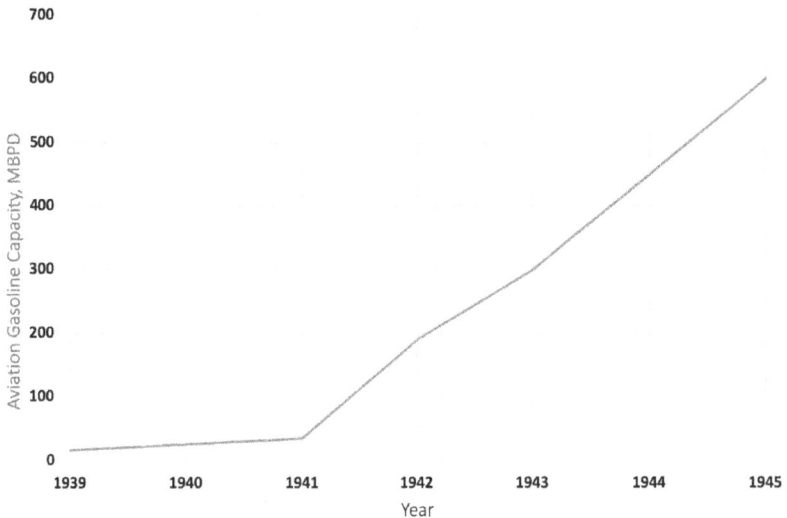

Figure 19. Aviation Gasoline Production Capacity [60]

The Japanese Army had occupied Malaysia and cut off the supply of natural rubber to the United States. Fortunately, the US had had the foresight to accumulate significant quantities of natural rubber in inventory. This inventory provided a stopgap measure meant to tide us over until a synthetic replacement was identified and produced commercially in large quantities as required. The problem was that an ever increasing number of military vehicles were rolling off the assembly lines requiring an increasing number of tires of all sizes. The crucial issue became making available enough rubber to enable production of a sufficient number of tires of all sizes to use in new equipment and as replacements for worn or failed tires. Since there was not an easily identifiable replacement for natural rubber, it became obvious that an alternate replacement for natural rubber would have to be developed and manufactured in large quantities to satisfy demand for tires.

It has to be said that the synthetic polymer was not as good as natural rubber but it was adequate. It also should be mentioned that present-day tires are manufactured with improved versions of the original styrene butadiene rubber, also known as SBR, which was developed during the war years as a result of R&D sponsored by the US government.

Once styrene and butadiene were identified as raw materials for the production of a natural rubber replacement for tire applications, it became essential to provide those raw materials in large quantities. It was imperative that manufacturing processes for both of these chemicals raw materials be developed and scaled up to enable production of commercial quantities in a reproducible and consistent manner.

The point here is that manufacturing synthetic rubber is not an easy thing, for it involves many different steps that have to be performed in a predetermined sequence in order to achieve the goal of manufacturing a synthetic replacement for natural rubber. Raw materials have to be of high purity in order to ensure consistent synthetic rubber product quality.

As in the case of aviation gasoline, the development of a manufacturing process to make synthetic rubber was the result of many long hours spent solving technical problems before scaling up to commercial size. Fortunately, the private sector and universities had begun experimentation in the field of polymer chemistry. These groups had established a small-scale pilot unit to demonstrate feasibility of a manufacturing process capable of producing a synthetic rubber. Nevertheless, additional engineering work had to be done to design, construct, and operate commercial-scale units capable of producing large quantities of rubbery material for use in manufacturing tires and other articles.

The story of TNT was similar to that of aviation gasoline and synthetic rubber. In all of these cases, there was close cooperation among industry and the scientific and engineering communities. Each of these technological developments presented specific challenges that had to be overcome in order to achieve a greater goal. In all cases, the technological developments resulted in new manufacturing processes and, more importantly, in the creation of job opportunities to make the American Dream reality for many individuals.

On the medical front, there were significant discoveries and commercial efforts to produce drugs that saved many lives by preventing infection of wounds. For example, the discovery of penicillin is attributed to Scottish Scientist Alexander Fleming in 1928. The problem was that Fleming was unable to make penicillin in sufficient quantity to be useful in medical practice. Penicillin, at that stage, was a laboratory curiosity and nothing more. Fleming's discovery remained dormant until a team of scientists at Oxford University rediscovered the medicinal powers of penicillin and attempted to convince British companies to undertake commercial production. These scientists were unable to do so because of the strain of Britain's war effort. The war, in effect, precluded British pharmaceutical companies from engaging in the development of a manufacturing process to produce penicillin in commercial quantities.

The story was different in the US, where the government solicited assistance from pharmaceutical companies to develop a production process for the production of the first "wonder drug" to treat infection. The appeal by the US government to US pharmaceutical companies was made in 1941. Scientists at Pfizer were convinced that penicillin could effectively treat infections so their company became one of the many pharmaceutical companies responding to the US government's appeal.

Scientists and engineers at Pfizer were able to develop a production process based on fermentation expertise developed by Pfizer as urged by scientist Jasper Kane. Pfizer's efforts were successful after many long hours of hard work. This effort was very risky, but Pfizer was determined to succeed. It was risky because it would require Pfizer to curtail production of other well-established products while it focused on the development of penicillin. It could also place the company's existing fermentation facilities in danger of becoming contaminated by the mobile penicillium spores. Pfizer invested millions of dollars, putting the assets of Pfizer stockholders at risk, to buy equipment and facilities needed for deep-tank fermentation. The process was very successful and soon Pfizer was producing five times more penicillin than originally anticipated. [61]

Pfizer agreed to allow its competitors to use the penicillin production process it had developed to satisfy the demand for this antibiotic. Most of Pfizer's competitors, however, were unable to match Pfizer's production rate or quality because they lacked fermentation expertise. As a result, Pfizer ended up supplying the major portion of the penicillin supplied to the US government.

It is worthwhile to learn about the contribution made by Pfizer in the penicillin story. The important point is that, unlike popular belief, Corporate America depends on the US government to define a need and to subsidize the research required to make new products. That was true not only in the penicillin case but also in the development of aviation gasoline, synthetic rubber, production of airplanes, etc. The story also teaches us that scientists and engineers regardless of whether employed in the corporate world, educational institutions, or by the government are able to work together in an industrial, government, educational labor setting to make the American Dream possible for all involved.

While most of the R&D work funded by the US government during World War II had military objectives, there were significant offshoots applicable to the civilian sector. A case in point was the work leading to the development of the atom bomb. The same technology that produced the atomic bomb was applicable in the medical field to treat cancer. It was also useful as a means of generating electricity. A more recent recognizable benefit derived from defense focused R&D during the Cold War was the Internet.

There were other benefits relating to electronic equipment such as computers, communications, and many more.

There are countless examples of very important contributions made by the scientific and engineering communities. These accomplishments represent effective collaboration among academic, corporate, and government laboratories to develop effective weapons system or to save lives during the war. The most notorious of these are the medical advances developed and implemented during the war years and the development of atomic weapons.

It is also worth noticing the very valuable contributions made by immigrants to these scientific efforts. The important point here is that Americans citizens whether by birth or naturalization had the best interest of this country at heart. It is, therefore, essential to recognize that all of these developments were made by individuals educated in scientific disciplines. In view of that, it is essential to emphasize the need to make the best educational opportunities available to all citizens to ensure the pool of technical talent is never exhausted.

The US depends on an uninterrupted supply of well-qualified scientists and engineers to sustain its technological leadership status. Consequently, the educational system has been charged with the duty of preparing primary and secondary students to pursue scientific and engineering majors in college. This goal recognizes the importance of an educational system grounded on science and mathematics. The educational system is and will continue to be the genesis of all future scientists and engineers. This requirement places an awesome responsibility on the educational system. But the educational system is not the only avenue available to supply the ever-increasing number of scientists and engineers. Obviously, immigration plays and will continue to play very important role in providing some of these scientists and engineers.

THEN AND NOW

It is important to recognize factors, policies, and tactics contributing to ending the Great Depression. Those same things can be adapted and implemented by present leaders to end any great recession such as the one we have had in 2009. If in the past these moves have been effective, then it is likely that the same strategies will be effective in a present or future case. If that proves out, then these tools can be added to the arsenal of weapons to battle future economic crises. Things that have been shown to be effective include: government spending, stimulation of manufacturing activities, common sense and fair regulations, an honest and fair financial system, a strong research and development commitment, a first-class educational system, a political system focused on needs of the electorate, and a cooperative attitude between labor and management ensuring manufacturing excellence.

Government spending is a major contributor to the economy as has been demonstrated by the impact it has had on the economic recovery from the Great Depression. It is the spark that starts job creation leading to reductions in unemployment. Job opportunities create a positive outlook that improves the entire economic climate that is so necessary to enhance consumer confidence. It dispels consumer pessimism and leads to greater consumer spending. Consumer spending stimulates demand and, in turn, manufacturing. Suppliers are immediately impacted, thus creating additional job opportunities.

Government expenditures during time of crisis have to be consistent. It may be necessary to increase government spending if the rate of unemployment fails to drop significantly below an anticipated target level within a reasonable period of time or if other sectors of the economy fail to be stimulated. It is naïve to think that government spending on infrastructure projects is the magic bullet leading to economic recovery. That is so because public projects tend to be slow starters and generate a limited number of new jobs. These projects also do not result in immediate demand for construction supplies. Consequently, they tend to have very little initial influence on other sectors of the economy. Manufacturing, on the other hand, has an immediate impact on many sectors of the economy. Manufacturing requires immediate supplies of raw materials and other components necessary to make the final product. Consequently, US government expenditures focused on acquisitions of manufactured goods tend to have the greatest positive influence on the speed of recovery and on job creation.

If instead of focusing on saving financial institutions during the 2009 crisis, the government had focused on reenergizing manufacturing activities then the outcome would have been different from what has been experienced. That reenergizing effect could have been be achieved by tax breaks to make possible the acquisition of automobiles, all sorts of machinery and airplanes, as well as in constructing new homes. Modernization and development of weapons systems would have been an ideal solution particularly since the country is engaged in fighting wars in Afghanistan and Iraq.

The government acted correctly but timidly when it provided financial benefits to encourage the replacement of gas guzzler automobiles with more fuel efficient ones. It should also have included in that policy the replacement of model automobiles as well as trucks older than those produced in the year 2005. This same policy could also have been extended to cover airplanes, machinery, and other capital assets employed in manufacturing activities. President Obama and President Roosevelt made the same mistake; President Roosevelt started spending to get us of the Depression but then reduced spending on account of fears and political pressures relating to the national debt. The result was the same in both cases causing unemployment to increase. President Obama should have increased expenditures to get the unemployment situation under control.

Industry by itself is unable to initiate an economic recovery because it will not spend one dime or hire workers unless it has a market for its product. On top of that, manufacturers and suppliers have to act in concert with other manufacturers to have a widespread result. This is an unlikely result. But, if consumers are unemployed, how will demand for manufactured goods be created? Corporations are interested only on making a profit, and that happens when there is demand for its products. In view of that, government expenditures on acquisition of products manufactured in this country are the only means of initiating an economic recovery.

A plan has to be formulated in cooperation with the industrial sector to determine the best way of to get people back to work in order to produce goods required by the government. Products purchased by the government have to be manufactured in this country rather in foreign locations to be effective. This plan has to focus on energizing manufacturing activities done by companies in this country, regardless of the national origin of the company. This means that automobile manufacturers such as Honda, Toyota, Nissan, and others should be encouraged to expand their production and to enjoy the benefits of being American manufacturers.

This plan should also encourage corporations to invest in new manufacturing facilities or in modernizing existing facilities to improve production cost and enhance manufacturing efficiency. Industry attains long-term benefits by this policy and so does the entire country. This policy leads to a potential for future higher profit margins and creates a snowball effect on manufacturers' suppliers. This also leads to job creation. This beneficial impact on Corporate America can also be achieved by common sense use of taxing, environmental, and other regulatory policies.

Similarly, the US government can use its power to regulate business activity in a positive manner rather than as a means of frustrating the best efforts of the private sector in creating jobs. For example, imposing unrealistic, nonsensical, and unattainable mandates issued by unaccountable regulatory agencies stifles manufacturing activities. This leads to manufacturing paralysis and forces Corporate America to move to foreign locations that are more manufacturing friendly. This ultimately kills job prospects for American Citizens.

There are many examples of regulatory mandates that adversely impact job creation. Among these are misguided environmental policies that stop industrial growth completely. Specifically, requirements to obtain licenses to build and operate new nuclear power plants result in delay and uncertainties in estimating initial investment; profitability cannot be estimated. Uncertainty is the worst enemy companies faced when making investments. If it becomes impossible to know when a project is going to be completed or in estimating its cost, then that set of circumstances kills the project. That is so simply because companies are unable to determine whether the initial investment will ever be recovered. That is the reason no new nuclear electrical power generating stations have been built in the US in the past twenty or so years. Construction of new nuclear power plants face long delays in getting environmental permits, and the result is to increase initial cost. Similarly, the so-called "cap and trade" proposal to limit carbon dioxide emissions will ultimately limit job creation and decimate manufacturing. How?

Let's illustrate the consequences of these poorly thought out regulations enacted by irresponsible and unaccountable bureaucrats in Washington. Cap and trade proposal refers to an idea where manufacturers including petroleum refiners are allowed to emit a certain amount of carbon dioxide, methane, and other chemical by-products. If the allowed limit is exceeded then these facilities have to buy additional permits to cover those emissions in much the same way as in the commodity markets. Allowable emission limits are lowered every year. Refiners are responsible not only for emissions from their refineries but also for carbon dioxide emissions from vehicles burning the amount of fuels produced by each of those companies.

This implies, therefore, that an exchange such as the Chicago Mercantile Exchange has to be created to handle the purchase and sale of these credits. Here are the problems with the cap and trade proposal. Refineries have not been very profitable over the past few years; consequently additional costs will make those refineries even less profitable. This means refiners will be precluded from operating because no one invests to get zero return. The credit exchange will be subject to manipulation in the same manner investment bankers manipulate financial institutions. Finally, as the level of allowable emissions limit decreases with time, fewer and fewer refiners will be able to meet emission requirements forcing them to shut down refineries and eliminate jobs thereby shattering the American Dream for many workers. But, fuel will still be required to operate motor vehicles thus forcing the importation of fuels from other countries and adding a financial burden on the country. How are we going to pay for these fuels if people are unemployed?

Another example is the idea of obstructing oil and gas exploration to such an extent that it basically prevents or, in many cases, ends any sort of exploration. The problem here is that bureaucrats are concerned about a problem that may or may not exist. Specifically, the recovery of natural gas from oil shale requires fracturing the shale to enable the release of gas trapped in pores within the shale; fracturing has been done for many years without problems. The fracturing is done using chemicals and water at high pressure. The concern is that continuous injection of water and chemical mixture will migrate to aquifers and contaminate these aquifers. It is a problem that needs to be addressed by a solution developed based on valid scientific and engineering concepts. But, before the problem can be addressed it is necessary to get data to understand the problem and solve it.

Bureaucrats are hindering all attempts at creating a sustainable job creation machine in the area of oil and gas exploration and production as well as in petroleum refining. There are many examples of negative bias against particular segments of the private sector in the Washington bureaucracy. The best example of that is the bias against oil and gas exploration that prevents exploration in many areas of the country. There is also a bias against petroleum refining that prevents construction of new refineries. The latest threat is the idea being floated to make refiners liable for carbon-dioxide emissions from refineries and users of refined fuels. Who is going to provide fuels for our transportation needs? Perhaps, Chinese refineries will provide such fuels without being subject to these nonsensical emission rules.

There are ways of addressing a problem and, at the same time, provide the means to help corporations to modernize manufacturing facilities. For example, the US government can enact common-sense regulations to lower emissions and then provide means for manufacturers to either buy the equipment required to achieve the emissions goal or pay a fine for failure to meet the goal. The US government can achieve both goals by allowing manufacturers, such as refiners, to immediately depreciate the cost of purchasing and installing new pollution-abatement equipment. This enables original-equipment manufacturers to order from suppliers, thereby increasing the demand for workers to staff suppliers' manufacturing sites.

There is, however, a downside to this scheme in that foreign competitors may try to get around this emissions-control scheme by not installing the equipment and thereby gaining an unfair cost advantage over US manufacturers. Obviously, this unfair advantage can be prevented by a requirement that all importers of goods into the US from foreign countries be able to certify conclusively that the goods have been manufactured under strict environmental compliance with US Standards. If they fail to do so then the US government should impose a duty equivalent to the cost of implementing the regulation.

Failure to conclusively show strict compliance with US EPA standards by foreign manufacturing facilities would lead to an import duty being levied on product coming into our country from an offending manufacturer. Foreign manufacturing facilities would be subject to inspection by US authorities to verify compliance. Why? First of all, this will level the playing field by eliminating unfair cost advantages resulting from compliance by our industry and noncompliance by foreign manufacturers. Secondly, this will ensure pollution levels generated in foreign nations are minimized. Finally, this action makes it clear to every nation in the world that if it wants to participate in the US market then it has to comply with US standards, including environmental and safety standards, and be able to prove their manufacturing facilities comply with US regulations.

This is a constructive manner of addressing problems and creating employment. Furthermore, the US government can go one step further and encourage manufacturers to jointly fund or work together in R&D programs to develop new technology addressing pollution problems. In that manner, a dual benefit would be created: jobs creation and building new manufacturing facilities built to make the new devices invented.

There is no question that unaccountable regulators have too much power that, in many cases, is detrimental to the industrial health of the country. Politicians have to shoulder the blame for creating these agencies and giving them the power to enact what, in effect, is the law of the land. Americans should demand their representatives make these agencies accountable to the people or, better yet, disempowered them.

Taxation is another tool that can be used to stimulate manufacturers. Tax policy can be used to encourage industrial modernization aimed at improving efficiency to lower production cost. It also can be used to penalize relocation of manufacturing facilities to foreign location by denying tax write off and offset provisions to US companies relocating manufacturing to foreign locations and selling their products in the US. On the flip side of the issue, foreign companies relocating to the US should be granted tax incentives.

Corporations do not react unless there is a cost involved or a profit to be made. The cost would have to be a fairness tax imposed on profits derived from manufacturing products by US companies in foreign countries and subsequently exported to be sold in the US. This is not an action intended to punish but rather to level the playing field. Notice that what is being advocated is not to limit choice available to Corporate America but only an action intended to demonstrate to US corporate leaders the impact their decisions have on the livelihood of people in this country. Taxation policy should be considered an instrument to protect the American Dream for all US Citizens.

The preeminent status of the US depends on sustaining its technological developments. Consequently, it is essential that our educational system be revitalized and improved countrywide to enable young people to perform in such a highly technical and competitive environment. The first step in achieving that revitalization is to eliminate political correctness and enforce discipline to create a learning environment in the classroom. Political correctness leads to mediocrity by keeping inept teachers on the payrolls while, in effect, discouraging qualified and dedicated teachers from staying in the classrooms.

Finally, there has to be a more agile regulatory system devised to ensure that all financial institutions act in a fair, transparent, and socially responsible manner free of gimmicks and unable to change contractual terms at will.

"AND SO, MY FELLOW AMERICANS:
ASK NOT WHAT YOUR COUNTRY CAN DO FOR YOU—
ASK WHAT YOU CAN DO FOR YOUR COUNTRY."

PRESIDENT JOHN KENNEDY
JANUARY 20, 1961

CHAPTER 6

PINNACLE OF SUCCESS

Corporate America was transformed completely during the course of World War II. Before the war, it had weathered a financial crisis - the Great Depression - over many years that drove many companies to the brink of bankruptcy. Some of these companies ended up bankrupt and out of business. Many other companies had manufacturing facilities that were either shut down or unable to restart production because of the lack of consumer demand for its product. After all, consumers were unemployed and unable to earn wages, and that lack of earning power prevented consumers from purchasing many types of manufactured goods such as cars and home appliances.

Lack of consumer demand during the Great Depression made it nearly impossible to restart manufacturing activities. The lack of demand, in turn, had a very significant impact on Corporate America's cash flow that prevented these companies from either employing anyone or investing in the business. This situation put an end to all investments, including those aimed at modernizing existing facilities or to undertake new R&D projects to develop new products and newer and more efficient manufacturing processes. In short, companies were in a very difficult position by being unable to produce anything because of lack of sales, and so were Americans. Companies could not and would not spend any money without that would not have a return on that investment. In short, since there was no consumer demand for product, companies had no demand for employees. The situation was difficult indeed, and companies were unable to project a return to better economic conditions.

The only alternative available to start a recovery from the Great Depression was demand from new sources other than consumers. Those new sources were either export markets or the US government itself. Economic conditions throughout the world were very similar to those in the US; therefore, the export market was not a viable alternative. The US government, on the other hand, had two alternatives available to it: either take over Corporate America completely or spend to acquire products made by the industrial sector to initiate an economic recovery.

Fortunately, the US government did not take over industry. Instead, it developed and financed a production plan to kick start manufacturing activities and encourage corporations to hire employees to produce products demanded by the government. This was at the advent of World War II. It was a time when Germany's hostile intentions toward its neighbors had become well known. That forced the US to start preparing for potential conflict in Europe and also to become a supplier to our potential European allies. As a result, the US government imposed price and production controls on corporations and consumers. It purchased large quantities of new armaments and other war materiel necessary for the conduct of the war. It also sponsored R&D to develop production processes for many things such as fuels, chemicals, metal alloys, electronics, weapons, and so on.

The increased level of government expenditures was the seed that transformed the industrial status of the nation from weak and barely viable to strong and very dynamic. In turn, industry completely changed the US. It made the US the preeminent military and industrial nation of the world it is today. In short, Corporate America and the US government had entered into a marriage of convenience that had materialized into a mutually dependent relationship for continued growth and dominance.

That interdependence between Corporate America and the US government continued to mature and strengthen during the period after World War II. There was no question that this marriage of convenience would experience the usual conflicts and disagreements present in any marriage. But, both the US government and the corporate sector, however, recognized that they needed and continue to need each other.

Individual citizens, on the other hand, became beneficiaries of this marriage. Citizens perfected the union in more or less the same way children of a marriage perfect the marriage. Citizens provided a motivation for both parties to continue to jointly grow stronger.

Achievements by the industrial sector were contributions and achievements of human beings employed by corporate entities. These individuals were the unsung heroes who labored long and hard to do what was needed to be done to ensure victory over our adversaries. Similarly, the US government depended on human beings for developing policy to strengthen the industrial sector and to provide political leadership to achieve that end.

The US government provided financial resources to purchase manufactured goods from Corporate America in order to wage war and help our allies. Those expenditures became the lifeline necessary to keep many corporations afloat and grow stronger. That cash flow fueled job-creation and led to a condition of full employment as reflected by an unemployment rate as low as 1 percent at one time during World War II. Undoubtedly, low rates of unemployment meant financial benefits for Americans who, in turn, made significant contributions to ensure that our country's needs were met while at the same time ensuring that employers became commercially successful in the process of providing those needs. This translated into a deeply held sense of loyalty that became a very valuable asset analogous to consumers' loyalty to a brand name.

Brand loyalty is well recognized as very valuable in marketing for it reflects quality, value, and consistency. All of these factors tend to differentiate between competing products; this is true even for products made by the same manufacturer but marketed under different store names etc. Brand loyalty becomes a sacred bond that, once broken, is very difficult and expensive to repair. This concept is now well understood by GM and other US car manufacturers who have lost market share on account of attempting to take advantage of customers by selling inferior products. Now those manufacturers that have broken that bond with consumers are facing an uphill battle to regain that loyalty and regain market share. Similarly, employee loyalty to their employers is a sacred and valuable bond that preserves an atmosphere of trust. This loyalty leads to growth and prosperity for employers and, in return, for employees.

POST-WORLD WAR II
STATUS QUO

The US defeated all of its enemies in the European and Pacific theaters. It did that decisively on battles at sea, on land, and in the air. It defeated our adversaries on the industrial front as well. And, it also achieved supremacy on the intellectual front as the direct result of many outstanding scientific and engineering developments leading to the scale up of laboratory discoveries to commercial production.

Technical know-how developed during the war years focused on solving challenging problems faced by the country at a very difficult time - war. These included shortages caused by lack of raw material in our country or embargoes of essential raw materials imposed by adversaries. One relevant case was the availability and importation of natural rubber to manufacture tires for airplanes, trucks, and other military vehicles. Malaysia was a large producer of natural rubber but was under Japanese occupation. The Japanese prevented Malaysia from exporting natural rubber to the US. The US responded to that challenge by discovering and manufacturing a synthetic substitute for natural rubber that became ideally suited for manufacturing tires, for example.

Technological achievements also led to a new source of power. The development of nuclear power led to development of nuclear or atomic weapons that are credited with ending the war against

Japan and saving many lives in the Pacific theater of operation. Ironically, it also provided an immeasurable number of medical benefits by becoming a tool to fight cancerous malignancies and for generating electrical power to light and heat our homes.

In short, the US had become an industrialized nation capable of supplying high-quality manufactured as well as agricultural goods not only to satisfy its internal needs but also those of the rest of the world. No other nation could do that!

The US had also attained a level of scientific and engineering supremacy unrivaled by any other nation in the history of the world. The US military had been transformed into the most powerful armed forces on the face of the earth. As a result of all these achievements, the US became the country other nations aspired to become. That supremacy was grounded on the industrial, agricultural, military, and scientific might of its institutions. In particular, it represented the achievements of the American people working in the private sector, academia, and the US government during the war years. That success represented the result of close cooperation among the US government, the private sector, and American workers. This trio became the key to success.

Technological supremacy of the US depended, and continues to depend, on the strength of its private sector, US government leadership, and the ingenuity of the American people. Consequently, if Corporate America were to become weak, then the US as a nation would lose its global preeminence and our individual American Dreams would be shattered. The private sector depended and presently depends on its employees to achieve this level of success. As a result, mutual loyalty between corporations and employees was the underlying key to success. Similarly, the US government depended on its political leaders to outline a plan turning the country in the direction of recovery and on the road to victory and prosperity.

These industrial, political and military achievements were the achievements of the American people because they are the heart and brains of government and private sector. These successes were enjoyed by both the private and public sectors and reflected

213

successes of American citizens regardless of race, country of origin, or whether native born or naturalized; they were all Americans.

US preeminence in the global arena was the outcome of a synergistic effect among government, labor, and management. It was the product of team rather than individual effort. It led to the creation of a bond strengthening the parties of the team and magnifying their contributions. That preeminence was a bond uniting the parties. It became a badge of honor and a source of pride for those individual human beings. This was made abundantly clear by the loyalty individual workers had developed for their employers. In other words, individual workers were proud to be associated with individual corporations.

Obviously, it would not have been possible for corporations acting on their own to achieve the degree of success that they had achieved by the end World War II. Similarly, labor would not have benefitted as much as it did without the US government purchasing goods produced by corporate employees. In fact, labor would not have been employed had the US government not been forced to purchase goods for the purpose of fighting the war. This tripartite enterprise demonstrated the truism that there is strength in unity. That was the lesson learned from World War II. It was a lesson that needed to be kept in mind as the country moved forward to the 1950s and beyond. That historical union and cooperation among labor, the private sector, and the US government were essential elements driving the US to its present leadership position.

Unfortunately, corporate arrogance led many industrial leaders to the erroneous conclusion that the same achievements would have been made by the industrial sector acting alone. In fact, corporations kept complaining about government interference when, in effect, the government was acting in a manner beneficial to the corporate financial wellbeing. In the decades after the war, corporations focused only on profitability without regard for the welfare of its employees. Consequently, employee loyalty began to deteriorate gradually. This deterioration was particularly obvious at the point many corporations began to move a significant portion of manufacturing facilities overseas.

By the mid-1980s and beyond, the concept of loyalty between a company and its employees had eroded significantly. It began to weaken as employees were laid off and manufacturing facilities moved to foreign locations. For example, there were many electronic manufacturers including those making TV sets in the US after the war. Among those TV manufacturers were Zenith, GE, RCA, and many others; but, now it is very difficult, if not impossible, to find a television manufacturer in the US. All TV sets, it seems are made in overseas locations, particularly China. The beneficiary of that manufacturing relocation has been China and not the US.

If that relocation trend continues unimpeded, the industrial private sector and the US would begin a downward trajectory toward third-world nation status. As a result, high-paying manufacturing jobs would be unavailable. This will adversely impact consumer spending and lower the standard of living to which we have become accustomed in the US. This will prevent Americans from purchasing consumer goods regardless of country of manufacture, thus decimating many companies including those of US origin.

The message to be derived from the breaking of this loyalty bond between corporate employers and American workers is simple. Corporations seem to be sending a simple message to workers, and workers should be sending their own response to that message. The message from Corporate America to its workers is: We want you as consumers and not as employees. In response, the workers should be : We do not want your products unless we are employed to produce it. It is a simple message that will have a very significant impact on the corporate world for it would reduce profits and, in turn, bonuses to corporate executives. That's the only way of ending corporate abuses.

Americans experienced unequaled prosperity during World War II in terms of earning power and job opportunities due to the strength of manufacturing in the country. The end of the war, however, brought an element of uncertainty to the employment picture. Changes would have to be made to adjust to conditions existing at the time. Clearly, the demand for manufactured goods would not be as high as it was during the war years. In fact, demand would be expected to decrease when compared to demand during the war years. Furthermore, the economy would have to make a transition from war production to manufacturing for civilian uses. Clearly, civilian demand would be much smaller than that required to satisfy the demand for manufactured goods destined for the war effort.

The transition from war production to production for civilian markets meant automobile factories had to be retooled from manufacturing airplanes and tanks over to production of automobiles and trucks. People questioned whether the excess production capacity built up during the war to satisfy war demands would continue to be fully utilized. If it were not, then that excess capacity would have to be shut down, causing surplus workers to lose their jobs. In other words, it would become necessary to find new markets for products made by Corporate America to prevent layoffs.

On top of the downsizing of industrial capacity, there would be a downsizing in the armed forces. This would compound the problem by increasing the number of potential workers competing for a reduced number of manufacturing jobs. It was a worrisome situation for workers, because they foresaw an undesirable transition from prosperity to uncertainty. It was also a worrisome situation for the entire country. Fortunately, the result was not as bad as had been anticipated. Consumers were willing to spend to acquire goods that they had been prevented from buying during the war years. And, the reconstruction of Europe and Japan opened up export markets, thus expanding demand for US manufactured goods.

There were several events that allayed the fear of the general labor population in regards to losing their jobs in a post-World War II environment. Educational benefits were made available to returning veterans under the GI Bill. This was a very valuable benefit and a very wise solution to a potentially devastating situation. These educational benefits to veterans were an investment by the US government on its people that eventually strengthened the nation and its institutions. It was a step that recognized the need and the means to provide a highly trained population to fill high-paying jobs that had been created by a very technically oriented industrial sector. It was an investment that would pay off many times in terms of higher earnings for the beneficiaries of that educational investment—returning veterans—and the US government. Higher earnings would enhance income tax receipts for the US government. Many veterans took advantage of that educational benefit, which enabled them to accept professional jobs and thus reduce competition for general manufacturing jobs.

The second factor was assistance provided to reconstruct European and Japanese industries that had been destroyed or damaged during the war years. Foreign aid would be predicated on making credit accessible to purchase US manufactured products such as machinery and agricultural goods. These goods were required to satisfy immediate needs in rebuilding industry and preventing widespread starvation. This provided an incentive to manufacture goods for those export markets. As a result, the US attained a leadership position in international commerce reflecting its production capability. It also reflected the decency and kindness of the American people and its government in recognizing and helping both friend and foe alike during a time of need.

US foreign aid was the driver for reconstructing the industrial and private sectors of many nations and for getting those nations back on their feet; this was done without expecting anything in return. It was true that the assistance provided was an outlet market for products from Corporate America. It was also true that this assistance enabled industries in those nations to become competitors to our national industries. In any event, this assistance enabled US industry to make the transition to a private-sector economy in a much smoother fashion than otherwise would have been possible. The industrial sector demonstrated its capability to become a major supplier to the entire world as well as to satisfy the demand of the US.

It turned out that all those factors had an effect on employment opportunities in the US as shown in Figure 20. The unemployment rate increased from approximately 4 percent to 6 percent as the economy shifted from a war footing over to one driven by consumers. In other words, the immediate impact of additional workers coming into the labor pool and reduced manufacturing activity was not as severe as had been anticipated considering the number of soldiers returning to civilian life. In fact, if population growth had not been into account then the unemployment rate would have been even higher than it was. This meant that the economy was creating more jobs than had been anticipated to lose at the end of the war when all clouds of uncertainty had been present. The resulting unemployment rate was still within the range of 2 percent to 7 percent considered "full employment" by most economists. In other words, the post-war economy was very dynamic and, in general, doing quite well.

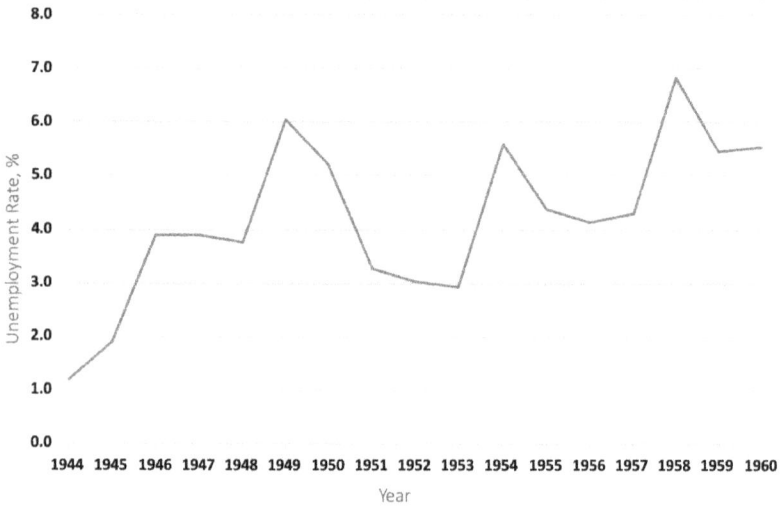

Figure 20. Post-World War II Unemployment Rate [62]

The Korean conflict added another dimension to this picture in terms of new challenges and demands for armaments and, more importantly, manpower. In effect, the number of workers available to compete for the number of jobs existing at the time diminished significantly to the extent of the number of people called for service in the armed forces. Paralleling that reduction in manpower was an increase in manufacturing activities to produce products required by the war effort. The challenge was to balance and satisfy the total military and private sector demands with available manufacturing capacity. This added another dimension to the equation showing Corporate America's flexibility in being able to simultaneously satisfy different markets. The enhanced level of manufacturing activities created new employment opportunities and reduced the unemployment rate as shown in Figure 20.

Obviously, as the Korean War continued, additional reductions in unemployment were attained. After the Korean War, the unemployment rate increased somewhat but did not reach a level higher than 7 percent during the decade of the 1950s, which was a very prosperous period in US history. That prosperity was based on factors that should be identified and replicated by our political and corporate leaders to enable a repeat performance in the second decade of the twenty-first century. This would be essential to maintain our national preeminence in the world and to enable our children and our children's children to share in the American Dream.

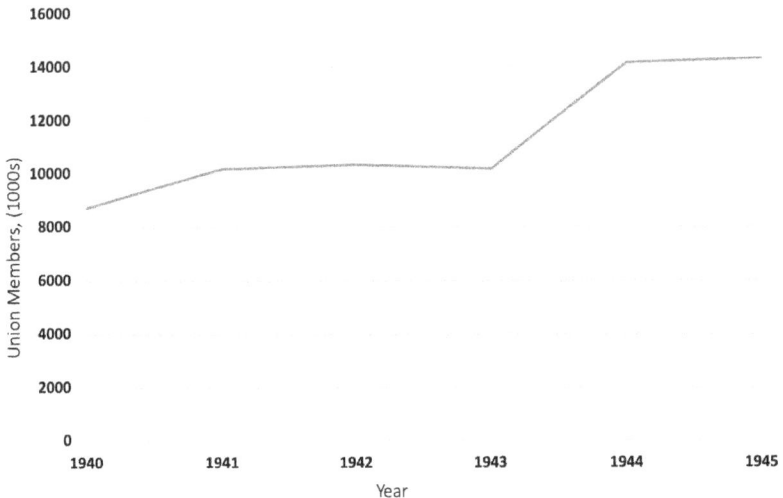

Figure 21. Fraction of Labor Represented by Unions [63]

Union membership, shown in Figure 21, increased steadily from 1935 to 1942 as a result of requirements imposed by the US government on its procurement contracts. Specifically, this growth was the outcome of the protections and rights granted to workers to unionize under the National Labor Relations Act of 1935.

Union membership remained fairly constant during the period from about 1945 to about 1963, indicating either a loss of union momentum or attainment of a saturation point in the labor movement. This could also be interpreted to indicate an unwillingness to become union members either because working conditions were satisfactory or on account of dissatisfaction with the union movement. Union membership began to decline steadily from 1960; that trend has continued to the present time. Was the decline in labor union membership a rejection of the ideals behind the labor movement or the result of being fed up by corrupt union bosses? Perhaps, it was a combination of both factors.

Corporate America was revitalized and reenergized during the period starting around 1938 and continuing through the war years. This revitalization process was the result of government spending on weapons procurement programs and developing technological know-how through its sponsorship of R&D efforts. Industry partnered with the US government in this program and made many significant contributions that resulted jobs creation. This partnership arrangement resulted in the deployment of corporate staffs to man operating facilities, manage R&D programs, and scale up laboratory developments into commercial products. The know-how developed was the product resulting from government expenditures under President Roosevelt's New Deal and massive expenditures to procure products necessary for the war effort.

It was during this period that US industry moved from the brink of bankruptcy to a very profitable position as shown in Figure 22. In fact, corporate profitability continued to improve from that point on to the mid-1950s and thereafter. US government expenditures, therefore, had saved the private sector. In view of that, US industry became indebted not only to the US government but also to its employees who trusted their employers and gave them their unconditional loyalty. More importantly, this success could become the pattern to follow in managing future economic crises.

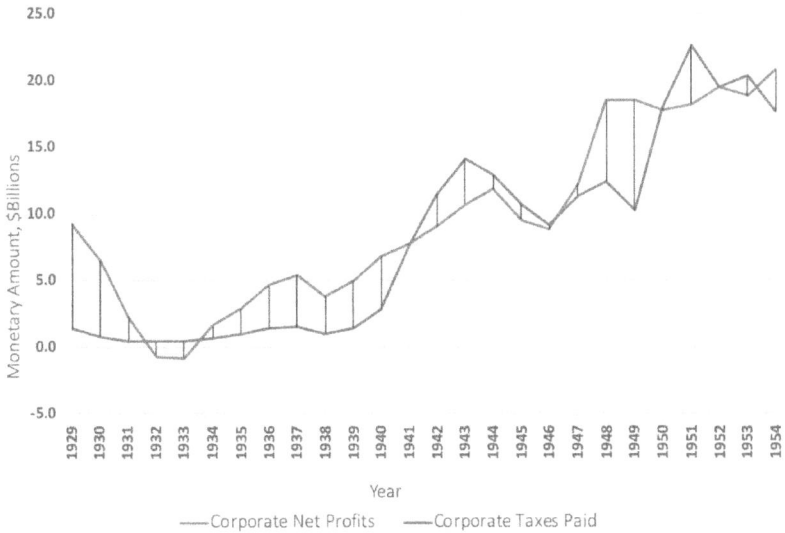

Figure 22. Corporate Profits and Income Taxes [64]

Corporate taxes paid to the US government are also included in Figure 22. Data in this figure show that the US government benefited from its investment in Corporate America. That benefit represented the increasing amount of taxes collected by the government. Taxes could be looked at as a return on the government investment in saving the industrial sector from financial disaster. It is worth noticing net corporate profits and tax receipts in the form of income taxes are more or less equal on an annual basis. Is this coincidental or intended to indicate equal sharing of profits among partners? The government probably had an even better return if taking into consideration income taxes paid by workers and the beneficial impact arising out of the multiplier effect corporate wages and expenditures for raw materials had on the rest of the economy.

Corporations always considered tax levies imposed by federal and state governments to be excessive. In view of that argument, it would be worthwhile to analyze the tax picture during the war years and soon thereafter to determine whether that argument had any validity. It was true that the tax imposed on Corporate America amounted to approximately 50 percent of the profits generated by Corporate America during the war years.

The question then would be: was a 50 percent tax rate excessive? First of all, it was reasonable to expect the US government would demand and get a return on its large investment to rescue the private industrial sector from the brink of bankruptcy during the Great Depression. Certainly corporations would have done the same. The magnitude of a reasonable return would need further investigation. Secondly, the US government invested in the development of new technology leading to more cost-effective manufacturing processes and the creation of new products. The results from this government investment made the future profit picture for industry much more attractive and certain. Unlike private companies that would have charged royalties to users of their proprietary technology, the US government did not charge any fee or royalties users of new technical know-how developed with federal funds. Thirdly, the US government was the largest buyer from industry, and it was acquiring those goods at a price that included a reasonable profit margin for producers. Finally, the US and state governments provided the entire infrastructure required to transport goods to the marketplace.

In view of benefits accruing to the private corporate sector from US government investment, would the 50 percent rate be considered excessive? It was obvious that tax receipts represented not only return on the government investment but also a payment for essential government services. In view of that, it would be difficult to argue that 50 percent was excessive considering benefits obtained by corporations. In fact, one could be argued that 50 percent tax rate was on the low side considering taxes would be assessed only on profits and not revenues.

Another way of looking at the 50 percent tax rate is to consider a fair return on profits from a partnership. Partners are equally liable for liabilities of the partnership and split profits in accordance with their investment in the partnership. No one can argue that the US government's investment in rescuing corporations from bankruptcy is insignificant. Neither can it be argued that corporate efforts are insignificant. Therefore, equally splitting profits between the two partners is a reasonable result. Regardless of individual opinions, income tax payments to the government represent nothing more than a fair return on investment and payment for designing, building, and operation of manufacturing facilities.

The US government was in partnership with the private industry to the extent it contributed money to design and build manufacturing facilities, to finance the purchase of capital equipment, to purchase the entire output from government owned manufacturing plants, and to sponsor R&D efforts to develop new weapons, products, and manufacturing processes. In essence, the government's role was that of a silent partner.

Labor, on the other hand, was the catalyst making the partnership viable and successful; it was rewarded by the wages it received for hard work. In other words, labor was playing an essential role as an investor contributing its sweat and tears in the form of hard work and loyalty to ensure success for the partnership. In return, labor expected corporate employers to keep rewarding it by an implied covenant and duty to continue manufacturing in this country. That corporate action would be sufficient to show loyalty to employees ensuring high-paying employment opportunities.

That tripartite arrangement made US industry powerful and successful, and it was a recipe for continuing that prosperity into the future. That industrial arrangement was the enabler making the US the preeminent nation it is. US workers as well as their employers became beneficiaries of untold prosperity. This was the ultimate expression of the American Dream as we know it today.

REVIVAL OF EUROPEAN AND JAPANESE INDUSTRIES

European and Japanese industries were in shambles at the end of World War II. The economies of those countries were weak and unable to undertake or finance a rebuilding process to bring about stability and vibrancy to their nations. A reconstruction process would be necessary to enable those countries to steer their economies on a path leading to better living conditions for their citizens. That would enable their population to enjoy the peace that had been so costly to attain. The industrial base of and many cities in those nations were either completely destroyed or heavily damaged. The national fiscal status was very shaky due to large expenditures of funds from their national treasures to acquire armaments and supplies for the war effort.

Most Europeans nations had incurred large debts purchasing weapons and food supplies from the US during the war. Those nations had been borrowing money from the US before and during the war. Consequently, their financial reserves were exhausted, and they did not have the monetary wherewithal to finance an industrial reconstruction effort. This presented a very difficult situation to enable arranging the required financing for the reconstruction process.

Unlike Europe and Japan, the US suffered no war damage to its cities or manufacturing facilities. In addition, the US emerged from the war in an enviable financial standing. In short, the US was in an excellent position to supply machinery, manufactured goods, and agricultural products to the rest of the world as well as providing financing to undertake reconstruction projects. Those credits would enable European nations, whether friend or foe, to purchase goods necessary to rebuild their cities, repair their infrastructure and rebuild their industrial base. The US had become the richest nation on the face of the earth and a lender to not only our allies at the time but also to our former enemies.

European and Japanese industries were in desperate need of

repairs to resume production. Repairs would require a long time to complete and expenditure of large sums of money to re-build and re-establish their industrial infrastructure. Old manufacturing facilities would have to be demolished and rebuilt incorporating, one would expect, the latest technological manufacturing know-how and processes. That reconstruction effort implied that a very detailed rebuilding plan would have to be prepared taking in consideration the extent of manufacturing and reconstruction effort required as well as funding necessary to achieve those ends. This plan would be the vehicle used to prioritize activities necessary to achieve goals with financial resources.

This was a very ambitious process that required prioritizing the rebuilding steps to maximize benefits to those societies. It was also a process defining a logical sequence for the rebuilding activities taking into account the financial resources available and the need to maximize benefits. Furthermore, this detailed plan had to be used to determine the rebuilding cost of these facilities and how the rebuilding would be financed. It was not an easy task.

National and international markets served by European and Japanese industries no longer existed; it was a chaotic situation for these countries. The US situation, on the other hand, dealt with the question of retooling existing manufacturing plants from war production over to private sector production. European and Japanese industry did not have to address the retooling question for in many cases the facilities no longer existed. The required tools necessary for initiating manufacturing activities had to be redesigned and rebuilt once again. In addition, new markets would have to be captured once production restarted. But, how these markets would be recaptured needed to be fully understood particularly in a situation where consumers were unemployed and unable to purchase products. And yet, consumers were in need of all kinds of basic goods to satisfy their daily living requirements.

Aerial bombardment had not only destroyed the industrial base but also leveled many of the cities. This caused untenable living conditions for the general population. In fact, many European and Japanese consumers had their homes destroyed and were bordering on starvation; some of them froze to death due to a hard winter and lack of fuel to heat homes.

Consumers were unable to earn regular wages and, consequently, local industry could not expect consumer spending to become the driver for the revitalization effort. In short, Corporate America's foreign competitors were unable to supply necessary products and food to alleviate living conditions for their local populations. Local governments were unable to finance a strong national reconstruction process or to finance the revitalization of its national industrial base.

In view of that dire situation, European and Japanese national industries were unable to generate cash flow required to finance necessary repairs and return to normal production. Furthermore, the national industrial base could not borrow from the national government or get the credit lines necessary to pay for repairs because the national governments had exhausted their national treasuries and were basically financially broke. The situation faced by these industries was very serious indeed.

The US was the only nation capable of providing financial credits necessary to undertake a rebuilding process of European and Japanese industries, cities, and infrastructure. Furthermore, the US was also capable of supplying the necessary manufactured and agricultural goods to get our allies and former enemies back on their feet. Consequently, the US was not only helping our allies and former enemies but it was also helping Corporate America to become the beneficiary of a very bad situation.

US government credits to foreign countries enabled US corporate entities to gain a very strong market position in global markets. In short, US industry would continue to enjoy prosperity for the foreseeable future. That prosperity guaranteed generation of sufficient cash flow to finance modernization and efficiency improvements projects to its manufacturing facilities. Those efforts would improve the long-term operating cost and profitability picture thus ensuring that US industry would sustain its growth and become a formidable competitor to modern European and Japanese industries. Modernization and efficiency improvement efforts would sustain future US corporate profits. In effect, the US government continued to help industry in the postwar period.

Prosperity was something US corporations enjoyed as an indirect result of US government intervention and not something expressly accomplished by itself. US corporations forecast prosperity lasting many years. This level of prosperity and profit generation would enable Corporate America to get ready to compete with the new facilities that, undoubtedly, would be rebuilt in Europe and Japan. At the same time, this modernization effort would make US industry the lowest-cost producer in the world. That, in and of itself, would definitely be a very significant advantage over European or Japanese competitors. Another advantage enjoyed by US corporations was access to all international markets. Those international markets provided the opportunity to gain recognition and loyalty from consumers on a global basis. That recognition was valuable in terms of telling consumers that a product carrying the "Made in USA" label stood for quality and consistency. That was an advantage that foreign competitors did not have due to their absence from those international markets.

On the political side of the European reconstruction effort, different views arose among the Allies on the definition and implementation of the program itself. Initially, the Allies were determined to punish Germany for twice starting a war: World War I and World War II. In fact, some of the allies advocated that the punishment should include reducing manufacturing activity to a level equal to approximately 50 percent of the German manufacturing capacity in 1938.

Punitive measures were proposed to prevent Germany from rearming and starting another conflict as it had done after World War I. That would have included destruction of weapons manufacturing facilities. Keep in mind that Germany had continued operating weapons manufacturing facilities up until the end of the war despite heavy aerial bombardment. Furthermore, it was contemplated that punishment would prohibit Germany from building manufacturing facilities capable of being converted or retooled for weapons production. In short, the allies wanted to see Germany become totally incapable of ever waging war again.

The victorious Allies were very resentful, and that displeasure against Germany and the German people was leading to the imposition of sanctions intended to bring Germany to its knees. A similar feeling had developed against Germany at the end of World War I, which historians think was one of the causes leading to World War II. As a result of this feeling in 1946, many German manufacturing facilities were disassembled and shipped to the Soviet Union and other places including the US. In addition, German technological developments were confiscated and taken over by the US and all the other allies. Among these were technological advances made on jet propulsion for airplanes and missiles.

The other side of that feeling of resentment against Germany was the recognition that Germany would become vulnerable to attacks by foreign invaders and former enemies. That was a very serious issue that needed to be addressed because Germany had many enemies that were very vocal in expressing their displeasure and in proposing punitive means to destroy it completely. In view of that, the relevant question became: Who would then defend Germany? The US assumed a leadership position in this regard upon learning that the Soviet Union intended to take over the entire world to spread communism. That was a contributing factor to the start of another conflict which would ultimately become more expensive than World War II. It was the start of the "Cold War" which was a conflict that would last for approximately forty years!

The destruction of German industry caused a significant number of German nationals to lose their jobs. This was not limited to positions in manufacturing lines but included the ranks of highly trained and very capable scientists and engineers who had been instrumental in developing so many important technological wonders leading to significant developments in jet propulsion, rocketry, chemicals, and other areas. The Soviet Union captured some of these scientists and engineers and relocated them to the Soviet Union. The US, likewise, got some of these highly qualified scientists and engineers and brought them to the US, where they were allowed to continue working on their developments.

German scientists and engineers became very important contributors to the US space program under the leadership of the National Aeronautics and Space Administration (NASA). Their contributions culminated in several landings on the moon by US astronauts. Given the hatred against Germany and its people after the war, it was expected that the situation in Germany would not improve and, in fact, would last a long time. Certainly, it did not improve for East Germans under the control of the Soviet Union. West Germany, however, chose a capitalist system and, unlike East Germany under the Soviet Union, became very prosperous. Upon reunification, Germany became and is today the most influential and richest European nation.

Allied nations had liberated different parts of Europe and had kept their troops stationed there after the war. This, in essence, led to a division that ended up splitting Europe among those who had occupied different parts of its territory. On the one side was the Soviet Union and on the other side were the US and its western Europeans allies. There were also deep-rooted ideological divisions further splitting the allies and, in turn, dividing European territory in accordance with the nationality and philosophical beliefs of those occupiers. This division was based on political demagoguery—the Soviet Union was championing communism and the US and its allies a system based on capitalism.

Europe became a divided continent after the war. It was divided on the basis of political philosophies. Soviet troops had reached as far west as the eastern half of Berlin and occupied all countries from its eastern German sector all the way to Russia. The Soviet Union intended all along to occupy those Eastern European countries, including occupied German territory to protect the Russian homeland from postwar foreign invaders. The geographical area under occupation would become a buffer zone to protect the Russian homeland. The reasoning was that Soviet troops would engage invaders in that buffer zone rather than in Russian territory thus preventing a repeat of the fierce fighting that led to more than 25 million Russian casualties during World War II. Implementation of that Soviet strategy led to annexation of all occupied countries as Soviet Republics and becoming part of the Soviet Union by force.

The Soviet Union installed a communist regime to govern occupied German territory and renamed it the German Democratic Republic. Annexation of captured territory east of Russia would prevent the emergence of a country capable of attacking from the west as had been done by Germany. In short, actions taken by the Soviet Union were meant to act as a barrier to protect the Soviet Union and to prevent a recurrence of fighting in Russia. It was Stalin's answer to a security concern. At the same time, this move subjugated people in Eastern Europe and condemned them to live under brutal dictatorial communist regimes controlled by Stalin and his henchmen.

The US and its Western European allies liberated Western European countries, including the western half of Germany and the western part of Berlin. The bulk of allies troops were stationed primarily in Western Germany. The Soviet occupied part of Germany, i.e., East Germany, before the war had produced much of the food consumed in all of Germany. The Soviet Union cut off food supply to the rest of Germany and precipitated serious concerns among the Allies that led to deterioration in relations with the United States and its allies. A further deterioration in relations between the allies resulted when Russia annexed Europeans countries ceded by Germany to Russia prior to entering World War II. Additionally, the Soviet Union proceeded to convert occupied European countries into satellite states under its control. These activities revealed the true intentions of the Soviet Union and led to a reevaluation effort on the part of the US and its allies in regards to European reconstruction.

It became painfully obvious that, unlike the US and its allies, the Soviet Union had ambitions of establishing a communist empire in occupied European countries. The Soviet Union was acting on the premise that it wanted secured borders along its western front, but the allies knew better. The Soviet Union instructed European countries under its control to refuse any assistance from the US. If those countries refused to follow the Soviet Union instructions then their leaders would be immediately summoned to Moscow for a meeting with Soviet leaders. This began a period of enslavement of Eastern European countries by the Soviet Union that lasted until the late 1980s.

The ideological divide was not limited to merely a political argument between communists and capitalists. It became much more than that. On the capitalist side of the argument, there were some countries that believed Germany should be severely punished. France, on the one hand, had twice suffered defeat at the hand of the German army. It wanted to see Germany unable to engage in another war. It also proposed to have all German industry destroyed and Germany converted into a pastoral state. France also wanted control over the German coal-producing areas as a means of recovering damages caused by Germans during two world wars. It, therefore, reasoned that by taking over the coal-producing areas Germany would be prevented from producing gasoline and diesel fuels to drive its war machine.

The French, perhaps, were basing their thinking on lessons learned after World War I. Germany, after being defeated, was later able to rearm and continue the fight after a cessation of hostilities lasting twenty years. German scientists and engineers developed technological know-how to produce fuels for its war machine from coal and had built several facilities to practice this technology on a large scale basis This was significant because it allowed Germany to become independent of foreign oil imports or interruptions in the delivery of fuels for its war effort. That know-how would enable Germany to wage war against France after World War I. France knew that if Germany were allowed to retain control over its coal reserves then Germany, once again, would be capable of attacking France at will. France did not want a repeat of what happened after WWI. That same technology would later be perfected and used in South Africa to avoid the effects of an international blockade preventing it from getting oil imports.

Belgium, Netherland, and Luxembourg (Benelux) took a different approach to that of France. These countries recognized that their economies were closely linked and dependent on the

German economy. If the German industrial base were to be destroyed, then their own national industries would suffer the same consequences. That would have the effect of rendering their economies totally ineffectual. In other words, anything that destroyed the German industrial base would have adverse consequences on the economies of the Benelux countries leading, possibly, to their total destruction. In view of that diversity of opinions, there was no simple answer on what to do with Germany.

Perhaps, the most influential factor changing the attitude of the US and its allies away from total destruction and toward allowing Germany to rebuild its industrial base was the hostility shown by the Soviet Union in its drive to impose communist systems on the rest of the Europe. There was no other alternative left but to challenge Soviet hostility head on. This meant rebuilding German industry and creating formidable competitors for US industry. But, that did not matter, because US industry was well established and it had a significant amount of lead time that the Europeans would have to overcome.

Political demagoguery and divisions complicated the European reconstruction picture. First of all, the Soviet Union had no intention of accepting any sort of aid to rebuild countries under its occupation. Secondly, European countries under Soviet control would become part of the Soviet Union regardless of nationalist ideals. Thirdly, the Soviet Union would not allow agricultural products grown in the eastern part of Germany under Soviet control to be shipped to the western side of Germany for the people to eat; the eastern part of Germany was focused on agriculture. This was a direct expression of the willingness of the Soviet Union to starve Germans living in the zones occupied by the US and its allies. The Soviet Union took this hard position hoping to cause upheaval that would result in the expulsion of western allies from their sectors. It was a threat showing Stalin's expansionist ideas, and it had to be contained.

Communist Parties in many European countries gained strength as a result of high unemployment, lack of job opportunities, food shortages, and poor living conditions. The Soviet Union saw this state of affairs as the ideal breeding ground for unrest that could potentially lead to additional territory gains in Europe. The Soviet Union encouraged members of the Communist Party to do whatever was necessary to expel the US and its allies from Europe, thereby creating the perfect environment for expanding the Soviet Union sphere of influence whether by free elections or otherwise. This painted an alarming picture calling on the US and its capitalist allies to reverse some of the original plans intended for Germany.

President Truman, acting on the advice of the Joint Chiefs of Staff, recognized that reconstruction of German industry was of great importance to US National Security. In view of that, President Truman signed into law "The Marshall Plan" on April 3, 1948. As a result, many of the production restrictions and rebuilding plans imposed on German heavy industry, such as the steel industry, were changed to more closely align with those security concerns.

The US and its Western European allies began negotiations on a plan to reconstruct European nations devastated by the war and to impede growth of the Soviet Union's sphere of influence. These negotiations involved developing a program providing aid to those nations, but there were some issues that needed clarification. Number one, the form of assistance had to be defined to secure support from the US Congress. Keep in mind that the US was the only nation capable of lending money to the rest of the world and supplying manufactured as well as agricultural goods for reconstruction and to prevent starvation. Secondly, there had to be a program detailing how much each affected nation would get from the US. Finally, the means of implementing such massive program had to be identified and authorized. Resolution of these issues took a considerable amount of time, thus delaying implementation of this massive reconstruction effort until the end of the second half of 1948.

Country	Annual Amount of Aid, $Millions			
	1948/1949	1949/1950	1950/1951	Cumulative
France	1085	691	520	2296
Germany	510	438	500	1448
Italy & Trieste	594	405	205	1204
United Kingdom	1316	921	1060	3297

Table 12 Marshall Plan Aid to Europe [65]

The total financial aid provided to European countries under the Marshall Plan amounted to approximately $13 billion. That assistance included aid to all European nations except the Soviet Union, Eastern European countries under Soviet control, and Spain. The Soviet Union and its satellite states had refused all aid from the US. The bulk of US aid went to four countries listed in Table 12. Additional funds estimated to be in the range of $9 billion had been spent by the US from 1945 to 1947 restoring infrastructure and assisting refugees. [66] This aid was given with the understanding that it would never have to be repaid except in the case of Germany which was obligated to repay the full amount. Germany was the beneficiary of partial loan forgiveness, but it repaid the entire balance due to the US by 1971.

On the other side of the world, there was another critical situation needing attention. This was the situation focusing on demilitarizing another of our World War II adversaries. In fact, this was the only adversary causing damage to US territory by an aerial attack on Pearl Harbor in the Hawaiian Islands. That attack drew the US into World War II and caused it to engage in fighting in both the European and Pacific fronts. Aerial attacks on Japanese territory by the US caused a lot of damage to Japanese military installations, industries, infrastructure, and cities. These aerial attacks culminated in the use of atomic weapons leading to wide devastation including the destruction of the cities of Hiroshima and Nagasaki.

The issue of greatest concern to the US was ensuring that Japan would never again be capable of rearming and attacking the US; this was similar to the sentiment held by France against Germany. Consequently, the Japanese reconstruction effort followed on a different path and approach compared to the one in Europe. In the Japanese case, the approach was composed of three different phases: punishment, revival of industry, and conclusion of a formal peace treaty. [67] As in the German case, the civilian population was on the brink of starvation, thus precipitating an immediate relief effort to prevent this situation from occurring; the US government supplied food to the Japanese government for distribution to the population.

The punishment phase included several parts. The emperor's power was stripped to that of a figurehead without political control and the parliament was given more power, thus converting the national government into a parliamentary system. A land reform was instituted by acquiring land from large landholders and then dividing it into smaller parcels for distribution to small farmers. This land-reform program was an effort to punish large landlords who had advocated war and a Japanese expansionist policy prior to and during World War II. A campaign was initiated to break up large business conglomerates and to transform the economy into a free-market capitalist system. Finally, the four main islands making up Japan as well as immediate adjacent islands were kept intact under US control, but Japanese occupied territory in Korea and other islands farther from the main Japanese mainland were divided among the Allies.

The breakup of large financial conglomerates known as Zaibatsu was intended to disable weapons production that could be used to start another military conflict. Furthermore, it was also intended to punish those industries that had supported the militarist government. Initially, 325 firms were scheduled to be dissolved, but then the number was reduced to nine when the US reversed course and decided that Japanese recovery was in the US national security interest, particularly in view of the emergence of communist regimes in China and North Korea. Companies that had been part of previous conglomerates were denied monopoly status and special privileges they had once enjoyed.

During the war, the Soviet Union did not engage in military activities in the Pacific theater of operations including the islands off Japan. Nevertheless, it declared war on Japan on August 9, 1945, which was five days before the Japanese surrendered. Soviet troops invaded and occupied the Kuril and Sakhalin Islands, which were then under Japanese control; these islands have been the subject of previous territorial claims by both Russia and Japan that continue to this date. This was another attempt by the Soviet Union to expand its eastern frontier, and it was consistent with its annexation actions in Europe.

In contrast to the massive amount of financial aid allocated to the European rebuilding effort, there was no similar assistance program developed for rebuilding Japan. The US attitude toward Japan changed significantly upon the takeover of China by the communists and the invasion of South Korea by North Korea under the tutelage of the Soviet Union. This overt action by communists made patently clear the Soviet's intention of spreading communism, thus becoming a threat to US national security.

The Japanese reconstruction effort had to switch from that of destroying or incapacitating its industrial might associated with its military to a reconstruction effort enabling Japan to become a major supplier to the Allied troops engaged in the Korean conflict. This led to the revitalization of Japanese industry under the sponsorship of the US government. Obviously, this was extremely beneficial to Japan and to its recovery effort in that it allowed the latest US technology to be transferred from the US to Japan.

Despite lack of a formal financial package from the US to assist Japan in its reconstruction effort, there were significant contributions provided by the US to assist in its recovery. One of the most important contributions was the restructuring of the Japanese government. When Soviet expansionism raised its ugly presence in Asia, the US became concerned about a communist takeover of Japan. In view of that, the US pledged to defend Japan against Soviet aggression. In effect, the US included Japan within its Asian defense perimeter, thereby assuring Japan that no threat by an outsider against Japanese soil would be unanswered. That defense treaty enabled Japan to divert military expenditures toward its reconstruction effort. The Japanese government would use military funds to finance business and industrial reconstruction activities for the private sector.

Why was there such a disparity in the financial value of war recovery assistance extended to European countries versus that given to Asian countries particularly Japan? Could this disparity have been based on the ethnicity of those countries? Could it have been based on prejudice arising from the discredited "Anglo Saxon Superiority" myth? Perhaps, that was part of the reason for the difference in treatment in the case of Japan versus Europe.

It would be worthwhile remembering that, at one time in our history, the US was opposed to immigration from all Asian countries. In fact, this opposition was aimed at immigrants from China and Japan under the Chinese Exclusion Act of 1882 and the Gentlemen's Agreement of 1907 signed by President Theodore Roosevelt and the Japanese Government, respectively. Perhaps, another reason was that, unlike our European enemies, Japan had been the only country that had attacked the US. It would be reasonable to think that the US would feel some resentment against Japan for that attack particularly at a time when the two governments were actively engaged in negotiations.

Both Germany and Japan underwent severe transformations and both became major economic world powers. Given that both of these nations had their industrial base demolished and their cities ruined during World War II, their recovery and ascendancy to economic power were phenomenal. It was a testament to the industriousness of their people. It was also the result of close cooperation among all sectors of their societies: national government, industry, and labor represented by their citizenry.

The government of both Germany and Japan provided low-interest loans to businesses as a means of encouraging growth and development. In the case of Germany, funds from the Marshall Plan were converted into local currency and loaned to businesses.

Those loans were then repaid to the government with interest and then further recycled as loans to other businesses. In the case of Japan, business borrowed extensively from banks that drew their funds from consumer savings.

This close cooperation between the national governments and industry led to the full recovery of the German and Japanese economies. Another very important factor in the recovery of both Japan and Germany was the availability of a large pool of highly educated technical people experienced in the handling of technology and scientific issues.

The GDPs of some European countries are listed in Table 13 for comparison with those of the US and Japan. Given the devastation in both Germany and Japan, one can assume that their GDPs for the year 1951 reflect a much higher level than those of 1945 when those nations were under intense aerial bombardments. West Germany's economic output increased 312 percent from 1947 to 1951, which is referred to by historians as the "German miracle." [69]

Year	Japan	USA	W. Germany	France	Britain
1951	14.2	328.4	28.5	35.1	41.4
1955	22.7	398.0	43.0	49.2	53.9
1960	39.1	503.8	70.7	60.0	71.9
1965	88.8	688.1	115.1	99.2	100.2
1970	203.1	992.7	184.6	145.5	124.0
1975	498.2	1549.2	418.2	339.0	234.5
1980	1040.1	2633.1	816.5	657.1	525.5

Table 13. Comparison of Gross Domestic Product [68]

The economic growth of both Germany and Japan is substantial as reflected by GDP. The other European countries also show growth but not of the same magnitude. For example, the GDP of Japan increased approximately seventy-three times and that of

Germany went up twenty-nine times. In comparison, the GDP of Britain increased only thirteen times while that of France went up nineteen times. The US GDP went up by a factor of eight during the same time period. Annual growth rates of the Japanese and German economies during the 1951 to 1980 period averaged 15 percent and 12 percent, respectively. Those are phenomenal growth rates compared to the US's 7 percent growth rate over the same period. These growth rates are even more exceptional when one takes into consideration the devastation experienced by both Germany and Japan, where the general population was on the brink of starvation.

There was a lesson to be learned from the economic miracles in both Japan and Germany after World War II. That was the same lesson that came out of the economic miracle leading the US economy out of the Great Depression. That lesson had as much relevance at that time as it did after the war or even today. It was a simple lesson, but was one that was overlooked or ignored by politicians and corporate leaders in the US as a tool to get the US economy back on track to recovery from the 2009 Great Recession in the US.

Simply stated the lesson was that the private sector could not by itself cause an economic recovery. The US government had to play a leading role just like it did during the Great Depression and World War II. The Japanese and German governments played, and continue to play, leading roles in the economy of both countries.

Corporate America, unlike its Japanese and German counterparts, tends to reject government participation under the disguise of the free enterprise system. In so doing, it creates the false impression that government involvement is something that interferes with the profit-making motive. Historical facts, however, indicate that close cooperation between government and Corporate America is an essential element strengthening the private industrial sector. US corporations would be powerless without such government assistance. A case in point would be the situation of airplane manufacturers that rely on US government's purchases of its aircrafts to keep the companies in business.

Corporate America loves to have government involvement in its business only when that involvement brings funding or serves as an insurance policy against risk or something to blame in the event of failure. Corporate America hates government interference when the company is profitable.

The terms "cooperation" and "involvement" should be clearly distinguished. While cooperation between government and corporations is essential, direct government involvement would be detrimental to the economic wellbeing of the nation or individual companies. In other words, the government's function is to facilitate business instead of controlling the operation of the business. The Japanese government, for example, facilitates international trade and industrial activities through the Ministry of International Trade and Industry (MITI), which is an agency created after World War II to enhance growth and economic development. The German government, on the other hand, to this day continues to lend money to businesses for growth and development. In contrast to the Japanese and German governments, the US government tends to over regulate business activities based on how the political winds are blowing.

Corporate America needs to carefully consider developing closer cooperation with the US government similar to what existed after the Great Depression and the period during and after World War II. It should be a relation based on mutual respect for the capabilities each party brings to the table rather than a unilateral relation only to benefit industry. Unlike Germany and Japan where there is close cooperation between industry and government to stimulate growth and economic development, the relationship between Corporate America and the US government is one that can best be described as a love–hate relationship.

Corporate America loves to accept funds from the US government to pursue difficult goals, but hates to pay taxes and is unwilling to credit the government for its contribution. It likes to complain about government interference in its business when the venture is profitable but says nothing when the government comes in to assist it in getting out of trouble. A case in point is saving

Chrysler from bankruptcy and repayment of that loan to get the government off the back of the same executives who caused the bankruptcy in the first place. There are many more examples including some recent cases showing this antagonism between Corporate America and the US government.

The US is the greatest industrial nation in the world, based on scientific and engineering achievements of its industrial base. Corporate America has recently chosen to follow a leading to reductions on the level of scientific and engineering staffs. This misguided policy will detrimentally impact not only industry itself but also on the US preeminent industrial status. In short it will lead to lower a lower standard of living for Americans who will see their American Dreams shattered once and for all.

That path misguided policy is based on reducing costs by eliminating or significantly curtailing R&D expenditures. R&D efforts that focus on developing newer and more efficient manufacturing processes should never be curtailed because, that is the lifeline of the corporation. Another detrimental practice is the reliance on financial gimmicks rather than scientific and engineering know-how to improve profitability. Finally, the relocation of manufacturing facilities to foreign countries to lower workers wages is destroying the country's manufacturing base, if it hasn't already done so.

Corporate America has chosen to side with greedy Wall Street financiers. That reliance has had an immediate impact on the so called "bottom line" of the company. Yes, Corporate America has seen an upsurge in its profits. That upswing in profits has increased the amount paid in bonuses to executives. Corporate America, however, is cutting its throat by focusing on the present rather than continuing its development to guarantee future profitability. Corporate Leaders don't care because they are only concerned about the present which is what determines their bonuses. Corporate executives do not care about the long term, because they assume they will not be there to personally benefit or suffer the consequences of their present decisions.

Corporate leaders ignore historical lessons that teach blind faith on greedy Wall Street financiers leads to financial disaster. This is the lesson that has to be learned from events leading to the Great Depression and also those leading to the Great Recession of 2009. Financial gimmicks create nothing of value or anything that can be sold for long periods of time.

Perhaps, business leaders have chosen to follow financiers' advice to get under the protective US government umbrella that has been so effective in rescuing failing banks and corporations from messes created by inept management as in the case of GM, Chrysler, AIG, CITI Bank and others. In the meantime, German and Japanese corporate leaders continue their reliance on science and engineering for new developments.

Unlike German and Japanese industry leaders that value scientific and engineering developments, Corporate America emphasizes financial matters; this is an issue relating to present versus future returns. These foreign corporate leaders know that reliance on scientific and engineering concepts is an essential element to sustain corporate profitability.

Corporate America should awaken and realize time is running out, and that is not too late to straighten out their companies to prevent their downfall. Wages become the basis for relocating manufacturing facilities by Corporate America to lower wages countries to lower cost. These corporations neglect to take into account that along with the transfer of manufacturing facilities goes the transfer of proprietary technological know-how. Once recipients of those changes become proficient using the new technology new manufacturing facilities are built using the same know-how to compete with the original corporate technology owners thus minimizing their future profitability. Corporate America runs to the US Government with the complain their proprietary technology has been stolen as in the allegations against China. Is there a sound basis for this allegation?

COLD WAR

Two distinct events defined US national identity and character. Those events reaffirmed the idea the US was a country that did not run away from challenges or adversity. The first event was the "Cold War" which was a term coined to represent the threat against our national self-interest by the expansionist goals of the Soviet Union. The second was the challenge created by the placement of an orbiting satellite by the Soviet Union and the implications of that act on US national security.

The US government played a leading role in challenging the private sector and American people to rally support for a policy aimed at preventing the Soviet Union from taking any hostile action against our country, our allies, and our freedoms. The US mustered its technical and financial resources to deal with this threat from the Soviet Union and refused to be threatened. A policy aimed at containing that threat was developed and implemented. As a result, the US defeated those threats and destroyed the Soviet Union without firing a single shot.

The Soviet Union failed to recognize that the US works best when it faces adversity; this was the same mistake made by Japan when it attacked Pearl Harbor. Yes, Admiral Yamamoto recognized that it was awaking a sleeping giant, but the Soviet Union failed to realize the giant was still awake after the end of World War II.

The Soviet Union did not understand that US was established by immigrants from all parts of the world who had faced extreme hardships in their home countries and in their new adopted country—the US. It did not recognize the US was a nation where those immigrants had overcome untold challenges in creating a nation founded on the belief that nothing was impossible to achieve. It did not understand that those citizens would repel all threats and would stand tall to protect the freedoms this country provided them. It did not understand that Americans, regardless of their ethnicity, would band together to defeat threats from the Soviet Union or any other adversary who dares to threaten our liberties.

It would become clear to the Soviet Union that no effort would be spared to overcome this period of adversity faced by our country. There was nothing to distract our attention from the traits that united all of us as Americans rather than as members of a separate ethnic or minority group. That trait made us strong as individuals and made Corporate America what it is today, thus making our country the preeminent industrial nation of the world that it is. That was the same resilience exhibited by our people when faced by an unprovoked attack on Pearl Harbor and the same spirit that guide us today solving difficult problems that threaten our piece of the American dream.

The Cold War began after the end of WWII when the Soviet Union blockaded Berlin intending to force the US and its allies to abandon their occupied sectors. Soviet leaders believed this action would leave the US no choice but to abandon occupied sectors. The Soviet Union planned to occupy German territory under the control of the US and its allies upon their departure. The Soviets assumed it would be able to reunite Germany upon departure by the US and its western Allies.

The Soviets, however, underestimated the resolve of the US and its western allies. The Soviets started a campaign intending to starve the German citizenry by eliminating shipments of agricultural goods to western Germany from the eastern part of Germany, which was the food producing region and was under Soviet control. That was not the only hostile action on the part of the Soviet Union against its former western allies.

The Soviets had also engaged in activities aimed at using the discontent of local European populations at the lack of jobs and poor living conditions to replace existing governments. They figured that those governments could be replaced by communist regimes under direct domination and control of the Soviets. The Soviet Union actively pursued that policy with the participation of Communist Parties that became very vocal in Western Europe organizing demonstrations against prevalent conditions. It was an effort to show to local population that capitalist ideology was decadent and unable to provide basic needs of the population.

Again, this was in line with communist doctrine the Soviet Union was trying to spread around the world.

The response from the US and its western allies to the Soviet blockade of Berlin was a massive relief effort implemented by an airlift of food, fuel, and other supplies. This demonstrated the importance of air power in dealing with Soviet threats. Transport planes rather than bombers or fighters were the means used to provide the airlift capability to defeat the blockade.

This demonstrated transport planes could be converted to civilian airliners to transport people comfortably and much faster than railroads. This became particularly important in the US where long distances were a fact of life as compared to Europe. This new use for transport planes identified a potential means for converting the aircraft industry from military purposes over to dual military and private-sector uses. US industry was in an ideal position to retool military aircraft production lines over to the production of transport planes for airline use. This enabled the aircraft industry to avoid a collapse when all contracts for military aircraft were cancelled at the end of the war.

The aircraft industry was geared to produce in excess of 50,000 airplanes per year and now would produce zero aircraft. Stopping all manufacturing activities at the end of World War II would have been disastrous for this industrial sector of the economy. The impact on employment would have been severe indeed. As a result, aircraft sales volume diminished from $16 billion in 1944 to $1.2 billion in 1947. [70] It became apparent that there was a potential for keeping the aircraft industry operational by retooling manufacturing production lines to produce transport planes rather than bombers or fighter aircrafts.

Soviet's actions in Asia were consistent with their actions in Europe. The Soviet Union had a peace treaty with Japan during World War II that was in effect until a few days before Japan surrendered. As a result of that treaty, the Soviet Union had a secured eastern border and did not have to fight in the Pacific theater against Japan. But, knowing that Japan was about to surrender, the Soviets suddenly decided to declare war against

Japan and attacked Japanese territory with the clear intention of grabbing territory to implement its expansionist policy. That hostile action on the part of the Soviet Union signaled a very important message to all future generations. That message was that the Soviet Union and communists could not and should not ever be trusted. There was a minor skirmish between Soviet troops and US troops caused by a US reconnaissance plane overflying one of the Japanese island occupied by Soviet troops.

Hostile Soviet actions raised eyebrows in Washington and the capital cities of our western allies. The Soviet Union and the western Allies had been partners in the war against Germany and had shared some common ideals. Now, it became apparent that the trust Western Allies had placed on Soviet leaders was misplaced. In fact, it became painfully obvious the Soviet Union and its communist leaders could not be trusted.

President Truman recognized the expansionist intentions of the Soviet Union and decided to take a stand against communist expansion in both Europe and Asia. Henceforth, the US and the Soviets would become opponents in many parts of the world. The end effect of that adversarial contest was to cause both parties to up the ante in response to the actions of the other side. That contest would not end until either party blinked or failed to respond.

The US reacted to the Soviet's blockade of West Berlin by ordering an airlift of fuel and food that rendered the blockade totally ineffective. It also implemented a plan to reconstruct the damage caused by war in Europe. This was the Marshall Plan, providing financial and technical assistance for the purpose of rebuilding Europe from the devastation it had suffered during the war years.

The Marshall Plan was so successful that local communist agitators and operatives were unable to elect communist- leaning politicians to take over any European country. That takeover of Europe had been anticipated and hoped for by Soviet leaders. The communists were defeated at the polls rather than on the battlefield. Europeans turned away from communist propaganda handing the local communist leaders and the Soviet camp its first defeat after the start of the Cold War. Unhappy with that outcome, the Soviet Union pursued other avenues to engage the US and its allies in an ideological war. That ideological battle would last close to fifty years, if we were to believe the Cold War ended with the collapse of the Soviet Union. Otherwise, the battle would continue.

Ideological battles spread from Europe over to Asia, raising concerns not only in the US but also among leaders of Asian allies. Ideological warfare was particularly important in Japan where the US was attempting to change the government structure and to reshape the economic and industrial stance of the nation away from military production. The US was also concerned about political developments in other parts of Asia, particularly in China where communist backed groups were actively grabbing more and more territory and placing it under communist regimes. One of the most alarming events was a regime change in China when the communists took over the government.

There were also concerns raised by North Korean actions against South Korea that clearly indicated North Korea's willingness to fight in order to effect Korean reunification under a single communist regime. As a result of that, the US reversed course on its reconstruction efforts in Japan. It decided to place Japan within its sphere of influence, thus ensuring that Japan would not fall to the communist side. This action by the US enabled Japan to divert its military expenditures to the private sector for the purpose of reconstructing its industrial base and infrastructure.

The Cold War was not a war in the classical meaning of the word. It was a war fought in terms of threats, economic competition, industrial spying, and military posturing. It was an ideological war between two distinct camps; the capitalist side headed by the US and its Western European Allies on the one side and the Communist bloc headed by the Soviet Union and its Eastern European Satellites on the other. In short, it was a war without battles. It was a war where the armies from the two main ideological camps kept watch on each other but fired no bullets. It was a war fought not between the Soviet army and the US army but rather a war fought by proxies of the two respective camps under the tutelage of the principals, i.e., nations that were backed or supported by either the Soviet or the US side. It was a war where these proxy nations engaged in battles in many parts of the world. In some cases, however, US military forces became involved in actual combat such as in Korean and Vietnam.

The US was the only nation with proven nuclear weapons at the end of World War II. The Soviet Union did not have atomic weapons until 1949. Consequently, the Soviets would not risk engaging the US in another conflict because it knew that if it did it would be annihilated.

Once the Soviet Union got the atomic weapon, then it became a situation where both sides could destroy the other. It was a situation where both parties knew that nuclear war was not winnable and would lead to the destruction of both parties.

So why were there no battles between the two main ideological contenders? It was simply that both sides in this conflict were afraid of each other because each side knew there would be no winners in such a conflict. Each side realized that their countries would be devastated. Both sides had vivid memories of the destruction caused to Hiroshima and Nagasaki by atomic weapons.

The acronym MAD, which stood for Mutually Assured Destruction, represented the reason neither side would engage in a direct war. Both sides knew that a direct military conflict would lead to the use of nuclear weapons. How, then, would the winner of the Cold War be determined? It had to be determined not by the outcome of battle but rather by implementation and soundness of ideas, technological developments, economic might, and financial strength. Based on those standards, the US was the clear winner of the first phase of the Cold War, but the Cold War did not end when the Soviet Union collapsed.

Phase two of the Cold War continues to this day. Russia has the same ambitions once held by the Soviet Union, and that is to take over the US. The Soviet Union has not been able to achieve that goal military, but now Russia is trying to achieve that objective by economic and scientific cooperation with the US.

The US has been fooled by Russia into believing it is now a

democratic country; it is not. It is a country ruled by communist sympathizers who have now clothed themselves as democratic communists. Russia may succeed in achieving its takeover goal if the present Obama administration allows it to assume a leadership position in space exploration. That will happen when the US grounds the Space Shuttle and relies on Russia to transport US Astronauts to the Space Station.

The US and its Allies formed an alliance known as the North Atlantic Treaty Organization, NATO, which originally included most of the Western European nations, Canada, and the US. The Soviet side, not to be outdone, brought together its satellites states in Eastern Europe and Russia under a pact known as the Warsaw Pact in order to ensure a military alliance capable of defending primarily Russia.

Satellites states were under no illusion that the main purpose of this Soviet alliance was to prevent a recurrence of fighting in Russian territory; each satellite state henceforth would provide the battlefields in the event Russia were to be attacked from the west. This buffer zone would absorb all territory casualties of war in much the same way as was the case in World War II when millions of Russians were killed by the attacking German army. Eastern Europeans nations had no choice but to join the Warsaw Pact, otherwise their government leaders would be replaced forcibly and their country placed under direct Soviet control. Government leaders would be interred in Soviet prisons or killed.

Although there were no battles between NATO and Warsaw Pact forces there were many battles fought by proxies of both the Soviet Union and the US. For example, the Berlin Blockade was one of those conflicts. Similarly, the Korean War was another conflict fought by troops under the tutelage of the Soviet Union and China, which again was acting in place of the Soviet Union. There were other wars in the Middle East, Africa, Latin America, and Asia. All of those conflicts were fought between troops or guerrillas backed by either the Soviet Union or the US. In the case of Korea and Vietnam, US military forces were actively involved in the fighting.

It was necessary to divert our attention to the impact the Cold War had on Corporate America. Obviously, a nation like the US would depend on its industrial might and resources to develop the most effective means and weapons to conduct a war. The US government undertook a campaign to, once again, spend taxpayers' funds to invent, develop, and produce new weapon systems to prosecute an ever more technically complicated war. It had to fund R&D efforts under the guidance of Corporate America to develop new weapon systems capable of ensuring that our freedoms are protected against the evil desires of the Soviet Union and its henchmen.

This also meant the US government had to have the financial means and wherewithal to complete the project. In other words, once the government began the process of developing these weapons, it had to stay the course for as long as it took. Corporate America benefitted from this continuous stream of government military expenditures, and grew stronger as a result in much the same way it did with World War II expenditures.

The R&D work necessary to discover and design new weapon systems led to new products and technologies for manufacturing those new products commercially. This process created new employment opportunities for Americans looking to realize their own particular piece of the American Dream. It also opened new horizons for Corporate America to develop additional products based on the original military development. This was beneficial to US industry.

A simple example would lead to a better understanding of the implications of what the US government was asking from the private sector. The government was asking the private sector to develop and build a new reconnaissance aircraft capable of flying at high altitudes and over long ranges without detection. This aircraft would be used to determine where Soviet weapons were stored and to monitor those sites continuously.

The design requirements for such airplane implied that new materials had to be developed to fabricate airframes capable of operating in very severe environmental conditions without failure.

It also meant new electronic navigation and mechanical equipment would have to be devised to enable operating the aircraft within very tight operating tolerances. Additionally, new fuels had to be developed to allow aircraft operation at very high altitudes. How about the photographic equipment to enable effective site monitoring? All of these problems represented new job creation opportunities that would benefit employees.

Materials of construction for such aircraft had to be invented. Those same materials of construction could then become available for use in other manufacturing applications where the properties if found to be suitable. New applications for those exotic materials included, for instance, civilian aircraft, thus benefitting Corporate America by adding a new potential income stream. The same was true for electronic navigation and photographic equipment, and these items would find application in the private sector such as in the case of GPS, now in the process of replacing paper maps.

It is obvious that US industry derives many benefits from direct government sponsored R&D. In many instances, the technology that is developed from such government sponsored research is applied in manufacturing goods for the private sector. If one assumes the government is interested only in the military applications then it is fair to assume that corporations would exploit private-sector applications.

The US government should definitely allow corporations to benefit from production and sale of consumer goods derived from government sponsored R&D results. These private sector uses should, however, be conditioned on manufacturing products in this country and payment of a license fee equivalent to some percentage of profits derived from product sales. In this manner, both industry and the US government benefit. The government recovers part of its investment in R&D. Industry, on the other hand, gets the opportunity to produce new products thus creating new profits streams. In no event should the US government allow industry to practice the new technology without payment of a license fee for it would represent a subsidy leading to the undesirable state of corporate welfare; industry would not allow competitors to use its technological know-how free of charge.

The answer as to whether use of newly derived technology should be licensed to industrial sources revolves around the issue of ownership. The know-how is probably developed by industrial sources with US government funds. It unquestionably raises the issue of intellectual property ownership and needs to be addressed in the contract between the corporate entity or entities and the US government. Is the technology owned by the US government exclusively or is it owned by both parties? If ownership is in the hands of the government, then will it license such technology to corporate entities for use in the private sector? Are these corporate entities obligated to pay the government a license fee or royalties for such use? In many cases, Corporate America pays nothing to the government for using such technology to manufacture goods destined for the private sector. The US government, however, should demand a license fee or royalty payments to recover its investment and generate funds for additional R&D funding.

If the technology is owned by the corporation in partnership with the US government, does Corporate America share profits derived from the use of that technology with the government? If not, why not? Certainly, corporations demand payment of royalties from users of licensed technology and prevent others from using such technology. In past instances, the government has allowed technology to be shared with competitors free of charge as done during World War II. This is done to enable production of large quantities at different locations to serve the national interest; that case does not represent corporate welfare. In the event use of the technology were considered corporate welfare, then corporate users would owe a debt of gratitude to all taxpayers payable only by creating jobs here in the US. In the event corporate users were to use that know-how to produce goods in foreign locations, the US government would be justified in prohibiting such use and imposing high license fees on users of such technology.

Let's describe a hypothetical situation. This is the case where the US government invests in an R&D program to develop a camera capable of taking photographs of the earth from outer space. One can immediately see the benefits that can be derived from such invention. It is able to photograph military sites with great accuracy and definition. But, the same physical principle incorporated in the military camera can be adapted to manufacture lenses and cameras with better resolutions and definition for television or regular photographic purposes for use by the general public. This is one example, but there are many more examples where the outcome of military or government-funded research has provided significant benefits to the public.

In the case of the camera just discussed, it is possible to imagine medical applications where it may be possible to miniaturize the camera to the extent necessary to allow insertion in the human body to photograph tumors or other medical malignancies. The point here is that these government developments have value, and Corporate America derives substantial benefit from using those discoveries developed at taxpayers' expense.

In light of the previous discussion, it becomes apparent that Corporate America should share with the US government profits derived directly from the sale of goods manufactured using results or discoveries from US government-sponsored R&D. The other alternative is to allow corporate users to acquire a license to use such discovery and pay the government a royalty or license fee for its use. In either case, the government would be able to continue to sponsor R&D efforts and partially recover that investment from the royalty income stream. That would reduce the direct annual contribution from taxpayers' funds. A license fee should not be confused with a tax. A license fee represents the recovery of an investment by the government, and it has nothing to do with taxes imposed on profits.

It is true that discoveries and developments resulting from US government-funded R&D represent the outcome of corporate efforts and the ideas of its employees. Companies might argue that, in view of that, they should be allowed to use technology free of charge because of its investment in the development particularly in using specialized facilities, employee knowledge, and so on. Nevertheless, the developments are the results of an effort that the corporation would not undertake without government funding; therefore, it seems that the technologies are developed for and owned by the government. In view of that, corporate users of the know-how should pay the government a fee to allow it to recover its investment.

The private corporate sector expenses its R&D costs, thus reducing its own income-tax liability to the US government. Additionally, if a corporate entity were to pay royalties to the US government, then it would also be able to expense those payments as an ongoing cost, and the net effect would be to further reduce its tax liability. Taxpayers expect government to spend taxpayers' funds wisely and not just for entitlements to the private sector, particularly when those corporations relocate manufacturing to foreign countries.

It has been mentioned that the most visible contributions of military and space expenditures have been the development of the internet. Another idea that has been discussed is collecting a license or royalty payable by Corporate America to the US government to enable recovery of funds spent on these programs. If the US government had imposed a license fee on internet providers based on their profit margins, the amount of money collected by the government would be sufficient to allow recovery of the initial investment and provide additional funds for other R&D projects? The amount of money involved would be substantial. In fact, it would be in the range of millions of dollars annually. Given the number of private sector off-shoots from government programs, it is conceivable that the total royalty or license fees payable to the government recovery would be in the range of billions of dollars annually.

Although there were no actual battles fought between US and Soviet troops during the Cold War, the cost of the Cold War was significant. One would have thought the lack of battles and the resulting lack of destruction would have had a tendency to minimize costs involved. But, in fact, the contrary was true.

Imagine engaging in a war where both sides are trying to intimidate their opponents. In such situation, one cannot underestimate rivals and assume that they are standing still. One, instead, assumes that the other side is developing weapons that will inflict a great deal of damage. That is particularly true when both sides in the contest have capabilities to use nuclear weapons. One would, therefore, think about possibilities of not only defeating the other side but of destroying its nuclear weapons prior to or immediately after launch. One would even go to the extreme of spending money to determine if the opponent is preparing an initial nuclear attack so that we would hit him first. That was the idea behind President Reagan's "Star Wars" defense strategy that not only scared the Soviets but also bankrupted them.

There are other examples illustrating the need to continue developing newer and better defense ideas or strategies to counteract hostile actions from our enemies. One such case was the development of the nuclear-powered aircraft. Supposedly, the anecdote goes, the Soviet Union was purposely misleading US Intelligence by leading it to believe the Soviet Union had actively pursued the development of such aircraft and, in fact, had flown such aircraft. It turned out this was a hoax perpetrated by the Soviet Union to divert US attention from other more realistic developments. The idea behind this trick by the Soviet Union was to force the US government to spend money to keep up with the Soviet Union.

The advantage of that aircraft was the capability of unlimited range without refueling. It certainly would have allowed Soviet bombers based in Soviet territory to fly to the US, bomb it, and return to a base within the Soviet Union. This would have obviated the need to have Soviet bases closer to the US for refueling purposes. It would also have allowed bombers to continue flying for an unlimited period of time ready to attack at a moment's notice.

The US, believing its military intelligence, undertook a development program to build a nuclear-powered bomber to counteract Soviet threats. The Soviet Union continued to feed misleading intelligence to the US side so that it would continue spending money on a program that would lead nowhere. Later on, it was discovered that the whole idea of a Soviet nuclear powered aircraft was a hoax. Nevertheless, the US spent significant amounts of money researching nuclear propulsion for aircrafts.

One can imagine the cost of pursuing a futile effort such as the case of the nuclear-powered bomber. But was it really a futile effort? Perhaps the whole program was a waste to some extent but not totally. Lessons learned from that program are very likely adaptable to advanced propulsion systems for other types of very sophisticated aircrafts. One can be sure that a lot of lessons learned from this program remain classified and are useful discoveries for the defense of our beloved nation. Yes, sometimes failure is a success.

In hindsight, the nuclear-powered aircraft anecdote is a funny tale. There are technical articles suggesting the existence of calculations leading to estimates for the number of sandwiches required to be kept onboard the aircraft to support military missions while minimizing landings and takeoffs, which are always the most critical aspects of flying. Other articles raise issues relating to crew isolation from harmful radiation effects. Furthermore, other issues focus on mitigating accidents occurring over populated areas. The result is that neither the Soviet Union nor the US ever built a nuclear-powered aircraft. Nevertheless, it is likely that the research program has provided a significant body of knowledge advancing nuclear propulsion, new metallurgical alloys, radiation protection, and many other aspects that have trickled into common use nowadays. In short, the nuclear-powered aircraft research program is not a total loss, but its cost is a substantial amount of money.

Now let's take a look at the cost of the Cold War from the perspective of our nation. US military expenditures are shown in Figure 23. Annual expenditures are plotted using two different valuation methods. The first is in terms of expenditures based on 1996 dollars. The second is plotted in terms of dollars spent annually; this is arrived at by using the Gross Domestic Product Deflator to convert 1996 dollars into equivalent dollars at the time of the expenditure. [71]

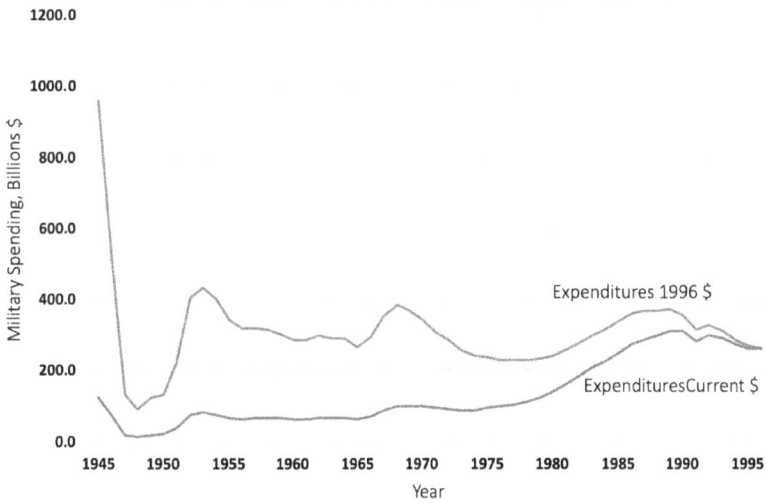

Figure 23. Annual Military during Cold War [72]

Data in Figure 23 include 1945 expenditures for World War II. Expenditures during the war are much higher than post World War II expenditures. World War II expenditures appear to be on the high side compared to subsequent expenditures. Those expenditures were high on account of the acquisition power of the 1945 dollar, which is equivalent to that of $7.50 in terms of 1996 dollars. That means that a 1996 US dollar only would have bought approximately $0.13 worth of goods during the war period. Expenditures prior to the 1947 included money up to the end of World War II, troop demobilization after the war, and some initial expenditure for European recovery prior to implementation of the Marshall Plan.

Military expenditures focusing on Cold War started becoming significant in 1947. On June 24, 1948, the Soviet Union imposed a blockade on Berlin, preventing road access from the west to supply Berlin with food, fuel, and other necessities; this was considered by many to be the start of the Cold War. The military airlift by the US and its Western Allies started at that time. Notice that military expenditures showed a declining trend up to 1948 when the trend reversed and military expenditures increased. Also note the declining trend starting around 1988–1989, which was when the Berlin Wall was torn down uniting citizens of East and West Germany for the first time since the end of World War II.

Some people consider the Cold War to have ended upon the disintegration of the Soviet Union around the mid-1980s to 1991. The question is: has the Cold War really ended? The author believes that the Cold War continues to the present time. Russia still has the same expansionist ambitions and continues to show the same tendencies held by the Soviet Union. One has to be skeptical of Russia's intention of being a credible partner for peace and international commerce particularly based on recent actions leading to the expropriation of assets owned by foreign and domestic oil companies. It has also shown a tendency to curtail natural gas supplies to European customers reminding us of the Berlin Blockade. Also recall the Soviet declaration of war against Japan a few days before its surrender.

US military expenditures during the 1947 to 1991 period amounted to $13.1 trillion in terms of 1996 dollars. [73] That level of military spending energized the economy and brought a lasting benefit to industry and US society in general. For example, in the 1950s and thereafter, there were over 40,000 defense contractors that considered the Department of Defense their best customer. [74] Obviously, these 40,000 plus contractors benefited, but those benefits did not stop with them. Those benefits trickled to their employees who, in turn, became dependent on military expenditures for their wages and realization of their piece of the American Dream. Those wages became consumer dollars to enhance demand for products manufactured by other corporations, and the cycle repeated itself many times. In other words, government expenditures had a multiplier effect on the whole economy.

If one assumes that each large defense contractor employs, on the average, 100 employees then one can easily estimate that the number of direct jobs created by these 40,000 defense contractors exceeded 4 million, which is on the low side. There are also indirect jobs created by companies on the periphery that provide services to the community of direct employees such as medical doctors, dentist, waiters, mechanics, automobile dealers, and so on and so forth. Typically, two to four indirect jobs are created for every direct job. In view of that, the total number of jobs is approximately 16 million jobs (4 million direct and 12 million indirect). That's quite a contribution! Are military expenditures important to create jobs? The answer is, without doubt, an unqualified yes. Are government expenditures a lifeline to the private sector? US government expenditures are definitely beneficial to Corporate America.

The benefits derived from government expenditures on the nation's economy can be estimated by taking into consideration the amount spent by employees of primary contractors directly as well as those indirectly impacted by expenditures to acquire automobiles, home appliances, houses, etc. The point is that military spending has a very significant impact not only on those industries dealing directly with the government but also on those industries indirectly supplying either goods to primary government contractors or to consumers. The total impact, therefore, amounts to several times the initial expenditure.

It is fair to say that not all the money spent by the government goes directly into R&D budgets. The expenditure may also include some amount for acquisition of some preliminary test models of the end product in the form of advanced fighter planes, warships, electronic equipment, etc.

It is also fair to say the government is not the only sponsor of corporate R&D. Corporations also sponsors their own R&D efforts. There are, however, distinguishing features between government and corporate-sponsored R&D. In general, government-sponsored R&D focuses primarily on concepts or ideas that might lead to new means of defending the nation against attacks from adversaries; this might be considered "blue sky" or "basic" R&D as illustrated by the work on the nuclear-powered airplane. This type of R&D has the potential of expanding technical frontiers of knowledge in medical applications to counteract biological attacks and in metallurgical discoveries leading to sophisticated alloys for specialized applications such as airframes.

Corporate America, on the other hand, focuses primarily on development part of the R&D function. This is mainly to improve existing processes and reduce production cost; this is typically considered "applied research." The portion of corporate R&D budgets dedicated to basic-research efforts is relatively small compared to applied-research efforts.

Pharmaceutical companies typically spend more on basic research than chemical or automobile companies; typically these companies spend in the range of 10 to 20 percent of total revenues on R&D. Chemical and petroleum companies expenditures on R&D efforts are in the range of 2 percent to 6 percent of revenues. [75] Corporate America tends to cut or significantly reduce R&D budgets to reduce costs, but that reduction in corporate R&D expenditures ends up being very costly in the long run.

SPACE RACE

The Space Race was another facet of the Cold War. It was and continues to be a program with dual purposes. Part of the program was focused on military ends and the other part was aimed at the civilian sector. The military side aimed at protecting our nation against evil desires of the former Soviet Union. The private-sector side complemented the military aspects and provided a vehicle for advancing our knowledge of outer space, aviation, and astronomy, while at the same time improving communications, providing storm warnings, advancing medical science, developing new composite materials and metallurgical alloys, and many other aspects that have proven extremely useful in many private-sector applications. In other words, the space program was responsible for many significant contributions improving our daily living conditions.

President Kennedy in a speech delivered at Rice University on September 12, 1962, recognized the importance of the Space Program to our nation. He challenged American scientists and engineers to build the means of going to the moon by the end of the 1960s. He said among other things that

"If this capsule history of our progress teaches us anything, it is that man, in his quest for knowledge and progress, is determined and cannot be deterred. The exploration of space will go ahead, whether we join in it or not, and it is one of the great adventures of all time, and no nation which expects to be the leader of other nations can expect to stay behind in this race for space.... .

Those who came before us made certain that this country rode the first waves of the industrial revolution, the first waves of modern invention, and the first wave of nuclear power, and this generation does not intend to founder in the backwash of the coming age of space. We mean to be a part of it--we mean to lead it. For the eyes of the world now look into space, to the moon and to the planets beyond, and we have vowed that we shall not see it governed by a hostile flag of conquest, but by a banner of freedom and peace. We have vowed that we shall not see space filled with weapons of mass destruction, but with instruments of knowledge and understanding....

We set sail on this new sea because there is new knowledge to be gained, and new rights to be won, and they must be won and used for the progress of all people. For space science, like nuclear science and all technology, has no conscience of its own. Whether it will become a force for good or ill depends on man, and only if the United States occupies a position of pre-eminence can we help decide whether this new ocean will be a sea of peace or a new terrifying theater of war....

Yet the vows of this Nation can only be fulfilled if we in this Nation are first, and, therefore, we intend to be first. In short, our leadership in science and industry, our hopes for peace and security, our obligations to ourselves as well as others, all requires us to make this effort, to solve these mysteries, to solve them for the good of all men, and to become the world's leading space-faring nation....

We choose to go to the moon. We choose to go to the moon in this decade and do the other things, not because they are easy, but because they are hard, because that goal will serve to organize and measure the best of our energies and skills, because that challenge is one that we are willing to accept, one we are unwilling to postpone, and one which we intend to win, and the others, too."...

President Kennedy recognized our nation had been challenged by the Soviet Union. At that time, the Soviet Union had an early lead in space exploration that became very apparent to everyone concerned. That advantage was a satellite that had been placed in orbit. That early Soviet lead had clear military implications indicating the Soviets were now in a position of strength. The Soviets were capable of threatening our nation and our own liberties. The implication was that the Soviet Union could now use a rocket to place in outer space a nuclear weapon capable of damaging or destroying our country. Recalling the bombings of London by German rockets during World War II made this possibility a very real concern. This was obviously a challenge arising out of the Cold War and was based on the Soviet Union's desire to spread communism and gain control over the US. It was a challenge that had to be faced head on, and President Kennedy provided leadership and federal funds to deal with this threat. President Kennedy was confident that the American space program would overcome that early lead and move ahead of the Soviets. We had done that before and we would do it again.

President Kennedy responded by upping the ante and challenging our scientists and engineers to not only overcome the Soviet lead in space but to exceed it. The US would do that by landing American astronauts on the moon by the end of the 1960s. This would tend to imply that the US would be able to not only land a man on the moon but also to use the moon as a base for military purposes. That was a very bold challenge but one that President Kennedy knew that we, as a nation, had to achieve. The challenge was meant to demonstrate to the world that the US would not crumble under any threat. It would demonstrate that the US was and would continue to be a technological and military leader in the full sense of the word. That same political leadership and attitude would be the magic bullet necessary to overcome the Great Recession of 2009. But, the magic bullet would have to be backed by technological and industrial developments rather than just plain political rhetoric and nonsense.

President Kennedy knew that US technical preeminence hung on the outcome of this challenge and was confident the US would, once again, be in a position to show the Soviet Union what was meant by the term "Yankee Ingenuity." On July 20, 1969, NASA landed a space capsule and two American astronauts on the surface of the moon. These astronauts planted the American flag on the moon and made each and every one of us proud to be an American. That's the only flag still flying on the surface of the moon to this day. During the following three years, ten additional American astronauts stepped on the moon surface. That was a significant achievement never again equaled by any other nation in the world.

Those achievements in outer space proved, once again, that the US was a technological leader in many fields, including the aerospace arena and, particularly, in space exploration. Landing on the moon was not a single lucky event but a feat repeated several times demonstrating to the Soviets that the first landing was not a mere coincidence. This was an achievement representing the collective efforts of sons and daughters of immigrants from all parts of the world. This also represented an achievement by scientists and engineers, who were either immigrants themselves or descendants of immigrants. Their contributions reaffirmed their ancestors' beliefs that the US was the land of opportunity where nothing was impossible to achieve. Those scientists and engineers in the Space Program achieved their American Dream, and made all of us proud. Obviously, this technical accomplishment dealt another defeat to the Soviet Union.

It became apparent early in the Cold War that the capabilities of military aircrafts were limited. The main limitation was flying range without refueling. The second was the altitude at which these airplanes could fly. Finally, there was a limitation on the ability to prevent detection. Ideally, a military aircraft would have unlimited flying range, be capable of flying above the reach of antiaircraft fire and missiles, and of flying without being detected by radar or other means.

Those technical requirements presented interesting challenges calling for new ideas and thinking. That led to much focused R&D efforts to achieve those objectives. The flying-range issue was being addressed by a very active program focused on harnessing nuclear power as a propulsion system. The nuclear-propulsion system would definitely overcome the range issue but there were many risks negating the apparent benefits. The other alternative was aerial refueling, which proved more practical than the nuclear option.

The capability to fly at very high altitudes was another issue requiring a significant level of R&D effort. This was required simply because of the nonexistence of materials capable of tolerating extreme environmental conditions present at high altitudes. New materials were developed for this particular application, but the issue did not end there. Being able to machine those materials to make required mechanical parts was also a concern. The capability to produce these exotic materials in the quantities required presented additional technical challenges.

Finally, the detection issue was important but if airplanes were capable of flying high enough then it would be impossible to shoot it down. The detection issue became a secondary issue until the Soviets used a missile to shoot down a U-2 reconnaissance aircraft. The answer to that was the development of another aircraft capable of flying above the range of then existing missiles; this was the SR-1 aircraft, which to this day remains a technological marvel. The SR-1 was not only capable of flying at high altitudes but it also had a long flying range. This achievement made it possible to fly approximately 3,000 miles without refueling. Less refueling at lower altitudes reduced vulnerability to missiles. Obviously, progress had been made, but a better way had to be found to enable better delivery of weapons with less exposure to ground fire or missiles.

Missiles did not have the limitations of military aircraft and required no pilot to guide it to its intended target and were very difficult to destroy. Germans scientists and engineers had designed and built workable rockets to deliver bombs over relatively long distances. The German armed forces pioneered the use of early rockets to bomb London during World War II. When World War II ended, German scientists and engineers were unemployed and some of them migrated to the US. Many of those scientists became actively involved in the US Space Program under NASA and continued their pioneering work on rockets in this country. It was also very likely that these scientists and engineers participated in the development of missiles destined for military applications just as much as they participated in the development of rockets for space exploration. Here was another example of immigrants coming to the US and contributing their best efforts to defend this country, to advance the technological base of the country and to keep US industry at the leading edge of technological development.

It was curious that a distinction between space exploration and military applications existed for these devices commonly known as rockets: it was a rocket if used for space exploration and a missile if used for military applications. Both rockets and missiles relied on the same physical propulsion system. Propelling rockets or missiles depended on a rearward ejection of hot gases in the form a jet stream, causing forward motion as a result. Perhaps, the distinction was meant to indicate that missiles were vehicles for delivering weapon systems.

The aerospace industry employed highly educated people. It was one of the largest employers of highly qualified technical personnel. Consequently, it was an industry that provided and continues to provide many high-paying job opportunities to many Americans. It was an industrial sector that ranked very high in terms of value for its manufactured products. It was an industry that positively contributed to our nation's balance of payment. The US was a world leader in the aerospace industry, but maintaining this leadership position depended on many factors. Some of these factors were within the control of Corporate America itself but there were others factors that were clearly outside Corporate America's control. In fact, the US government had a significant input in maintaining leadership in the aerospace industry.

The US should has an interest in protecting the aerospace industry for its obvious defense and commercial value to the nation. Yet, recent actions by government officials have clouded that picture and have clearly undermined continued US supremacy in the aerospace industry. They have done that by recommending procurement of a tanker aircraft for the US Air Force from a foreign supplier instead of a very qualified US supplier. This is an example of actions by US government officials undermining our own industry and raising a question as to whether these officials are being bribed. This case has been extensively discussed in the press, and it involves bids for the tanker aircraft submitted by Boeing, a US aircraft manufacturer, and Airbus which is a European manufacturer.

Purchase specifications for this tanker for the US Air Force are written in a confusing manner. Boeing asked for clarifications and got misleading information intended to put Boeing at a disadvantage thus tilting the aircraft selection in favor of Airbus. Airbus, as expected, wins the bid for the tanker. Boeing complained, questioning the bidding process, and irregularities become apparent. Specifications are reissued, and it is expected Boeing will get the contract to supply tanker planes to the US Air Force. The Airbus group decided to drop out of the bidding for this type aircraft because they knew Airbus has never produced a tanker aircraft. How then can the US government buy such aircraft from Airbus? How can the US government justify buying an unproven aircraft for use in our national defense when Boeing tanker aircrafts have demonstrated reliability over a long period of operational history?

US government officials in the tanker procurement example clearly undermined our local aircraft manufacturers. If the truth were known, it would very likely be proven that procurement officials acted to protect their own personal financial interests. They probably acted either in response to payments and gifts from Airbus lobbyists or to secure an employment position with the foreign supplier upon departure from government service. Those actions were clearly beyond the control of Corporate America. What was clearly within the control of the corporation was the right to file a complaint challenging the award, which Boeing Aircraft did.

In many cases, manufacturers shoot themselves in the foot. Case in point is the procurement of foreign manufactured parts of the composite airframe for the Boeing 787 airliner. The manufacturers would say that this type of activity is required to enable it to participate in global markets. Perhaps, that is a consideration, but that action does not ensure sales of that aircraft to airlines in that country. It would be hard to imagine that the situation described would happen. Airlines purchase aircraft based on their needs and cost of the airplane. Obviously, performance and other technical considerations enter into the evaluation process leading to the selection of the aircraft to be purchased.

Now, let's look at the other side to determine if there are detrimental impacts accruing to Boeing from this sort of activity. There are press reports indicating deliveries of Boeing 787 aircraft have been delayed on account of technical and quality problems associated with the composite airframe and other components manufactured in foreign locations. That, obviously, has a detrimental impact on Boeing's profitability.

Consider, for example, the situation where Boeing engages a foreign supplier to produce a special component or part for a particular type of aircraft. That foreign supplier has to learn from Boeing how to manufacture the required part. Boeing teaches the foreign producer how to manufacture the part properly. Once that skill is learned then it can be used to produce the same sophisticated part for Boeing's competitors. Who loses? Who pays for the training? Who benefits? Does this action lead to additional aircraft sales from Boeing to the country where some of these components are manufactured? A "yes" answer is very unlikely.

There are some alarming statistics about what the future holds for the US aerospace industry. The number of aerospace employees declined from 1.3 million Americans in 1985 to 796,000 in 1995. That is an alarming trend indicating the aircraft manufacturing sector is losing its importance on a global basis. Part of that decline may be due to a misguided policy of sharing manufacturing of aircraft components on a global basis.

In 1985, aircraft manufacturing employed 8.8 percent of the total number of people in manufacturing but by 1995 this number had been reduced to 4.3percent. There was a similar declining trend in the number of scientists and engineers employed in the aerospace industry. In 1985, 20 percent of the total number of scientists and engineers in the country were employed in the aerospace industry, but by 1999 that number was down to 7 percent. [76]

The declining number of manufacturing workers and scientists in the aerospace industry raises a red flag pointing to the same trend in other manufacturing sectors of the economy. The picture that comes from looking at these manufacturing data is that US manufacturing is under attack. It is fighting for its life, and it is presently in a deep comatose state. If that trend is allowed to continue, then that will lead the US on the road to the status of a third-world country. Manufacturing is essential to US economic health. Unfortunately, many politicians have done their best to ignore these data.

Corporate executives continue to relocate US manufacturing activities to foreign countries to enhance their own financial position. These executives are greedy financiers interested only in their financial wellbeing. These, unlike previous executives, have no concern for the long-term health of the companies they lead. They are destroying US manufacturing from within their own corporations. Government officials are attacking US manufacturing from the outside by purchasing goods destined for national defense from foreign suppliers as the Boeing tanker case demonstrates. The future of US manufacturing in general looks bleak and will become insignificant unless corrective actions are taken quickly and effectively. If the US loses its manufacturing capability, then we all would suffer and the result would be relegated to the rank of a national tragedy.

The declining trend shown in aerospace manufacturing is also a fact of life in other manufacturing sectors of the US economy. That is a troubling tendency for it points to a considerable reduction in the number of high-paying manufacturing employment opportunities becoming available for Americans. The lack of those high-paying jobs will adversely affect our standard of living. And, many Americans will see their American Dream shattered by irresponsible actions by both corporate executives and government officials. The US will end up suffering the consequences as its global manufacturing and technical preeminence diminishes. The result will be a reduction in the global influence of the US.

It is worth pointing out that aircraft manufacturing is one area in which the US balance of payment still is in positive territory. But, it is an area that is being challenged constantly by foreign companies, and if corporate entities as well as the government do not rise to this challenge, then the importance of the US aircraft industry will be relegated to irrelevance. US aerospace industry preeminence will diminish in much the same way as have US steel, automobile, and textile companies.

Detrimental actions of US government officials in the tanker aircraft case are not limited to lower-rank officials. President Obama has done the same thing in terminating many programs at NASA. He is basing his actions on the idea of sharing costs with international partners to reduce the cost of these programs. Cost reductions have not been very successful for US Industry as demonstrated by the increasing number of industrial accidents and damage to the environment. He is ignoring the fact that the US is the only nation that has gone to the moon. The US is in a position to gain nothing from the international partners, while those partners get access to the crown jewels of US technology. In particular, the president justifies not extending the Space Shuttle Program on the basis that the US can depend on our Russian friends to transport our astronauts to the Space Station. President Obama is either ignoring or has failed to learn lessons from past dealings with Russians such as those concluded during World War II when Russia needed US assistance. Democratic communist Russians will never refused to take whatever is given to them so long as you give them something that is in their interest to take. At the point where you have nothing to offer or give, they will dump you and give you nothing in return. That will be the result if President Obama's ideas on the space program are allowed to stand. If that happens, for all practical purposes, Russia would be the clear winner of the Space Race.

Present Russian leaders, like former Soviet leaders, are still trying to overtake and convert the US into another satellite republic. Russians are still operating under a Cold War mentality. Recent acts speak louder than the soothing words from its democratic communist leaders. For example, Russia wants to join the global economy, but its behavior in cancelling or blocking natural gas deliveries to European nations under existing contracts tells a different story. It wants to reduce nuclear weapons and prevent rogue nations from acquiring them, but it supports Iran's nuclear ambitions and fails to join the rest of the world in opposing Iran's nuclear threats. It threatens and invades its neighbors, thus showing its expansionist ideals are still in effect and ready to be implemented.

What's different now in the Russian behavior? Does current Russian behavior indicate that the Cold War has ended? Can the US ignore those clear threats from current Russians leaders? In light of those activities, can the US depend on Russians to give our astronauts rides to the space station? Furthermore, can we trust our Russian democratic communist friends to allow our presence in the Space Station once our astronauts are totally dependent on Russians to give them a ride? The author believes that Russians will not honor any agreement with the US in regards to the Space Station just like they failed to honor agreements concluded during and after World War II. The US is the only nation that honors its agreements.

Regardless of our opinions, Russians are still operating as if the Cold War were still a fact of life. There are many Russians in position of governmental authority who have not changed their communist beliefs. These so called "Democratic Communists" are still of the opinion the US needs to be converted to the communist system. We as Americans need to wake up and act decisively, as President Ronald Reagan did to ensure that we are not fooled by our naiveté. Russians certainly have fooled our government officials, and that needs to be corrected at the polls during the next rounds of elections; Russians, however, have not fooled the American people.

One of the reasons President Obama is recommending termination of many NASA programs is that he feels the programs are very expensive. He feels the country needs to reduce spending. This is a position contrary to what the country really needs as shown by historical data. Well, let's look at facts and determine whether that is a valid reason. NASA's annual budget is in the range of $18 billion. [77] NASA uses budgeted funds to conduct research programs focusing on future space exploration and aerospace developments. It also pays for operations under existing programs and activities performed in accordance with programs under its jurisdiction. The president, perhaps, is concerned about the magnitude of expenditures and, like the rest of the corporate executives, sees those expenditures as a waste of money. He sees that as something that can be postponed or totally eliminated because it is not impacting the bottom line of the nation now. This position fails to recognize that R&D, which is covered by a significant portion of NASA expenditures, does not provide immediate benefits but rather provides benefits for the future as demonstrated by the contributions made under NASA previous R&D programs.

Perhaps he feels the way he does because he fails to understand benefits derived from discoveries and technologies developed by NASA. This is an attitude held in common with corporate leaders who also fail to understand the value of their corporate R&D to their future corporate profitability. The plain truth is that the president, like corporate leaders, neither understands nor knows the true value of R&D in general and in particular NASA's contributions to the welfare of this nation. The attitude of corporate leaders toward R&D is understandable on the basis R&D expenditures reduce short-term profits thus reducing bonuses for executives. But, the president does not get a bonus based on the nations' profit position. So what is the basis for the president opposition to NASA's programs? NASA needs to become more proactive in telling the president and the rest of the nation about its contributions to ensure that everyone understands why we need to continue funding NASA.

Perhaps, NASA needs to embark on a public relations campaign to demonstrate how its technology development efforts have made significant contributions in the miniaturization of surgical equipment making surgery less invasive and less prone to complications. NASA needs to point out how the space program has improved communications, storm warnings, and other things that we as Americans take for granted today. Perhaps, NASA can use concrete examples to educate our political leaders and demonstrate conclusively to the American people the value NASA funding brings to the nation, the American people, and the people of the entire world. Perhaps NASA can use the testimony of knowledgeable people in this very important undertaking to make its case once and for all. One such individual is G. Scott Hubbard, professor of aeronautics and astronautics at Stanford University and former director of the NASA Ames Research Center. [78]

Professor Hubbard has estimated that for every dollar spent on the space program, the US economy gets eight dollars in economic benefits. Compare the return from an investment in NASA against the return resulting from the infusion of taxpayer funds to revive failed financial institutions causing the Great Recession of 2009. Based on NASA's annual budget of approximately $20 billion, that national investment returns about $160 billion to the US economy! The same amount given to failed banks and financial institutions have returned nothing to the nation, unless you count the number of Americans losing their homes a benefit.

The US government gave failed financial institutions responsible for the financial debacle of 2009 hundreds of billions of dollars. What has the nation gotten in return? The nation received no return from that huge infusion of taxpayer funds to failed financial institutions. Those failed financial institutions used taxpayer funds to reward their executives for the collapse of the institutions they were managing. Banks' executives distributed $20 billion of our taxpayer dollars as bonuses among inept executives who caused the banks and US economy to collapse in the first place. That $20 billion dollars could have been better spent on funding NASA to get a return.

Corporate executives driving failed banks and financial institutions into the ground got a bonus from the US government that really amounted to robbery of taxpayers' funds. They together with politicians who facilitated that robbery ought to be indicted and prosecuted for stealing taxpayers' funds. They should be barred from ever again holding a management position at any financial institution and politicians should be barred from ever again seeking another elective office.

Federal regulators failed to detect inconsistencies in the books of financial institutions they supposedly regulated. These regulators have also had their performance rewarded with bonuses. [79] This adds insult to injury for these were the same regulators, who, charged with the duty of determining whether these financial institutions were playing by the rules or cooking the books, failed miserably in the performance of their statutory duties. How could they be rewarded? What kind of example are these inept and corrupt officials providing to our children?

It is clear that they failed to perform their duties properly by results on the economy and failure of many financial institutions. Had they performed their duties they would have uncovered all of the shenanigans that led those institutions to the brink of bankruptcy. Obviously, those regulators have been doing a poor job for a long time because this financial failure is not the result of a single event but rather the result of multiple events. Why reward them instead of firing them. This clearly points to similarities in practices employed both in the corporate world and the US government to reward ineptness and irresponsibility.

Rewarding poor performance sends the message that mediocrity or failure to do your job is not only acceptable but also profitable. Regulators who have failed to detect books of these financial institutions have been cooked to the detriment of their clients and to the benefit of executives. What lesson does that sent to young people? The answer is simple. It tells them that lying, cheating, and stealing are acceptable and profitable forms of behavior. Furthermore, it signals that the search for excellence in performing our jobs is nonsense, for it is something that goes unrewarded. Obviously, that is not the case in the Space Program where so many talented and qualified individuals labor long and hard to ensure success in every mission.

If the private sector and the US government continue to encourage mediocrity, then it will not be long before our nation achieves self-destruction and third-world status. Is that what the general population wants? The author believes that the majority of Americans want to continue on the pursuit of excellence. We want our nation to stay the course on the journey to global preeminence.

The author further believes that the US as a whole has to change from the practice of political correctness. We have to become blunt and tell it like it is regardless of consequences. We have become so accustomed to political correctness that we are failing to recognize the facts as they are. Our children are not being properly educated, and we say that's okay. Our corporate leaders are stealing from their corporations, and we accept that. Our political leaders are enriching themselves by serving lobbyists and special interest, and we say it is okay. Well, it is time to say those things are not okay.

We have to chart a new course to educate our children that all of this political correctness justifying corruption, ineptness, and mediocrity is not okay. We have to teach them to be responsible and to act ethically. The same has to be done to change the present culture of corruption, ineptness, and greed so prevalent among corporate and political leaders. We have to instill in all our people a sense of responsibility and accountability for all of their individual actions. We need to reward ethics, responsibility, and competence instead of unethical behavior, irresponsibility, and incompetence. That is the prescription for preserving our portion of the American Dream and ensuring preeminence for our country.

COLLAPSE OF THE SOVIET UNION

There were many internal as well as external steps leading to the collapse of the Soviet Union. Internal factors included lack of truthfulness in communications between political leaders and population, ineptness of political leaders, ethnic conflicts, economic inefficiencies, corruption, and political repression.

The main external cause of the Soviet Union collapse was the pressure exerted by President Reagan's Strategic Defense Initiative (SDI), which was commonly known as the Star Wars initiative. That initiative set very high goals that seemed almost unachievable. But, based on the US record of technological achievement, the Soviet Union did not want to risk having those goals become real.

Under this defense initiative, the US would use ground and space-based systems to shoot down incoming Soviet nuclear ballistic missiles. It would do so immediately upon after Soviet missiles were launched, thus preventing delivery of nuclear weapons and causing potential destruction of the launch site by the weapons themselves. This was a very ambitious defense initiative on the part of the US to defend against nuclear ballistic missile attacks; the US began to invest to make these goals reality. The Soviets recognized the US was serious about this new technology and also successes the US had had on aeronautics and space. The Soviet Union realized it would have to spend large amounts of money it did not have in order to counteract the impact of this US initiative; that would certainly bankrupt the Soviet Union. Perhaps, President Reagan was using the same philosophy the Soviet Union had used against the US when it encouraged the US to undertake development of a nuclear-powered aircraft. In any event, the Star War Initiative was a bluff, but it was a very effective bluff. It forced the Soviet Union to realize it could not continue spending money on weapons while there were shortages of food and other consumer necessities. It was a bluff that contributed to the demise of the Soviet Union.

In 1985, Mikhail Gorbachev was elected general secretary of the Communist Party of the Soviet Union after three previous Soviet leaders had died within a period of three years. Gorbachev was a reformer. He, unlike previous communist leaders, realized that reforms were needed to improve living conditions to ensure survival of the communist system in the Soviet Union. He initiated reforms including economic and political reforms aimed at correcting previous policies and governmental practices. He, however, underestimated the reaction from the general population and ended up losing control of the policies during the implementation phase. [80]

Reforms introduced by Gorbachev included a policy known as "Glasnost" which purported to deal with Soviet citizenry in an open and truthful manner. This policy infuriated the average citizen when they learned that former Soviet leaders had lied to them regarding communist achievements. The level of brutality used by government leaders against opponents and in suppressing opposition also became known. Communist leaders had reshaped the historical record to ensure it agreed with their side of the story. The second reform was a policy known as "perestroika" that attempted to restructure the Soviet economic system to make it more efficient.

Gorbachev recognized that, in order to improve the Soviet communist system, certain changes had to be made in the political apparatus. He envisioned changes including the introduction of democratic concepts and a power shift in the Politburo from the old communist guard over to younger political reformers; the Politburo was analogous to the US Congress or the British Parliament. Gorbachev believed that electing younger political reformers to the Politburo directly by the citizenry rather than by the old communist guard would enable reforms to be implemented quicker. This would grant him power to introduce and implement necessary reforms for the purpose of improving living conditions for the general population.

These democratic reforms, however, backfired and a period of instability followed as the general population demanded more reforms and faster implementation. There were ethnic conflicts that tore apart the fabric of Soviet society. Those conflicts had their genesis on forced relocations of entire ethnic groups, Russian nationalism, and belief of Russian superiority over other ethnic groups. A similar effect would have resulted in the US by forcibly implementing the Anglo Saxon superiority myth. These reforms eventually led to the downfall of Gorbachev in a coup d'état that resulted in the dissolution of the Soviet Union and replacement of Gorbachev by Boris Yeltsin. The results of these ethnic conflicts were very disastrous not only to Russia but also to Soviet satellites. A case in point was the disaster caused by ethnic conflicts and the fragmentation that occurred in Yugoslavia and the civilian casualties and suffering resulting from those conflicts in many parts of those satellites.

Gorbachev was credited with leading events resulting in the total collapse of the Soviet Union. That position, however, failed to acknowledge contributions made by US President Ronald Reagan who, in effect, played a leading role in causing the downfall of the Soviet Union. President Reagan's role was simply to define a very expensive program that, if developed and proven successful, would have rendered Soviet nuclear or missiles attacks against the US very difficult if not impossible to carry out. The Reagan's defense initiative would have forced the Soviet Union to either develop a workable alternative to trump the US program or realize the insanity of continuing on that path and abandoning it. The Soviets realized that their economy could not afford such a program and resolved to change their course of actions to address other concerns providing greater benefit to the general population.

In addition to the Defense Initiative, President Reagan knew the Soviet Union relied on sales of natural gas and crude oil to generate funds in terms of hard currency to keep its economy going. He, therefore, decided to implement the second prong of his approach at ending the Cold War. That approach involved exerting US influence to cause the price of oil and natural gas to decline. This had the intended result of denying funds to pursue funding R&D programs to counteract the US Strategic Defense Initiative. Concurrent with that approach, President Reagan secured funding to finance the first few preliminary steps of the Strategic Defense Initiative. That action convinced the Soviets leadership that the US was serious about developing the required technology to ensure success of this program. The Soviets realized the US had the technological wherewithal and now the funds to fully undertake this effort. In fact, some contracts were awarded in furtherance of this effort. The price of crude oil and natural gas dropped, and that seemed to have had some effect on the Soviets.

Natural gas prices, shown in Figure 24, showed an increasing price trend starting in 1976 or thereabouts. In fact, the increase was very significant; it increased from less than one dollar per thousand cubic feet to close to three dollars per thousand cubic feet. Considering the Soviet Union was a significant natural gas producer, this increase in prices had a very positive impact on the amount of hard currency income available to the Soviets. But, then natural gas prices began to decline and stabilized at a lower price. It was not until 2001 that another increasing trend developed. This significantly reduced the amount of hard currency available to fund weapons programs. President Reagan was getting the results he expected from exertion of US influence on oil and natural gas producing countries.

US Natural Gas Well Head Prices

Figure 24 Historical Gas Prices [81]

Crude oil prices shown in Figure 25, on the other hand, increased from approximately twelve dollars per barrel in 1976 or so all the way to close to forty dollars per barrel in 1981. This increase was partly due to an oil embargo by members of the Organization of Petroleum Exporting Countries (OPEC) in the late 1970s. The Soviet Union – now Russia - while not a member of OPEC became a beneficiary of OPEC actions in increasing crude prices during the 1970's. The benefits obtained by the Soviets resulting from doubling oil prices were significant; this had the effect of enhancing the stream of hard currency income. But, something happened to cause natural gas and crude prices to decline around the mid-1980s. The declining price of natural gas and oil prevented the Soviet Union from undertaking an effort to enhance its military capability in response to the US initiative.

Were the reductions in natural gas and oil prices the direct result of President Reagan's effort at exerting US global influence? It would be easy to imagine discussions between President Reagan and political leaders of oil and gas producing nations resulted in the observed price reductions. Regardless of the true cause for the reduction in energy prices, the Strategic Defense Initiative was funded by the US. The Soviet Union, on the other hand, was facing a shortage of funds resulting from lower revenues from oil and natural gas sales. Lower natural gas and crude oil prices certainly had a significant influence on the collapse Soviet Union. This was particularly true at a time when Gorbachev was trying to implement reforms in the Soviet Union. As a result of the shortage of funds, Gorbachev decided to focus on reforming the system rather than on funding a strategy to counteract the Star War Initiative. Gorbachev had wisely recognized the level of discontent in the general population that could lead to civil unrest, as it obviously did by toppling him.

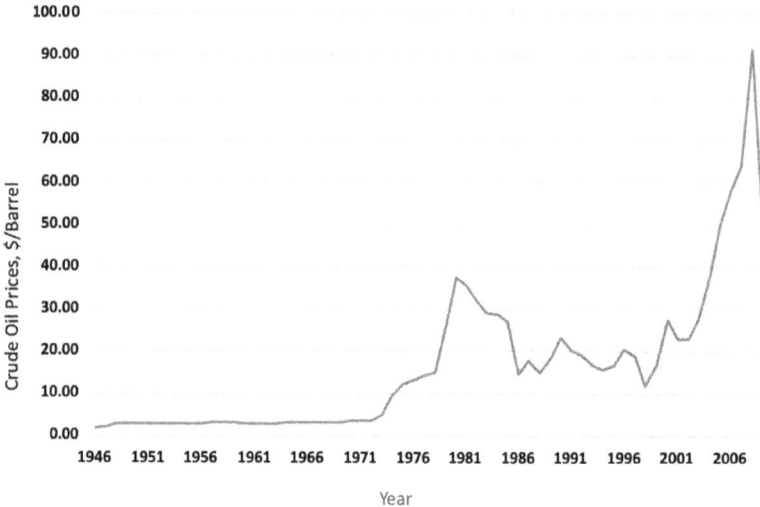

Figure 25 Historical Crude Oil Prices [82]

Are there lessons to be learned from the collapse of the Soviet Union? That is a fair question to ask. First of all, the issue of false communications between politicians and the citizenry is an important element that should be kept in politicians' mind. That issue parallels the present situation in the US where politicians are not truthful in regards to communications with constituents. Politicians tend to disclose only those things that benefit them. Case in point is the present health care legislation passed by Congress and known as Obama Care. Republicans tell you one part of the story, and Democrats tell you a completely different story. The result is that neither Republicans nor Democrats are telling a truthful story. The truth is somewhere between the stories told by both parties, but nobody knows for sure. In any event, this legislation is over 2,000 pages long and neither Republicans nor Democrats have ever read it or, if they have, they have certainly failed to understand it.

Another issue is the one relating to politicians remaining in office for life; this situation like the Politburo situation leads to a brain-dead congress composed of mummified legislators in our case unable to improve anything within the country. Corruption is the result of having professional politicians perpetuating themselves in office for life. Professional politicians begin to think they own the place and are essential. These mummies begin to believe service longetivity should be rewarded in terms of pay, or more appropriately, bribes to get them to act; that is something that benefits only politicians. There are other lessons on simplifying or eliminating political bureaucracy. Finally, it is worth keeping in mind the dismemberment of Yugoslavia was the result of ethnic conflicts; the same could happen in the US if politicians continue fueling class warfare between rich and poor instead of providing educational opportunities for the poor to become wealthy. Finally, US influence played a major role in the collapse of the Soviet Union. That US influence was the direct result of US technological and manufacturing strength. US influence will diminish significantly if Corporate America continues on its path to self-destruction.

Referring to data shown in Figure 23, military expenditures started to increase about the time President Reagan assumed office. Military expenditures reached a plateau by the mid-1980s and began to decline shortly after that. This leveling in military spending occurred about the time Gorbachev was named general secretary of the Communist Party, and it had become obvious that he had run into problems implementing his reform program. US defense spending continued to decline until the mid-1990s as shown in the same figure, and that had a profound impact on corporate performance.

The US was the clear Cold War winner. It became obvious that many, if not all, Eastern European countries that had been under Soviet control rejected communist ideology. What was not clear was how Russians felt about the Cold War outcome. Many of them felt that democracy was not a workable system, particularly those who had seen their livelihood affected negatively. In the US, however, it was felt that the US should be in a position to extract a "peace dividend" enabling it to reduce military expenditures and dedicating those funds to other purposes. That view was in agreement with US isolationist attitude prevailing in the country after the end of World War I. Unfortunately, that perspective provided nothing but a false sense of security.

IMPACT ON CORPORATE AMERICA

The period after World War II was a period of uncertainty and change. The uncertainty came as a result of not knowing how the private sector would sustain manufacturing activities in peace time to sustain wartime employment level and production capacity. Change came about as a result of having to retool manufacturing facilities to enable production of goods destined for general consumption and export markets. It turned out, contrary to expectations and fears, that the post war period was one of prosperity as consumers demanded goods such as automobiles that they had been unable to acquire as a result of restrictions imposed on them during the war years. Corporations expanded marketing efforts into the export markets to assist in reconstruction efforts underway in Europe and Japan. Entrance into export markets resulted, therefore, in continuous prosperity for Corporate America as industrial employment opportunities and demand for goods became more plentiful.

The immediate post war period was followed by the Cold War and the Space Race. It was during those years that many great technological discoveries were made that expanded our existing frontiers all the way to outer space. This led to the development of many new products for use in medical applications, weather forecasting, aerospace, and so on. New discoveries ended up becoming new products and creating consumer demand for those products thereby extending the prosperity to the 1980s.

The collapse of the Soviet Union marked a turning point for the US government and the US industrial sector. Government and corporate officials became complacent and led to a paradigm shift in the way things would be done henceforth.

The government assumed all of our enemies were defeated. As a result, the US government reduced defense spending thus cutting off the fuel supply from the R&D engine that had proven so successful at invigorating the private sector and the entire nation to reach for the stars and attain incredible achievements. Those achievements included development of a technological base making our nation the most powerful industrial and military nation in the world. Many high-paying manufacturing jobs were created that enhanced the standard of living of our citizens. Unfortunately, the US Government reduced spending that had been so successful at creating national wealth.

Corporate America, on the other hand, saw the emerging picture and decided to undergo some changes of its own. It wanted to continue deriving maximum profits but saw reduction in government spending as a threat to its profitability. It became lazy and complacent and switched its allegiance from science and engineering over to financial gimmicks.

Corporate America wanted to generate profits and do nothing other than rely on hot air and financial gimmicks to inflate profits. That led to malicious greed or insatiable avarice. Corruption became the instrument creating imaginary profits and wealth by any means necessary regardless of consequences. In other words, corruption was a means to the end—bribing government and regulatory officials to overlook illegal or prohibited activity. This level of corruption and greed has not been limited to corporate officials but it has spread to officials at all government levels.

Corruption feeding on an insatiable greed is the leading cause for the financial crisis of 2009. It is also responsible for the collapse of the Soviet Union. It is ironic that the collapse of the Soviet Union would coincide with the beginning of a sequence of events leading, unless reversed, to the collapse of Corporate America. It is ironic that Corporate America's role in the Cold War led to the collapse of the Soviet Union, and now the result of that achievement ends up placing Corporate America on the road to its demise.

Rebuilding European and Japanese industries had very significant positive effects on US industry. On the one hand, it benefitted from being a supplier of goods and services during the rebuilding phase of the European and Japanese reconstruction efforts. On the other hand, the reconstruction effort resulted in the revival of formidable competitors for US industry. Obviously, the US government had a say regarding what these revitalized industries could or could not produce; this protected US industry to some extent during this period and its immediate future. For example, German industry pioneered the development and production of military jet aircrafts during the war, but Germany was prohibited from continuing work on this development or extending that technology to the production of civilian aircrafts.

The ban on production of jet aircrafts would have severe repercussions on European manufacturing of transport aircraft or use by airlines. That benefited US manufacturers. Although formidable competitors were revitalized, US companies had a significant amount of lead time to continue and extend its technical and commercial leadership position.

The initial phase of European and Japanese reconstruction was beneficial in providing new markets for US manufactured products destined for the private sector. Supplying private-sector goods mitigated to some extent the impact of discontinuing or totally stopping the massive supply of military goods to European allies during the war. Corporate America also profited by gaining market share in the consumer-products sector. That initial gain in consumer goods had enormous future growth potential as European and Japanese consumers expanded their demand for those products.

US companies gained a beachfront in Europe and Japan, enabling it to establish alliances with local companies for the purpose of licensing manufacturing processes and, perhaps, to partner in the building and operation of manufacturing facilities to supply goods to markets nearer Europe or Japan. These alliances provided some beneficial marketing privileges to these companies. Ending World War II was a great thing in terms of providing a peaceful and stable economic climate, but it also presented risks and challenges that American companies had to address and overcome to continue providing stability and prosperity to employees back in the US.

On the other hand, commercial threats and risks presented by reconstruction efforts undertaken in Europe and Japan to Corporate America had to be addressed. It meant simply that the US government would be assisting in the revival of foreign competitors to Corporate America; it was a risk addressed with active participation from US industry. The risk was new foreign producers would return to the market, albeit at a future date, but in a reinvigorated form to compete against US companies. The cooperation between US and foreign companies enabled the foreign companies to learn how US companies operated. That knowledge would benefit them for at least two reasons. First, foreign companies would be in a very good position to improve their operations with American know-how. Secondly, these foreign companies would learn how American companies act in the market place and the foreign companies would be better prepared to react.

Newly rebuilt European and Japanese factories and industries would be capable of undercutting US companies in several respects. First of all, foreign companies would be operating new and more efficient plants return to the market to compete against older and possibly less efficient US manufacturing plants. Those new foreign facilities would become more productive than US counterparts once they got past the initial bugs and learned to operate those facilities optimally. The new industries would employ local workers who had been unemployed for a while and were desperate to start earning a living once again. This presented an advantageous situation to be selective in selecting workers to staff its plants and also to avoid wage escalation thus reducing production costs versus those prevailing in the US. Finally, products of emerging European and Japanese industries would be favored by local consumers in those countries. That would be expected on account of the fact that foreign industries were now in a position to provide employment opportunities to nationals of those countries.

US industry would face significant challenges competing with both European and Japanese companies in their local markets. There were many possibilities to mitigate preferences for local companies. For example, US companies, based on their local market share, could build manufacturing facilities to satisfy local markets and use the local labor pool to equalize production costs versus those of European and Japanese competitors. US companies could overcome preference for the local companies on the basis of product quality, after-sale service, and reputation from prior performance.

Obviously, this situation presented a great opportunity and a great challenge to US companies. In fact, the reconstruction effort got underway in Europe and Japan, and it became a defining moment for US corporations. Corporate America had to establish a plan addressing future contingencies that potentially could be very costly in terms of market share and profitability. US corporations rose to the occasion and demonstrated they were up to par and unafraid to face future competition. They based that assessment on the strength of their R&D capabilities and efforts, on manufacturing know-how, on marketing and customer service expertise, and on financial strength.

The reconstruction of Europe and Japan brought a period of profitability and stability for US corporations. This made the transition from war production to production for the private sector smoother. It represented a period of change and, no doubt, there were pundits predicting high unemployment rates and an end to prosperity for all Americans. Those predictions did not come true, and in effect, the opposite happened. It was a period during which corporate profitability increased, as shown in Figure 22, during the period from 1946 to 1950 and leveling at a very robust rate for the next several years. This, no doubt, reflected a period of great prosperity with potentially no end in sight.

Labor Unions failed to increase membership as shown in Figure 20, were in the range of 4 percent to 6 percent considered by economists to be "full employment". This could be interpreted to mean labor relations were good. But, there were alarming red flags looming in the horizon that should have been noticed by Corporate America. Those flags showed amazing recoveries by both Germany and Japan; industry in both of these countries would become formidable competitors for US industry. One such example was the growth rate in the Japanese and German GDPs, as shown in Table 13, which grew at approximately twice the rate of US GDP growth during the 1951 to 1980 period (15 percent to 12 percent for Japan and Germany, respectively vs. 7 percent for the US).

There were intervening events brought about by actions and threats from the Soviet Union that, once again, led US industry and the US government to forge a strong relationship promoting closer cooperation; this relationship further strengthened US corporations. This was the beginning of the Cold War and the conflicts caused by the main ideological rivals: the Soviet Union and the US. These events resulted in massive expenditures for the purpose of developing new military hardware. Military programs transitioned to a space-exploration program that demanded innovative solutions to very complicated technical problems. The Cold War had a stabilizing effect on employment and prevented further economic deterioration as had been feared at the end of World War II; this strengthened the bond between Corporate America and its employees. It was also instrumental in enhancing Corporate America's profitability outlook for years.

Figure 26 shows a long period of uninterrupted Corporate America profitability. More importantly, the figure shows an upward trend in corporate profitability leading to a protracted period of prosperity. It is important to note that the level of corporate profitability appears to be independent of wars or other major conflicts faced by our nation since the end of World War II. It also seems to be independent of criminal terrorist attack suffered by our nation on September 11, 2001. In fact, it seems corporate profitability grew unimpeded until about the beginning of the 2009 financial crisis. Corporate profitability ensured prosperity not only for corporations, but also for its employees and for our nation.

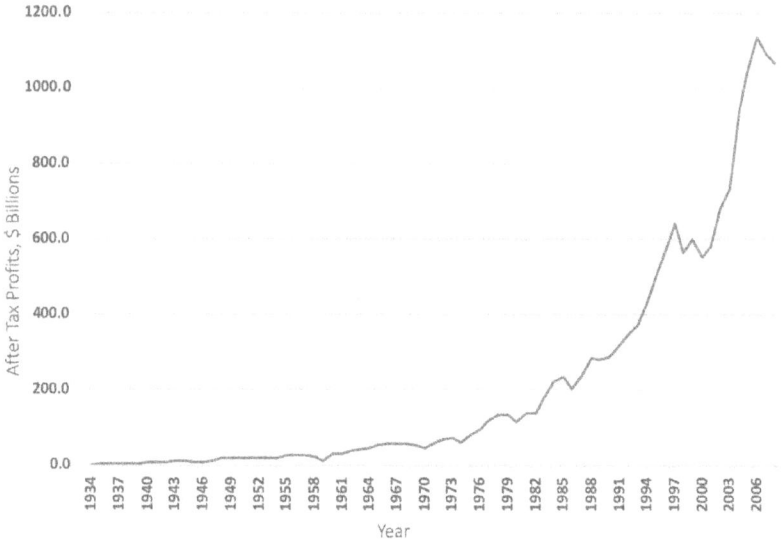

Figure 26 Annual Corporate America Profitability [83]

Continuous prosperity fostered a period of corporate arrogance among executives. Examples of this arrogant attitude included a false sense of invincibility and complacency that, in turn, led to inaction and reluctance to continue investing in R&D efforts to improve manufacturing processes and reduce operating cost. Corporate leaders began to rely on outsourcing as a means of reducing operating cost. That attitude on the part of corporate leaders placed companies on the road to mediocrity that eventually would cause their downfall.

Complacency among corporate and government leaders led to an unquenchable thirst for power and money driving them to cheating, lying, and stealing. The result of corporate greed was to look out for personal interests rather than the wellbeing of the corporate entity. Executives became egomaniacs in search of financial benefits for themselves. In the search for personal financial success, they became concerned only of the short term thus neglecting the long-term outlook for their companies. This attitude had unwanted and undesirable consequences for the corporation they led as many of those corporations began to suffer financial disaster. At that point, corporate executives began to realize what their competitors had known all along; it revealed these corporate executives were not as good or as invincible as their egos led them to believe. This had grave consequences not only for Corporate America but for its employees and our nation.

In conclusion, the period after World War II was a very prosperous era for US industry, corporate employees, and the US in general. It was a period when the US industrial sector was propelled to new heights in terms of profitability. It was a time when the US became a major supplier not only to satisfy US demand but demand of the entire world. It was a period leading to great successes in developing new manufacturing processes. It was a period leading to introduction of new products that would benefit the entire human race. It was a favorable situation resulting in the creation of an untold number of high-paying manufacturing jobs for Americans. It was a time when US companies were transforming the US into a preeminent technological and manufacturing powerhouse in the world.

Corporate America employees, in turn, were the beneficiaries of untold prosperity. That allowed them to spend on consumer goods to make their living conditions more enjoyable. In so doing, consumers stimulated further manufacturing activities ensuring continuity in the prosperity cycle. The US government also benefitted from this prosperity from an ever-increasing income stream generated through collection of income taxes. This is the recipe that needs to be repeated now in order to get the US out of the Great Recession of 2009. Then and only then will Americans be able to, once again, dream and see their American Dream realized.

CHAPTER 7
STARING INTO
THE ABYSS

Up to this point, discussion has focused on development and growth of Corporate America. It is a fascinating story tracing the emergence of US industry from a humble beginning to the point of becoming the envy of the entire industrial world. Immigrants have contributed to that development from the very beginning of being actual vehicles used to transfer technology from European countries to our nation. They have also contributed by their early efforts at establishing a local industrial know-how base tailored specifically to address difficult conditions present in the US. That early period of learning and initial implementation is followed by a period of growth and prosperity that foreshadows a period of great economic suffering and misery. The Great Depression, as that period is commonly known, is the result of unchecked greed and corruption on the part of corporate officials, particularly by financial institutions and financiers. Excessive corporate greed leads to the creation of an imaginary bubble based on nothing substantial but only imaginary expectations. It is a bubble based on financial gimmicks and tricks to enrich a segment of the population at the expense of the rest of the nation consumers and institutions. Avarice inflates the bubble until it reaches a point of no return and it bursts.

The US government, at that time, allows industry to operate freely without interference and able to anything or whatever it wants to do. Consequently, the government has no interest in regulating industry; it in the purest type of a free-enterprise system.

That freedom to operate is abused, and as a result, a system has to be devised to control corporate excesses. The Great Depression, therefore, is caused by irresponsible actions of corporate entities and officials. Consequently, it becomes obvious the US government has to engage and play a leading role in regulating the private sector. This is necessary to prevent recurrence of abuses that have resulted in financial catastrophe. The government also has to act to get the country's economy back on the road to recovery. That effort succeeds to some extent, but it is not the cure-all everyone expects it to be. The initial attempt at changing the economic environment is structured around public jobs in constructing or repairing the infrastructure of the country. This early effort is successful to some extent, but it is not the magic bullet that ends the Depression. It isn't until manufacturing is reenergized to produce armaments necessary to fight and defeat World War II enemies that the economy begins to show some signs of improvement. Manufacturing becomes, therefore, the magic bullet that kills the Great Depression.

The US government's role in regulating the economy expands from its early involvement in the 1930s. This becomes obvious during and after World War II. That expansion includes establishment of an R&D network responsible for transforming the US into a technological and industrial powerhouse. The R&D network includes universities and corporate laboratories. Labor is the glue holding the whole program together. In summary, this period showed the kind of success that is attained by close cooperation among Corporate America, the US government, and labor. That tripartite team effort is very successful up until the mid-1980s when something happens to cause the whole arrangement to begin showing some early signs of stress and rifts.

The present discussion looks at sources of stress and impacts those stresses have had in leading Corporate America to the brink of collapse. In some cases, conditions leading to the present financial disaster are the same conditions that led to the Great Depression.

It is obvious that lessons from the Great Depression have not been completely understood. Failure to learn those lessons have culminated in the Great Recessions of 2009. The true cost of that failure may not become as apparent as one would have hoped, but certainly it may even be more costly than it is anticipated. Results of financial gimmicks and corruption present in our corporate and government circles point to a slow move by Corporate America into the abyss of its own demise unless corrected. But, we all know that Corporate America is not going down the abyss by itself; it is dragging all of us and the nation down the same road. We all depend on Corporate America to make our American Dream reality, and that reliance is failing us. This is a very disturbing concern because the US is being driven into the ranks of third-world nations. Some leading politicians are presently advocating this path for our nation. Is that we want?

Each one of us has accumulated vast amounts of information, knowledge, and memories in the inner confines of our minds. At some particular point, those pieces of information are accessed for the purpose of determining how to address current situations. Those pieces of information provide a basis for comparing and evaluating present existing conditions or situations against stored data on similar events we have personally witnessed. That is one way of evaluating the transformation Corporate America has undergone in the past twenty years or so, causing the largest and most devastating economic crisis since the Great Depression of the 1930s.

The Great Recession of 2009, as the present situation is commonly known, has significantly affected the lives of many Americans and has seen many companies driven to the brink of bankruptcy or even into liquidation. Corporations once considered powerful and invincible are no longer in existence or have been rendered powerless and irrelevant. Many American companies that are once idolized as leaders in their field on a worldwide basis are no longer able to compete with German or Japanese counterparts. In many cases, these former industrial icons are losing the battle against competitors.

GM is a case in point. It has lost significant market share to foreign competitors and has been forced to seek bankruptcy protection, while Toyota has overtaken GM's market leadership. The US government is forced to rescue GM to prevent it from going out of business. Toyota transforms itself and achieves a remarkable recovery from extensive aerial bombings damage caused by World War II. GM, however, suffers no war damage but instead it is devastated by its own management. In other words, GM suffers devastation at the hands of inept and corrupt management. Those same inept managers are incapable of returning GM to its past glory. As a result, GM has to rely on the US government to get it out of its comatose state. Chrysler is another example with a history of multiple bankruptcy filings. The first time around, Chrysler is returned to economic viability by a capable leader. After a few years of operation, there is a management change and, once again, bankruptcy or sale is the only alternative open to it. That is shameful and to have that situation repeated is a complete and unforgivable disgrace.

This crisis shatters the dreams of many American families. It is also of the level of corporate ineptitude on the part of executives and management. Corporate America has to change operating philosophy and management attitude to sustain its viability. And, like Toyota, GM can regain its glory by concentrating on quality of its product, regaining employees' loyalty, and connecting with customers. It is a simple recipe that has been ignored by an arrogant management interested only in satisfying their short-term avarice without regard for the effect that avarice has on the corporate entity, employees, or customers.

Our memories remind each of us of times when Corporate America supply goods to every corner of the world. It reminds us of times when Corporate America supply technology to foreign companies that are devastated during World War II. Those memories are a reminder of a time many consider ideal—a time firmly etched in our consciences because of the prosperity that our citizenry and the whole country enjoy; a time when high-paying manufacturing jobs are plentiful; a time when people enjoy a high standard of living; a time when employers count on the loyalty of employees; a time when national leaders provide a long-term vision and leadership to achieve unimaginable goals; a time when national leaders exhort each of us to put forth our best effort to overcome national crises; a time when Corporate America is at the pinnacle of its glory; a time when Corporate America is strong; and a time when the label "Made in The USA" stands for quality and value. Now all of that has disappeared. Those are the times we refer to as the "Good Old Days" and are the times providing teachable moments to identify techniques or tools to counteract present economic adversity.

That is the way to make the American Dream something that is achievable by our children and our children's children once again. Such is the case now as we witness a situation that has been developing in the corporate and political institutions of our nation since the mid-1980s, when the Cold War supposedly ends. It is a situation that has changed moral and ethical standards leading to abuses and corruption without regard for collateral damage resulting from abuses of corporate or political power.

These abuses culminate in corporate fraud of unimaginable proportions. And, when the perpetrators are caught, they show an unwillingness to accept responsibility for their failures or lack of action. Instead of rewarding our corporate leaders on the basis of performance excellence, corporate America continues to reward them for ineptitude and inaction. Regulatory agencies charged with the duty of preventing these abuses look the other way and allow these abuses to continue unabated. Why? Simply because regulators and lawmakers are beneficiaries of bribes and gifts from the very corporations they are charged to watch. Imagine rewarding a wolf for eating the chickens it is supposed to protect. That describes the situation we currently are experiencing in the US. But, luckily, this situation can be remedied.

Corporate and political leaders have been working hard over the past twenty to thirty years or so to undermine the solid foundation on which Corporate America and this nation depend for prosperity. They are committed to destroying the solid foundation inherited from those who have worked hard to make Corporate America strong and successful. This has been done not to improve efficiency of Corporate America or the leadership of our nation but rather to benefit Wall Street and the leaders of financial institutions, politicians, regulators, and corporate leaders. Obviously, in any situation there are winners and losers, and it so happens that the losers, in this case, are the citizens who end up paying these corporate transgressions by losing their homes, their jobs, and their retirement benefits; these are members of the "Silent Majority" that need to become very vocal and loud to regain control over the course of our economy and to put an end to corporate and governmental abuses.

This situation describes a problem that has been brewing for years and now has reached a point requiring immediate attention to correct. It is a problem that adversely affects the economic welfare of millions of Americans who depend on Corporate America for their livelihood. It is a problem that causes economic uncertainty with potentially devastating consequences. It is also a problem that affects the leadership position of our nation as it struggles to avoid adverse consequences from the downfall of Corporate America. A corporate downfall of this magnitude would definitely lead to the demise of our nation's preeminent global position. Those are bad omens for not only our citizens who will see their individual American Dream shatter but also for our country and, perhaps, the whole world. Inaction is not an option in this case because it will cause US power and influence to diminish. It will also transform the US into an undeveloped third-world nation. That is really something not one of us wants, but that's where we are headed unless effective corrective action is implemented quickly. It is essential to inject corrective medicine to reverse government and corporate policies and procedures that have led Corporate America to the precipice of decadence and failure.

We see the corrupting power of corporate officials and their paid lobbyists in bribing politicians and regulators. That effort ensures actions of political leaders make it easy for corporate officials to achieve objectives regardless of consequences on the entire nation. It is time to paraphrase President Kennedy eloquent words cautioning against selfishness and instead to focus our efforts on the greater common good rather than on greed or avarice. The point is to:

Ask not what the corporation can do for you, but instead ask what you can do for the corporation, fellow employees, shareholders, and country.

The 2009 economic and financial situation reflects lack of leadership both in the corporate and political arenas. It is the result of unchecked and compounded corporate avarice and corruption leading to a disastrous situation that, eventually, affects all of us. It is an issue challenging each one of us to put aside differences separating us and, instead concentrate on similarities uniting us. This is the best way of correcting this economic disaster. It demands action on the part of each one of us to reverse actions of corrupt and greedy corporate and political leaders. Success in this matter is an achievable goal that ultimately strengthens our nation as shown by the prosperity achieved after the Great Depression. What kind of action is required? It is necessary to demand our authorities investigate misdeeds threatening the present financial situation and to penalize perpetrators under criminal statutes ensuring that this situation does not ever occur again.

Political and corporate leaders have ignored morality and ethics in the performance of daily activities. And, yet, they are rewarded. Citizens see daily abuses of corporate and political power and fail to take a stand against those abuses. Political leaders fail to enact effective legislation and to enforce existing regulations to prevent this level of corruption. Why is that the case? The answer is simply that legislators and regulators are paid by corrupt corporate officials, via lobbyists, to encourage them to look the other way. Consequently, this failure to act fuels further abuses as our political and corporate leaders begin to believe their actions are acceptable and beyond reprehension. In short, there is a three-party system at play in this context: corporations, government, and citizens. Each of those parties shares a certain degree of blame for what ails our economic system and threatens our prosperity; these are reviewed in subsequent sections along with their contributions to our economic malaise.

Causes of this corporate malaise are discussed individually in the sections that follow. In the next chapter, suggestions are made to reverse those destructive actions and ensure Corporate America remains viable and profitable for the long term. That is the only way to guarantee sustainability of the American Dream and US world preeminence and influence.

EXECUTIVE COMPENSATION

Executive compensation is an issue that comes to the forefront of any debate regarding bailouts of financial institutions and corporations. It is a matter that raises tempers and emotions because of the level of manipulation and corruption involved. It is believed high salaries and bonuses are necessary to attract and retain the best qualified managers for Corporate America. At the same time, one finds corporate performance and financial results achieved by Corporate America are not outstanding, particularly in the last twenty years or so. End results achieved by many of these corporations, however, tend to negate the validity of arguments advocating high salaries to attract the best and most qualified managers.

Many corporations have gone bankrupt and many others have lost market share to foreign competitors under the watchful eyes of highly paid executives. Corporate executives defend this poor performance on a disadvantage relating to competition against foreign corporations manufacturing overseas where supposedly wages are lower. Let's accept that, but what about foreign companies that are manufacturing in the US and still are beating our home-grown companies. Many foreign automobile producers manufacture in the US and employ American labor to beat and yet they do better than GM and other US car companies. It seems that the real reason is not the lower manufacturing cost enjoyed by foreign producers but management style —plain and simple. So if that's the case, then that raises doubts about the quality of management. Are Corporate America highly paid executives the best and brightest money can buy?

The argument can be made present-day executives have gotten to their positions not because of merit but rather because they have never disagreed with superiors. If that is the case, then what we have is a breeding ground for inept executives. This situation is analogous to a cancerous growth infecting a small part first but then spreading very quickly to cause a lot of damage. During the growth period, the malignancy may not be detected. Once it is detected, however, it needs to be removed quickly and without leaving any piece of the malignancy behind. That reflects the management situation in Corporate America today. These inept managers need to be removed to reenergize companies and to enable them to reach for the stars.

A typical corporate employee on his first day of employment is required to sign several corporate documents. The first one is a secrecy agreement binding employees to a duty to protect corporate confidential information. The second is an informational document detailing important corporate policies. That second document tells employees, in great detail, what behavior is expected as well as consequences for violating those policies. Consequences range from a simple reprimand all the way to termination of employment. Stealing, drug use, and conflicts of interests are among the reasons one typically finds as being offenses leading to termination. Furthermore, typical employees are required to devote all of their energies to the performance of corporate duties and are precluded from performing similar duties for a second employer.

The rule on conflict of interest, one would think, prevents typical corporate employees from earning a second salary or stipend from other corporations or dividing their loyalty among two or more different employers. Perhaps, this rule on conflict of interest is well grounded on the wise old saying and philosophy precluding serving two masters adequately. Engineers, for example, are on call around the clock to solve plant problems whenever necessary regardless of time of day. That rule, however, does not appear to apply to corporate executives who, on a routine basis, serve on multiple corporate boards of directors. Executives acting as directors perform duties for another employer and earn a significant amount of compensation from those outside activities.

If a corporate executive attends a board meeting at another company where he serves as a director then that executive is inaccessible to his primary employer for as long as the board meeting lasts. The primary employer of that executive is, therefore, paying for services it is not getting. The executive is, therefore, dividing his loyalty between two masters. How, then, can those executives claim that they are available at all times to conduct business for their primary employer? Have they not divided their time to the detriment of their primary master? Engineers would be fired if they were to perform any duty for another employer. Something is wrong with unequal enforcement conflict of interest rules that supposedly apply to all employees rank; it does not apply to high level executives.

If an engineer goes on assignment to another company to perform a service, that engineer is unable to collect a fee for the performance of such service. In fact, the engineer's employer may charge the second company a fee higher than the engineer earns. Why is it that executives are able to keep the fee given as payment for serving on a board other than its own corporate board and engineers are not allowed the same right? Why is the engineer unable to even get the differential between what he earns and what his company gets paid for the performance of such service under assignment from the corporation? Who is enforcing the rule? How can one executive serve two masters at the same time? This situation suggests a conflict damaging corporate interest. Why is that allowed?

Shareholders should demand corporate entities adopt strict rules precluding executives from undertaking consulting activities, including serving on outside boards of directors, for other corporations regardless of the nature of the business of those other corporations. Lawmakers are always looking for opportunities to enact new legislation; this would be fertile ground for such legislative effort. Political leaders should enact legislation to prohibit this type of activity because of the potential it has to adversely impact a broader segment of the economy. One such concern would be possibilities interactions to create monopolies and generate price-fixing ideas. Legislation should penalize corporations allowing its executives to serve on multiple corporate boards.

Table 14 lists corporate executives of some of the largest US Corporations. Look at their compensation level and the results these executives have achieved for the corporation that rewards them so generously. Pundits say it is necessary to pay high salaries to attract the best talent available. Data above tend to indicate that, contrary to expectations, high salaries attract the least qualified and most inept executives. A disconnect clearly exist between what Corporate America needs in terms of talent and in the quality of executives it gets. Corporations aim at profitability goals but it fails to explain to its executives that it means "corporate profitability and not individual profitability."

Executive	Title	Company	Severance Pay, $ Million	Impact on Company
Charles Prince	CEO	Citigroup	42+	Bankruptcy.
Edward Whitacre	CEO	ATT	158.5	ATT underperformed vs. peer group. Now at GM
Bob Nardelli	CEO	Home Depot	210	Home Depot low performer compared to Lowe
Lee Raymond	CEO	ExxonMobil	351	Declining proven oil reserves
James W. Stewart	CEO	BJ Services (Baker-Hughes)	92+	Negative stocks returns last 5 years.

Table 14 Typical Corporate America Leaders [84]

It is inconceivable to think a corporation would want to be

driven into bankruptcy protection. But, why do corporations fail to him inept executive or force them to resign or prior to reaching that result? And on top of that, companies grant failed executive large exit bonuses. Are these companies grateful for being driven into bankruptcy? Something is wrong with Corporate America in this regard.

Who evaluates executive performance in an objective manner? Who tells the CEO he is a worthless manager and leader? Shareholders are precluded from doing that because the deck is stacked in favor of the corporation and its executives; the CEO in a corporation is king. Other executives will not say anything on account of "diplomatic political correctness" and to avoid risking losing their jobs or future chances for career advancement. In other words, corporations reward mediocrity and ineptness. Certainly, it is not a good practice or in the radar screens of underlings to criticize superiors particularly those who aspire to be heirs to the CEO.

How can this situation continue to be tolerated? The present Executive-selection system is one based on political correctness encouraging ineptitude and mediocrity. Corporate executives below the CEO are always chosen for their willingness to agree with the boss! Underlings will never disagree with the boss, and the boss likes that attitude and rewards them for their loyalty. Consequently, if a thief is at the helm of the corporation then you have a bunch of co-conspirators willing to wait their turn to line their own pockets; corporate performance does not improve over the long term and major surgery is required to reverse this corporate cancerous malignancy.

The list in the table is just a sampling, and it is not meant to be all inclusive. Excluded from this listing are many other executives who are presently doing untold damage to their companies and being well compensated for performing poorly. In short, excessive executive compensation data show that measure is not a reflection of good management skills. It is merely a reflection and lack of good sense on the part of a mismanaged company without direction.

Also excluded from the listing are executives who truly deserve to be paid more than they are presently getting because the corporation is benefiting greatly from their services. There are many executives within Corporate America who are literally worth their weight in gold. One such executive is Steve Jobs of Apple, Inc. There are others executives who really outperform for the companies and its shareholders and yet their compensation is not alarming. Corporate America really needs higher caliber executives to lead it away from the road to collapse.

There is nothing wrong about compensating executives for a job well done and for improving corporate profitability. Perhaps guidelines can be developed to determine reasonable levels of executive compensation. These guidelines should take into consideration contributions made by executives in pursuing efficiency, reducing production costs, growth, and profitability improvements over the long term rather than the immediate short term, which usually means that only the executive benefits. Executive compensation guidelines should reflect a relationship between salaries paid to typical employees of the company and that paid to executives. This proposal would recognize that profitability is not the result of a single individual but rather the achievement of a team. Both typical employees and executives contribute to the welfare of the company. Corporations work on team basis, and the salaries of the team members should be proportionate to their duties. Perhaps the fairest way to determine executive compensation would be to determine an average salary among all company employees and reward executives by paying them a multiple of that salary average; that method would recognize contributions made by all employees and assign a multiple of that average on the basis responsibility and achievement of results.

The list of executives in Table 14 is not all inclusive but rather a representative group among those who are considered "too valuable and overpaid" by Corporate America. Most of these executives are failures in terms of corporate results, and, yet, Corporate America rewards them handsomely and continues to argue that they must be highly compensated to prevent losing them. If that's a true reflection of Corporate America's attitude toward executive compensation, then the logical conclusion is that Corporate America is in trouble and in need of immediate corrective action to prevent it from its own destruction. Perhaps some of these highly paid and valuable executives should be exported to China, as a form of foreign aid, to help Chinese companies.

As evidence of their true worth, it is worthwhile to focus on the testimony of Mr. Charles Prince—former CEO of Citigroup—and Mr. Jack Rubin—a member of the board of directors of Citigroup and former US Treasury Secretary. These highly paid executives are unwilling to accept responsibility for failures at Citigroup and admit they had nothing to do with that. In view of that, one wonders if these executives would have had an issue accepting payment for the performance of their duties at Citigroup. Their testimony tends to relieve them of all responsibility on the basis they have been unaware of any and all activities going on at Citigroup; that is hard to swallow. How then can they accept payment and a bonus check for doing something they are not even aware they are doing? Either they are a bunch of liars or are complete idiots. Something is wrong with the system when you allow the situation at Citigroup to go on unpunished and, at the same time, sentence a person to fifty years in prison for stealing the equivalent of two dollars worth of milk to feed his children. And, yet the US government rescues Citigroup from financial disaster but does nothing to help the individual stealing milk for his children. Using the logic advanced by these executives, lawmakers should be rewarded with a vacation in jail for not imposing conditions on the Citigroup rescue package.

It is more likely, however, that executives and their underlings are the ones holding Corporate America hostage. That would explain why US corporations fail to dismiss these inept and corrupt executives. Given the record of abuse in executive compensation and less than stellar corporate performance, it is apparent that something needs to change to correct the situation preventing dismissal of these inept executives. It is incumbent, therefore, on all of us as stockholders, employees, and American citizens to end this situation. How can this be done?

It can simply be done by exercising our rights to change political and corporate leaders through the power of our votes and consumer dollars. We can change our spending habits to achieve what corporate executives are unable or unwilling to do. And, in so doing, we can force a change on corporate culture and get rid of these inept egomaniacs. This simple action will prevent the downfall of Corporate America and the loss of our country's technical and commercial preeminence in the world. Similarly we can use our power to vote to get rid of corrupt and inept lawmakers and regulators.

Let's briefly highlight some of the contributions made by these highly paid executives. Mr. Charles Prince is the CEO most responsible for driving Citigroup to the brink of bankruptcy. He is the CEO who caused many Citigroup's shareholders to lose their life's savings. He is the one who saw many of Citigroup's employees lose their livelihood. In short, Mr. Prince is one of those failed bank executives considered among the leading architects of the financial meltdown of the economy. He and other CEOs of the largest and most respected banks in the US and in the world were driving their institutions to the edge of bankruptcy. The US government unwisely stepped in to save those failed institutions and rewarded their inept leaders. The US government bailed out the institutions and made it possible for the executives to be rewarded by getting their hands on bailout funds. Despite being unable to steer Citigroup away from economic disaster and potential collapse, Prince was well compensated and rewarded for very poor performance. But compared to others on the list his compensation package is a bargain.

Edward Whitacre was the CEO at AT&T, which was an underperforming company as compared to its industrial peers and the Standard & Poor 500 Index. In fact, AT&T stock prices failed to appreciate during his tenure and, at one point, AT&T stock traded at a level equivalent to 67 percent of the value of the company. [85] Mr. Whitacre was rewarded with a very generous retirement package. In fact, he was even rewarded by the US government by being named to lead the rescue of GM for the benefit of taxpayers.

305

Would taxpayers be able to get better results from Mr. Whitacre at GM than he provided to AT&T? Based on his AT&T performance, taxpayers would end up getting the wrong end of the stick. What was the real reason for nominating Mr. Whitacre to rescue GM when he could not do the same for AT&T? Perhaps the real reason was that Mr. Whitacre contributed heavily to the Democratic Party or because US government's officials believed GM was moribund and needed to be put out of its misery. Certainly, the appointment was not based on merit.

Robert Nardelli's tenure as Home Depot CEO resulted in the loss of market share, alienation of executives, and the downplaying of customer service. Home Depot became a retailing powerhouse on the strength of its customer service; therefore, downplaying customer service and eliminating employees was tantamount to killing the goose that laid the golden egg. It was, therefore, not unexpected that moves initiated by Mr. Nardelli would significantly reduce market share. Consequently, Home Depot's stock price languished, and the company underperformed as compared to Lowe's. The board of directors, nevertheless, provided him with an excellent and unreasonable compensation package to get rid of Mr. Nardelli. The board of directors should have followed Mr. Nardelli out the door. [86] Mr. Nardelli had the dubious distinction of being named one of the "Worst American CEOs of All Times" by CNBC. [87]

Mr. Lee Raymond's compensation package from ExxonMobil clearly indicated that executive compensation is being abused and out of control. Is that not a fact? His retirement package amounted to a golden parachute of unimaginable proportions. Was it a fair in terms of Mr. Raymond's contribution to ExxonMobil? The answer was a definite and unqualified "no." ExxonMobil based its reward to Mr. Raymond on the strength of 2005 profits amounting to approximately $36 billion. The relevant issue was not the magnitude of the profits but rather Mr. Raymond's contribution to generating those profits. It would be fair to say that Mr. Raymond had nothing to do with the magnitude of those profits; those profits were due to a 50 percent increase in the selling price of oil and natural gas. Luckily, Mr. Raymond was not at ExxonMobil when the prices of oil and gas declined shortly after his departure. The tragedy behind this obscene salary was that, during Mr. Raymond's tenure, ExxonMobil proven reserves of natural gas and oil declined. Would a reasonable person, investor, or employee believe that ExxonMobil's future would be brighter after his departure? It would be more likely that they would conclude that ExxonMobil's future was cloudy at best. On second thought, if the price of oil had decreased, then Mr. Raymond would have been equally well rewarded for not allowing oil prices to go down further!

Mr. James W. Stewart's contributions to his corporation, Baker Hughes, are negative returns that eventually would have driven the company into bankruptcy. His contributions are nothing more than admission tickets to bankruptcy court. And, if that's not the case then those negative returns represent cheating on income tax returns. In any event, those returns should have triggered alarms and raised questions about this executive within the company Board of Directors. Two questions come to mind. How can the Board Directors not be aware of these results and fire this loser? The other question is why the Board of Directors rewards this inept executive with such a generous retirement package? The retirement package given to this inept executive is not commensurate with his contributions unless company it is meant to reward ineptitude. The Board of Directors as a unit and individually should be held liable to shareholders for breach of a duty owed to shareholders to ensure oversight of performance. In view of this continuous stream of negative returns, the company should have fired Mr. Stewart and every single member of the board.

Executive compensation has two components or elements: a base salary and a bonus based on meeting or exceeding a set of predefined corporate performance criteria. In most cases, the predefined criteria include such things as return on investment, profit margin, stock price, and others measurements. Executives become eligible for bonuses and other benefits if and only if they achieve these performance criteria. In Baker Hughes' case, the criteria included to go out of business and waste shareholders money.

In some cases, stock price may be included as an objective to meet to get a performance bonus. This objective may be met in several different ways. The preferred method would be one due to successes in company financial and operating performance that attracts attention from market forces and result in a price increase. An alternate method is for the company to purchase its own shares of stock in the open market to reduce the number of shares in the market; this stock purchase causes the remaining shares of stock to increase in price. Companies normally buy shares of their own stock with excess capital on hand because management considers prevailing market price to be on the low side; management considers this to be a good investment. The net effect of this stock transaction is to increase the price of the company stock. There is nothing wrong with this practice, but the practice may achieve indirectly what could not be achieved directly, i.e., performance excellence. Nevertheless, this practice may provide a means for executives to manipulate stock prices for their financial benefit.

Mr. James Mulva, ConocoPhillips's CEO, stresses reliance on financial returns. [88] He proposes to sell assets to generate cash for the purpose of buying back shares of stock, thus artificially inflating share prices and thereby rewarding shareholders with the profit generated by the higher stock prices. This rhetoric sounds good, but what is the real impact of this decision? First of all, stock prices increase in the short-term as a result of selling oil and gas production acreage, reserves, or properties. The long-term impact is a reduction in company value resulting from lower oil and gas reserves. The CEO benefits because now stock prices are within the acceptable range triggering a bonus award. The CEO gets his bonus award in terms of restricted stock that he can sell upon retirement or satisfying some other condition. He then goes ahead and sells some shares of stock and makes a large profit and then retires. At that point he could care less what happens to the corporation. The point is that this CEO cares only about his own benefit regardless of impact on ConocoPhillips. The stockholders now realize a short benefit upon selling the shares of stock, but they will fail to realize long-term benefits from owning ConocoPhillips shares of stock.

Taking that logic to an extreme, it becomes apparent that destroying a company is a very easy task and those executives are being rewarded for doing exactly that. In view of that, what does the future hold for Corporate America? More importantly, what does the future look like for Corporate America's employees? How does this type of activity impact our nation?

How is executive compensation determined? It is simply based on the "You scratch my back and I'll scratch yours" principle. This principle simply states that compensation is not based on merit but on the "good ole boy" network, which is alive and well entrenched in the higher echelons of Corporate America. This system works simply by nominating outside directors to an executive compensation committee. These outside directors are supposed to show a degree of fairness and independence, but the facts are different.

Executives from one company become directors at multiple companies, which directly enhance their compensation as previously discussed. They become outside directors to that second company and are eligible to serve on the compensation committee. Now, here is where a conflict of interest arises. The executive from the first company invites his counterparts from the second company where he serves as an outside director to become a board of director member at his company, and very likely will serve as a member of the executive compensation committee. Do you think either executive will vote to reduce the compensation of any of his corporate executive buddies? Do you get an idea how the good ole boy system works to the detriment of Corporate America? Who has the right to complain about this fraudulent corporate behavior? It looks like these directors have a very intricate and workable arrangement to manipulate executive compensation. This corrupt and unethical behavior goes on unchallenged in Corporate America, and there is no way to legislatively prohibit it, because of the bribes passed on to politicians by friendly corporate lobbyists.

What's even more outrageous than the simple determination of a salary and bonus target as guidelines for corporate executive compensation is the recent trends in compensation committee decisions to award cash [89] rather than shares of stocks or share options for good performance. Cash awards remove all risks of stock-price fluctuations leading to reductions for the executive. In other words, the compensation committee actions really represent a bias for executives, disregarding all risks for the corporation. Does that give you a warm feeling about the continuing viability of Corporate America? Is that not the ultimate reflection of loyalty under the "you scratch my back and I'll scratch yours" principle? Who is going to win and who is going to be the loser?

We as shareholders and citizens have more power than we think to eliminate abuses we are currently witnessing in the political as well as the corporate arenas. That power is based on casting our votes, which unfortunately not many of us do. First of all, we can effect corporate change by first reforming the political system. We cannot cause corporate change unless we reform our political system. Why is that?

Politicians enact legislation to regulate corporate behavior. Corporate America, in turn, bribes politicians ensuring passage of favorable laws. The flip side precludes enactment of laws that are considered unfavorable to the corporate sector because the do not want to bite the hands that feeds them regardless of impact on constituents. Therefore, our votes and actually voting are the only weapons at our disposal to effect political and corporate change, which is essential to improve our society and our individual wellbeing.

Our political votes should be used to replace incumbents in every election. Consumer spending is our economic weapon against corporate abuses. Shareholders also have the weapon of voting against proposed corporate slate of directors and also corporate proposals. Keeping in mind that corporate votes are stacked against shareholders and in favor of management, it is essential that all shareholders vote and that the majority vote against the proposed slate.

Despite recent financial conditions leading to an economic meltdown, executives' compensation packages have continued to increase. It seems nothing causes a reduction in the amount received by executives in terms of bonuses. Executive compensation appears to be independent of company performance. It is independent of company economic condition and the nation's economic difficulties and immune to collapsing stock prices. It seems that executives' compensation packages are immune to everything. In fact, one wonders if driving a company to bankruptcy would be grounds for enhancing compensation packages for executives.

The compensation package of some CEOs increased over 50 percent from 2008 to 2009 despite prevailing unemployment rates in excess of 10 percent, greater than 50 percent reduction in stock prices, greater than 50 percent reduction in the Dow Industrial Average, greater than 40 percent losses in the value of 401(k) plans employees rely on for retirement, and reductions in company valuation exceeding 40 percent. Executive compensation is not only excessive but obscene. It indicates that the system used in determining executive compensation is broken and in need of urgent repairs to be reformed.

Despite high cost of corporate executive retirement packages, it has become customary for retiring executives to continue to demand continuation of fringe benefits beyond normal retirement. Many retired corporate executives demand and get free tickets to sports and cultural events and, at times, air transportation. When do these abuses end? When is the corporate umbilical cord cut off? It is morally repugnant to see these former executives continue to milk the corporation for the last penny. Is it possible that, at some point, corporations would become liable for the funeral expenses of their retired executives? How about continuing the obligation to provide free tickets to sports and cultural events for the surviving spouses, children, and grandchildren? When do these abuses end?

CORPORATE COST CUTTING

Corporate America has become obsessed with cost cutting since the mid-1980s. The declared motivation behind these campaigns is to enhance corporate profitability, a laudable goal. But results of these exercises indicate the real motivation is personnel reductions rather than an improvement in profitability.

Profitability depends on many different factors including raw material consumption, utilities usage, labor costs, sales volume, and many others factors. There is no question that cost cutting is a worthwhile exercise that should always be on the minds of everyone in the corporation. That is a necessary activity to enhance efficiency and ensure long-term corporate viability. But, the methodology used in pursuing cost-reduction activities has been wrong. Most corporations have focused exclusively on reducing labor costs without improving the efficiency of the process or operation. Employee reductions result in a minuscule cost reduction, but the operation continues just as inefficient as it was before the cut in personnel. In other words, labor costs are a very small part of the total cost picture. As a result, Corporate America fails to achieve its cost-reduction goal. In fact, it can be argued that every corporation that has reduced personnel to cut cost has shot itself in the foot by cutting off the source and flow of ideas generated by its employees. Employees are the ones who provide ideas leading to real cost reductions and efficiency improvements, and they are being eliminated.

Cuts in R&D spending and reductions in technical and plant operating personnel are also damaging to corporations. Each of these groups has a very important role to play—R&D develops new products, technical staffs develop manufacturing processes, and operating personnel improve manufacturing operations by discovering unused capacity inherent in operating equipment to improve efficiency. What are the consequences of personnel cuts? The consequences are no improvements in operation, no new products, and a greater potential for industrial accidents.

R&D benefits are reflected in many cases in the number of

innovations produced. Innovations are normally protected by applying for patents. It is worth noting Corporate America has been granted fewer than half of the total number of US patents issued in the last couple of years. [90] It may be argued that patents are not a valid indicator of future profitability, which may be true to some extent. That may be due in part to the fact that many patents do not really represent a viable product or describe an entire manufacturing process or, for that matter, represent something that is of commercial value. On the other hand, there are patents that are considered very valuable such as for example patents on compositions of matter and typical products such as Nylon. It is also true that many corporations prefer to avoid the cost of patenting and, instead, choose to protect their technological developments by keeping them secret. The trend, however, represents a change from a historical perspective indicating, more likely than not, a real change in corporate attitude toward R&D—to less R&D.

There are many valid reasons for choosing patenting over secrecy as a means of protecting technological developments. A patent is valid only for a certain period of time (twenty years) and after that period the technological jewel belongs in the public domain and anybody can practice the invention. On the other hand, relying on secrecy is risky for once the secret is disclosed it can no longer be protected.

Relying on secrecy to protect intellectual property can be extremely risky and costly over the long run. A fired DuPont employee [91] has recently been convicted of selling proprietary information pertaining to the Kevlar manufacturing process to a South Korean company—Kolon Industries Inc. Kevlar is a fiber five times stronger than steel. It is used in applications ranging from body armor to brake pads. It is a billion-dollar business for DuPont. Now, the South Korean company is manufacturing a product similar to Kevlar and competing with DuPont's Kevlar. Obviously, this represents a very significant loss for DuPont. The guilty ex-DuPont employee has been sentenced to eighteen months in prison and ordered to pay approximately $186,000 in restitution to DuPont. Is that a sufficient amount to make DuPont whole?

Possibly not, but that's all DuPont is going to get. This case clearly illustrates that once the horse is out of the barn there is nothing else one can do to bring it back or reclaim the loss. The South Korean company has capitalized on DuPont's loss very quickly.

Corporations have several strategic reasons for pursuing patent applications. It may be that corporations want to protect new products, processes, or designs. The intent may be to keep competitors away from a field of interest to the corporation or to force a competitor to spend money unnecessarily on a worthless pursuit. Regardless of the philosophical reasons for seeking patent protection, it is more likely than not that Corporate America has received fewer patents as a direct result of reductions in R&D expenditures than of any other cause. Reductions in R&D lead to fewer patentable technological achievements and newer products. If that's the case, then there are bad implications for the future of Corporate America's profitability. Foreign competitors continue to spend on R&D, and these efforts will be, and are, rewarded in terms of future profitability. The bad omen in this picture is that US corporations are facing a very real threat from foreign competitors challenging its future technical leadership. It is preferable and cheaper for companies to lead rather than follow.

Technical staffs have been reduced significantly in the past twenty years or so. These reductions have adversely impacted the number of students pursuing scientific and engineering educations. This means that the future supply of qualified scientists and engineers available to Corporate America will not be sufficient to support corporate growth. This, in turn, will prevent Corporate America from revitalizing itself once it realizes how it has shot itself in the foot. US corporations will have to rely on immigration to fill the gap in the number of engineers required to satisfy the demand.

Engineering is the one discipline relied upon by developing and developed nations to improve manufacturing, reduce operating costs, and lead the way to real economic development and growth. Developing nations realize the importance of engineers, but Corporate America prefers to get rid of engineers and rely on financial gimmicks that lead nowhere. Developed nations, including the US, have achieved their present status based on engineering developments, and the US still needs engineering to continue and maintain its development status. Corporate America, however, fails to realize that its future is closely linked to engineering developments to advance on its developing journey. An adequate supply of engineers is a necessity in order to sustain corporate profitability and ensure that the US remains preeminent on a worldwide basis.

Corporate America shot itself in the foot many times and now regrets the adverse consequences of its actions. A case in point is the situation many multinational oil companies are experiencing. Oil prices have more than doubled in the period from 1976 to 1980 as a result of an oil embargo against the US. Consequently, oil companies have become very profitable. These higher oil prices justify large expenditures to explore, find, and produce more oil, thus increasing reserves and future profitability. As a result, oil companies increase the hiring of oil exploration professionals and engineers. When oil prices decline, oil companies react by reducing the number of trained professionals in many scientific and engineering fields to reduce costs. Reduction in demand for technical personnel impacts college enrollment particularly those who are pursuing scientific and engineering careers. Undoubtedly, oil prices will increase but available personnel is now limited.

Terminated employees have to work to earn a living to support their families. They pursue employment opportunities with national oil companies and exploration service companies taking with them all the knowledge base multinational oil companies rely to make new discoveries and develop efficient methods of commercial l oil production in the first place. Executives in the multinational oil companies fail to realize these employees, and not the corporation, are the ones finding oil as well as developing new oil exploration and production concepts. Corporations would be unable to find and produce one drop of oil unless they have access to a technically competent staff. In fact, employees are the keepers and developers of the corporate technological portfolio. In short, companies lose their know-how when they terminate technical professionals. Financiers running these multinational companies and advocating cost reductions never realize the extent of their loss until it is too late to recover.

Multinational oil companies approached national oil companies to offer expertise in oil exploration in exchange for a share of the oil production or oil field. These multinational oil companies were turned down by the national oil companies. The multinationals were rejected on account of being able to get similar expertise from terminated employees and service companies without the need to share oil production. Those employees that were terminated by multinational oil companies were now employed by national oil companies and service companies. It was no longer necessary for national oil companies to share ownership of producing field with multinational companies. Consequently, multinationals oil companies found very few opportunities for exploration and complained about being unable to expand exploration acreage. Multinational oil companies created the means that came back to haunt and prevent them from getting exploration acreage. Similar situations were faced in other industries, but not to the same extent as multinational oil companies. These companies dug their own graves when they failed to recognize the value of their professional staffs and decided to terminate them.

Another consequence of cost reductions is a higher incidence of accidents occurring in chemical plants and refineries. These accidents have resulted in loss of many lives and damage to private property and the environment. The root cause of these accidents is twofold; operating manufacturing plants with very lean staffs and fatigue. Operating staffs are forced to focus on too many activities, ignoring smaller details that are essential to maintain a safe operating environment. It can also be attributed to unqualified contract maintenance employees doing unfamiliar and dangerous activities and bypassing established operating and maintenance procedures specific to the chemical or refining process to safely complete the work. This is not limited to oil refineries and chemical companies; it also applies to other industries.

Corporate cost-cutting campaigns without exception focus on getting rid of people. In particular, they get rid of older people earning the higher salaries. But, those older highly compensated people are the ones who know the most about the operation and have the most experience about safe operation. Consequently, the ones remaining are those who are less experienced and more prone to overlook or ignore details that lead to industrial accidents. Older, experienced people can easily recognize problems that younger, inexperienced people often ignore; those are the little things that converge into a situation ripe for an accident.

Toyota Motors recently had a massive recall of approximately 8 million cars. It forced Toyota to stop all manufacturing facilities and sales operations in order to focus all of its efforts on repairing customers' cars. This was a very expensive alternative for the manufacturer continued to pay wages to all workers without receiving any income. It was also expensive in terms of the damage caused to Toyota's quality reputation and the loss in market share with bad repercussions for future profitability. Toyota lost its market dominance as its market share decreased by approximately 40 percent. The total loss suffered by Toyota as a result of this incident would amount to hundreds of millions of dollars. On top of that, it had to offer rebates of at least $1,000, a first for Toyota, off the price of each car in order to revitalize sales. Rebates of this magnitude would add more hundreds of millions of dollars to the cost. In total, Toyota's loss in this episode would be in the range of billions of dollars. All of this loss was due to cost cutting. [92] It was something that could have been avoided if Toyota had not kept on insisting on annual cost reductions from suppliers.

Jim Press, who was Toyota top US Executive, became concerned about the impact cost cutting was having on vehicle quality and expressed that feeling to Toyota's top management in Japan. But his warning fell on deaf ears. Toyota continued on the path to further growth that demanded additional cost reductions from its parts suppliers. Eventually, the demand for additional cost cutting had an impact on product quality, leading to premature mechanical failures and resulting in customer's complaints. Mr. Press expressed his frustration at a recent interview with Bloomberg News by saying: "The root cause of their problems is that the company was hijacked, some years ago, by anti-(Toyoda) family, financially oriented pirates" [93]

Did Toyota benefit from this cost cutting exercise? The answer was clearly no, but the damage was already done. One thing differentiating Toyota from other automobile producers was the recognition of its mistake and its apology to purchasers of its vehicles. Time would tell whether Toyota would be able to recover its market share. But, one thing was for sure and that was that Toyota incurred significant expenses in recovering from this cost-cutting exercise. The total cost of that exercise would be overwhelming. In fact, it would very likely exceed the savings by a very wide margin. Only Toyota would be able to tell if the value of this cost cutting exercise exceeded the damages it faced.

Mr. Press's statement raises several important points not only relevant to Toyota but also to other American corporations in general. How many companies within the Corporate America umbrella have been hijacked by these "financially oriented pirates" and been run down? How many of these corporations have faced or are facing bankruptcy and extinction because of these financiers? Has Corporate America learned anything to stay away from the next round of bankruptcy filings?

Toyota faced a disaster caused by technical problems not clearly understood or fully resolved. It recognized that this disaster could have been prevented by maintaining its focus on engineering quality rather than on demanding more cost reductions from parts suppliers. It was acceptable to reduce parts cost but not at the expense of quality or parts performance. Continuous cost reduction demands from manufacturers to parts suppliers would not only reduce cost, but also would reduce quality. The cost of the part was commensurate with what goes into the part to make it functional and that in not would influence parts cost. The financial impact of the crisis Toyota faced were definitely very high. And the resulting lawsuits from unhappy customers would add even more cost to Toyota's balance sheet. It was estimated that the total cost impact to Toyota would be in the range of $3 billion.

Anyone who has ever been employed by a corporation within

the past twenty to thirty years recognizes cost reduction patterns followed by corporate entities. The pattern is the same in the corporate field regardless of activity or management style; this makes one wonder whether it is a message learned from business school professors or business consultants preaching the same message to management engaged in different corporate endeavors.

The first step is done with great fanfare and includes the CEO announcing the company would undertake an exercise aimed at reducing cost. The CEO provides details as to the amount of cost reduction expected and how it would be achieved. In all cases, the company offers a severance package amounting to a payment of one or two weeks for every year of service to the company; this is a cost to the company. The CEO announces that it needs a given number of volunteers willing to take the severance package and leave the company by not later than a designated date. Notice the CEO always knows the amount of cost reduction the company has to achieve. The CEO appears to know every detail about the operation, but when an accident happens he knows absolutely nothing about the cost to the company. He will also be the provider of good news indicating those early projections have been achieved. But, there is no independent verification of claims or data to substantiate achieving the initial cost reductions goals.

What happens in these cost reductions situations? Typically the best people, mainly those who are sure of their capabilities and competence, accept the severance package and go on to find another position at a different company. The company also design severance packages to attract older, more experienced and higher paid individuals because that action has the most impact on the cost-cutting exercise. People who remain behind are the less competent people who are not completely sure they will be able to find a position at a different company or those who are basically the "yes" men who are basically politicians; they know for sure they are unqualified to perform any useful work other than shout to the boss: "How great thou art!."

Bear in mind, a company incurs a significant initial expense in getting rid of these employees. Do corporations ever recover that initial expense? If you believe the CEO, corporations always recover that expense. But, then, another cost cutting situation is announced because the first one is not enough to achieve the total cost reduction the company required. Does that make you suspicious about the real outcome from the first exercise?

The company gets the designated number of volunteers and, once again, retains the least productive and qualified people; this basically dooms the company. Executives do not recognize the fallacy of these cost-reduction exercises and the adverse consequences these activities have on the company. Those same executives are not even able to determine if anticipated savings are achieved, and for sure they fail to tell the troops or shareholders whether anticipated reductions are achieved. If asked about these reductions, executives would always indicate the exercise is successful. In many cases, anticipated savings never materialize. But the cost of the severance package is something that cannot be denied; in many cases that severance cost exceeds savings anticipated or obtained. But, who cares? Certainly, executives do not care because it is not their money.

Has anybody ever heard an executive admit failure of cost-cutting exercise? If that were true then it would be a rare and unexpected admission. Toyota Motors, however, may be the first company admitting failure in its cost-cutting drive. Perhaps, it would be desirable for other corporations to learn from Toyota and tell shareholders the real outcome of their cost-cutting exercises. Regardless of results for the corporation, executives declare success and reward themselves. When the corporation finds the results are not positive, it has no resort to any remedy for the executives have already cashed on their bonuses and are now happily retired or milking another company.

Another subtle but real problem arising out of cost-reduction exercises is the impact on retention of older and experienced personnel. There is no question that, in general, the earning capacity of any person increases with experience and age. As Corporate America focuses its cost reductions on number of employees, it becomes apparent that older employees are the highest paid and therefore the more likely to be terminated or severed from the company's employee roster. The higher the compensation, the more difficult it is to find employment. It is for that reason that anybody older than forty-five or fifty years old experiences difficulties in finding adequate employment. It does happen but it takes time. Older employees are selling their knowledge, and it takes a while to find a buyer for that knowledge. Corporate America simply does not value the experience older employees bring to the table; the less-experienced employees tend to get into more operating difficulties that potentially could cause accidents. And, if the truth were told, it would be apparent that the older and higher-paid employees provide better, faster, and cheaper solutions to problems than younger, less-experienced people.

In many instances, Corporate America soon realizes it needs the experienced people it has severed. In that situation, Corporate America rehires them under contract; this action calls into question the judgment of corporate executives. Former experienced employees come back earning the same or higher salary. Where are the savings in this picture? It appears that Corporate America and its executives really do not know what is required to make the corporation tick.

Most, if not all, corporate cost-cutting drives end up reducing the number of employees at the company. This reduction in has a deleterious impact on employees who remain employed. The reason is obvious. Those who remain must do their assigned duties and also do the work of those who were laid off. In other words, the same work has to be done, but fewer employees are available to do it. This additional workload leads to stress and eventually impacts workers' morale and health. There is another consequence to overworked personnel, which is the adverse impact on operating safety. It is a fact that overworked workers are less alert or attentive to safety; cutting corners is the result, thus maximizing risks for dangerous situations to occur. Loss of life and damage to property and the environment are the results, as has been clearly demonstrated.

Corporate executives point to productivity improvements resulting from reductions in force. It is true that the work gets done. Consequently, more work is being done by fewer workers. That, by definition, is an improvement in worker productivity. Is that productivity enhancement a lasting or temporary benefit? It is a temporary benefit that lasts until overworked personnel leave their jobs. Workers get frustrated and do the additional work during hard economic times to continue earning a living to support their families. When the economic situation turns around, those so-called "more productive workers" leave the company to pursue other employment opportunities. Then, the company has to hire and train new workers, and these new workers are not as productive as the ones who left voluntarily. Consequently, worker productivity plunges. On top of that, new workers have to be trained, thus forcing companies to spend significant amount of resources on training.

There have been several newspapers and magazine articles reporting results of surveys on workers' satisfaction with their present employers. These results indicate more than 50 percent of presently employed workers will leave their present employers when economic conditions improve. This is bad news for Corporate America for it means that Corporate America will not be as productive as expected and that will adversely impact the production cost picture.

In short, results from typical cost-cutting exercises undertaken by US companies have failed to reduce production costs over the long term. But, corporate executives are not interested in the long-term wellbeing of the company; they are interested only in short-term results that provide a justification to enhance their bonus awards. Those corporate executives get their bonuses and leave the resulting mess to somebody else to fix. The mess is addressed by another crop of executives incapable of solving the problem leading to the conclusion that operating cost is too high and the company must relocate to a foreign country to survive. This is one factor contributing to the destruction of Corporate America and making it less competitive on a worldwide basis. There is nothing wrong with Corporate America except its inept management. Replace management, and things will improve in much the same way improvements are achieved by replacing the coach of a losing athletic team with a more competent coach; notice that the same players stay, and often the team begins to win more games.

LEVERAGED BUYOUTS (LBOS) AND MERGERS

Leveraged buyouts (LBOs) and corporate mergers are two means used by Corporate America to get rid of competitors. These are very destructive mechanisms that amount to declarations of corporate war among competing corporate entities. Only one of these battling companies survives this corporate battle, but the victor survives with financial wounds threatening its own survival. The result to society as a whole is very costly in terms of closing manufacturing facilities, leading to loss of job opportunities and unemployment. In many cases, the costs to the victor of this corporate war are considerable, for it results in a large financial burden that the surviving company may not be able to overcome in a short period of time. In fact, the survivor may end up limping along slowly on the road to bankruptcy or another merger.

In a typical LBO, a corporate buyer secures funding for the purpose of acquiring a corporation using loans and high-yield bonds. The key here is securing a loan, but that loan will have to be ultimately repaid causing financial hardships. Corporate targets for LBOs are typically companies that have steady and stable cash flows, valuable corporate assets in terms of plants, equipment, and valuable real estate but depressed stock prices. In the opinion of the acquirer, stock prices of the acquired entity do not reflect the true value of the corporation when corporate assets are taken into consideration.

Furthermore, the acquiring company sees huge potential opportunities for substantial cost reductions that may or may be realized. In other words, companies that do not show their true value in financial terms or who fail to load their balance sheet with excess debt become targets for takeovers. The acquiring party risks very little of its own money to make the acquisition. It premises principal and interest loan payments due on cash flows of the acquired company. In other words, the acquired company is saddled with acquisition debt, and all risk is on that company; bear in mind that prior to the acquisition the acquired company may have been a profitable debt-free company. Interest rates become an important factor on the outcome of the LBO.

There were many LBOs in the 1980s, particularly in the second half of the decade. In that decade, interest rates, were represented by prime rate and appeared to be declining and so was the inflation rate as shown in Figure 27. Prime rate, as used herein, is the interest rate charged by banks to their most creditworthy customers. Obviously, less creditworthy customers pay higher rates. In this case, prime rate is used as a reference point for the sake of this discussion.

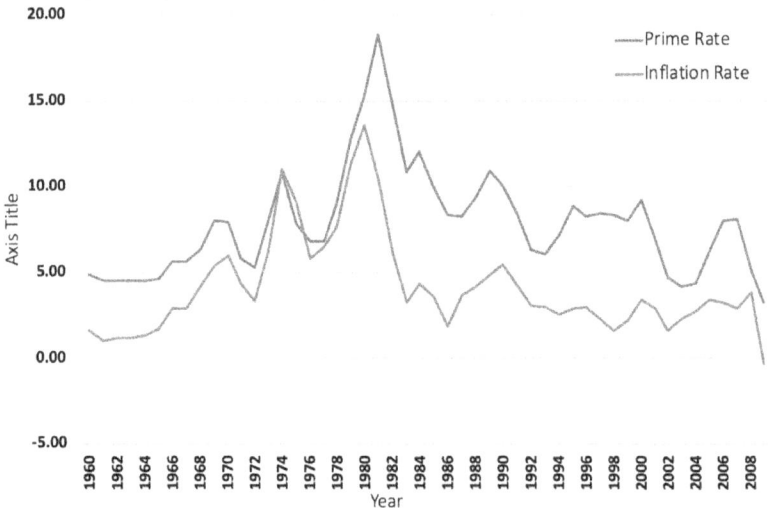

Figure 27. Inflation [94] and Prime Rates. [95]

LBO promoters secure financing for the buyout using a combination of loans and issuance of high-yield bonds. The high-yield bonds are sold to investors who immediately realize a high return based on interest rate paid by the bond; this is particularly true if the bond interest rate is higher than prevailing interest rates. Bondholders realize a second benefit in the situation in which prevailing interest rates show a declining trend; this is so because bond value increases with declining interest rates. Let's illustrate this inverse relationship between bond value and interest rate with a simple example.

Assume a $10,000 bond is issued, paying an interest rate of 8 percent per year; these values are fixed until bond maturity. This means the bondholder gets $800 per year worth of interest. Now assume interest rates increase to 10 percent per year causing the 8 percent bond owner to want to get more interest on his $10,000 original investment. What can he do? He can sell the bond. But, the new buyer wants to get 10 percent return on his investment, meaning that the bond value would have to be $8,000 instead of $10,000, i.e., 10 percent of $8,000 equals the original interest payable under the existing terms of the bond which is unchangeable. This is so because bondholders cannot arbitrarily change the terms of the bond but rather they must change the value of the bond to reflect actual market conditions. When interest rates decline bond value increases.

What happened in the case of many of LBOs in the 1980s was that as long as the interest rates were declining everyone was happy, because the value of the bond was increasing. But, the Federal Reserve Bank (the Fed) began to increase interest rates to rein in inflation starting around 1988. That increase in interest rate caused problems for everyone involved. The company now had to refinance at a higher interest rate, thereby increasing its costs. The bondholder, on the other hand, faced a reduction in the value of his bond if he were to sell it. In many cases, the company could not absorb this added cost, because it was loaded with debt and its cash flow was insufficient to support that level of debt at the higher interest rate.

The only easy thing to do was to sell assets or reduce cost by reducing personnel. Notice the impact on the unemployment rate caused by LBOs in the 1980s and the Fed action with respect to controlling inflation as shown in Figure 28. Notice that this increase in unemployment coincided with the rise in prime rate around 1988. Assets the company could sell were the best and most valuable assets, which caused the company to retain its lower-value assets, thus diminishing the true worth of the corporation. Taken to their logical conclusion, LBOs became very destructive financial gimmicks. This was the situation experienced by Pan American World Airways as it dismembered itself by selling the most valuable pieces of the company and retaining the worthless pieces of the company that could not be given away.

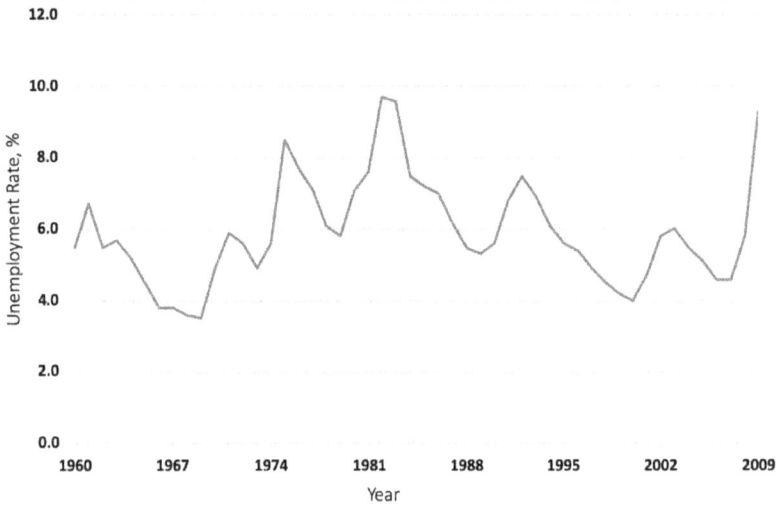

Figure 28. Annual Unemployment Rate. [96]

A typical procedures followed in LBO transactions include a promoter approaching a corporation and disclosing intentions to take over the corporation. At that point, one of two things happens. In the first instance, the corporation declines to accept the takeover offer and attempts to pays off the LBO promoter a certain amount of money to compensate him for his efforts and to keep corporate management in place. In the second case, the corporation is taken over by the LBO promoter and then is saddled with the entire debt incurred in the buyout. In many cases, this action forces the corporation to sell assets and reduce staff. Since the promoter has very little capital at risk, the risk is totally on the target corporation and the benefits are all for the LBO promoter. There are many examples of corporations that have failed or gone bankrupt as a result of LBOs such as Federated Department Stores, Revco Drug Stores, and many others.

A business merger, on the other hand, is another destructive mechanism promoted by financiers or by internal company executives to acquire or combine one corporate entity with another. It is used for several different purposes, including growth, expanding product range, overcoming weaknesses, or eliminating competitors. The success rate of mergers and acquisitions is very low. In fact, some studies peg the failure rate at 50 to 70 percent, which reflects a very poor track record indeed. [97] Despite low success rate, mergers and acquisitions activity has increased over the past twenty years, primarily to satisfy demands from Wall Street financiers for higher corporate revenues and profits.

What is the real motivation behind LBOs and mergers? Why such a low success rate? Those are very important questions. For the financier the advantages are obvious—when he risks very little and stands to make a substantial amount of money in commissions, payoffs, or profits from the corporations involved in these transactions.

Companies undertake mergers based on a variety of reasons. In many instances, companies looking to expand look at view competitors as a means of achieving a growth goal either by adding new products or simply by getting the market share of that competitor. In other cases, companies merge to balance or complement product lines of each individual company. Finally, mergers occur to eliminate a weakness in the acquiring company. In any case, high mergers failure rate indicates that mergers are consummated without extensive knowledge of the attributes of the acquired company.

Upon completion of the merger, market share and revenue stream of the combined company are larger than those of the individual companies. Profit margin, however, does not necessary increase in a manner commensurate with the larger revenue stream. As a result, the next step is to increase profits of the combined company to pay off the debt incurred as a result of the acquisition. The best way to achieve that is by integrating staffs of the two individual corporations and eliminating duplicate corporate staff functions. That's where problems start. Which corporate staff functions will be eliminated? An alternative is to sell assets to raise capital for use in payment of incurred debts and get rid of staff manning divested properties.

Functions performed by administrative staffs are consolidated under the umbrella of a single company. Obviously, this integration process defines what functions are required and decides how those functions will be performed and by whom. This leads to redundancies that are eliminated by terminating many employees in order to reduce operating cost and enhance corporate profitability. The next step is addressing who will perform the required functions, which leads to the issue of employee redundancy and who will be terminated? Who is more likely to be terminated? Are the employees of the acquiring corporation more likely or less likely to be terminated?

Employees of the acquired corporation are more likely to be terminated because they are the vanquished parties and as such have to accept the consequences of being defeated. The number of job losses is considerable as shown by the acquisition of Wyeth by Pfizer, which was projected to result in the termination of more than 19,000 employees and the closing of several manufacturing facilities. [98]

The acquiring company insists its established policies and work procedures be followed. Employees of the acquiring companies are familiar with those work practices, but employees of the acquired company are unfamiliar with those policies and procedures and require training. Training adds an element of cost that can be bypassed if training were to be avoided. This, therefore, becomes a justification for getting rid of employees from the acquired company. It is a fact that very few employees of the acquired company are considered essential and remain with the acquiring company. In particular, executives of the acquired company who have agreed to be taken over in the first place are very likely to remain in the new company payroll. Other executives of the acquired company are given large payouts and leave very happily. But, that creates a morale problem among remaining workers. The problem is that employees facing termination have some know-how or specific knowledge essential to operations of the acquired company. The integration process continues to identify redundancies throughout the company that lead to more terminations.

Problems arising after the acquisition are many. They stem from a lack of understanding of individual corporate philosophy that has made the target company profitable and attractive to the acquiring company in the first place. In other words, the acquiring company fails to understand that employees of the acquired company are the lifeline and brains of the company acquired. It is those employees who have made the target company attractive by their collective achievements. Corporate culture plays a very important role in achieving goals and making the corporation a place where people want to work. Terminating those acquired company employees or changing corporate culture or philosophy will lead to adverse impacts on performance. Let's illustrate with a simple example.

A company may provide a lot of leeway to its employees to implement ideas while another company may be dictatorial and totally opposed to implementing new ideas. If the acquiring company falls under the category of being dictatorial, then frustration will set in and employee morale will suffer. Frustration will impact workers' performance, causing a stellar company to lose its motivational drive. Undoubtedly, this leads to a transformation from a stellar to a second-tiered company in a very short period of time. In other words, low employee morale leads to poor performance that affects the bottom line or profitability of the new company.

Taking this line of reasoning to a logical conclusion, one can easily see how profitability of the acquired company begins to deteriorate. Consequently, the acquiring company achieves the goal of turning a profitable company with stellar performance into a loser and therefore justifying the sale of the acquired company. But, the value of a once stellar performing company suffers significantly to the detriment of the acquirer. In short, this is a typical process that leads to a dismemberment of the acquired corporation. Executives of the acquiring corporation will never admit their role in destroying the corporation but, rather, insist that the acquisition is always a success. This is analogous to the situation that exists in corporate cost-cutting campaigns.

In very rare occasions, the acquiring corporation indirectly admits its error in going ahead with the acquisition. One such instance was the acquisition of Union Carbide by Dow Chemical in 1999. That acquisition caused many Union Carbide employees to lose their jobs or to be replaced by Dow employees. On top of that, many Union Carbide operations were either sold or shutdown to generate cash to pay for the acquisition or to reduce operating cost. A valid question would be: what attracted Dow Chemical to justify the acquisition of Union Carbide in the first place?

Undoubtedly, the board of directors of Dow Chemical probably thought of the same question and could not satisfactorily answer that question. In fact, they probably discovered that the acquisition was a losing proposition right from the beginning. Based on that determination, Dow Chemical decided to terminate the executive blamed for the aftereffects of the acquisition. That executive was Mike Parker, who was the successor to the acquiring CEO William Stavropoulos. Mr. Stavropoulus was the CEO who engineered the acquisition and, upon his retirement, left the resulting mess to Mike Parker to fix and take blame for any failure. In other words, Mr. Parker became the sacrificial lamb for Mr. Stavropoulos's mistake. What was even sadder and harder to comprehend was Dow board of directors' action in returning Mr. Stavropoulus to the CEO post of Dow Chemical Company. A press release from Dow announced Mr. Stavropoulos's triumphant return to Dow as followed:

> *"Dow announced today that its board of directors has elected William S. Stavropoulos as president and chief executive officer, succeeding Michael D. Parker. The firing of Michael Parker is solely on the basis of poor financial performance of the company.*

The sudden firing has definitely nothing whatsoever to do with the intense criticism that has been building of Dow and Parker's attempts to spin the company's responsibility in Bhopal as "absolutely nothing to do with us."

Obviously Dow's image had been under increasing fire in recent months from assorted stakeholders but, according to Dow spokesperson Bob Questra, [99] *disappointing share value is only "a result of the former CEO's poor math skills."*

Worth noticing in the above statement from Dow regarding the firing of Mr. Parker was the reason for the firing. Dow blamed Mr. Parker for poor financial performance of the company and returned Mr. Stavropoulos to reward him for the mess he created.

The sad thing was that Dow Chemical did not learn a lesson from its acquisition of Union Carbide. In fact, Dow acquired Rohm and Haas in 2009 on the justification that Rohm and Haas focused on production of specialty products that sell for higher prices than commodity products made by Dow Chemical. Rohm and Haas employees would face a similar fate to that faced by former Union Carbide's employees.

Rohm and Haas would be dismembered in much the same way Union Carbide was dismembered, and Dow's executives would be rewarded for getting rid of a competitor, albeit at a high price. Perhaps, Mr. Andrew Liveris who as CEO engineered the acquisition of Rohm and Haas would retire before the board realized the end effect of the Rohm and Haas acquisition. No doubt, Mr. Liveris would expect to return to the Dow CEO position in a triumphant manner as in Mr. Stavropoulus' case. While many employees would lose their jobs, Mr. Stavropoulus and other executives at both Dow and Rohm and Haas would be rewarded for putting this great success and achievement; Rohm and Haas would cease to exist.

In short, LBOs and mergers and acquisitions are two different mechanisms to achieve the same end, which is the destruction of Corporate America. This shatters the American Dream for a lot of hard-working, decent, and honest individuals who labor hard and honestly to make Corporate America successful.

BALANCE OF PAYMENTS

The US balance of payments represents the difference in value between all goods and services imported into the US and those exported from the US. Agricultural and manufactured products as well as crude oil are typical products exported and imported, respectively. Historical trends in US trade balance are depicted in Figure 29. Data indicate the US imports more than it exports, which reflects a negative trade balance as shown in the figure. This widening trade imbalance means more dollars are leaving the country than are brought into the country. How long can the US tolerate this imbalance is a good question to ponder? Do you think you can do the same in your own households meaning you will spend more than you earn?

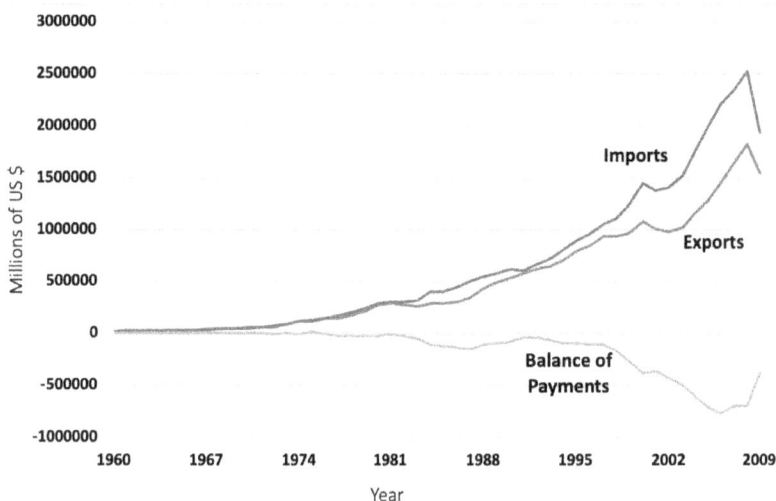

Figure 29. US Balance of Payments. [100]

The growing trade imbalance represents a disturbing trend raising many valid questions in our minds. This trade imbalance indicates the US is a debtor, and the magnitude of the debt increases on a yearly basis. These are issues resulting in consequences that citizens must evaluate based on our own personal experiences running our own households. It is essential that we send a signal to elected government officials and Corporate America expressing our dissatisfaction with the current state of affairs. Why is that so important? Do you think this is a good situation to be in? How long can this situation last before creditors cut us off?

It is important because it implies one of two things. It indicates that either the US is unable to satisfy its domestic demand with domestically manufactured products or the US does not have the capability to produce those products. If the problem is insufficient manufacturing capacity, then the answer is to expand existing capacity and employ more people to do that. If, on the other hand, the problem is that no manufacturing capacity or that manufacturing capacity has been relocated to a foreign country, then the relevant question to ask is: why has that situation been allowed to exist? It means that either Corporate America has failed to expand to keep up with growing domestic demand or has decided to move its manufacturing facilities out of the country. In either case, the result is bad for current and future employment opportunities.

Regardless of motivation for failing to meet domestic demand with locally manufactured product, US manufacturing is the loser. Ultimately, American workers end up on the losing end of this scheme because high-paying manufacturing jobs become scarcer. The US loses because its industrial might becomes less significant. This, in turn, paints a very disturbing picture of what's coming as the standard of living for Americans declines. This implies that many citizens will be unable to purchase goods and services for lack of jobs thus limiting earning and purchasing capacity. In short, continuing on this path will lead to the loss of US industrial preeminence and third word status for the US. US citizens will see their American Dreams shattered and that will lead to desperation and even civil unrest. It is a scary but realistic picture.

This alarming trend has to be reversed to prevent an economic catastrophe in the US. Keep in mind that corporate executives are the culprits creating this alarming situation. They are the ones responsible for relocating manufacturing facilities to China and other foreign countries. The Chinese are not forcing these executives to move there; the Chinese are merely facilitating the move. The US government is also responsible for allowing manufacturers to deduct the cost of R&D investment from their corporate income-tax liability and by subsidizing corporate moves to China to manufacture products developed from R&D efforts. This situation has to change before the US loses, if it hasn't already done so, its capability to scale up from laboratory results to commercial production. The net result is loss of US technological and manufacturing base to China. The US will pay for this loss.

Components of trade include goods and services. Figure 30 shows the magnitude of both of these components. The service component includes financial and technical services, among other things, and shows a positive balance of trade, which is good. However, the magnitude of the services component pales in comparison to the magnitude of the goods components, which includes oil imports and manufactured as well as agricultural goods.

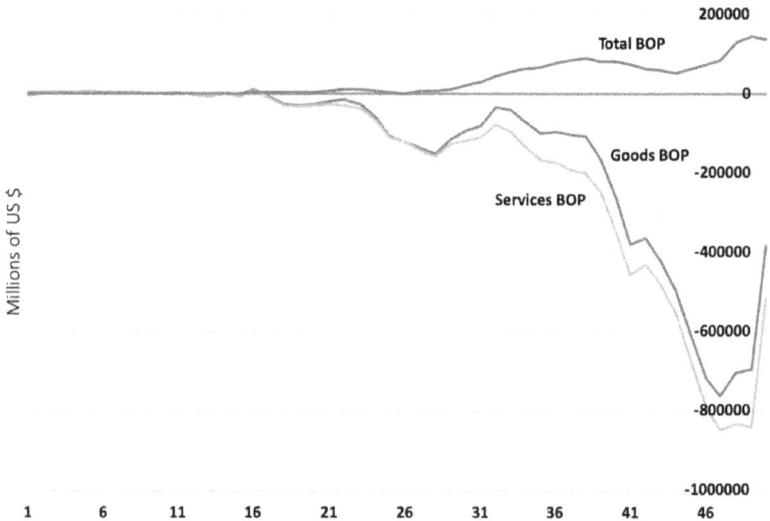

Figure 30. Balance of Payments (BOP) Breakdown. [101]

The goods component, however, shows an ever-increasing trend in the negative direction, meaning the US is buying more than it is selling. This obviously represents a decline in the level of manufacturing activity in the US. That reduction in manufacturing results in fewer higher-paying jobs becoming available to Americans. How, then, is consumer spending to be energized to get the economy back on track when the number of higher-paying manufacturing jobs is declining? Most service jobs are not high-paying jobs since a high percentage of those jobs are minimum-wage jobs.

Increasing the minimum wage is not the answer, because all that does is to diminish the availability of minimum-wage jobs. The unemployment problem has to be resolved by eliminating tax loopholes that enable manufacturing relocation. One way of doing that is to impose heavy duties on imports of goods from countries that unfairly subsidize manufacturing companies. These duties should take into consideration the cost included in US manufactured goods to satisfy US regulatory requirements.

It is apparent from data in the figure the services component has leveled off and it is not increasing as fast as the goods component. The conclusion, therefore, is that the US does not have additional capacity to rely on providing more services to reverse the trade imbalance; it has to increase manufacturing to enable it to reverse the trend. A reversal in these trends are shown in this figure appear to occur around 2007 when US economic conditions begin to deteriorate as result of the mortgage crisis created by greedy financiers. In other words, the trend reversal is not due to increased manufacturing activity but rather poor economic conditions prevailing in the country.

There are many well-meaning economists and government officials who brag about job creation to show to the American people that the policies of the Obama administration are generating jobs; census jobs are typical examples of jobs generated by the Obama Administration; these are temporary jobs. It is acceptable to generate employment opportunities in the service sector of the economy so long as it is recognized service jobs are normally low-paying jobs that are unable to sustain the standard of living the majority of Americans have become accustomed to. In other words, that is not happening. Perhaps, this is the intended end of taking from the rich to give to the poor. Maybe that's the meaning of real change under the Obama Administration. In effect, we all are getting poorer. Let's focus on implementing policies aiming to make all of us rich instead of poor!

Crude-oil imports amount to approximately 3.5 billion barrels per year. The historical values of this import component are shown in Figure 31. It is a significant expenditure is needed for power generation, manufacturing, and as a source of fuel and raw materials for the chemical industry. This level of oil consumption is necessary to sustain US economic activity. In view of that, if the US does not produce sufficient quantities of oil, then that quantity has to be imported. That is necessary to sustain and maintain our standard of living. The importation of crude oil can be reduced to some extent, but not totally eliminated, by producing more oil and natural gas in the US. This requires expanding oil exploration and production, but this will be a long-term solution. In any event, this should not, however, be misinterpreted as a call to exclude development and use of other energy sources including nuclear, geothermal, wind, etc. or to totally eliminate oil imports.

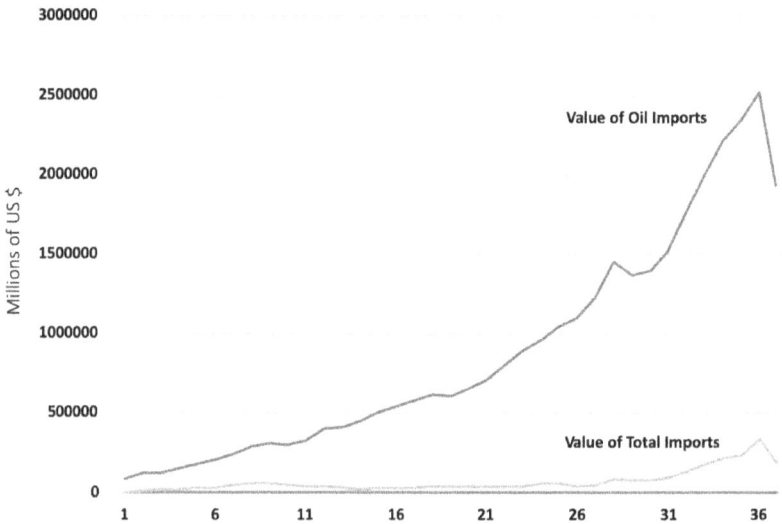

Figure 31. Value of Oil Imports [102]

Oil and gas exploration and production should be encouraged and undertaken to create additional employment opportunities and to reduce reliance on oil imports to some extent thus benefiting the US balance of payments. A benefit derived from oil and gas exploration is the creation of high-paying job opportunities for the American people, which is an opportunity that should not be dismissed. The Obama administration has imposed a moratorium to prevent deep-water drilling in the Gulf of Mexico. That will have bad consequences for the US. That policy will lead to job losses.

As consumers, we all have experienced rising gasoline prices resulting from higher crude-oil prices. Figure 32 shows historical crude oil prices showing a tendency to increase in the long-term. Obviously, there are normal day to day price fluctuations, but oil prices continue to trend upwards and will continue to do so over the long-term. This affects the component of trade attributed to crude oil and resulting in more dollars going out of the US. Consequently, investments in oil and gas exploration will pay substantial returns and ensure fewer dollars leave the country to pay for these oil imports.

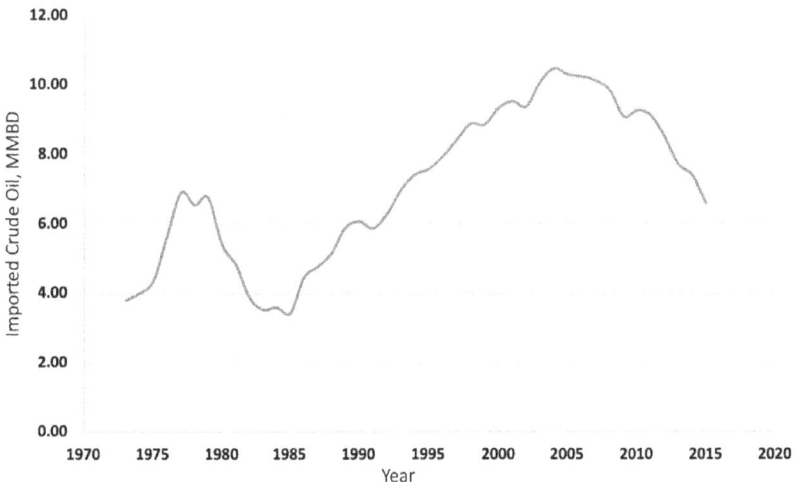

Figure 32. Historical Crude Oil Prices [103]

A subtle benefit of oil and gas exploration is national security. It is no secret the US buys crude oil from some countries that wish us harm including Iran and Venezuela. In addition, the US is in a very precarious situation risking damage to our industrial sector by oil embargoes imposed by rogue regimes. The US has experienced oil embargoes in the past and has witnessed the resulting damage to our economy. In short, the US cannot afford to be held hostage to dictators and fanatics. It is difficult to understand why the US places itself in such a situation when it has sufficient hydrocarbon reserves to satisfy its needs.

The US should increase exploration to increase production of hydrocarbons from new oil and natural-gas discoveries. The US also has significant reserves of oil shale and coal to reduce dependency on imports. The financial burden of this oil dependency amounts to approximately $350 billion a year, assuming oil prices at $100 a barrel, which is not an insignificant amount of money by any means. In view of that, it is difficult to justify the Obama's administration position on oil exploration because of the damage it is causing on the employment and balance-of-payment fronts.

MORALS AND ETHICAL STANDARDS

Corporate America executives and government officials are increasingly being exposed to be people lacking moral and ethical standards. Perhaps, this reflects feelings and attitudes of an extremely small minority within our American society. But, it does not reflect the beliefs, attitudes, and feelings of American society as a whole. American society is composed primarily of kind, God fearing, hard-working, decent, and honest people who are concerned more about the welfare of neighbors than they are about their own wellbeing.

The kindness and goodness of the American people has always been demonstrated by their reactions to natural disasters causing damage and extreme human suffering. American are always the first to respond generously regardless of location in the world, race, religion, language, or political beliefs. It is at those times that the kindness of the American people becomes evident. Unfortunately, Americans are always criticized and ostracized by many groups around the world. But, like the God fearing people they are, the American people turn their cheeks and allowed detractors to strike again. And, more importantly, are the first to respond once again to subsequent disasters even if it is in the same place where they are the subject of criticism. That's a human quality only noble people possess.

It is also true that not all Americans are good, decent, ethical, and moral. There is a very small minority of people who most Americans would not normally consider ideal role models for their children because of their moral and ethical standards. Among those unethical and immoral individuals are many corporate and government officials who are caught stealing from their corporations or from the government itself and many others who should be caught.

Mr. Leo Dennis Kozlowski was the CEO of Tyco International. He was accused and convicted in 2005 of stealing in excess of $100 million from the corporation he ran as if he owned it. His $30 million New York City apartment was paid for by Tyco. [104] The shower curtain supposedly cost $6,000 and, once again, was paid by Tyco. His actions and behavior revealed a pattern of arrogance exhibiting lack of human decency. The extent Mr. Kozlowski would go to milk the corporation dry at the expense of shareholders, employees, and US government was, is and will forever be repugnant to any kind of human decency. Did he pay any tax on these excesses? He probably failed to report his income and pay his fair share of income tax on income stolen from the corporation. Perhaps, he thought he deserved all of these benefits because the corporation was there to satisfy all of his needs and avarice. Tyco also footed the $2 million bill for an extravagant birthday party for his second wife, who left him after he was sent to prison. Wow! Perhaps, he believed he was an indispensable manager who deserved everything he stole. Even better, he probably was considered one of those indispensable managers who were too good for the company to lose.

Ken Lay and Jeffrey Skilling were two CEOs convicted of the massive fraud scheme causing the downfall of Enron. These two highly compensated executives drove Enron to bankruptcy and to disappear from the face of the earth. Mr. Ken Lay died before being formally sentenced; consequently, he never served any prison time. Mr. Skilling was sentenced to prison and is presently serving his term in federal prison. Unfortunately, the implosion of Enron also resulted in the loss of many jobs and retirement savings of many families.

There were many more CEOs who were thieves disguised as honorable individuals. But the greatest thief of all times among these dishonest CEOs was Mr. Bernard Madoff who ran a $65 billion Ponzi scheme that almost caused the global financial system to collapse.

Mr. Madoff was considered a pillar of the investment community, and, at one time, had served as a nonexecutive chairman of the NASDAQ stock exchange. No doubt, he would be called to address many high-society meetings to show what a respectable and trusted financial wizard looked like. Yet, he was nothing but a thief disguised as a respectable financier. There are many more like him among the corporate ranks that have never been caught.

There are corporate executives who are major drug users and pushers. For instance, Mr. Charles Gasparino in his book The Sellout discloses a conversation that occurred when Mr. James Cayne, former chairman and CEO of Bear Stearns, interviews Mr. Larry Friedlander for a position at Bear Stearns. Mr. Cayne is portrayed as trying to attract Mr. Friedlander at all cost and, at one point in the interview, supposedly tells Mr. Friedlander that one of the benefits of working for him is being able to get the best pot (marijuana) available in New York City. Mr. Cayne brags not only about his ability to get a prohibited drug and use it but also shows his willingness to share the illicit substance. Is that not a criminal activity? [105] If any poor individual were to utter those words and show convincingly that he uses and distributes illicit drugs, that poor individual would have been sentenced to rot in prison. Is this an example of equal justice for all?

Another example is the massive fraud allegedly committed by Goldman Sachs in subprime mortgages dealings. Goldman Sachs is not the party committing the offenses; executives and their underlings at Goldman Sachs are the ones responsible for this fraud. This is the subject matter of civil -fraud charges filed by the Securities and Exchange Commission against Goldman Sachs. [106]

It is alleged Goldman Sachs marketed securities to customers while, at the same time, betting these securities would fail to the detriment of customers and other innocent investors. The US government further alleges that Goldman Sachs engages in a conspiracy with Paulson & Co.—a prominent hedge fund— to devise this fraudulent scheme by issuing collateralized debt obligations (CDOs). Why aren't all Goldman Sachs executives charged under the indictment? Corporations act through their executives. Therefore, its executives should be charged and sent to prison. These CDOs are to be backed by subprime mortgages through insurance-like contracts. Those contracts would rise in value as the bonds issued by Goldman Sachs declined or as mortgage defaults increased. [107] In any event, Goldman Sachs would win.

It is further alleged Paulson & Co helped the Goldman Sachs team to select the subprime mortgages. Presumably, the selected subprime mortgages would be those having the highest probability of failing. This would ensure that the whole scheme would become a self-fulfilling prophecy, guaranteeing excellent returns for Goldman Sachs and Paulson & Co. Investors would lose their investment for sure. Goldman sells these risky securities tied to subprime mortgages to investors without disclosing its involvement with Paulson & Co, and the securities failed to the detriment of investors. [108] Goldman benefits from this scheme and so does Paulson & Co, which collected $20 billion when the securities fail as expected. The investors, however, are the big losers in this case. No doubt executives also benefitted. Why aren't these executives in prison? Why has the US government not placed a lien on all property and assets owned by both Goldman Sachs and Paulson & Co. and their executives to ensure investors are made whole from this fraud?

There is no question corporate leaders have deviated from accepted moral and ethical norms and standards. In the past, Corporate America has relied on its ethical and moral compass to guide its growth and to develop business relationships with clients and customers. Recent corporate executive behavior from some companies within the Corporate America umbrella has shocked the conscience of reasonable individuals in our society. Yet those corporate executives are failing to accept any blame or responsibility; they are showing no remorse.

What does that say about corporate leaders? It is obvious that, regardless of whether or not ethical and / or moral standards exist within US corporations, many of their executives are clearly acting in an unethical and immoral manner. Corporate leaders must have a sense of right and wrong to guide not only their business activities but also their personal behavior. In the absence of ethical and moral standards, Corporate America risks losing its reputation and harming its ability to conduct business that is so essential to its future profitability. It seems that corporate executives have an insatiable appetite for money, regardless of source, to line their pockets. Can Corporate America earn the trust of its business partners and customers and continue to exist and grow under these circumstances?

Walter Forbes, former chairman of Cendant Corp, was convicted and sentenced in 2007 to 121.5 years in prison for the largest accounting fraud of the 1990s. The fraud scheme perpetrated by Mr. Forbes cost Cendant—a large real-estate and travel company— in excess of $3 billion. His ex-wife was ordered to transfer back property to recover money for Cendant and its shareholders. [109]

In the past, corporate leaders have served as role models for our children. Now, it is unlikely anyone would urge his children to emulate corporate leaders. In fact, the only role model these leaders can play and play well is that of thieves who get away with their crimes. That has to be one of the lowest point in US Corporate history. If left unchecked, this activity will destroy Corporate America and stain the image of the US. That will be a disastrous consequence for all of us and we will become victims. Nevertheless, this type of activity reflects on our children who learn that is possible to steal and get away with it. They also learn that crime does pay in many cases. Is that what we, as parents, want our children to learn?

One hears about all this fraudulent activity against Corporate America and its customers. It is activity perpetrated by corporate executives and internal corporate sources. One cannot help but wonder how is this type of activity allowed to continue? All corporations pay huge sums of money to independent auditors ensuring that fraudulent activity is uncovered, and yet it is not. How is that possible? Independent auditors, like executives, are probably involved in covering up such activity. They know what is going on but do not want to risk losing business from the corporations employing them. In view of that, they keep their mouths shut and move on to claim they were unaware of what was going in the corporation. Should not shareholders ask: What are auditors getting paid for?

If auditors were asked what they did for the corporation, they would detail a long list of activities to justify their huge paycheck, but in essence, they do nothing. That has been proven to be the case in the Enron debacle, in the Bernard Madoff scheme, in the Tyco Corp case, and many others similar cases. It is a scary situation. How can anybody trust audited and certified financial documents issued by corporations to investors? In view of all this criminal activity going on in Corporate America, why is it that the Securities and Exchange Commission fails to detect this behavior and indict higher-ups in order to stop this very harmful and destructive situation?

It seems that executives lack moral and ethical values and are only interested in making money for themselves. This feeling is well expressed in emails exchanges between Mr. Fabrice Tourre, who is the only individual charged by the SEC in the fraud case against Goldman Sachs and his girlfriend Marine Serres. This is the case arising from the sale of investment securities backed by subprime mortgages that were secretly intended to fail. In one such email exchange [110] dated June 2007, Mr. Tourre wrote: "Just made it to the country of your favorite clients! I'm managed (sic) to sell a few abacus bonds to widows and orphans that I ran into at the airport, apparently these Belgians adore synthetic abs cdo2."

Earlier in 2007, in an email to a friend, Mr. Tourre expressed belief that the product he helped create was crumbling:

"It's bizarre I have the sensation of coming each day to work and re-living the same agony- a little like a bad dream that repeats itself. In sum, I am trading a product which a month ago was worth $100 and which today is only worth $93 and which on average is losing 25 cents a day... That doesn't seem like a lot but when you take into account that we buy and sell these things that have nominal amounts that are worth billions, well it adds up to a lot of money."

The only motivation is to make money regardless of consequences. That's the mindset of corporate executives and the consequences of that avarice lead to collapse of the company. It does that because customers like you and me do not want to deal with thieves. As a result of the corporate collapse, a lot of innocent Americans lose their homes, retirement savings, and their jobs. Executives, on the other hand, are rewarded with big bonuses. Regulatory agencies employees fail to detect any wrong doing or look the other way so as not to offend potential future employers.

Something is wrong with this picture! In essence, this state of affairs amounts to lawful robbery. How can the US government justify this activity and extend a helping hand to these financial institutions run by thieves to bail them out of trouble but do not do the same for citizens? Is it because these entities are too big to fail or because they are too influential and knowledgeable of political realities to blackmail politicians and force them to act? Politicians would get the message and prevent many financial institutions to survive so politicians can continue to benefit from financial contributions made by Goldman Sachs and others. Many constituents believe most politicians are not interested in their interests but rather are only interested in protecting their own interest.

UNWILLINGNESS TO ACCEPT RESPONSIBILITY

Corporate executives and political leaders have consistently been reluctant to accept responsibility for their acts. In the past, founders of companies and executives in those companies not only accepted responsibility in the roles they played but built on their failures to make Corporate America even more successful; the new reality is otherwise. It is a new phenomenon. This reluctance includes a failure to be held accountable for knowing anything about what goes on within the corporation they lead. How can that position be realistic and credible? If executives are unaware of what goes on within the company and earn huge salaries for that then either these executives are liars or are stealing from the company. Which is it? It can be argued they are thieves because they admit to be doing nothing to earn huge salaries. In short, they are drawing a huge salary under false pretenses and committing fraud at the minimum or plainly stealing from the company.

Corporate losses, bankruptcy, fraud, and a multitude of other detrimental impacts on the corporation and shareholders are some of the results for which executives refuse to be held accountable. When it comes time to draw a paycheck or a bonus award, executives line up to brag about their contributions to the company. Then, they try to convince everyone that, without their presence and efforts, the corporation would not have been able to perform as it did. It is beyond belief that these executives want to get credit for good corporate results but are unwilling to take credit for bad results. Maybe that's the reason they are so successful. If any executive or human being does not admit difficulties or failures then that is a good indication he is doing nothing! Unlike the old financial slogan relating to "earning it the old fashion way", current executives want to be compensated for not earning it.

Unwillingness to accept responsibility is widespread in our society today, and it is leading to socioeconomic problems. For instance, independent corporate auditors are charged with the duty of auditing corporate accounts for the benefit of corporate owners i.e., the shareholders. Auditors, however, are unwilling to accept responsibility for failing to discover or notify shareholders of upcoming problems; they just want to be well compensated for not performing the services they are hired to do. Investors, customers, employees, and suppliers rely on the accuracy of audited results to make decisions impacting their own finances. If investors cannot rely on audited results, how can they determine whether corporate books represent a fair picture of the financial status of the corporation? The job of auditors is to determine whether the corporate books are being cooked to the detriment of the corporation and those who depend on it. If they cannot ensure accuracy of results, then they should decline payment from the corporation. Auditors should also understand that their primary allegiance is to stockholders and not corporate executives. Since executives hold the purse strings, who do auditors pledge allegiance to?

Despite being well compensated, auditors either fail to perform their duties or willingly participate in the cooking of the corporate books. The next step is to claim they are unable to find anything wrong with the books and sideline accountability. They do that by claiming they could not be expected to know everything going on within the corporation. Isn't that the reason they are getting paid? That is an argument that holds very little water. For instance, in the case of Enron, auditors knew what was going on and accepted what Enron told them instead of checking the facts. It should be mentioned that one of the arguments behind the recommendation by the board of directors to retain the services of an auditing is that these auditors supposedly know what is happening within the company. If that's not the case then either the board of directors or the auditors are lying; perhaps, a more accurate description is that both parties are lying.

Similarly, regulators are charged with the duty of protecting consumers, investors, and workers. Regulators also refuse to accept responsibility for performance shortcomings. In short, everyone is passing the buck. When it comes time to get paid, however, everybody shows up to be rewarded and to receive a check while bragging about their contributions. At that time, everyone is willing to accept a check. And, not one of them refuses to accept payment on account of not having done what they are supposedly being paid to do for the corporation.

Elected officials are also reluctant to accept responsibility for corruption in government and within governmental agencies. This becomes particularly apparent when these politicians are caught with their hands in the cookie jar. How many times have you seen a video showing a politician accepting a bribe only to be denied later as an intentional entrapment by the FBI? How many times do you hear of a politician getting caught accepting illegal contributions or vacation trips as bribes and denying with a straight face they are being bribed? They simply claim to be acting undercover to help the FBI investigate corruption? There are times when politicians blame their staffs for accepting illegal contributions or trips, but the politicians rather than the staff are the ones enjoying the trips and spending the money. And, they refuse to declare those bribes as taxable income because they never knew it was income. In other words, it is something that their staff did without their knowledge. Had they known, they would have been happy to pay taxes due.

It never fails to amaze people when elected officials involved in a scandal claim they have been set up. And, yes how many times the supposedly ethical transgression is overlooked or simply dismissed by colleagues in the US Senate or US House of Representatives. These transgressions are ignored by their political colleagues simply because the rest of them do not want to be exposed to the same scrutiny. Those remaining officials who are not caught with their hands in the cookie jar are just as guilty as the one who gets caught. That's the reality in political life. Elected officials are very easily tempted by money offered by lobbyists and are corrupted. That's part of the reason for the suggestion to vote them out at every election.

Unwillingness to accept responsibility and accountability is endemic in our present-day society, particularly among the younger generations, creating many socioeconomic problems. Perhaps, this is due to the idea of winning, to be number one, and to strive for success, regardless of cost. That motivation leads to rejection of failure. At the same time, that belief fails to recognize that, at times, failure is a mechanism leading to success. In other words, it is not important how one fails; what is important is how and how many times one gets up.

For instance, Henry Ford founded Ford Motor Company after experiencing many financial difficulties that drove him personally to the brink of bankruptcy. He got up many times and tried again until he became successful. Persistence paid. There were many other similar stories indicating that failure was only bad when people experiencing it failed to get up and try something else. In short, it would be worth keeping in mind the idea that when you are down on the floor the only way you can look at is at the stars. That would indicate that the sky is the limit.

Look at the disturbing trend shown in Figure 33 pointing to the increasing number of children younger than eighteen years of age being raised by their grandparents. This disturbing trend indicates an increasing number of children are being abandoned by their parents. Thank God for grandparents! The failure of parents to accept responsibility for the care of their children imposes a heavy burden on grandparents. What would happen to these children if grandparents were unwilling to accept the awesome responsibility of properly raising these abandoned children? That would impose a significant financial burden on taxpayers and not ensure a successful outcome.

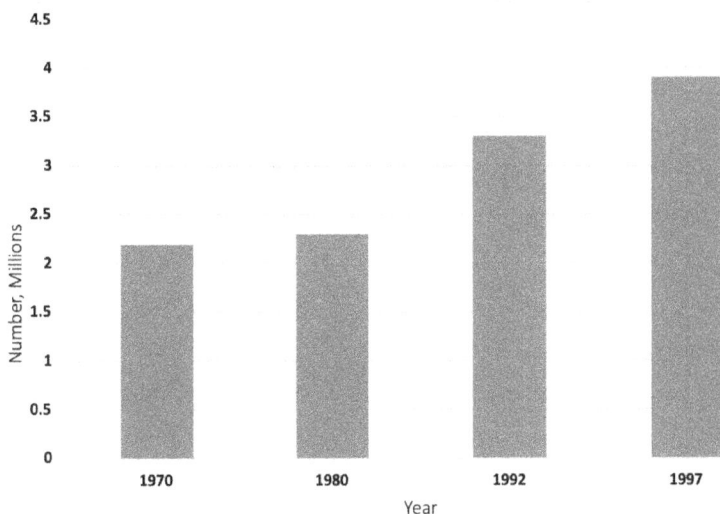

Figure 33 Minor Children Living with Grandparents [111]

These abandoned children would have to be raised by the states, creating an even bigger socioeconomic problem. Grandparents who are burdened with that responsibility accept that duty willingly to keep their family units intact. But it is an unwanted or even unaffordable heavy financial burden imposed on the elderly at a time when they have access only to limited funds. It happens at a point in their lives of these elderly folks when they should be enjoying their retirement years instead of actively caring for young grandchildren. The result of this trend is that more than 2.6 million grandparents nationwide are raising grandchildren, which represents an increase of more than 6 percent since 2005. Parents end up being incarcerated for drug use or criminal activity, become mentally ill, or experience further financial problems. Eventually, the state has to step in and provide financial assistance to the grandparents. The children are the victims of this sad situation, and in many cases this situation leads to undesirable consequences.

The pattern described by the actions of grandparents in accepting responsibility for the family unit and grandchildren indicates previous generations willingly accept responsibility unlike members of younger generations. If the unwillingness to accept responsibility is present in the family nucleus, what can be expected to be present in the corporate and government environments? Failure to accept responsibility and refusal to be held accountable ends up burdening someone else. That burden leads to a final consequence shared by society. In the case of parents abandoning their children, those deadbeat parents relieve themselves of financial and personal responsibility but do not extinguishing it completely. Someone else has to step up and assume that financial and personal burden.

Parents, corporate executive, auditors, and government officials absolve themselves of any and all responsibility thus placing a heavy financial burden on grandparents, investors, customers, and constituents. Why should society allow this practice to continue? Why not hold these parties accountable and subject to liability, including long prison terms to deter this practice? Why not confiscate property and assets from these offending parties to cover the cost of their irresponsibility? The act of confiscating assets from offenders would compensate society for the consequences of their acts. That would be the best mechanism at our disposal to teach responsibility.

Corporate and government institutions operate in a broken environment in need of major reforms. There are no consequences or punishment for actions of deadbeat corporate executives, regulators, politicians, and parents. In fact, the system rewards them. Look at bonuses paid with taxpayers' funds that are awarded to dishonest individuals responsible for the Great Recession of 2009. The system should be rewarding innocent investors, customers, and grandparents.

Should the government lend money at favorable rates to failing financial institutions to reward executives causing the failure? Should it not, instead, take legal action to get back hard-earned taxpayers' funds and proceed to confiscate assets from those individuals who are responsible for creating the mess? Money is the only language these crooks understand. It is now time to reverse the game they have been playing, and play the game with their money rather than money belonging to somebody else. It is only when these executives realize they are risking their own money that they will become more responsible and accountable not only to themselves but also to rest of us.

The US experiences a financial meltdown created by greedy bankers who risk investors' money and not their own. That excessive risk-taking activity brings many of the large and most powerful financial institutions to the brink of bankruptcy, forcing some of those institutions to collapse. Those that survived that cataclysmic downfall have to be bailed out with taxpayers' funds. That downfall is a situation that does not happen overnight. It is something that starts and compounds itself over a period of time to reach a disastrous climax.

One has to question roles rating institutions play that are supposedly charged with the duty of overseeing the viability of those institutions. In particular, rating institutions issue opinions regarding creditworthiness of securities. Now we find that these supposedly independent rating agencies have been colluding with banks to disguise the true risk of investments opportunities marketed by their banks clients. In other words, the rating agencies have been issuing a "safe" rating on investments securities that, in reality, are extremely unsafe. Banks pay these agencies hefty fees for this fraud. Shouldn't investors have the right to confiscate assets from these agencies and banks to be compensated for their losses?

How well has the Securities and Exchange Commission (SEC) performed its regulatory role of ensuring financial institutions are operating in a transparent and ethical manner? That statutory duty is imposed on the SEC. This massive fraud is perpetrated by financial institutions against the investment community and the entire nation. It would not have occurred if the SEC had done its job properly or professionally.

Instead of monitoring financial institutions performance, it was recently disclosed SEC regulators were watching pornographic movies on government issued computers. [112] They were watching these pornographic movies while the industry was collapsing and investors were losing their hard-earned dollars. In fact, the SEC's inspector general conducted probes and found many abuses throughout the agency. For example, a senior attorney at SEC's Washington's headquarters spent up to eight hours a day looking and downloading pornography. In another instance, an accountant was blocked more than 16,000 times in a month from visiting pornographic websites. These were not the only cases uncovered by the inspector general. There were other examples where regulators were not performing their jobs while getting paid to do so.

The salaries of many of these nonperforming regulatory agencies employees were in excess of $200,000 per year. This clearly demonstrated how the best, brightest, and more talented people at the SEC earn a living. [113] It would be fair to enquire whether these highly paid, worthless individuals were charging the SEC the cost of providing popcorn to make the film watching activity more enjoyable. It would be fair to say, therefore, that while the regulators were watching pornographic movies the financial institutions under their jurisdictions were going under. In fact, many innocent investors were suffering the effects of fraud allowed to go on by nonperforming regulators. Many individual investors watched their life's savings depleted and their lives ruined during this irresponsible action by the SEC. Isn't that enough to request the US government undertake legal action to punish these nonperforming and irresponsible regulators?

In a chamber of the Capitol in Washington DC, high level Corporate America executives were testifying on the causes of the ecological disaster brewing from the oil spill in the Gulf of Mexico. Present at the hearing were high-level executives including the CEOs of BP, Transocean, and Halliburton. The companies represented by these individuals were the oil well owner, driller, and the company providing technical services, respectively. All you could see from the televised picture was a trio of high-level executives pointing the finger at each other, and yet no one was willing to admit that any of these companies or its employees played any part in causing the problem. What a tragedy! If all of these executives believed the work was done competently, then what was the cause of the well blowout? Someone must had done or failed to do something to cause the event leading to the spill and ecological disaster? If this tragedy had been an act of God, then it would have been desirable to know that. There was no need to run away from problems. It would have been better to explain difficulties these companies face and the hard work being done by their employees to solve the problem.

It would have been a much better picture to see these highly paid individuals acknowledge a problem existed and that it was being addressed. It would have been better to reassure the nation that they were more concerned about solving the problem than in engaging in rhetorical exercises to absolve their companies from any and all liability. In fact, their performance at the hearing showed the nation that the industry is run by incompetents, and that is not a fair assessment of the oil and gas industry. It certainly is not a fair representation of the capabilities of the highly talented, technically competent, and dedicated group of employees employed by oil companies. Their performance brought shame to the oil and gas industry in general. That shame should be place on the heads of the inept and incompetent executives at that hearing. Since that time, it is fair to say BP has acted honorably by facing consequences of its acts and addressing the problem.

If the idea of pointing fingers was to assign blame, then it would have been better to look for the person or persons who were responsible for cutting corners. It would have been better to admit cutting corners to reduce drilling cost and to expedite the well-drilling process without regards for consequences. This was obviously done as shown by facts that became public knowledge subsequent to the accident. Unfortunately, cutting corners did not pay off. It had not paid in the past and will not pay in the future.

As a result of that accident, exploration in the Gulf of Mexico for oil and gas is placed on hold. Many oil companies working in the Gulf lose millions of dollars. Employment opportunities are shut down for many residents suffering the impact of the spill and losing their jobs. At the same time, BP and its partners are facing additional liability resulting from their irresponsible actions. In short, the effort at passing the buck has not worked for BP or its partners. Let's hope they learn from this debacle and do a better job in the future.

It would have been much better to be truthful at the time of the hearing. They should have told legislators and the entire nation that oil exploration and production at those depths and conditions in the Gulf of Mexico is a technically challenging but necessary exercise. It is challenging because new technology has to be developed, and it will be developed. At the same time, it is a necessary activity ensuring the wellbeing of our entire nation in terms of national security and job creation for many people. Exploration and production activity at those depths is analogous to developing the means to go to the moon. It is a very risky business but worth doing. It would have been better to admit that industry does not have answers to all problems, but it is learning. Lessons from this disaster will lead to solutions to ensure future success at meeting the nation's energy needs safely.

One of my industrial mentors once asked me about my work activities; at that time I was a young engineer engaged in R&D activities. I told this gentleman that I had a lot on my plate, that I was trying different things to solve problems, and that I was concerned that some of the ideas I was planning to try might fail. He stopped me right there and told me something I will never forget. He told me something which I considered very a philosophical and witty statement. He said: "Don't be afraid to fail. That tells me you are doing something. If you fail twice using the same idea then I know you are stupid, and I will fire you." The point was that you had to learn from your mistakes. That applies to BP as much as it does to me and everyone else.

The idea of refusing to accept responsibility is not limited to the corporate world or the government. It is something that pervades all segments of our society. Children always find an excuse to avoid responsibility. When a child throws a baseball and accidentally breaks a glass window, you are very likely to hear from the perpetrator that the window got in the way of the ball. You hear parents blame teachers for the poor grades their child gets instead of blaming themselves for failing to show interest in their child's education or blame the child himself for failure to do his school work. Perhaps, the teacher is a lousy teacher, but if that is the case then there it is the parents' duty to let school officials know that fact.

CORPORATE LOBBYING

The right to petition the government is clearly recognized in the First Amendment to the US Constitution. It is that right that foundation for lobbying. The First Amendment states:

> *"Congress shall make no law respecting an establishment of religion, or prohibiting the free exercise thereof; or abridging the freedom of speech, or of the press; or the right of the people peaceably to assemble, and to petition the Government for a redress of grievances"* [114]

It is true that citizens have a constitutional right to petition the government and lobby their elected officials, but this right is not explicitly extended to corporations, which are only juridical person and not a citizen in the sense of being a human being. Nevertheless, corporations have used this right to appeal to legislators to receive redress to some problem they may be having that impairs their operations. There is nothing wrong with that so long as corporate lobbyists do not grant legislators money or gifts in exchange for action on their behalf even if it means acting contrary to constituents' interests. An example of this is the situation where lobbyists bribe legislators to enact legislation reducing the interest rate payable by financial institutions to their savings account customers. And, that is not the only example. It is undeniable that politicians prefer to follow the views of those who pay them. In other words, the Golden Rule is alive and well in getting the attention of and securing access to elected officials. The Golden Rule simply states that those who have the gold rule. Consequently, citizens are at a disadvantage to get elected officials to hear their petitions when they have to compete with lobbyists who shower politicians with gifts and money. Normally, citizens do not pay politicians or shower them with gifts, money, trips, or special mortgage deals at the bank. The First Amendment does not contemplate any sort of payment to elected officials as a precondition to hearing our petition. Yet, that is an essential requirement in today's environment particularly when corporate lobbyists are involved.

If the absence of payments from constituents, politicians do not get excited about views held by constituents unless there is an election is on the horizon. That is so because at those times they need constituents' votes to remain on the gravy train. When elections are over, the grace period granted by politicians to hear constituents' grievances is closed and remains only partially open until the next election. Upon termination of the grace period, politicians' ears are tuned to lobbyists' request. It is a shame that elected public officials prefer to follow the wishes of lobbyists rather than those of their constituents. One can understand why. Lobbyists fund their campaigns and provide them with gifts, trips, and many other financial benefits that allow pos to have a more luxurious life.

Citizens know politicians will violate their individual trust, and this breach of trust causes frustration on the part of constituents. Instead of voting out those who violate their trust, constituents refuse to cast their votes, and they justify that action on the idea that it does not do any good to vote. If, instead of abstaining from voting, citizens were to consistently vote even if it means voting for a candidate from a different party then the situation would be entirely different. There would be no more frustrations.

Politicians would understand perfectly well that, unless they satisfy the majority of constituents, they would be denied a return trip to Washington or any other government office.

A more efficient method of expressing individual frustration at elected officials would be to cast votes against those who ignore the wishes and views of constituents. If that were done, politicians would soon learn to listen to their constituents and enact legislation more closely representing the interests of the people rather than those of lobbyists representing special interest groups. Unfortunately, only a very small percentage of eligible voters cast their votes regularly. Politicians recognize that, and so all they need to do to perpetuate themselves in office is to convince a very small minority of constituents. Financial support from lobbyists goes a long way to get the views of incumbents across, via paid political advertisement, to the very small minority of voters required for reelection.

Table 15 lists contributions received by members of the US Senate from 2007 to the second quarter of 2009. Notice Senator John McCain is the one receiving the largest amount on account of being a candidate for the US presidency. Notice also that these contributions are being handed out to politicians directly from insurance and pharmaceutical companies or indirectly through their lobbyists. Those financial contributions are intended to ensure that whatever legislation is proposed or passed regarding medical insurance or anything having to do with medical care truly reflects the best interests of those companies regardless of the impact on constituents.

Considering the recent debate on health care and the failure to enact any sort of health-care legislation during the past one hundred years or so, it becomes apparent that money talks. It is also interesting to note that health-care costs have continued to escalate without any logical explanation, interference, or objection from US government sources or our elected officials. Considering insurance companies deny coverage to anyone who develops any kind of ailment or files a claim to recover medical expenditures supposedly covered by the insurance policy, it is ironic to see how splendid these insurance companies are with politicians.

Republicans		Democrats	
John McCain	$900,930	Max Baucus	$453,649
Mitch McConnell	$513,772	Arlen Specter	$225,528
Pat Roberts	$130,620	Chris Dodd	$187,758
Susan M. Collins	$69,216	Mark Udall	$155,175
John Cornyn	$62,850	Mary L. Landrieu	$102,800
Chuck Grassley	$78,450	Mark Warner	$131,100
Richard Burr	$40,798	Michael Bennett	$39,200
Saxby Chambers	$48,050	Patty Murray	$92,300
Mike Crapo	$46,650	Mark Pryor	$45,350
Mike Enzi	$51,762	Tom Udall	$24,950
Orrin G. Hatch	$35,800	Barbara Boxer	$12,793
Alexander Lamar	$25,900	Byron L. Dorgan	$27,086
John Barrasso	$22,100	Al Franken	$15,900
Lindsey Graham	$19,350	Kirsten Gillibrand	$11,150
Jeff Sessions	$12,000	Tom Harkin	$30,150
Roger Wicker	$17,300	John Kerry	$19,150
		Amy Klobuchar	$13,800
		Frank R. Lautenberg	$23,350
		Blanche Lincoln	$15,250
		Jack Reed	$51,650
		Harry Reid	$33,089
		Jay Rockefeller	$15,000
		Jeanne Shaheen	$19,600
		Debbie Stabenow	$29,750

Table 15. Contributions from Health Lobbyists [115]

Politicians have been aware of these problems for years and yet have ignored them completely on account of financial contributions received from these special interest groups. Who is protecting the public? Certainly, neither elected nor regulatory officials show any interest in addressing this problem simply because it would be harmful to their financial interest. Now, if voters were to express their will through their votes, then the result would be completely different.

Lobbyists and their clients have donated approximately $4 million to US senators. Obviously, the people who cannot afford insurance coverage are unable to match corporate political contributions this magnitude. As a result, lawmakers turn a deaf ear to the plight of defenseless sick children whose poor families cannot afford health insurance and have to do with second-class or maybe fifth-class health care. And, yet, those people are Americans. This is clearly the outcome of applying the Golden Rule to the detriment of the general citizenry. Something is wrong with the system. The preamble to the US Constitution provides:

> 'We the People of the United States, in Order to form a more perfect Union, establish Justice, insure domestic Tranquility, provide for the common defense, promote the general Welfare, and secure the Blessings of Liberty to ourselves and our Posterity, do ordain and establish this Constitution for the United States of America.'

One wonders about the meaning of "general Welfare." It seems clear the US Constitution imposes a duty on the US government to promote the general welfare, and it would be illogical to think that health care and the health of the general population are excluded from the term general welfare. If healthcare is included within that constitutional provision, why has the government failed to address this issue in a meaningful way? It is an issue that needs to be addressed.

Nothing is mentioned about paying for health care, which is a different issue. Clearly, someone has to pay for health care. But, the fundamental question is: why does the US government allows insurance companies to deny coverage on the basis of preexisting conditions? The answer is clear: special interest groups, primarily those representing insurance companies, medical organizations, and pharmaceutical companies, are opposed to having lawmakers address that issue. Unlike special interest groups that are able to bribe politicians to prevent action but cannot elect politicians; individual citizens can trump all of that money donated to politicians by them their votes and thus employment.

It is difficult to understand why the richest nation in the world cannot afford and has been unwilling to provide medical insurance coverage to treat children. It is disgraceful when we read press reports showing that child mortality in the US is higher than in many undeveloped and poor nations in the world. For instance, twenty years ago, the US ranked twenty ninth in child mortality rate but the latest data on child mortality shows the US losing ground on this very important issue. The US now ranks forty second, according to data analyzed by the Institute of Health Metrics and Evaluation at the University of Washington. The US ranked behind much of Europe as well as the United Arab Emirates, Cuba, and Chile. [116]

If children represent the future of our nation, then it is fair to conclude that we in the US are not adequately providing a means of ensuring a bright future. We fail to provide medical insurance to ensure the health of all of our children. This is very selfish attitude on our part. Those of us who can pay for medical insurance to cover our children ignore the fact that the health of all children is paramount importance to our future as a nation. High abortion rates tend to denigrate the value of children to our future. We better wake up or we are going to find ourselves unable to sustain a bright future for our nation.

Selfless grandparents raising children abandoned by their parents understand the value of children to our future. Perhaps, we need to learn a lesson from those elderly folks who do their best with limited financial resources to ensure children are provided for. They do not want to risk losing a single child who, if allowed to grow and be educated, becomes the discoverer of a cure for cancer or another similar dreadful disease. Let's learn from them.

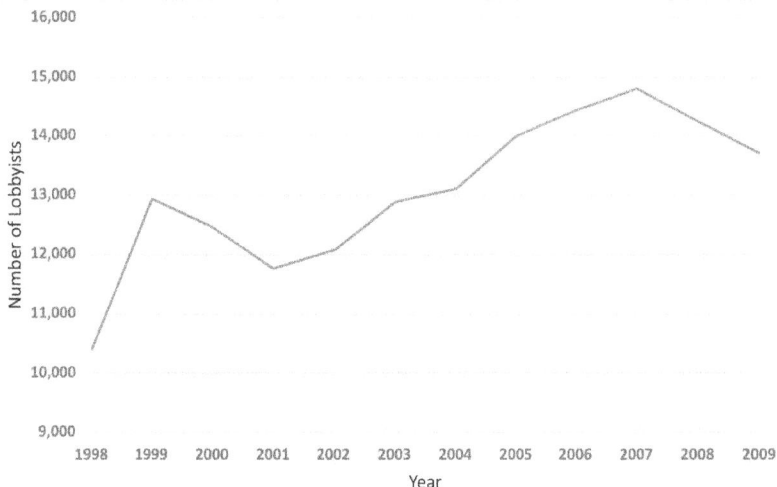

Figure 34. Number of Lobbyists [117]

Figure 34 shows an increasing trend in the number of lobbyists reflecting a 40 percent rise in the number of lobbyists from 1998 to 2009. This indicates that the future is not going to bring many favorable changes for citizens based on historical facts. In short, one can expect legislation that is either proposed or enacted would allow corporate abuses to continue to the detriment of individuals.

Lobbying expenditures continue to increase as shown in Figure 35. This means politicians will continue to favor issues advocated by lobbyists rather than constituents. That is true not only on the subject of health care but also on other issues of importance to the general population. That includes legislation making it possible and easier for manufacturers to relocate manufacturing facilities to foreign countries, which would be detrimental to the general population. If lawmakers are paid off then they will view requests of special interests favorably and accommodate their needs. That pattern has to be reversed and can only be reversed by the power of our individual votes, which are more powerful than all the money spent by special interest groups on politicians.

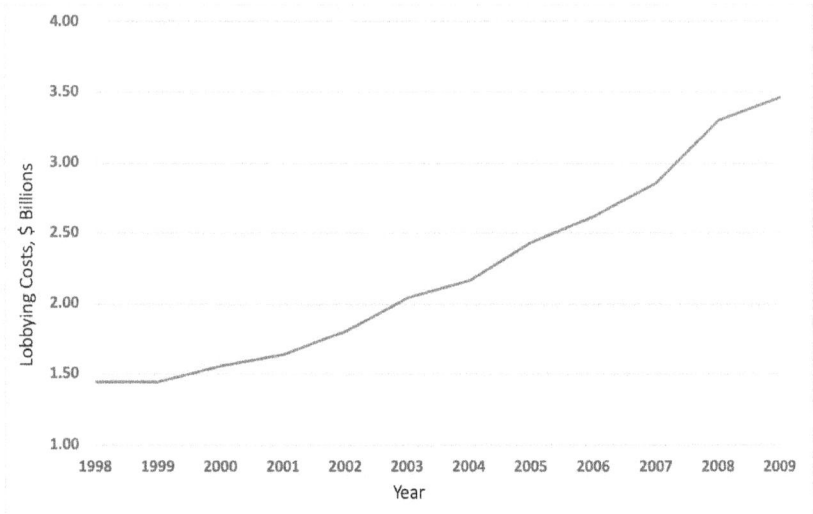

Figure 35. Annual Lobbying Expenditures [118]

On the issue of health care, politicians have indicated a desire to provide a health-care plan similar to what all politicians in Washington get. Yet, they pass Obama Care in a bill that is more than 2,000 pages long. They know no one is either going to read this proposed legislation, including lawmakers themselves, or understand the goal of the legislation. If their desire is what they say it is, why not say so in a one-page bill? Politicians prefer to write longer bills to make it easier to hide favors being granted to special interest groups in the midst of this voluminous legislation. Legislators do not want to face voters with facts, and that is the best way of addressing that issue. The intent of legislators is to overcome voters' objections by preventing them from getting the truth.

They do not want transparency, because that would reveal the level of corruption present in our government. The author is not a legislative wizard but one who believes health-care legislation could have been made more transparent and simpler to read by all voters. For example why not pass a bill saying the following:

"All American Citizens shall have access to a medical insurance plan of the same scope and coverage provided to US Senators, Representatives, and any other US government Official. The cost of that coverage shall be identical to that paid by all present recipients of said insurance coverage.

Insurance companies shall be precluded from denying coverage to any American on the basis of preexisting medical conditions or to impose a life cap on such coverage".

The growing trend in corporate contributions becomes more disturbing now that the US Supreme Court has ruled in a five to four decision that free-speech grants groups like corporations and labor unions the right to directly subsidize political campaigns. Presumably, this will allow unlimited corporate contributions [119] thus drowning the voices of the American people. Justice Stevens writing for dissenting justices expressed an opinion that more accurately represents the true outcome of the ruling in these words: [120] "The notion that the First Amendment dictated [today's ruling] is, in my judgment, profoundly misguided,

The net effect of that ruling will be to encourage corporate contributions to advance the agenda of special interest groups at the expense of consumers and voters. This will be done now to influence the debate going on in both the US Senate and US House of Representatives on financial reform or to prevent enactment of effective legislation to curb abuses in the financial sector. Lobbyists for financial institutions know that now is the ideal time to achieve those objectives when politicians are facing elections and need money to conduct campaigns.

Contrary to the message lobbyist want to send to politicians, constituents have the means to send an even louder message. Voters can do so by voting all the incumbents up for reelection out of office and demanding that new elected representatives and senators enact legislation overruling the US Supreme Court decision as their first act in Washington, D.C.

There is no question that large corporate expenditures on lobbying efforts get the attention of legislators to the detriment of constituents. The reason corporate lobbyists get the attention of legislators is simply the power to pay legislators or give them gifts and pay for vacation trips. It is not because these lawmakers are good speakers, good looking, well dressed or anything else. It is simply that they are passing out money to get something in return. Money and expensive gifts get the attention of lawmakers, but individual citizens are unable to provide the same things to legislators. Consequently, citizens are at a disadvantage when dealing with legislators as compared to corporate lobbyists and the special interests they represent. Something has to be done to level the playing field so that citizens and corporations alike have the same opportunity to bring their petitions to legislators.

There is no way legislators are going to restrict lobbying expenditures anytime soon, because that would be tantamount to killing the goose that lays the golden egg. Are citizens then up a creek without a paddle? Quite the contrary is true.

There are several ways to eliminate the buying of political favors for the benefits of corporations. The first would be to require incumbents release certified records on contributors and the amounts contributed. Failure to show such records prior to elections would indicate they are hiding something and would automatically signal voters not to vote for those individuals who are basically lying to constituents. The second would be to force introduction of a bill requiring transparency in financing elections. Any incumbent who fails to vote in favor of such a bill would be targeted for removal at the next election. The third way would be to collect information on corporations and their lobbying habits. This should include determining how much money is being spent by corporations on lobbying activities, the lobbying goal, and the incumbents who are the beneficiaries of such lobbying. If corporations fail to curtail lobbying efforts voluntarily then voters as consumers should boycott those corporations and refuse to purchase their products.

Removal of gifts and money from the picture would enable citizens and corporations to have equal access to legislators. That would enable constituents the opportunity to have their views heard as contemplated in the US Constitution.

REGULATORY SYSTEM
GONE BERSERK

The US system of government is based on the idea the will of the people is of paramount importance. It must be accorded the respect it deserves and honored by all government officials, particularly elected officials. The US Constitution provides a mechanism empowering constituents to express their views through the electoral process. This process includes the requirement that every member of the House of Representatives must face constituents every other year to be reelected for a two-year term of office. Similarly, one third of all US Senators must face constituents every other year; this is done to ensure all these elected officials understanding what constituents want.

If the views of voters and politicians align, then politicians get elected but not otherwise. Elected officials get a fairly good idea of their constituents' views and constituents elect only those politicians who represent the views of the majority of the people.

In practice, however, the system does not really work that way. When a significant number of voters are either frustrated by actions of politicians or refuse to vote altogether, that underlying premise may be wrong. If constituents fail to vote and make their views known on the erroneous assumption a given politician may not be elected, then the outcome of the election may be contrary to their true wishes. In fact, that politician may gain an advantage when voters who oppose them stay out of the election. The result of that action is that the incumbent has neutralized voters who oppose him. This action gets rid of voters who oppose the incumbent and those f ; that action favors the incumbent. If voters really wanted favoring the incumbent come ahead. Unhappy constituents should show their frustrations and disappointment with the incumbent by voting for the opposing candidate instead of refusing to cast their votes at that particular election. In that event, constituents lose twice: once when they fail to cast their votes against incumbents and, secondly, when the politician remains in office and continues to not represent his constituents.

Notice the founding fathers required all members of the US House of Representatives to stand before the electorate every other year. This was based on the idea that constituents would have a chance to straighten out any lawmaker whose performance in office failed to comport with the will of voters. More importantly, that made it possible to change lawmakers more easily in the event they failed to address constituents' concerns. Senators, on the other hand, are not required to stand before voters as frequently; one third of all senators is reelected every two years thus having a moderating impact on changing the course of the nation. Senators were not elected directly by constituents until passage of the 17th Amendment to the US Constitution. Up until that time, senators were elected by state legislatures. The founding fathers in prescribing this procedure intended for the senate to have a moderating impact on drastic changes in the political system of the nation. In other words, they wanted to have the Senate focus on the long term and the House of Representatives to have a short term outlook for the nation.

Election frequency is a mechanism to correct misalignments in representing constituents' interests. That enables constituents to reelect politicians if citizens agree he or she has performed in accordance with their wishes or to vote them out otherwise. If politicians follow the views of their constituents then any legislation that is passed by the US Congress and signed into law by the president represents the will of the American people. In many cases, however, lobbyists come into the picture to grease politicians' palms and to force politicians to favor special interest groups even when advocated results are contrary to the wishes of constituents. That's part of the problem with tolerating lobbyists' financial contributions to lawmakers.

Legislation has been passed by the US Congress delineating policy objectives and delegating enforcement authority to many administrative agencies. Delegation of authority from the US Congress to administrative agencies includes legislative power to enact and issue rules required for implementation of the will of the people as well as enforcement authority. That administrative agency system traces its heritage to the early days of our federal government under the US Constitution when particular agencies were entrusted with the administration of custom laws, regulation of ocean-going vessels, coastal trading, and payment of veterans' pensions.

These governmental agencies have grown in parallel with the nation's development, based on the need for expert knowledge of a particular subject matter, specialization, and continuity in enactment and administration of rules based on that expertise. Regardless of good intentions behind the establishment of these regulatory agencies, there is always the threat of creating a bureaucratic monster that will, through its legislative and enforcement powers, lead to undesirable and oppressive results contrary to will of the people. That feeling has been expressed very well by J. O. Boyd in the Iowa Bar Review in these very eloquent words: [121]

> *"Government by bureaucracies has all the weaknesses of an autocracy and few of its advantages. Continued growth of bureaucracy will mean the doom of democracy. The destruction of all progress, the complete bankruptcy of free government, and eventually will lead to fascism or some form of totalitarianism".*

It is undisputed some administrative agencies have had a positive impact on the growth of our industrial might. But, these agencies have become bureaucratic and unresponsive to the needs for continued industrial development. In fact, it can be argued that this system has caused and will continue to cause more harm than good to future economic developments and growth. It is for that reason that these administrative agencies must be closely scrutinized and, if necessary disbanded.

The US Constitution provides for a legitimate government composed of three separate but equal branches performing a separate functions subject to the control and accountable to the people; it does not provide for the creation of totally independent and unaccountable agencies with the same powers as the three branches of government. Creation of these agencies represents an early attempt to delegate authority to an independent legislative and judicial body out of citizens' control. If our elected officials are not qualified to deal with specific problems then the solution is to elect people who would be qualified and capable of dealing with problems on behalf of constituents. This is a problem that has become endemic to the government and made our government a dysfunctional government. The most recent example of this is the creation of a committee composed of senators and congressman to cut expenditures from the federal budget. Keep in mind congress has failed to pass a budget for the past two to three years and spending is out of control; this is evidence members of Congress are unable or unwilling to act to solve a basic problem.

In many cases, administrative agencies are entrusted with the power to enact and enforce rules. The resulting rules are passed without taking into consideration any harm those rules might possibly cause. The American people have always intended to balance benefits against harm. It is undisputed Americans would not allow enactment of a rule doing more harm than good. This suggests a cost-benefit analysis is always necessary to ensure benefits exceed costs. There has to be a balance between the benefit the rules aim to achieve and the resulting harm caused by enforcement. If the benefit exceeds the harm, then the rule should be enacted and not otherwise. One must also keep in mind, that there is no way to totally eliminate risk. In view of that, the cost involved has to be no more than that required to achieve an acceptable level of risk and nothing more.

In a way, it can be said Congress is passing responsibility to a group of unaccountable bureaucrats who may have hidden agendas. Those hidden agendas based on personal biases rather than on the will of informed constituents should never play a role in passing any kind of administrative rules. If we allow bureaucrats to follow their individual agendas, they may act in a manner inconsistent with the will of the people or contrary to the goals of the legislation passed by congress. Let's illustrate.

The Environmental Protection Agency is charged with the duty of ensuring our living environment is protected. In some cases, the EPA has gone beyond the call of duty without taking into consideration the best alternative for the people. In these cases, the EPA has bounced ideas that, if implemented as proposed, would result in the loss of jobs to the detriment of people. There is no question that people would be opposed to any regulation that threatens their best interest without achieving a major benefit. But the agencies go ahead and implement the rules regardless of consequences. The agency may argue that it achieves a benefit by eliminating all cancer causing emissions, but that would require eliminating all jobs in a particular sector of the economy. That would be something the public will not stand for. In other words, there is always a risk that a segment of our population will contract cancer regardless of what is done; that risk cannot be totally eliminated. That then becomes the basis for discussing what an acceptable level of risk is.

One such proposal is the idea being advanced by EPA to control carbon-dioxide emissions to supposedly prevent global warming. Leighton Steward--a noted geologist and at one time a believer that carbon dioxide caused global warming-- argues that the scientific evidence available does not support EPA's conclusion. In fact, it has been shown that proponents of carbon dioxide emissions control are basing their opinions on fraudulent scientific data showing an impact on global warming when that cannot be clearly established by scientific means. Mr. Steward argues, based on scientific evidence, that carbon dioxide is not the culprit. In fact, he concludes higher levels of carbon dioxide than those presently detected are needed to sustain and expand plant growth. [122] Initially, President Obama has favored this type of legislation. Now, he has reversed his position and has asked the EPA to delay implementation of these rules; it is a good thing the president realized his mistake [123]. But that sudden reversal calls into question his judgment and his dedication to job creation. The only reason he is postponing implementation is because he wants to retain his job without regards for the impact these idiotic rules based on voodoo-scientific nonsense would have on employment opportunities for Americans.

Notwithstanding the discrepancy on the interpretation of scientific evidence, EPA's knee-jerk reaction has been to declare carbon-dioxide emissions harmful, thus raising a question on the validity of such claims. If such emissions are indeed harmful, then why has EPA failed to influence the Food and Drug Administration to immediately outlaw the use of carbon dioxide in soft drinks? If those emissions are harmful as alleged, then how is EPA proposing to deal with the issue of plant growth? What is EPA proposing to use in the photosynthesis process to enable normal plant growth?

The US Congress has not acted to address global warning or even to indicate its intention of acting in this matter. Opposition to legislation on this matter has been raised by some lawmakers indicating that the will of the people is not clear. Notwithstanding clear direction from citizens, EPA unilaterally signals its intent to enact and implement some very punitive rules in regards to carbon-dioxide emissions. Implementation of these proposed regulations were would result in the loss of a significant number of jobs and of employment opportunities in the refining and petrochemical sectors of the economy. What is the basis for this EPA action? The EPA action clearly represents the actions of environmental fanatics rather than the will of the majority of the people who have their financial and economic interest under a continuing by these arbitrary and capricious EPA actions.

If the scheme proposed by EPA to address carbon-dioxide emissions were implemented, then refineries would have to invest in equipment to reduce carbon-dioxide emissions from refineries and spend money to enable those who buy gasoline and other fuels to emit carbon dioxide emissions from the burning of these fuels. This is absurd! The refining business is not very profitable. Consequently, this action would lead to reductions in petroleum refining activity and the loss of employment opportunities at refineries and petrochemical plants. In fact, it may lead these companies to close shop and move to other countries. So what does that achieve? China and India are not imposing similar limits on their refineries or petrochemical plants causing US industry to be at a disadvantage in this regard. Implementation of these EPA standards would lead to a very costly situation providing very few, if any, benefits. In case of war, how are US military forces going to ensure fuels supply? Implementation of these rules would also possibly lead to fuel shortages for our cars. Is that what we want?

In another instance, administrative agencies promulgate so many rules and regulations that enforcement becomes difficult, if not impossible, due to lack of understanding the legalese used. Let's illustrate this by examining an Occupational Safety and Health Administration (OSHA) description of what constitutes a safe ladder. In particular, let's look at the standards they have enacted and promulgated for a "Safe Step Ladder" found in the Code of Federal Regulations. [124]

1926.1053(a) General. The following requirements apply to all ladders as indicated, including job-made ladders.

1926.1053(a)(1) Ladders shall be capable of supporting the following loads without failure:

1926.1053(a)(1)(i) Each self-supporting portable ladder: At least four times the maximum intended load, except that each extra-heavy-duty type 1A metal or plastic ladder shall sustain at least 3.3 time the maximum intended load. The ability of a ladder to sustain the loads indicated in this paragraph shall be determined by applying or transmitting the requisite load to the ladder in a downward vertical direction. Ladders built and tested in conformance with the applicable provisions of appendix A of this subpart will be deemed to meet this requirement.

1926.1053(a)(1)(ii) Each portable ladder that is not self-supporting: At least four times the maximum intended load, except that each extra-heavy-duty type 1A metal or plastic ladders shall sustain at least 3.3 times the maximum intended load. The ability of a ladder to sustain the loads indicated in this paragraph shall be determined by applying or transmitting the requisite load to the ladder in a downward vertical direction when the ladder is placed at an angle of 75 1/2 degrees from the horizontal. Ladders built and tested in conformance with the applicable provisions of appendix A will be deemed to meet this requirement.

1926.1053(a)(2) Ladder rungs, cleats, and steps shall be parallel, level, and uniformly spaced when the ladder is in position for use.

1926.1053(a)(3)(i) Rungs, cleats, and steps of portable ladders (except as provided below) and fixed ladders (including individual-rung/step ladders) shall be spaced not less than 10 inches (25 cm) apart, nor more than 14 inches (36 cm) apart, as measured between center lines of the rungs, cleats and steps.

1926.1053(a)(3)(ii) Rungs, cleats, and steps of step stools shall be not less than 8 inches (20 cm) apart, nor more than 12 inches (31 cm) apart, as measured between center lines of the rungs, cleats, and steps.

1926.1053(a)(3)(iii) Rungs, cleats, and steps of the base section of extension trestle ladders shall be not less than 8 inches (20 cm) nor more than 18 inches (46 cm) apart, as measured between center lines of the rungs, cleats, and steps. The rung spacing on the extension section of the extension trestle ladder shall be not less than 6 inches (15 cm) nor more than 12 inches (31 cm), as measured between center lines of the rungs, cleats, and steps.

As shown above, the writers of these regulations spend an awful lot of time describing in minute details what constitutes a "safe ladder" for use in the workplace. It is apparent from the legalese used in these regulations that lawyers rather than engineers or people knowledgeable in the field of building or using ladders are the authors of these regulations. This raises the question: are these lawyers really qualified to design ladders? These attorneys probably do not know what a safe ladder looks like. It would have been much better to provide a mechanical drawing that includes all of these details, which would have made it easier to read and follow in a manufacturing or operating setting.

Would it not be much preferable to have people engaged in the design and construction of ladders develop ideas that would result in fewer accidents from the use of ladders? Are step ladders manufactured in other countries following different specifications or standards safer or less safe than step ladders manufactured in accordance with US Standards as dictated by these regulations?

The previous example applies only to a simple tool that has been in used for many years. Imagine the situation where the working environment requires the use of thousands of tools and machinery. In that case, you have a complete mess that leads to confusion and misapplication of rules. Misapplication of rules leads to heavy fines and frustrations on the part of manufacturers who, after a while, decide to give up dealing with all of this nonsense and decide to relocate their manufacturing facilities to foreign countries to avoid all of these frustrations. That result is detrimental to employees who end up losing their job, to our nation that loses manufacturing plants, and to our nation's balance of payments when imported ladders come into the country.

Would it not be better to require that tools used in the workplace be designed with safety in mind and allow innovative ideas to be developed to create better tools? Would it not be better to focus OSHA's attention on analyzing safety concerns brought up by the users of the tools who are very adept at identifying all of the safety shortcomings? In other words, the author believes that it would be more productive to lay out a general safety policy requiring individual initiative to develop innovative ideas. The problem then becomes one of encouraging parties to address concern in an open atmosphere without reprisals.

Many of these regulatory agencies promulgate rules and then assume that everything will be okay. Regulators relax and fail to focus on determining the causes leading to the same results those agencies are trying to prevent. In many cases, regulators are very lax about inspections and enforcement of rules, and then accidents happen. It would be better to investigate accidents, to learn their root causes, and to derive lessons that can be applied to prevent future accidents. That would ensure implementation of corrective action quickly and effectively to solve future problems. If corrective steps are not put in place, then the agency should take punitive action and impose heavy monetary fines and jail terms to prevent future abuses.

Recent coal mine accidents clearly demonstrate what is wrong with the US regulatory system and, in particular, its specific shortcomings. There have been many instances in which methane in coal mines have exceeded safe concentration. It has been shown repeatedly that, if safe levels of methane are exceeded, then there is a greater probability of accidents. Despite that knowledge, mine owners continue to operate mines without concern for employees and continue to hide data from regulators showing the dangerous situations that exists in coal mines. It is not surprising that explosions occur and result in the loss of many lives. The workers are exposed to this dangerous situation, and, if they complain to the owners, they are fired. The regulators are there but cannot stop the operation in the mines, because they lack authority to do that. Instead of passing so many unenforceable rules, empower employees to shut down the mines in the event methane concentrations exceed a safe level. Define that safe level and enforce the rule. That will solve the problem and prevent many funerals.

Effective enforcement means having the authority to stop mining operations any time a dangerous situation is detected. It also means granting the authority to employees to bring up safety concerns to employers and regulators without fear of reprisal or loss of jobs. Unless regulators have authority to act quickly to prevent accidents, workers will continue to be killed. Regulations on paper are meaningless unless there are means of enforcing those regulations. Legalese will not solve problems, and it would be too late to prevent accidents after they occur and cause fatalities and damage to property and the environment. Agencies have to become proactive rather than reactive in solving problems under their legal jurisdiction. There are hundreds of legislative acts and hundreds of regulations relating to mine safety, and yet miners continue to die; every state and the federal government has such legislation in the books. Why do miners continue to die? What's the benefit of all of these legislation and regulations?

The author believes mine owners need to understand the danger involved and the commitment of federal regulatory agencies to safety in coal mines. It is obvious that one way to address this issue is to encourage miners to report unsafe situations to the owners and federal regulatory agencies directly without fear of reprisal from mine owners. Upon receiving a complaint from workers, the agency should immediately inspect the mine and shut it down if it finds an unsafe situation. In other words, the only way to get the attention of some of these mine owners is to get hold of their wallets, and shutting down the mine will impact owners' wallets. If workers abuse this honor system then they should also be heavily penalized. In order for the system to work, it has to be a fair system applicable to both parties equally.

Based on the author's professional experience, most companies have safety cultures and strictly adhere to safety procedures. Companies understand that safety is intended to minimize to the maximum extent possible endangering life or assets; companies know the cost of accidents. However, there are companies that are focused on cutting costs and neglect operating procedures leading to safety related incidents and accidents. Those companies will change their operating philosophy only when it becomes obvious regulatory agencies will actively enforced regulations and penalize not only corporations but also executives and immediate supervisors with heavy fines and jail times; that will help them focus their attention.

Inspection and enforcement have the effect of demonstrating to companies that cutting corners is very costly. By the same token, regulatory agencies should avoid enacting unnecessary rules to drive companies out of business or merely to penalize the lack compliance for the sake of compliance. This is a process that has to be a collaborative process ensuring minimum disruptions.

A common sense approach will prevent industry from leaving to more friendly and less regulated operating environments. Excessive regulation of industrial activities leads to relocation of manufacturing facilities from our shores to foreign countries where the climate is more tolerant and not as restrictive. There is no question that regulations are essential to protect workers, the environment and a myriad of other issues, but it has to be a system based on common sense.

Regulatory agencies spent a lot of time unnecessarily describing how to do everything in minute detail, which is unproductive and costly to industry. Instead, these agencies should spend more time developing a collaborative culture to achieve the overall objectives of the regulations without adding unnecessary cost or unjustly penalizing minor violations of undecipherable regulations. Lack of enforcement of existing regulations has become painfully obvious in the failure of financial institutions under the watchful eye of the Securities and Exchange Commission. Where were the regulators when these financial institutions were engaged in fraudulent schemes? The same is true in other sectors of the economy.

The author believes every dog is entitled to one bite but only one bite. Once, however, the dog shows a propensity to bite as a result of the first bite then it has to be stopped immediately and prevented, at all costs, from biting again. The situation is similar in the regulatory arena. This means regulatory agencies should give wide latitude to Corporate America to develop and implement creative new solutions to achieve policy objectives detailed in law passed by congress as an expression of the will of the people. That latitude should grant companies more room to develop profitable and simple solutions to existing problems that are the subject of the regulation and in implementing those solutions. In addition, this proposal would give Corporate America the opportunity to develop solutions to a common problem faced by many other companies. This would result in raising the potential for marketing these new technologies, processes, or products to a broader group of companies. The result would be potentially a new source of cash flow for the company solving the problem.

The author recalls a technical meeting during which an engineer from a photographic-film manufacturer describes a solution to an emissions problem. The problem involves cleaning exhaust gases from a stack located in the photographic-film manufacturing complex. This engineer brags about being able to recover substantial amounts of silver from the stack. That makes the solution to the problem a very profitable outcome for the film-manufacturing plant. That same approach can be followed in every manufacturing facility. It is a question of taking a new approach to solve problems by focusing on the potential for profit rather than on forcing an unwanted expenditure on something that may not work.

On the other side of the coin is the issue of enforcement to ensure companies that fail to address or to ignore the issue are scrutinized strictly and penalized heavily, particularly after the first incident. Remember that every dog is entitled to the first bite, and that's it. Penalties have to include shutting down the offending facility if necessary to gain the attention of management. Reductions in profits or costs increases get the attention of management, and it is the only way to enforce some of these regulations for example enforcement of safety regulations in coal mines. At the same time, regulators have to be realistic as to what can and cannot be achieved and therefore draft regulations in a manner intended to show that limits required are achievable and not merely illusory.

I had a very interesting personal experience on "effective enforcement" of environmental regulations. During a visit to a petrochemical plant in Belgium, I was attending a meeting and the plant manager was constantly barging into the meeting and requesting an update on what was transpiring. Obviously, very little progress was made due to constant interruptions by this intrusive plant manager. When the meeting resumed after lunch, the plant manager failed to appear, and so his absence prompted me to ask a question on his whereabouts. I was informed the plant manager, along with the complex manager and the vice-president of chemicals, together with some other people, had been taken to prison for dumping some chemicals into Antwerp harbor. Furthermore, I was told that I would be unable to see the plant manager until his release from prison sometime on Monday after an initial appearance in front of a magistrate. On subsequent visits, I noticed a very strong commitment that focused on preventing emissions.

Comparing the situation described in the Belgian case with the mining disasters in West Virginia and Kentucky, where many lives are lost, one notices several differences. It is apparent that Belgian authorities are believers in strong enforcement and that strong enforcement is effective to prevent further occurrences. Mine owners, on the other hand, have been warned several times. Fines have been imposed as a result of these violations, and those fines have remained unpaid for several years while the mine owner to buys time to create a new rule or even overthrows the judicial system in the state thus getting away from paying the fine. In the meantime, deceased miners' families suffer the consequences of violations while the owners continue to line their pockets. This situation plainly indicates that US regulatory agencies are very lax about enforcement. Unlike Belgian authorities, US authorities assume everything will be fine after issuing a citation. Belgians, on the other hand, know everything will be fine after effective enforcement.

The results in the approach taken by these two governmental authorities are obvious. Mine owners and operators in the US continue to ignore warnings and citations with impunity. Miners continue to die as a result of these violations. Violations are ignored by the mining company and thrown out by judges who are bribed by the mining company CEO. Something is wrong with that picture. While the CEO is telling reporters that the company is concerned about the safety of its employees, the story comes out that the mining company has been issued many citations for the same violations causing the death of coal miners.

Administrative agencies created by the US Congress perform some beneficial services by developing expertise in a particular field of interest. A problem is created when regulatory agencies exceed the authority granted to them by Congress—in fact, this may hinder the activity the agency was supposed to perform.

In many instances, these agencies adopt rules imposing unachievable limits. These limits are determined on the basis of bias or simply as an incentive to do better than it is feasible. Obviously, achievement of unattainable and unrealistic goals costs money that could be better spent expanding manufacturing activities or researching new solutions to the problem. Undesirable consequences on employment levels are also a consequence of unnecessary regulation as President Obama has recently discovered.

It would be better and more effective if regulators were to rely on common sense rather than bias. The goal would be achieved with minimum disruption to industrial activity. And, this would encourage cooperative efforts rather than adversarial confrontations. This would require taking into consideration the economic impact of the rule prior to its implementation.

Regulatory agencies should rely more on the expertise of operating companies to achieve goals. This means describing a broad goal and asking companies to achieve that goal by whatever means possible; it does not have to be achieved by a prescribed manner. The regulatory agency should have the power to expect results or given feedback on why the regulation is unachievable in terms of realistic scientific and financial data within a given period of time. If it does not get cooperation from industrial sources, then the agency would be able to go ahead and enact the rule as it wishes. That mechanism would provide an incentive to develop new technology to address problems under consideration or generate comments based on facts as to why the goals behind the regulation are unachievable. Let's illustrate that with a hypothetical example.

Suppose an administrative agency asks aerospace companies to reduce fuel consumption by airliners by 60 percent in a period of two years. The response very likely would be a rejection because these companies know that the people who drafted these regulations did not know the total amount of energy required to get these airplanes airborne and flying. The response would be different if the agency were to ask the aerospace companies to provide a program to reduce fuel consumption to the maximum extent possible achievable with existing or newly developed technology. The difference in approach is significant. In the first case, companies are told what to do by people who, very likely, do not know what they are talking about. The second approach relies on those who know what to do to provide practical solutions. The advantage is a wider range of alternatives for different companies to implement depending on their economic status. The agency now has a broad range of solutions available to address the problem. It can favor one approach or allow multiple approaches. In any event, the problem gets solved. And, that's what we want.

A controversy has been brewing in Texas between the Environmental Protection Agency and Texas Commission on Environmental Quality (TCEQ) since 2009. The controversy revolves around the methodology to be followed in calculating emissions for the purpose of issuing construction and operating permits to petrochemical plants and refineries. The EPA has asserted that the methodology used by TCEQ allows the chemical industry and refineries to emit unmeasured amounts of toxins. TCEQ disagrees and has told EPA that its methodology achieves the same reductions on a plant-wide basis rather than in an individual section of the plant. If the level of emissions is achieved, then what does it matter if the methodology used in solving the problem is different? The real crux of the problem seems to be politics and the private agenda of Regional EPA chief Al Armendariz, who has a record of environmental activism against TCEQ. This kind of behavior is repulsive.

Mr. Armendariz has gone to the extent of threatening to take over all permits being issued to chemical plants and refineries by federalizing the permit process, and has done so in some cases. His real motive is to shut down chemical plants and refineries and to increase unemployment for Texans who failed to vote for President Obama. Is that a proper governmental function? I submit Mr. Armendariz should disqualify himself based on his bias and desire to get even for previous battle scars suffered in combat actions against TCEQ. This is matter that is now being litigated in the courts. Perhaps, President Obama's change of mind regarding environmental regulations will lead Mr. Armendariz to resign thus preventing disastrous results on employment opportunities. In that case, President Obama might get some votes in Texas.

WASTEFUL GOVERNMENT EXPENDITURES

The US government spends a significant amount of money unnecessarily. In fact, it wastes a lot of taxpayer money on projects that are going nowhere or are simply projects that benefit no one except special interests groups actively bribing politicians.

The US government is now engaged in building a wall on the border with Mexico, and it has spent close to a billion dollars building it under the misguided pretense of protecting our borders. This wall has not been completed yet, and so it is expected that additional funds will have to be spent to complete the project. The question that should be asked is whether the border protection excuse is valid? It is very likely that the real reasons behind construction of the wall are hypocrisy and the need to divert attention from a problem nobody wants to address. Why?

Nobody on our southern border is threatening the US. The real reason the wall is being built is to stop immigrants crossing our southern border from Mexico and other Latin American countries. Supposedly, the wall will stop the inflow of immigrants; that logic fails to take into consideration the root cause of the immigration problem, which is demand for low-cost labor for agricultural work. Proponents of the wall ignore the fact that tunnels can be built under the wall, as has been shown on many occasions.

These new immigrants unlike previous immigrants are arriving from countries neighboring our southern border. Unfortunately, the new immigrants are not Anglo Saxons. But they are also contributors to our nation's welfare. These new immigrants from our southern border are poor agricultural workers who find employment doing the work local workers do not want to do. They find employment picking agricultural crops that we demand for our sustenance. They also perform jobs in construction that nobody else wants to do. Are these the people who are threatening our borders? It is hard to believe that these immigrants, poor though they may be, are the enemies or invaders of the United States that they are portrayed to be. Are these immigrants the reason for the protection required by the wall under construction in our southern border? In fact, many of these illegal aliens volunteer for service in our military forces earning the right to become US citizens or dying in the battlefields of Iraq and Afghanistan without ever enjoying the benefits of US Citizenship. In view of that, does anybody believe the assertion the US is being threatened on the southern front? Are these the people threatening our nation?

It is hypocritical of our national leaders to back construction of this shameful wall, particularly in view of the words used by President Ronald Reagan encouraging General Secretary of the Soviet Union Mikhail Gorbachev to tear down the Berlin Wall. President Reagan addressed Mr. Gorbachev in these very eloquent words:

> *"We welcome change and openness; for we believe that freedom and security go together, that the advance of human liberty can only strengthen the cause of world peace. There is one sign the Soviets can make that would be unmistakable, that would advance dramatically the cause of freedom and peace. General Secretary Gorbachev, if you seek peace, if you seek prosperity for the Soviet Union and Eastern Europe, if you seek liberalization, come here to this gate. Mr. Gorbachev, open this gate. Mr. Gorbachev, tear down this wall!"* [125]

In like manner, we, as citizens of this great country, should ask our political leaders to tear down this wall under construction on our southern border and to level with us. These political leaders and hate mongers express the desires of lobbyists and racists; those expressions of hate and racism are not on the basis of justice and truth but political correctness. Republicans talk about dealing with illegal immigration, but don't want to deny farmers a source of cheap labor. Democrats, on the other hand, also talk about eliminating illegal immigration but want to continue getting votes from Hispanics. Consequently, no one does anything. This is the best example of political correctness. Politicians do not want to be wrong and offend a constituency. Consequently, nothing is done.

The construction of the wall is an effort by politicians to divert attention from a problem. It reminds the author of the reason Argentineans generals running the government justified going to war against Great Britain over the Falkland Island. The generals were hoping to divert the attention of the people from the economic problem over to the war effort. Needless to say, the generals lost the war. Similarly, our politicians will suffer a moral defeat over the construction of this wall and force the nation to spend a huge amount of money unnecessarily.

Politicians are talking from both sides of their mouths as they try to keep the wall building project going without addressing the real issue, which is the demand for low-wage laborers to fill jobs in agriculture or other undesirable sectors. If the government wanted to address the immigration issue correctly, they would be going after employers of these illegal immigrants for the purpose of exploiting them by paying low wages. Politicians, however, would never do that because those employers contribute to their campaigns, and it is in their best interest to keep this farce going.

It is a fact that these poor agricultural workers come to our country because our agricultural sector is willing to employ them in order to reduce labor costs. Those immigrants are paid less than minimum wages while performing very difficult jobs of harvesting agricultural products. It is a fact that farm owners rely on these workers because they cannot find local workers to perform the same duty. Are these immigrants threatening our borders? It is more likely that the real truth is that they are helping our agricultural sector. If the truth were to be told, it would become obvious that farmers need these workers. So why not address the issue head on?

The second hole for wasteful spending is the cost of incarcerating non-violent, young people who get caught in possession of small amounts of illicit drugs or consuming those illicit drugs. These young people are sent to penal institutions where they become hardened criminals and, then, are returned to society after serving their sentence. Since these people now have a criminal record, they become unemployable. Consequently, criminal skills they learn in prison become the means to earn a living in our society. Those who are incarcerated become totally dependent on the state instead of being productive taxpayers, which adds a burden to our society and creates a future problem; this is a waste of valuable resources.

Those who avoid getting caught are the lucky ones. Former President Bill Clinton is one of the lucky ones; he has admitted smoking marijuana without inhaling. Yet, he has served as president of the United States. This is a serious, costly problem in need of a solution aimed at solving the problem rather than creating a bigger problem. It is a problem that has been misunderstood and the consequences of those actions cannot be ignored. Why isn't the problem addressed directly?

The drug and immigration problems are not addressed for a very simple reason. These problems are left unsolved because the amount of money involved is so large and beneficial to special interests. In the drug case, there are many influential people in high positions who are benefitting financially from the problem and don't want it solved. In both the drug and immigration cases, the country chooses to attack the problem from the supply side rather than from the demand perspective.

In the drug case, the US spends significant sums of money spraying herbicides on drug plants in foreign countries. The spraying of herbicides on those countries amounts to chemical terrorism, costing hundreds of millions of dollars annually. This does not take into consideration environmental damage done to fertile land and to the health of local populations. Spraying herbicides on those countries engenders hatred against our nation. That hatred is the result of destroying a valuable crop to the detriment of the grower. Imagine how our local farmers would feel if some foreign power were to come over their land and destroy their crops; that's the same feeling those people have when they see their marijuana crops destroyed. If the demand for marijuana were eliminated, no one would grow it. Plain and simple!

In the immigration case, the results are similar. Immigrants cross the border because jobs are available here. They are detained and incarcerated, thus becoming totally dependent on the state and adding another financial burden on our government. Let's address the issue by developing a just system wherein farmers are able to hire foreign agricultural workers when needed under a guest program designed to pair employers and employees for the benefit of both parties. This alternative method would avoid the unnecessary expense of alien incarceration and deportation.

Funds saved by eliminating these wasteful expenditures can be better spent on drug treatment, rehabilitation, and education. This alternative would get people ready for positions in the workplace to man jobs created by a continuously developing and dynamic economy. Turning that wasteful spending into an educational investment would return many benefits to our society as a whole, including higher tax revenues, reduction in crime rate, and higher standard of living for all citizens.

Reducing or eliminating problems resulting in wasteful spending would have a snowball effect on reducing spending on other problems and generating government revenues. For example, rehabilitation of non-violent offenders or drug users would lead to a reduction in crime and lower incarceration costs. Is that not a better alternative for the money currently being wasted on just two problems--drugs and immigration? The magnitude of wasteful spending is astronomical considering the number of worthless projects funded.

These changes in policy would also have the added benefit of reducing the cost of government. Reductions in the cost of running the government would lead to potential reductions in income-tax requirements. This, therefore, would leave more money in the hands of consumers to spend acquiring new products or savings for the purpose of future spending. That added consumer spending would result in larger demands for manufactured goods, including large items such as cars that, in turn would result in more employment. The higher level of employment would mean more people pay income taxes and thus increase the revenue pool available to the government. Under this scenario, everyone wins! Politicians, instead of developing a common sense approach to problems, prefer to create new crimes to extend incarceration.

We all have household budgets to guide our expenditures. We all make difficult decisions to maximize benefits derived from our expenditures. That's us. Our legislators, however, do not share the same desires to maximize benefits when funding projects for the government. They figure it is not their money, so it can be spent in any way possible, regardless of benefit to constituents. The only benefit they are trying to maximize is their benefit.

Legislators fail to realize that the federal budget represents expenditure of taxpayers' funds. Taxpayers' funds represent a comingling of funds from every part of the nation that has been entrusted to the government for the benefit of the whole nation and not just for one small part of the nation. Taxpayers expect elected officials to spend those funds wisely and in such a way as to derive maximum benefit for the entire nation.

Given that lawmakers spent taxpayers' funds to perpetuate themselves in office, something has to be done to eliminate wasteful federal spending. Several things come to mind to rank the order of importance that should be placed on expenditures by the federal government. Number one, defense spending is essential to protect our nation from those who wish us ill. Number two, educational expenditures should rank very high so as to enable the country to have access to a qualified pool of people capable of manning technical jobs our technological industrial sector creates. Number three, since our people are our most valuable resource, then health expenditures should be given the level of importance that goes with that. Number four should be reserved for creating jobs for the general population. Notice this ranking results in jobs from defense expenditures, education to prepare our people for better jobs, and health care to enable people to work.

All expenditures for projects in infrastructure should be proposed by an independent nonpartisan agency of the government, such as the US Army Corps of Engineers. Expenditures for projects in a given congressional district should be funded not on the basis of politics or political influence but rather on the basis of need. Additionally, all expenditures should be clearly designated in spending bills and not hidden or attached to general spending bills in order to ensure passage by holding the general spending bill hostage to the wishes of particular influential lawmakers. Pork-barrel spending authorizations should stand on merits rather than political influence. Taxpayers have the right to see how their dollars are spent and the reason for that spending.

There is no question these proposals are idealistic in nature; lawmakers would never pass anything that prevents them from having control and power over taxpayers' funds. There is, however, a mechanism to turn this idealism into a pragmatic approach. It has been said that every dog is entitled to one bite. That concept applies as much to legislators as anybody else. In view of that, legislators should be given the first opportunity to implement these suggestions. In the event, they fail to do so, citizens ought to band together to draft and pass an amendment to the US Constitution requiring a balanced budget as is the case in every state of the Union. The other alternative would be to require all bills authorizing expenditures to pass both houses of congress by a majority of 80 percent.

EDUCATIONAL SYSTEM

Corporate America needs a continuous pool of well-educated people trained in many disciplines, particularly in scientific and engineering fields. These are the people who will replace retiring workers or become the new workers coming into the manpower pool due to population growth. The educational system plays a leading role in preparing the younger population thus enabling them to continue their post-secondary education at universities.

Corporate America hires many university graduates, including scientists and engineers to make significant contributions to our country's development. This development is something that has its roots in R&D discoveries, which essential building blocks to sustain our industrial base and expand Corporate America's leadership position and that of the entire nation. It is in this fashion that industrial development of the nation is rejuvenated and strengthened.

Growth and profits generated from new developments provide funding for both existing and new operations. This leads to job creation to support our ever-growing population. That is a recipe followed by not only Corporate America to advance our national industrial development but also by other countries in the world undergoing similar developments.

The term "developed country" is perhaps a bit misleading to the extent it provides a false sense of security. Development is a continuing process; it never ends. If it were to end, competing countries would overtake the country pausing in its development efforts. Once you fall behind, then it becomes extremely expensive and difficult to catch up.

It is extremely important to realize that the leadership positions held by Corporate America and that of our nation depends on continuing that development journey. If we fail to continue and expand our efforts in that regard, then Corporate America would see its technical leadership position challenged and overtaken by foreign counterparts. If that happens, then our nation technical preeminence in the world will decline, and the US will cease to be the power it is today. It is essential, therefore, for the US to maintain and expand its R&D efforts to strengthen its technical leadership position in the world. Look at the outcome of German and Japanese development efforts after World War II as examples of what can be achieved.

The responsibility to maintain technical excellence places an awesome burden on the educational system of the entire US and not just that of a given state. This implies that education has to be addressed nationwide. In other words, our students must excel in all subject matters. In particular, our students must excel in science and mathematics in order to enable the US as a whole to sustain its global technological leadership.

US students, however, presently rank behind foreign students in science and mathematics proficiency. That standing must improve if the US is to remain a technological force in the world. The educational system must emphasize science and mathematics in primary and secondary schools' curricula to enable graduates to pursue careers in scientific and engineering fields. It is not a question of competition between states but rather it is a worldwide competition for future jobs. This is a tall order for the educational system to accomplish. It is something that is essential for the survival of the US as a major international industrial power.

Nelson Mandela recognized the importance of education and the overwhelming responsibility it placed on the educational system. He stated his conclusion in terms of the impact education has on changing the world. Mr. Mandela said: "Education is the most powerful weapon which you can use to change the world. [126]

The educational system is a system composed of many different but equally important parts. It includes teachers who do their best to challenge and encourage students to reach for the stars. It is teachers who plant the seed of learning and see the product of those efforts as students flourish. It is teachers who dedicate their lives to benefit our whole society by educating students who will, in turn, change the world and improve our surroundings and daily lives.

We all fondly remember teachers who encouraged each of

us along the way to develop to our full potential. The author is no exception, for I have been encouraged by many teachers who inspired me to reach for the stars. This constant encouragement has allowed me to defy my blindness and metaphorically broaden my field of vision at a time when I could barely see in front of me.

There are many excellent teachers throughout the nation who are dedicated to educating our future industrial and political leaders. Those teachers have influenced and continue to influence young minds for the benefit of our whole nation and, specifically, Corporate America. We, as a nation, owe a great debt of gratitude to those teachers. It is incumbent, therefore, on all of us to support efforts teachers make on a daily basis and to reinforce the educational system so that our students gain a competitive advantage over students from other developed and developing nations. Good teachers have essential roles to play, and the whole nation must strive to attract and retain only those teachers who demonstrate an attitude toward excellence. The jobs of teachers and mothers are the hardest and least-paid jobs in our nation. Good teachers are essential for our nation's success. We must recognize they must be better compensated.

Let's examine some facts to determine the present status of the US educational system and to map a strategy to improve it. Data in Table 16 show that our eighth-grade students are not as proficient in math and science as eight graders from many of our Asian competitors. That's an alarming conclusion in view of the importance of math and science to our technological society.

Country/State	8th Graders Proficient in Math and Science, %	Country/State	8th Graders Proficient in Math and Science, %
Singapore	73	Netherlands	38
Hong Kong	66	CT	35
Korea	65	NY	30
Taiwan	61	Slovakia	28
Japan	57	Russia	27
Mass	51	CA	24
SD	41	AL	18
NJ	40	MS	14

Table 16 US vs. Other Countries Students [127]

Assessments of academic proficiency among developed nations belonging to the Organization for Economic Cooperation and Development (OECD) show the performance of our high school graduates to range anywhere from mediocre to poor. Results from the Programme for International Student Achievement (PISA), which is a test administered to students within the OECD, reveal the standing of US fifteen-year-old students compared to their counterparts from the other OECD countries. [128] These results are from the 2006 PISA assessment administered in 2006, except for the reading and problem-solving literacy results, which come from the 2003 test.

These test results indicate US students rank: fifteenth among twenty-nine OECD countries in reading literacy, twenty-first of thirty OECD countries in scientific literacy, twenty-fifth of thirty OECD countries in mathematics literacy, and twenty-fourth of twenty-nine OECD in problem-solving literacy. Unless the US educational system better prepares students for college and the workplace, the downward trend to decadence will continue or accelerate. This downward trend will worsen the rankings and place the US at an economic competitive disadvantage compared to our present trading partners. This trend, in turn, threatens the technological leadership standing of the US. This situation would make it very difficult to attract new investments by Corporate America or foreign companies planning to come to our shores. Simply put, industrial development ceases as industries pursue locations where the labor force is better educationally prepared. The situation is dangerous for each one of us because it threatens our standard of living as we know it today. Furthermore, this trend has to be reversed if the American Dream is to survive.

Another disturbing trend shown by data in Table 16 is the disparity in math and science proficiency among students from within the United States. Notice that Massachusetts students rank the highest among all states. But, the competition is not an internal national competition among students representing each of the states but rather a worldwide competition among US students and their foreign counterparts. The US is clearly losing that competition. Those states with the lowest rankings reflect the results of a failing educational system, and that makes it extremely difficult to attract new industry or to create new job opportunities there.

One might ask what causes the poor standing among US students. Several things come to mind in regard to this issue. The first has to do with the financial support provided for education. Secondly, the competence of teachers has to be scrutinized very carefully for they are entrusted with the very important task of educating our youngsters to compete on a worldwide basis. Thirdly, it becomes incumbent on all of us to attract and retain competent teachers. Finally, it is extremely important that the educational system reduce wasteful spending to enable more funds to be dedicated to educating students rather than spending on administrative or bureaucratic side of education.

It has been said that our future depends on our children. If our children are unable to compete internationally on account of a poor educational background, then our future is cloudy at best. That situation has to be reversed to brighten our future and to sustain our own American Dream and the nation's global preeminence.

Table 17 shows typical amounts spent per student in many nations as compared to similar educational expenditures in the US. Notice that the US spends a significant amount of money. In fact, it spends significantly more per student than many other nations. It appears that, while the US is spending a higher amount than many other nations, it is not getting a good return on that investment based on proficiency results in science and math.

Country	Expenditures, US $ per Student	Country	Expenditures, US $ per Student
Switzerland	9348	Netherlands	5304
Austria	8163	United Kingdom	5230
United States	7764	Israel	5115
Norway	7343	Portugal	4636
Denmark	7200	Spain	4274
France	6605	Ireland	3934
Italy	6458	Greece	3287
Germany	6209	Czech Republic	3182
Japan	5890	Hungary	2140
Australia	5830	Thailand	1177
Sweden	5648		

Table 17 Secondary School Spending per Student [129]

It is obvious other nations do a better job than the US in preparing their students in science and mathematics at a lower cost. There are no easy comparisons to be made with data in the two previous tables shown here. The Netherlands, for example, spends approximately 30 percent less than the US on a per student basis, and yet the science and math proficiency results for Dutch students exceed the results attained by US students from many states.

Country	2008 Per Capita GDP, US $ [103]	Teacher Starting Salary, % Per Capita GDP, [104]	Teacher Starting Salary, US $ [104]
South Korea	27939	141	39394
Germany	35613	141	50214
Netherlands	40850	99	40442
Hong Kong	43922	97	42604
United Kingdom	35445	95	33673
Australia	35677	95	33893
Finland	35426	95	33655
Singapore	49288	95	46824
Belgium	34493	92	31734
United States	46716	81	37840

Table 18 Teacher Starting Salaries [130]

Why is that? Perhaps, the answer lies in how the money allocated for education is spent. A portion of the expenditure is allocated to teacher salaries and the balance goes into administrative costs and other expenditures. Now let's look at starting salaries data for teachers in some of these countries. Data in Table 18 indicate the Netherlands pays its teachers a higher starting salary than the US. In fact, the US pays the lowest teachers' starting salaries compared to many countries. Is it possible that a correlation exist between teachers' salaries and students' performance? Certainly, higher teachers' salaries would attract better qualified teachers to the classroom. That would also be an incentive to retain better and more competent teachers in the classroom. Better qualified teachers would have a significant positive impact on the educational process, leading to improvements of the product from the educational system

If starting teachers' salaries in the US are lower than those in many other parts of the world then, in general, it is possible to conclude those countries place a higher value on education than we do. But, it is also a fact that the US is spending more on education than many of our competitors. So, where is the rest of the money spent? A significant portion of the balance is spent on administrative functions and creating a bureaucracy that does nothing to improve the quality of education or improve the quality of the product delivered by the US educational system. A lot of money is spent by every city in every state for superintendents and other administrators manning the many small educational districts located throughout individual states. These small districts could be more efficiently run by being absorbed within larger districts or, even better, within a central, statewide, educational authority capable of allocating funds equally rather on the basis of real-estate property value. That option would ensure equal educational opportunities for all of the state's residents rather than favoring those who live in richer sections of the state.

What is at stake here is more than the education of all of our youngsters. We are talking about the future of our country. Therefore, it is essential for all US students to have access to a good education regardless of where they happen to live or their family financial status. The US needs every student in every state and city to contribute to the best of his or her abilities to ensure our nation advances its development and sustains its leadership position in the world for everyone's benefit. Students from one state or section of a state are not competing against students from a different section of the state or on an interstate basis; they are competing on an international basis, and we are losing that battle. That trend needs to be reversed to ensure that everyone enjoys the American Dream and our nation's prosperity flourishes.

It is no secret the US places more emphasis on athletics than it does on academics. This means that significant amount of money is spent on athletic facilities and salaries for coaches. This activity, while useful and desirable, is one that should be undertaken outside of the academic realm. It is an activity that brings enjoyment to our youngsters and encourages their competitive spirits. But you cannot compete in our technological world unless you are soundly grounded in academic subjects. Students should be encouraged to excel first in academics and then in athletics and not the other way around. There are too many examples of youngsters graduating from secondary schools and colleges who fail to become professional athletes and who are unable to either write or read. That is a sad commentary for our educational system, for it has failed the individual students and the entire nation.

There is no question that professional athletes get very high salaries. That attracts the attention of youngsters who hope to also be able to earn similar amounts. Those high salaries become a good incentive for exploitation by coaches, who cause youngsters to focus on athletics rather than academics. The fact of the matter is that most college athletes fail to become professional athletes and, at the same time, fail to take advantage of the educational opportunities granted them. Consequently, at the end of their academic careers, very few of these athletic students become professional athletes and are unqualified or ill prepared for decent jobs or to earn a living. Coaches and universities are doing a disservice to these student athletes. In many cases, these athletes fail to graduate. It is a waste of human talent!

Universities encourage this behavior because of the amount of money involved in athletic activities, demonstrating, once again, that money corrupts. Based on this example, can the rest of society expect better treatment? It would indeed be unusual to expect ethical and moral behavior from all members of society when we see the power of money and lobbyists influencing the behavior of our most sacrosanct institutions. Universities should focus on providing a well-rounded education to enable students to earn a decent living. Athletic directors and coaches should be role models to encourage students to achieve in both athletics and academic endeavors. They should not use their positions to exploit and enslave students for it is true that those who fail to get a good education become slaves to their stupidity. Remember that a mind is a terrible thing to waste. Universities and coaches are no different from corporate executives who fail to accept responsibility for their actions.

Another discouraging fact in the American educational system is reliance on computers. Computers are great tools, but schools should focus on teaching basics principles before students can move on to the use of computers. Let's look at a typical example of the damage being done by excessive reliance on computers. Go to any store and run a very simple test to determine whether the mathematical abilities of the cashier meet acceptable standards. When you are told how much you owe, let's say $9.57, give the cashier a $10.00 bill. As soon as the cashier enters the $10.00, the cash register displays the correct amount to return to you, which is $0.43. Now, just before the cashier gives you the $0.43, offer to give the cashier $0.57 so that she can give a $1 bill back. Watch what happens. Nine out of ten times the cashier won't know what to do. Cashiers cannot tell you how much is owed to you and the cash register cannot be used to provide the answer. Cashiers are totally lost, and their facial expressions show their disappointment and frustrations. Now, run the same test in the middle of an underdeveloped country using an illiterate street vendor. What is the result? Ten out ten times the correct amount will be refunded to you. What does that tell you about the quality of our children's education?

At the same time, it must be realized that education is not a process occurring only during school hours and under the control of teachers. Education is a process that continues throughout the whole day and year; it is a never ending process. In view of that, parents have a fundamental role to play in their children's education.

Education is considered a state function rather than a federal function. In order to perform this educational duty, many states are subdivided into local school districts drawing funding from taxes imposed on local property; local districts are managed by local school administrators. This situation raises two points of concern. One is that there is a potential for unequal educational expenditures on a statewide basis and also on an intrastate basis. The second point of concern is the excessive bureaucracy that is part of the present educational system. Administrative educational bureaucracy contributes nothing to the educational of our children, and it should be trimmed.

In view of that, it would be better to have the educational system financed on a national basis. This proposal would remove the disparity in funding educational activities based on property value. It, however, would have to be adjusted for actual differences in cost of living prevailing in the individual states. The federal government should be the provider of educational standards to be achieved by all students regardless of states; this means that education would be considered a federal rather than a state function. The states would be tasked with the duty of creating a nonpartisan educational agency staffed by educators and not politicians to manage local schools and to set goals for excellence in the educational product.

Excellent teachers are required to educate our children and achieve excellent results. These teachers have to be selected on the basis of merit and not on anything else. They have to be well compensated in order to attract and retain the best professional people to undertake the task of turning the educational system around. This would enable our children to compete on an international basis and to do well. It is an essential part of sustaining our industrial might and national preeminence.

Academics rather than athletics' must be emphasized. This does not mean, however, that athletics would be relegated to the ranks of the forgotten. It does mean that athletics it would have to be part of after school activities. This would ensure that all students get a quality education enabling them to earn a living, even if they fail to secure a position in a professional athletic team after completing his education.

It is also worthwhile to consider a lesser reliance on computers to educate our youngsters. Why? There is a tendency for people to accept computer answers without challenge. The answer a computer returns represents the quality of the data you provide. A computer will return nonsensical answers if the data input to it is nonsense. Our youngsters need to rely on their minds and experience to determine when the answer is reasonable, and they should be able to provide a close approximation to the true answer regardless of whether or not they have access to a computer. Our students must be able to perform even when electrical power is lost or the batteries in their computers are discharged

LOW VOTER TURNOUT
AT ELECTIONS

There is a tendency on the part of many citizens to withhold their votes on the erroneous assumption that by doing so they express displeasure and frustration with elected officials. They then turn around and complain about unfair governmental actions, abuse of political power, corruption, and many other things ailing our society; these folks fail to recognize that by not voting to affirmatively express their desires and needs and elect unrepentant and undesired legislators. Citizens are frustrated when they see elected officials undergo a transformation upon arrival in Washington or the individual states capital, leading to a complete reversal of their views on issues promised to be dealt with during the campaign. No wonder constituents are frustrated for they know their elected officials are liars who will not deliver on campaign promises.

In many instances, this unwanted change by politicians is the result of having to repay a debt incurred during the campaign that, once elected, becomes due. In most cases, these newly minted legislators rely on gifts and political contributions from lobbyists who are advocating the views of special-interest groups, and these views are contrary to the views held by constituents. If legislators accept contributions to pay campaign expenses, they become indebted to lobbyists and must vote in favor of positions advocated by lobbyists regardless irrespective of their feelings about the issue at bar or constituents' point of view . In a way, this is similar to legalized blackmail, but the legislators have no choice except to accept a friendly offer from lobbyists to either vote for lobbyists' or face no more political campaign contributions from friendly lobbyists in the future. In view of that, these supposedly representatives of the people ignore pleads made to constituents in exchange for votes.

Voters feel abandoned until the next elections when these elected officials once again appear before them to make amends with the population in order to get their votes to stay on the gravy train. Citizens believe their votes have no value, but the contrary is true. Instead of complaining, all of us should exercise our power to elect politicians who are more in tune with our needs and desires than with their own personal financial concerns and greed. It may take more than one election to get rid of politicians who fail to stick with the voters. The issue with campaign contributions and the cost of campaigning raises a very interesting point demanding a solution in terms of effective campaign reforms with teeth.

Table 19 shows data on the percentage of eligible voters that exercise their civic duty to vote both during presidential elections and midterm elections. Voting is a civic responsibility we have to elect the best people to represent our views; it is a fundamental tool that can be used to reform and reshape our governments to align its performance to satisfy our ideals and needs and improve our lives. It is a right citizens of many other nations would love to have to get rid of tyrannical regimes.

Year	Presidential Election Turnout, %	Year	Mid-Term Election Turnout, %
1960	63.1	1962	47.3
1964	61.9	1966	48.4
1968	60.8	1970	46.6
1972	55.2	1974	38.2
1976	53.6	1978	37.2
1980	52.6	1982	39.8
1984	53.1	1986	36.4
1988	50.1	1990	36.5
1992	55.1	1994	38.8
1996	49.1	1998	36.4
2000	51.3	2002	37.0
2004	55.3	2006	37.1
2008	56.8		

Table 19. Voter Turnout [131]

It is worth noticing from such data that roughly 50 percent of eligible voters exercise their right to vote every four years at presidential elections. Also notice that there is a steady decline in the number of voters exercising this constitutional right from 1960 on. Why is that?

Voters tend to be unconcerned about issues of the day except at those times when something occurs that affects them in a very detrimental manner. Consequently, voters are involved in the political process only when something happens to trigger an interest in a particular issue. In order to be effective, the right to vote must be exercised on a consistent basis to let politicians know they are being watched and evaluated by those who hire them to work for a given period of time. If politicians know they are being evaluated on a continuous basis then that evaluation will cause them to be more responsive; lobbyists keep in constant contact with politicians soon learn that unacceptable performance leads to drop of financial support.

Take a look at voter turnout for mid-term elections. It is simply incomprehensible that voters fail to provide feedback to politicians regarding their performance in office. Voters have the opportunity to change the course embarked on by a newly elected president if they exercise their voting power to vote out incumbents supporting presidential policies in disagreement with the will of the people. And, the first opportunity to do that happens at a midterm election two years after the inauguration of a new president.

There is no need to get frustrated or upset at the conduct of officials carrying out governmental affairs. There is no need for term limit amendments. That is a myth created by politicians to perpetuate themselves in office, because they know that appropriate legislation will neither be introduced nor enacted into law. How many believe a congressman or representative will introduce legislation to kick him out of his job? Considering how long the debate on terms limits has been going on in the US and the results obtained, one would have to conclude it would never happen or would be highly unlikely. Is that proposition a myth? If it is a myth to rely on politicians do away with their jobs. It is not a myth for voters to ensure undeserving inept politicians lose their jobs for poor performance. All voters need to do is to vote incumbents out of office at the next election. This is particularly true when politicians begin to feel comfortable in their jobs and abuse political power or enrich themselves through corruption. If voters were to exercise their right to vote more frequently and consistently, government leaders would act differently and we would have better representation of our interests rather than theirs. It is, therefore, essential to exercise our votes regularly and carefully to ensure our government is a truly representative government of the people, by the people, and for the people.

Candidates for president, governor, senator, representative, and many others stand before voters at presidential election times. Mid-term elections are just as important because these provide a vehicle for the citizenry to either approve or reject actions taken by our legislators with respect to the policies of a new president and his administration. If we fail to proactively show them our agreement or displeasure at the way they are representing us, then they assume they are doing a great job and continue doing what they are doing. And, what has been the result? The result is corruption at all levels of government.

Elected officials can do things legally that neither you nor I can do; if we were to do those things we would be subjected to prosecution and jail times. For instance, members of congress are not subject to insider-trading penalties. This means they can get privileged information unavailable to the rest of us and use that information for their financial benefit in buying or selling stocks and other securities. If you and I were to do that, we would end up in prison and lose any profits derived from those transactions. And what do politicians get for doing the same thing? They get to go to the bank and make a very handsome deposit to their savings accounts. Why do we as voters allow that to continue? Is that an example of equal justice under law?

No, it is not. It is an example of hypocrisy, immorality, and the application of a dual system of justice that prevails in our political system. Politicians think they are above the law. And, you know what? They are. They are above the law because we let them abuse political power and break the law they themselves write to punish citizens and exempt themselves. One example of that is Obama Care which applies to citizens. This law results in many significant changes in the cost of health insurance while limiting access to doctors of one's choice; this health care law does not apply to politicians. Why is that?

Elections are the customary means provided by our founding fathers to get a government that is a government of the people, by the people, and for the people. It is not a government of politicians, by politicians, and for politicians. It is the means to ensure equal justice under law. It is what makes our government responsive to our needs. Voting grants us the power to tell the politicians who the real bosses are. Certainly, it gives us the power to let them know that we have the power to fire them if they do not perform according to our needs. It is not the lobbyists who keep lawmakers in power, it is us!

Our votes are powerful tools to end political oppression, and our consumer dollars are the equivalent weapons to prevent oppression from Corporate America. Instead of getting upset when fellow citizens lose their jobs resulting from relocation of local manufacturing facilities to foreign countries, we should use our consumer dollars to boycott products made by the relocating company. Make no mistake the relocation of manufacturing facilities is done for the purpose of increasing profitability. We have the power to deny the company the expected profitability by refusing to buy its product.

The primary concern of relocating companies is to increase profit margin without regards to how that goal is achieved. These companies close local manufacturing facilities, terminate workers, relocate to foreign countries, and force foreign workers to work under inhumane conditions to earn enslaving wages. The power of our consumer dollars is not be underestimated. We can ensure relocating companies are denied access to our consumer dollars by refusing to purchase its products. If we do that, the offending company will soon get the message. At the same time, we should buy products made by companies that create job opportunities in the good ole USA. As consumers, we all should be aware of corporate behavior that either harms or helps our fellow citizens, and we should be ready to retaliate against corporate abuses. It is always amazing to see foreign companies establish manufacturing facilities in the United States and create jobs for our citizens. On the flip side of that, one finds many local companies making the same product line relocating moving overseas and terminating employees. Why is that? Our consumer dollars should be used to reward those companies that create jobs for our citizens and penalize those that relocate. Our motto should be:

"If you don't want us as employees, we don't want you as supplier of any goods we buy".

In short, all of us have two very powerful tools at our disposal to express discontent with the political and corporate status quo. The first is the right to elect politicians who truly represent the views of the majority of voters. That right is exercised by casting our votes at all general elections. The right to vote also implies the right to withhold our votes from incumbents who fail to represent the views of the majority; this, in essence, amounts to firing them from their political jobs. The second weapon at our disposal is the power of our consumer dollars. We can use our purchasing power to get Corporate America's attention. Given that money is the only thing Corporate America understands and cares about, it is definitely possible to influence Corporate America's actions by using this tool against them..

Our purchasing power can be used to express our discontent with their corporate behavior. How? That can be done simply by not purchasing products made by any offending company. That action immediately impacts the corporate entity's so-called "bottom line" and elicit an immediate reaction to resolve the situation. The reaction would normally be to agree with consumer demands to either stop foreign manufacturing or to suffer great losses. Corporate officials know what is involved and the cost of failing to react.

Why don't displaced workers use their dollars to put an end to corporate abuses? The answer is simply that we, as citizens and consumers are complacent and happy with our situation. In view of that, we do not want to get involved in somebody else's business. But, if we don't get involved we may not have another chance when we ourselves become affected by similar abuse. It is best to stop the abuse as soon as it is discovered. That would establish the fact we as consumers and citizens are unwilling to continue tolerating corporate or political abuses.

If we were to stop purchasing goods manufactured in foreign facilities by Corporate America, that action would send a very strong message and force Corporate America to rethink the policy leading to relocation away from the US. If we were to do that, do you think any company manufacturing and selling goods in the US would relocate to a foreign location? The answer is clearly "no," because corporate executives know that the market for those goods is here in the US and not in foreign countries. Do you think manufacturers of popular American brands of shoes and shirts would continue relocating to foreign locations? Corporate America, however, should not be discouraged from building and operating foreign manufacturing facilities to create or satisfy local demand for Corporate America product or to become more efficient and flexible in satisfying demands of both the US and foreign markets.

Japanese and Korean car manufacturers have definitely demonstrated the US is an excellent location for manufacturing and selling their products. What do these foreign manufacturers see or know that our corporate leaders fail to see or know? Why is Corporate America so reluctant to expand manufacturing when foreign manufacturers are expanding here in the country? Consumers should cast their votes of confidence in terms of consumer dollars for products made in the USA regardless of the nationality of the company. Those foreign companies want us as employees and we want them as our suppliers. Think about that. Why don't we do that instead of complaining about job losses?

Is it worth complaining about our politicians when we take no part in electing them? We need to vote and spend our consumer dollars consistent with our desires and interests rather than being frustrated. In summary, do not underestimate the power of your vote and the power of your consumer dollars. Use those tools to get your message across.

In the United States, we enjoy rights that no other country in the world provides to its citizens. The US Constitution grants us freedoms citizens of other nations in the world cannot exercise for fear of incarceration. In many cases, we take these rights and freedoms for granted. We need to be more proactive in order to protect those rights for us, our children, and our children's children.

Our country was founded by immigrants who left their native countries because of political, religious, or economic reasons. They knew what it meant to be separated from their families, to be deprived of their liberties, to have their properties stolen or confiscated, to being enslaved by tyrants, and to be unable to practice their religion. Our forefathers wanted to ensure their descendants would not endure the same atrocities they had suffered in their native countries. That was the primary reason for codifying those rights in our US Constitution ensuring future generations would be able to enjoy them. Among those precious rights was the right to vote for political leaders to represent individual citizens and their rights. Notwithstanding the codification of those rights, our founding fathers went further to ensure their protection from tyrants.

The problem with our society is that we have never been deprived of any rights. Consequently, we do not know what it means to have right taken away from us. Consider, for example, living under a communist regime where you are told who you are going to vote for, when you are going to vote, and what will happen if you fail to follow instructions. Do you think that deprivation or constant reminders of what to do would make you realize the value of your electoral vote? I can assure you the right to vote is a sacred right, and you should exercise it as often as possible.

The outcome of events in Eastern Europe and the former Soviet Union after the people were given a bit of freedom was the collapse of tyrannical communist regimes that for a long time had enslaved them. Had people living in communist countries been given the right to vote freely at an earlier date, they would have toppled all communist regimes and kicked communist leaders out of office sooner than they did. That would have been clear proof of the power derived from voting.

What do you think the outcome would be if the peoples of North Korea and Cuba were given the right to freely elect their government representatives? Do you think those communist regimes would stay in power? Those regimes would not last twenty seconds in power. That's the value of your votes. Exercise it frequently so you won't be deprived of it by a tyrant or dictator.

Beware of how you use your right to vote. Vote for the best candidate regardless of political affiliation. Do not become a political fanatic affiliated with a particular party that does not even represent your views. You should be neither a Republican nor a Democrat. Be an independent voter and let your loyalty be placed on the candidate who best represents your views and who draws a picture of the nation that agrees with the picture you have in your mind for this nation. Second, if the candidate changes his vision of the nation as soon as he is elected, then you need to remind him of the original picture and vote him out of office at the next election. Third, any candidate who raises huge sums of money outside his district should never be elected to represent that district, because his heart is where the money is at and that's not in the district he supposedly represents. Fourth, beware of any candidate who spends huge amounts of his own money; he is going to line his pockets quickly to recover his initial investment. Finally, do not be fooled by rhetoric and sexy slogans; that's indicative of an intention to impress but not to be held accountable for changes to his campaign promises.

I leave you with one thought for your consideration. Do you know of anyone who would spend $10,000 to get a job that lasts for two years and pays only $100 per year? If I were considering spending my money to get a job, I certainly would not spend more than I expect to earn in salary. Certainly, I do not do that when investing in anything. I buy stocks because I expect to earn a profit on my investment. I do not intentionally invest to lose, and I think most people do that. Politicians invest their money and expect a return. Most of them expect to use other people's money to achieve their ends, which is to become wealthy at our expense. Those who spent their own money expect a return to repay their investment and earn a return.

ILLEGAL IMMIGRATION MYTHS

The United States is a country discovered, populated, and developed by immigrants from all nations of the world. History teaches the US is transformed from an agricultural nation to one that is heavily industrialized by a steady influx of immigrants. They contribute their talents to overcome problems and make their new living environment more adaptable to their needs. In fact, early immigrants recognize opportunities to grow larger quantities of food and other essential goods needed to improve living conditions and satisfy the needs of a growing population. That leads to the establishment of many businesses to make available proven solutions to common problems. Many of these immigrants realize that there are suitable conditions available in their new country to adapt concepts developed in Europe during the industrial revolution to industrialize the new nation and solve some of the problems they encounter. This teaches that immigrants are the ones revitalizing the country.

Manufacturing technology is developed, creating a launch pad for the establishment of factories that eventually lead to demand for larger number of immigrants to man jobs created in that fashion. That early industrialization effort has a significant impact on infrastructure development, education, and transportation. This is so because of needs created by manufacturing activities including the need to transport goods to markets. Roads are built to satisfy that need. The transformation of the nation as a result of this industrial activity is nothing short of spectacular.

The US throughout its history has been very attractive to immigrants from all parts of the world. It has always been considered the land of opportunity. In the early days, vast amounts of productive land from coast to coast and low population density, as compared to many European nations, provides incentives to immigration. Those two factors attract migration initially from many northwestern European nations to the US. Many of the early immigrants come to the US seeking refuge from religious and political persecution as well as to improve their economic status. The same reasons drive present immigrants.

As the industrialization pace accelerates, other opportunities are identified leading to further growth and creation of more employment opportunities. The standard of living of the general population continues to improve on a yearly basis. In short, Corporate America is built on the efforts and contributions of immigrants from all parts of the world. That is the story of immigration in a nutshell. In short, immigrants have always come to the US in order to contribute and not to siphon the fruits of society. In fact, it is fair to say that immigration is a blessing to the US for it revitalizes the nation.

Immigrants, throughout recorded US history, have been major contributors not only to industrialization effort but also to every part of society, including making major contributions to space exploration and defense of our nation. Recent immigrants are no different from previous immigrants. The only difference is the color of the skin and their economic and educational status. But, they, too, can and will contribute.

Regardless of the reasons for their migration to the US, immigrants have always been industrious and self-reliant; they are the fundamental reasons the US is what it is today. In other words, immigrants always have had a desire and motivation to succeed. That attitude has led to creation of new manufacturing processes, new products, and new job opportunities for the rest of us. That motivational engine has driven this country to higher and higher goals; it is the same incentive that drives us to reach for the stars and to go to the moon when others are unable to do so. In pursuing those goals, immigrants have started new industries benefitting the rest of us.

The demand for workers has always been the engine driving the influx of immigrants to this country. This is particularly true when there are plenty of employment opportunities available in our country and lack of jobs in their home countries. Those conditions prevail at various times during this nation's history, and in all of those instances workers migrate to our shores. In the early years of our nation's history, good economic conditions opened the immigration spigot and workers flow into the US from many European countries. Bad economic conditions in the US, on the other hand, close the immigration spigot. That is a very simple concept to understand. And, it is the situation that exists today with the so-called illegal immigration issue.

Why are agricultural workers from countries south of our Mexican border eager to come to the US? They come because of demand for their service in the US is high while the demand for their services in their own countries is not as high. Similarly, limited employment opportunities in Europe cause German and other European scientists and engineers to migrate to the US at the end of World War II. When conditions improved in Europe, European scientists and engineers cease their migration to the US. That same motivation driving European scientists to emigrate is the incentive causing agricultural workers from south of the border to come into the US with or without proper documentation.

The incentive for risking everything, including their lives, is the demand for their services in this country; these agricultural workers would not come if jobs were unavailable or if adequate jobs were available in their home countries. It is, therefore, obvious that the immigration issue is driven by lack of local workers for the jobs available. In reality, that's the situation prevailing in the US presently.

In order for immigration to occur, favorable economic conditions must exist in the host country. Those conditions must include job opportunities. At the same time, the reverse situation must exist in the home country, i.e., lack of job opportunities. Jobs available in the US must pay higher wages than comparable jobs in the home country. These are the conditions attracting workers to the US from countries where there are no job opportunities. Have you ever heard of massive migration of workers to a poor nation lacking jobs?

This is a simple concept that applies to all types of workers. German scientists and engineers migrated to the US to earn a living that they could not earn in their home countries after World War II. Now, economic conditions in Europe are favorable, and you find very few, if any, scientists or engineers from Europe migrating to the US. In short, the same motivation driving Europeans scientists and engineers after World War II to migrate to the US also motivates agricultural workers migrating from the Mexican border to the US. Agricultural jobs are available in the US, and these jobs go unfilled because local workers are either not interested in filling those positions or the workers are not there. In any event, the demand for agricultural workers is there. Farm workers are basically satisfying a demand for their services.

It is undisputed farmers and many industrial concerns are unable to find workers to do the jobs required to be done. This is a particularly acute problem at harvest time when crops need to be harvested or they will spoil. There are jobs available in meat packing plants and other low-paying industrial jobs. Employers are motivated by the payment of low wages to reduce costs and maximize profits. Very few, if any, local workers are willing to accept those jobs at the wages employers are willing to pay. Consequently, employers must look at employees other than local workers; the crops have to be picked. Illegal immigrants are willing to work for the wages paid because those wages are higher than comparable wages in their countries. Instead of demonizing poor, uneducated, agricultural workers, who cross our southern border illegally, let's praise them and try to address the immigration problem as it should be addressed in a fair and just manner.

Illegal immigration is the result of failed federal immigration policies and the unwillingness of legislators and regulators to address that issue. Farmers need workers to harvest agricultural crops; otherwise their agricultural produce would rot in the fields. If crops rot because of lack of workers, the result would be an increase in agricultural products prices beyond all reasonable bounds. So what can be done to address the problem?

The problem is a demand for approximately 400,000 unskilled workers. Those jobs are low-wage jobs available for a limited amount of time in agriculture and other industrial sectors; these are jobs that our citizens do not want to do. Legal immigration is one solution that can be implemented through a guest-worker program. The US government, however, issues 5,000 permits [131] annually authorizing unskilled immigrants to enter the country legally. The authorized number of immigrants entering the country annually is insufficient to satisfy the total demand for these workers. Why is the government limiting the number of legal permits to such a low number? How is the 395,000 job deficit addressed?

Economic theory predicts that when demand for workers exceeds supply wages increase. When demand for workers reaches 400,000 and only 5,000 workers are legally available, wages should increase. That's not the result our agricultural employers want to see develop. They like to pay the lowest wages possible in order to maximize profits. Restricting the influx of unskilled agricultural workers to 5,000 and turning a blind eye to illegal immigration, help farmers achieve their goal of keeping wages low. They do that by denying 395,000 illegal workers the right to a permit. If the government were to issue 400,000 permits, then employers would have to pay adequate wages. But if more than 395,000 workers suddenly show up to apply for jobs then the tendency would be for wages to decline. It is also relevant to keep in mind that illegal immigrants can be deported anytime, including those times when they demand higher wages from employers. The point here is that there is an incentive to restrict availability of agricultural workers. There is no incentive to resolve the issue legislatively, and politicians of both parties benefit from that situation. Republicans keep getting financial contributions from the agricultural lobby by restricting immigration and Democrats benefit by increasing the number of potential voters. In short, illegal immigrants are not threatening our nation; they are helping our nation.

Let's think about the illegal immigration problem in a logical and methodical way to define motivations of the parties involved. Employers want an abundant supply of workers to drive down wages. If the US government were to authorize 400,000 unskilled workers, then the demand would be satisfied, but employers would be required to pay minimum wages. In addition, employers would be obligated to collect income taxes and pay workers on a regular basis, and there would be no chance of cheating workers out of their wages under threat of deportation. That situation would not be desirable to agricultural employers. The ideal situation for employers would be the case when an insufficient number of unskilled workers are authorized to come. In that case, large numbers of workers cross the border illegally, leading to an oversupply of unskilled workers. Over abundant supply of unskilled workers drives wages down, which is what employers want. Is there a possibility that agricultural concerns may be influencing the immigration policy of the US as far as availability of unskilled workers is concerned? The answer is definitely "yes."

Employers want to pay lower than minimum wages, if possible, to enhance profit margins. Workers, on the other hand, want to be high wages commensurate with job duties. Local workers do not think on-going agricultural wages are sufficiently high to compensate them for the hard work required to be done. That is the reason local US workers do not want those jobs. As the supply of foreign workers increases, wages decrease. The point here is that employers have an incentive to seek a higher number of illegal immigrants in order to lower wages they are willing to pay, and those employers would do anything in their power to get their way. That includes bribing elected officials to prevent action on immigration reform. Doesn't that explain the present immigration situation? It appears, therefore, the illegal immigration issue is a myth perpetuated by political rhetoric, lack of facts, and an unwillingness to address the issue. How can that be?

The illegal immigration issue is not an immigration issue but rather a wage issue. It is an issue created by collusion between government and employers. Keep in mind that money talks, and when it talks, corrupt politicians and public officials government at all levels listen. Employers have only to bribe or contribute, as is known in politically correct terms, either directly or indirectly through lobbyists, to reelect great public servants" and ensure employers are rewarded for their financial contributions. As long as employers pay, immigration officials limit the number of work permits issued thus restricting availability of agricultural workers. That action, in turn, increases illegal immigration. As long as the number of workers exceeds the number of jobs available, wages decrease, and that satisfies employers. Isn't that right?

Everyone is happy at the outcome. Politicians deliver on their promise to employers thus earning further financial contributions or bribes. Employers get an overabundance of illegal workers to be abused by paying them low wages and enslaving them under the threat of deportation. Undocumented workers, on the other hand, are the losers to some extent. They get a job that pays higher than comparable wages in the native countries, but they lose to the extent they are subject to prison terms, deportation, and loss of wages if immigration finds them illegally here in the country. The US as a nation loses because taxpayers' funds are wasted in this type of activity to benefit the agricultural lobby. But, politicians do not care about that; they have their bribes safely in their bank accounts. The rhetoric from politicians would indicate illegal immigration is bad, but the alternative may be an undesirable situation because of the resulting higher prices for agricultural products.

Illegal immigration is not the answer, because it leads to many undesirable consequences. Among these are human trafficking, drug smuggling, and many other types of criminal activity. Assuming 400,000 jobs are available, it is not difficult to imagine that there would be at least two individuals crossing the border illegally for every job available. Some of these poor and uneducated people risk everything, including their lives, to be able to work and earn sufficient money to support their families back in their home countries. The reality is that not all of them will be able to get jobs. So what do the ones who fail to get jobs do? Well, they know how to cross the border undetected, and that skill is valuable when used to transport illegal workers or smuggle drugs. That's the result of a failure to address a simple problem.

History teaches that prohibition is not the answer to anything. That is as true of immigration as it of prohibiting consumption of alcoholic beverages as was done in the 1920s. So if prohibition is not the answer, what is? One potential approach is to have a guest-worker program enabling immigrants to legally come to the country for a temporary period of time and then return to their home countries on the expiration of such period or when the purpose of the temporary stay is accomplished. Unless our elected and government officials address the problem now, it would become a much bigger problem as the demand for low-skill workers increases to the level of 8.1 million as projected by the Bureau of Labor Statistics for 2018. [132]

A resolution to this problem faces strong opposition from agricultural and other low-wage employers. That is so because the result would tend to drive agricultural wages up beyond present levels. Rising wages would increase employers operating costs, increase product prices, and reduce profit margins. Employers would not hesitate to bribe politicians and government officials to prevent that from happening. Perhaps, that is the real reason there is no incentive to solve the illegal immigration problem. Bishop Mandell Creighton's admonition on the corrupting effect of power can be paraphrased in the following terms: Money tends to corrupt, and access to a lot of money corrupts absolutely.

Illegal immigration boils down to an issue between employer and worker. The employer is either a US citizen or an American corporation; the worker is a humble, uneducated, and undocumented foreign worker. The employer is protected by US law, while the worker is violating US law. The employer is probably a financial contributor to the reelection of politicians, while the worker is a powerless and an un-influential individual barely earning enough money to make ends meet. Employers do not suffer any consequences for breaking the law, while the worker who already breaking the law is subject to deportation and/or imprisonment. This is the perfect situation for exploitation of human beings. In many instances, employers retain unpaid wages or pay taxes when illegal immigrants are deported.

Immigration of illegal workers is the result of failed federal immigration policies preventing the establishment of legal means to supply sufficient workers to satisfy agricultural employers' demand. In the absence of legal procedures to address a shortage of workers, employers will employ available workers regardless of immigration status. It is essential to control the border, and that can be done simply by issuing permits to guest workers to enter the country legally when needed and ensuring an orderly return to their native countries upon expiration of the permit. The present situation implies that there is no motivation to end this problem. Politicians spend taxpayers' money unnecessarily building walls that will not stop the traffic of illegal immigrants. They spend taxpayers' funds in establishing and running a modern concentration camp where undocumented workers are exposed to all kinds of indignities by a zealous sheriff in Arizona.

It is hypocritical on the part of our government and elected officials to talk about human-rights violations in foreign countries when similar human-rights violations occur on our own doorstep with impunity. We see illegal immigrants coming to this country and providing a service that no one else wants to perform. In many instances, those illegal immigrants start living normal lives including having children who become native US citizens by virtue of birth; those children are not illegal immigrants but US citizens. The tragedy is that, in many instances, parents are deported because of their illegal status and the children are separated from their parents regardless of age.

There are instances when people motivated by racism and ethnicity advocate denial of US citizenship to children born in the US on account of being the children of illegal immigrants. It would be worthwhile to note the reaction from these same people when they have to pay extremely high prices for vegetables and fruits because illegal immigrants are unavailable to pick those vegetables in the field. Perhaps those ill-meaning citizens advocate that position on the basis of skin color, which is racial discrimination. They fail to recognize that many of their parents and grandparents also came to this country under the same conditions. Does that remind you of the Anglo Saxon superiority myth? How about the Holocaust? If that's not a human-rights violation, what is? How about the inhumane treatment detained illegal immigrants receive in prison and concentration camp run by Arizona Sheriff Joe Arpaio? Are the US attorney general and other federal and state officials doing something to stop these abuses?

The immigration problem is a problem that needs to be addressed now in a fair and equitable manner to prevent tragedies such as the separation of US born little children from their illegal-immigrant parents facing or undergoing deportation. An equitable solution to that problem would benefit employers and workers alike, as well as the government. Employers would benefit to the extent that workers become readily available when needed to do the required jobs. This would allow farmers to save their harvest and earn a living to support their families. Workers, likewise, would benefit by receiving wages in the amount prescribed by law and by having the legal right to ensure employers pay them their justly earned wages. The government would benefit by collecting income taxes and avoiding expenses involved in incarcerating immigrants and deporting them, which are considerable amounts.

Is there a motivation to stop or solve the illegal immigration problem? The answer is clearly no. Republicans and democrats talk about the problem but fail to do anything about the problem. Republicans have no incentive in stopping the flow of illegal immigration because they do not want farm owners to be forced to pay higher wages; they want the status quo to continue. Democrats want to get votes from Hispanics and are afraid to stop the flow and jeopardize those votes. President Obama, on the other hand, wakes up and realizes that he is about to lose the Hispanic vote for failure to keep his promise to find a way to solve the problem; he has done nothing to solve the problem. All of the sudden, President Obama instructs immigration officials to deport only those illegal immigrants who have committed crimes or have the propensity to engage in criminal activities. That's hypocrisy at its best. Why could he not do that earlier? The answer is that election time is coming and he needs the Hispanic vote to keep his job. Hispanics ought to deny him their votes for being so inept and ineffectual.

If the US government were really interested in solving the illegal immigration issue, it would be able to do so very easily and very quickly. The one and only thing it needs to do is to penalize with heavy fines and prison terms employers who fail to ensure workers are here legally. That solution would very likely be objectionable on the basis of penalizing upright members of our society who contribute financially to elected officials. Think about it. It is all political hypocrisy. We as human beings should demand our elected officials solve the immigration problem and solve it quickly.

But, there is really no incentive to solve the problem. This is well understood by elected officials who adhere to the teachings of the golden rule in that they know "He who has the gold rules." Guess who has the gold? And, guess who wants the gold? Now, do you get the picture why the immigration problem remains unsolved? It is put on the back burner simply because not solving it favors employers, and elected official dare not bite the hand that feeds them.

There are several prongs to the immigration problem. The first is the issue of what to do with those workers who have been here in the United States for a significant length of time and have established roots in this nation. Those "illegal" residents or immigrants or whatever you want to call them have to be brought into the mainstream of our society. These people are gainfully employed and have been holding that status for many years. They are not surplus workers; they are needed at their jobs; otherwise, they would have been fired. If they are needed, let's recognize that fact. Long-term illegal residents have established homes in the US and many have had children born in the US who are native US citizens. How can the US, in view of that, deport the parents and let the children become practical orphans and wards of the state or nation? That is not the US everyone in the world knows.

The second prong of the immigration issue is to institute a guest-worker program ensuring employers and employees satisfy each other needs equitably. A program of this nature would allow immigrants the right to come and work for a specific period of time and then return home after the job is done.

The third prong is to shift the burden to show authorization to work in the country from the illegal immigrant over to the employers. This means that, instead of arresting the illegal immigrant for the simple act of working, employers would be subject to arrest and heavy fines for employing unauthorized illegal immigrants as workers.

Consider the case of an employer hiring illegal workers. If the employer fails to verify these workers are authorized to work in this country, then he would be subject to a fine meant to inflict financial pain and, on top of that, be subject to a multiyear prison term. Do you think that would be an effective deterrent in eliminating illegal immigration? You better believe it would be. The employer would not risk prison terms and/or a heavy fine to reduce his cost and improve his profit margin. As it is now the employer risks nothing and continues to do the same thing because it has nothing to lose.

As you can see, the illegal immigration problem is nothing more than a myth. It is a myth that has been concocted to shift responsibility and blame from the employer to the employee. Let's end this hypocrisy. Let's impose criminal liability where it clearly belongs.

OVERALL RESULTS

There is no question the continuing viability of US industry is threatened. It is threatened by many elements from within the industry itself and from US legislators and regulators, and from outside sources. The elements encompassing these threats have been listed; these are the forces pushing many of our industries to the edge of a precipice leading to their downfall.

It is no secret that many industrial sectors have been wiped out as a result of poor management decisions. Examples include ceding market share to foreign competitors as was done by US automakers on the pretext US companies would concentrate on the most profitable markets; that decision resulted in losses in market share for all sectors of the makers. It is what pushed Toyota to replace GM as the largest global auto producer. But that logic is not limited to automakers; take a look at electronics, home appliances, telephones, etc. Why is that?

There are many reasons causing US industries to lose the battle against foreign competitors. The most fundamental ones are corruption and greed of corporate and government officials. Corruption and avarice, or insatiable greed, have been responsible for the downfall of many empires and very likely will bring our industrial and financial institutions to their knees. If that happens, then our individual and collective American Dreams would be shattered and cause our standard of living to diminish to the level of undeveloped countries. That would severely impact the global influence and preeminence enjoyed by our country.

It is obvious the motivation of corporate executives is to enrich themselves regardless of what happens to the corporations they lead. That unquenchable level of greed blinds corporate executives to the point of believing the corporation is there for their financial benefit and to disregard potential adverse impacts on shareholders, who are the true owners of the company. In so doing, they are violating the fiduciary duty owed to shareholders, but that does not stop them. Since the deck is stacked against shareholders, they know there will be no consequences for their actions. Executives tend to forget the corporation owes a duty to employees, customers, and the nation itself; the corporation is not their personal property. We need to remind these executives there will be consequences for their actions, and we can show them the impact of those consequences.

Executives abuse corporate power by granting themselves high compensation packages regardless of their contributions or lack thereof or their adverse impact on the corporation. They want to milk the company dry and extract maximum amounts of money in terms of bonuses and salaries to sustain their standard of living after they leave the corporation. Whatever happens to the corporation after they leave as a result of their actions is immaterial to them; it is no longer their problem. This means they create a mess a successor may not able to fix, which may cause the company to go under or suffer significant financial losses.

Corporate officials are only concerned about their interests first and foremost; they focus on the short term to enhance their compensation package and leave the long-term viability of the company to somebody else. They reduce operating costs by eliminating jobs, and they grow their market share of their company by acquiring competitors. There are no cases of reductions in production cost or growth in market share resulting from enhancement in manufacturing efficiency or introductions of new products. That's the reason you see so many foreign competitors coming to the US and beating our industrial leaders. That's the primary reason US companies are losing market share to more efficient and productive foreign producers.

Executives bribe politicians, regulators, rating agencies employees, and whoever gets in their way to achieve their own financial ends without concern for ethics or morals. And yet, they are unwilling to accept responsibility for those acts. There are plenty of illustrations of this point. For example, some financial institutions become very friendly with regulators and lawmakers. These institutions grant these government officials special deals on mortgages for their homes, for example. These favors tend to cause legislators and regulators to overlook problems within the corporate structure, even if it means financial ruin for their constituents.

Legislators and regulators prostitute themselves by accepting bribes from corporate officials through lobbyists. Like corporate executives, these government officials are unwilling to accept responsibility for their acts even when it is obvious they are complicit in the final catastrophic result; witness the recent case where banking officials get $20 billion of taxpayers' funds to reward themselves for causing the financial crisis. Legislators acted in a fashion intended to show their indignation about the result but continue to follow orders from corporate masters. In so doing, lawmakers demonstrate a lack of concern for taxpayers' funds lent to these institutions that may never be repaid. They, like their corporate lobbyist handlers, are only interested in their own financial wellbeing.

Citizens have the power to rein these corporate and political abuses, but, as a result of frustration, fail to use tools available to them to end these corporate and political abuses. There are two powerful weapons to end these abuses. The first is the power to vote for their representatives. This power to vote is also the power to get rid of unworthy politicians. Let's use our power to vote regularly to get rid of worthless and corrupt politicians and get our government back.

Citizens also have the power of their consumer dollars. Consumer spending is a very powerful weapon to get the attention of corporate entities and officials. Consumer dollars can be used to get rid of inept and corrupt corporate executives who are driving our corporations out of our country and into bankruptcy. Consumer dollars should be used to send a strong message to corporate officials. That message is simply that relocating manufacturing facilities overseas is an indication they don't want us as employees. If that's the case, then we don't want them as suppliers of our goods.

Politicians, like their corporate counterparts, abuse power. A case in point is the power to spend taxpayers' funds. They abuse that power by using it as an instrument at their disposal to enhance their own individual financial wellbeing. This they hope to achieve by attracting political contributions and courting special favors from special interest-groups, better known as their corporate masters. Politicians are nothing more than cheap prostitutes. Their actions can and should be stopped by our collective power to elect and remove officials.

There are some politicians who are honorable, but these are very few. In many cases, politician disguise themselves as a sheep when, in reality, they are a big, bad, wolf hungry for taxpayers' money to enrich himself. He is disguised, waiting for an opportunity to accept bribes to come around knocking on his door. At that point, he shows his true colors and opens the door to financial security and loses all interest in voters.

Another factor causing our corporations to lag behind foreign competitors is the poor educational background of our students. There is no question that products from our educational system are of poor quality. These students are unable to solve simple math and science problems as required by our highly technical industries. These are industries requiring good grounding in math and science. Unless the quality of US students improves, our companies would have a difficult time competing with foreign companies that have access to better-qualified people. There is no question this issue needs to be addressed.

CHAPTER 8
FAILURE IS NOT
AN OPTION

Our nation faces a very difficult economic situation based on lack of confidence. In the past, America has been blessed with many great entertainers, military and political leaders, scientists, and outstanding entrepreneurs. Among these are people such as Bob Hope, Johnny Cash, Henry Ford, George Patton, John F. Kennedy and many others in all fields of endeavor. These are people who motivated our nation with their actions to reach for the stars and to go to the moon. In so doing, the nation becomes a better place for all. These are the people who laid a solid foundation for this great country and brought hope and cash to all Americans. Now, we have lost all hope and have no cash to buy a Ford. The existing situation has to be reversed to restore confidence and hope to our people and to provide the opportunities to earn cash to buy the products that are made here in the US of A.

Ford Motor Co is an example of a company that has been turned around not by the efforts of government officials but rather by excellent management and the sweat and tears of hard working American workers. Similarly, we find Chrysler and General Motors have been turned around. In both of those cases, the US government has influenced economic results those companies are achieving. In the meantime, we find auto workers, whether at Ford, GM or Chrysler, regaining their hope and confidence in the future of the US. Furthermore, those workers and companies are having a positive impact on their suppliers. That is the story behind the urging by the author to political leaders to help manufacturers get back on their feet because that is the only way we as a nation will get back on our feet.

In the case of automotive companies previously cited, both the private and public sector come together to save these icons of American industry. Labor is also instrumental in achieving those results. The point here is that we can achieve miracles when we as a nation are united and focused on solving a problem. We have to regain that same sense of unity and purpose to achieve similar results in all economic sectors impacting Americans. Remember we float or sink together. There is no other way.

The US is in the midst of an economic crisis very similar, if not identical, to the situation that prevailed at the time of the Great Depression. Unlike the strong leadership of President Franklin D, Roosevelt, President Obama has not decided to focus his attention on the issues that need immediate attention. The same attitude is shared by all other political leaders including senators and congressmen. Those leaders have chosen to divert the attention of the American people from the number one issue affecting our country – lack of job opportunities - to other issues of lesser importance. They have done that to improve their reelection process but, in fact, the only thing they achieve is to improve chances of being defeated.

We need strong political leaders to guide this nation out of the depth of this horrendous hole the US economy is in. We find political leaders defining themselves as either republicans or democrats first and foremost. But, then you discover that divisions do not end there. Some of them are extreme right or left republicans or democrats. Additionally, you find these so called political leaders are extremely parochial and are focused primarily on their own interest without regards for the interest of the nation as a whole. Their motto in everything they do is: "What's in it for me"?

Politicians neither talk to one another nor trust each other. Each of them is focused on opposing ideas advance by any and all members of the opposite party regardless of merit. It is their way or the highway, and that is not politics, which the art of compromising to achieve results. They do not agree on anything because they want the president to fail. Wow! The only thing they are achieving is causing the whole nation to fail. Yes, the president is going to fail in his reelection effort, but so will they. And, more importantly, we as Americans are going to fail. That is a path to certain destruction.

It is time for politicians to get rid of all those labels and realize that the only label they need to wrap themselves with is the label of being an American. So what harm is there in turning the situation around and improving President Obama's chances of reelection. That same result will be achieved by congressmen and senators. There is no harm in improving the situation for all Americans. President Clinton, in his first term, was not as effective as he was during his second term; the American people benefitted from keeping President Clinton in power, and the same can be true with President Obama. The important point here is to forget about our differences and concentrate on the things that unite us. This is simple request can lead to wonderful results in terms of civility and achievements necessary to make this country the shining star it has always been until it began to lose some of its luster from all the dickering, political rhetoric, and nonsense dividing us. Americans can no longer afford to be divided. If we fail to unite and compromise with one another our country and our corporate institutions will fall in much the same manner as that causing the collapse of historical empires.

The crisis this country is facing is a very dangerous crisis for it can lead to very drastic and risky political situations. We all know lack of jobs is the problem. When people do not have jobs, they get desperate and lose hope. Simply stated, citizens see their families suffering and find themselves in a position of being unable to do anything about that suffering. That is a perfect situation for political and civil unrest in the country. This is the same situation that has seen revolutions in the Arab world leading to the overthrow of political despots and the killing of many innocent people. That is the situation the US found itself in during the Great Depression when communist agitators began a campaign to create social unrest within our society. That is the same situation prevailing in Europe at the end of WWII. At that time, communist saboteurs under the direct guidance of Stalin begin to overthrow all European governments and to bring them under the control of the Soviet Union.

The US gradually transforms itself from an isolationist laissez faire stance in both economic and world affairs over to being a major player in both economic and international aspects. During the depression the government realizes it needs to address the desperate economic situation existing at that time. It reacts to the Soviet challenge aimed at destabilizing European economies and their government to improve post war economic conditions and prevent domination by the Soviet Union. It also intervenes in the Arab world to improve conditions and prevent the killing of many innocent civilians. The point is that strong leadership from our president and political leaders similar to that exhibited by President Roosevelt is needed to overcome desperate economic and political situation, particularly in view of the US status as a world superpower. It is time, therefore, for our political leaders to end all divisions and act decisively to achieve results.

The unemployment rate in the US is 9.1 percent; this level of unemployment has not changed significantly for many months. If one were to define the meaning of the term "unemployment rate" and how that number is determined, one would realize that what we are seeing in that number is the tip of an iceberg. That number is reported monthly, and every time it is reported one hears how many people apply for unemployment compensation and how many jobs are created. Economists get excited when a lower number of people apply for unemployment benefits. We fail to take into consideration the lower number of people filing may imply that many people have exhausted all unemployment benefits they are entitled to receive. In other words, the rate of unemployment we hear does not include unemployed workers who have given up looking for jobs because there are none available, or people who have lost everything and become homeless on account of not being able to get a job, or the people who have had to take any kind of employment to earn a few dollars to get food, or those who are no longer eligible for benefits. Lack of employment is a human tragedy, and it is the number one problem facing this nation. It is the issue that will destroy this nation unless the government acts. The US as a whole has to come together and act decisively in this situation.

It is true that there are many problems that this nation must address. The number one problem is, once again, lack of jobs. In short, all other problems are of secondary in importance to the unemployment problem. So, what does President Obama and other politicians do to address this problem? First of all, they divert public's attention by focusing their efforts and all of their energies on less important issues. They concentrate on healthcare, for example. They pass a healthcare law that is basically jammed down the throats of political opponents thus setting the stage for revenge when the opposition takes over. They focus on financial reform and other less worthy issues and engage in a big battle over the budget thus ignoring the number one issue is jobs creation. Why do they do that? The answer is simple. Politicians have jobs and are earning a living doing absolutely nothing worthwhile for the general public. So long as they have jobs and get their usual financial contributions from lobbyists, they are happy. Their constituents, however, are suffering, but these politicians could care less about their constituents' suffering. They only care about constituents when they need votes to retain their jobs.

Let's talk about the battle of the budget and how that battle tells the American people politicians do not have a clue as to how to address the unemployment problem. Some politicians tell you that the private sector has the power to create jobs. They also point out the fact corporate coffers are overflowing with money that could be spent to create jobs but it is not. They ignore, however, a truism and that is that the private sector will not spend a dime unless there is demand for their products. It is obvious that unemployed consumers cannot buy products to cause the private sector to create jobs. And, companies are not employing even though these companies have more than sufficient funds to pay workers. Consequently, we find ourselves in a vicious cycle that only the government can break.

The government can create tax incentives to provide financial incentives to have companies hire people, but companies do not need money; they need demand for their products. But that is exactly the point politicians and their advisers fail to understand, and it is apparent from the political debate around the battle of the budget. The government needs to create demand for products and it can do that by placing orders for electronic equipment, airplanes, cars, battleships, paper, and many other articles of commerce. Those products will be the engine to drive the hiring process. So there is a contradiction here in terms of trying to prevent focused government expending when, in fact, what is needed at this time is government demands for products. Once that is done the unemployment rate would decline paying and, more importantly, the number of employed people and paying taxes would rise to increase government revenues.

On the one hand, we find democrats saying let's spend on infrastructure projects, welfare, clean energy, and pet projects. Democrats want to raise taxes to continue their spending habits. Republicans, on the other hand, are opposed to any spending because they realize expenditures will cause the debt limit on the national debt to be exceeded. In fact, republicans want to cut spending and not raise taxes. In the opinion of the author, both democrats and republicans are partly wrong in their views. Infrastructure projects and welfare are not be the magic bullets needed to kill this disastrous economic situation. This is obvious from disappointing results obtained by financing shovel ready projects when it becomes evident those shovel ready projects were not ready as the president and his political allies thought. The government sponsors a program to encourage replacement of older cars with newer models to encourage manufacturing and it is effective in getting manufacturing workers back on the job. In view of that, politicians should have learned that creating manufacturing jobs would be much more effective than financing infrastructure projects. That does not mean, however, that infrastructure projects should be totally ignored. The point is the government has to set priorities to obtain the biggest bang for the money spent.

The battle of the budget showed lack of understanding on the part of the majority of politicians in Washington. It was a real simple issue under discussion to authorize an expansion in the debt limit to enable payment of purchases previously authorized by congress and signed into law by the president. The situation would be analogous to charging purchases on a credit card and refusing to pay the debt on account of having exceeded the credit limit on the card after additional purchases. The outcome of the budget battle was the downgrading of the national debt of the US with the potential consequence of having to pay higher interest rates to refinance the debt. That battle achieved nothing except to clearly show the stupidity of our legislators. The time that was wasted in fighting this battle should have been better spent on developing ideas to create jobs.

The budget battle also revealed a very disturbing flaw in our government. It showed congressmen and senators could not agree on any solution. Consequently, it showed the government to be a dysfunctional government. As an admission of that, a super committee composed of members of the same legislative bodies that failed to solve the problem in the first round was appointed to try solving it. The disturbing concern arising out of this debate was the fact that our political leaders admitted they did not know how to do anything and abdicated responsibility by passing the buck to a committee. In view of that, why didn't they replace that worthless and incapable group of legislators with a new group capable of solving it. Why would taxpayers continue paying these inept legislators a salary? It would be worthwhile firing all these legislators to save taxpayers' money to pay part of our national debt in the process.

Let's look at some facts. Corporate coffers are full of money, but corporations are unwilling to spend any money. The US government continues to place a lid on additional expenditures. Consumers do not have money to spend because of the lack of jobs. What are we to do? Politicians point to corporate coffers and urge corporations to expand. The corporate response is that they are accountable to shareholders and do not want to waste their money. Consumers continue to look for jobs but cannot find any. What's the solution? Are we to continue drinking tea and point fingers anyplace but where they should be pointed? Keep in mind that when you point one finger in any direction there are three fingers pointed directly at you.

Politicians fail to realize that the only party capable of starting an economic recovery in this country is the government. It is true expenditures will increase and that may have an impact on the national debt. But, they fail to understand inaction would be just as detrimental to the national debt and provide no benefits to turn the situation around and increase revenues to repay the national debt. It is preferable, therefore, to spend and create jobs that would ultimately result in an increase in government revenues to the extent new employees pay income taxes and reduce unemployment compensation payments. The role of government in that situation is to focus on programs that have the capability to kick start the recovery. A lesson learned from the Great Depression is that manufacturing is the sector of the economy capable of having greatest and fastest impact on the recovery. The program encouraging replacing gas guzzlers with new more efficient new cars is a good valuable action. Instead of doing that, President Obama and his political allies continue to debate the same old programs shown to have been ineffective. There are other programs requiring no government expenditure and cause companies to spend their money and hire workers. For example, oil and natural gas companies are willing and financially capable to undertake that responsibility by engaging in exploration activities; unfortunately, the government does everything it can to prevent that from occurring.

Government spending should be used to replace existing older weapons systems with newer systems. It should also sponsor work to develop even better systems. Expenditures on R&D efforts will keep our country at the leading edge of technology and create new products useful for production of civilian goods and create the motivation for additional manufacturing in this country. Improving aviation control system and replacement of older electronic equipment used by government agencies. These are just some examples of goods and services that government needs and should buy now.

In addition to government spending, there should be new policies developed to improve many government functions and improve conditions creating the motivation for job creating new job opportunities and satisfy the needs of the nation. Included among these are: 1) a national energy policy, 2) an innovation policy, 3) a corporate policy, 4) a regulatory agency overhaul, and 5) a tax fairness policy. Congressional work should start immediately on all of these policies to create jobs. Let me describe what I envision these policies to address.

NATIONAL ENERGY POLICY

The US is a heavily industrialized country that depends on energy for manufacturing, raw materials, transportation and day to day activities of the general population. It is a country that is blessed with ample reserves of coal, oil and gas as well as other hydrocarbon sources. It consumes approximately 19 million barrels of crude oil on a daily basis, and this amount of imported oil represents about half of the total usage of crude. The point here is that the US is a large energy consumer and it is blessed with ample sources of supply that remained undiscovered. The US has large unexplored acreage that potentially could make the US totally independent of imported oil. The unfortunate fact is that much of that acreage is off limits to exploration. Oil imports cost the US approximately one half of a trillion dollars a year, which is a significant amount of money. More importantly, it indicates that without oil the US cannot function. Additionally, this amount of oil is coming from sources not always friendly to the US meaning that at some point in time the US may be cut off from this supply and cause tremendous economic damage to our country economic well being.

How can we allow our nation to be so vulnerable to external enemies? The question becomes why rely on imported oil while huge areas holding potentially large amount of oil and natural gas remain unexplored? The amount of money spent on imported oil is a significant negative contributor to the US balance of payments; that amount of money would be better spent on US produced crude oil and get a bigger impact on jobs creation. In short, there are many benefits directly attributed to crude and natural gas exploration and production. These include energy independence, creation of high paying jobs, and revenue for the government.

The US chemical industry is dependent on natural gas liquids and gas for raw materials. It is an industry that contributes positively to our balance of payment. It employs a very large number of Americans and it is a positive contributor to a positive balance of payment. Unfortunately, lack of raw materials at affordable prices has forced the industry to expand in the Middle East instead of our country. That chemical industry migration to the Middle East has been somewhat reversed by recent natural gas discoveries. As a result, chemical companies announce production expansions in many US locations that are having or will have a positive impact on jobs creation. The point here is that oil and gas exploration is a means to create high paying jobs for Americans not only in the petroleum industry but also in other industrial sectors.

Transportation is responsible for approximately 50 percent of the total oil consumption. This sector relies heavily on oil and gas for fuel; there are no sources of fuel to satisfy transportation demands for fuel. It is a fact that we are not going to be able to replace internal combustion engines with solar power engines in the near future; that may happen in a very distant future. We may not be able to afford a solar powered automobile. We need action now and now and not rely on rhetoric or what may or may not come in the distant future.

It is no secret the oil industry is one of the least understood industries in the country. People buy gasoline and diesel fuel, but they do not know anything about difficulties and costs involved in producing oil and gas. They see the price of gasoline rising and they blame the industry for that. They think that the industry has total control over the supply of crude, which is not true. In fact, oil prices are not set by the US oil industry; prices are set by international markets. The industry has to buy oil from national oil companies at international prices. The other thing is that demand for oil is increasing particularly in India and China. If we don't encourage our oil companies to undertake additional exploration and production efforts to expand our sources of supply then we are risking not being able to get sufficient crude to satisfy our needs. Keep in mind that other parts of the world are also growing their demand for energy and that present supply is limited, which is a prescription for higher crude and gasoline prices. That is the reality and we better get used to that. If we want energy and gasoline at affordable prices, then the only thing we can do is to explore and find new sources of oil and gas. It is simple as that.

You don't hear anything about nuclear powered automobiles. The government is encouraging development of electric cars. Politicians think this is a means to reduce our reliance on crude oil. The public assumes that it is a viable solution to our transportation needs. They fail to ask a very simple question: where is the electricity coming from? It is very likely that electricity powering those electric vehicles is being generated by gas fired power plants. The point is that politicians do not fully understand the importance of crude oil and natural gas to the well being of this nation. Consequently, they do things that threaten the very existence of the oil and gas industry and, in so doing threaten our way of life.

There is a very well known secret, and that is the oil industry is under attack by politicians and environmentalists. What other source of raw materials and transportation fuels are available to replace the oil industry with? Coal is a possibility, but it is a well known fact that the coal industry is also under attack from several sources including environmentalists. The author does not believe nuclear industry is a viable alternative in the US particularly after the nuclear accident in Japan. We need to be mindful of our environment and means to protect it. At the same time, we need to let people know that no oil company does intentionally harm the environment. In fact, when events have occurred causing significant damages to the environment, these companies have admitted responsibility and done their best to remedy the situation as demonstrated most recently by BP in the Gulf of Mexico.

It is important for us to take an objective look at our energy and raw materials needs. As economies of many nations bounce back from recession, the supply of fuels and raw materials is constrained and prices increase. What impact is that going to have on the US economy? Do we need to do something about that to minimize or totally eliminate adverse impacts to the US economy? You better believe that we need to be prepared for such a situation to arise otherwise we will be facing another economic crisis. That is the objective behind development of a realistic energy policy.

A realistic and objective energy policy will identify all means of generating electric power and providing raw materials for all of our needs. At the same time, obstacles in providing the energy sources would become apparent and strategies developed to overcome those obstacles. It is no longer possible to say wind or any other source of renewable power will totally replace oil and gas. Once that conclusion is apparent, then one can speculate on the contribution from each source of energy source and ensure we secure a source in case those renewable sources fail to meet our expectations. It should be realized that it takes time to get new energy sources on line so we better plan well in advance to overcome future problems that in the not too distant future will become present problems.

The energy policy should evaluate all sources capable of supplying all energy required to satisfy our needs. It should not exclude any sources but let's not place all of our hopes on a single source, which is what President Obama is basically doing. He is a big proponent of renewable sources of energy. He is opposed to the oil and gas industry and has done his part to throw obstacles in the path of exploration and production efforts in the Gulf of Mexico, which is one of the most promising areas in the US for additional oil production. The EPA is also another enemy of hydrocarbon usage particularly and it shows its hatred for the industry by proposals to penalize companies for carbon dioxide emissions. Those environmental fanatics ought to be forced to work in non-air conditioned offices in the middle of the desert to appreciate the effect of their opposition to hydrocarbon fuels. Those are some of the conditions oil companies workers encounter everyday to supply the energy needs to keep the air conditioners going for environmentalist to complain about.

A realistic energy policy is an essential tool to jobs creation. This is so because it will define our needs and convince people of the need to produce oil and gas. As a result of that exercise, it would become apparent high paying jobs can be created not only in oil and gas exploration and production sectors but also in other sectors of the economy; keep in mind coal production can also add jobs. That is exactly what the US needs at this point to create jobs, secure our future, and put a dent on the economic crisis we are facing.

E. J. Salmon

INNOVATION POLICY

The US is an innovative, if not the most innovative, country in the world. Unlike the former Soviet Union where scientists and engineers are afraid to fail, US corporate culture encourages risk taking in order to commercialized scientific and engineering discoveries. That characterization is evident not only by the intricate products it develops and commercializes but also by the variety of products it develops and makes available throughout all sectors of the economy. It is also a country that works best under pressure as demonstrated by the reaction to the Pearl Harbor attack and subsequent events leading to the defeat of those who attacked us. A similar situation arose when the Soviet Union placed a satellite in an orbit around the earth; the US response to that challenge is to land men on the moon; it does that not once but several times clearly showing it is not a lucky event but one unique event that remains unmatched by other nations. In the process of developing technology to travel to the moon, many new products become available to help people in many sectors of daily life such as, for example, miniaturization of medical devices for surgical applications. Given those two factors, it would be naïve and shortsighted not to use that capability to get the country back on a firm footing and on the road to recovery from this horrendous recession that is causing so much pain to our families. Innovation is the secret weapon that the US needs to deploy once again to improve our economic outlook and establish trust and confidence among all parties involved – government, labor and private industry. Americans need both hope and cash. There is no better way than to create wealth through innovation.

There are many problems that we as nation face and must solve. One group of people among our citizenry solves all problems by outlawing the activity that supposedly creates the problem. That is a very dangerous group for they believe in controlling all of our processes including our intellect; this seems to be the preferred mechanism in the former Soviet Union. The other side is a group that believes problems should be defined and an incentive provided to solve them. The author believes that the second group is more attuned with his own personal views. It is all a question of perspective, and I happen to believe that all the problems we are facing are problems created by man and solvable by pragmatic individuals willing to work hard on a solution.

There is no question the US relies heavily on the use of crude oil, natural gas, and coal to generate electrical power for its industrial and transportation needs. In fact, one can predict and follow economic activities by keeping an eye on the price of crude oil. When economic activity accelerates, crude oil prices increase. Higher crude prices result in higher gasoline prices. When we do not a job and have to buy gasoline to go to work, it is a difficult situation that may call for adjustments to our buying practices; in some cases it may become necessary to reduce food purchases. This example clearly illustrates the importance of energy availability and price. The downside to energy usage is the fact burning hydrocarbon fuels produces carbon dioxide and that leads to an environmental problem. It is believed that carbon dioxide is affecting climate change.

Given our reliance on hydrocarbons fuels for energy and the detrimental environmental effects of carbon dioxide production from those fuels, what should we do? Should we totally ban the use of any and all hydrocarbons fuels? If the use of hydrocarbon fuels were banned then we would eliminate a problem but create a bigger problem. We would eliminate the problem associated with carbon dioxide production but, at the same time, do away with a source of raw materials for uses by pharmaceutical, food, and chemical industry. There are some politicians who advocate this route on account of carbon dioxide production. What these politicians fail to take into consideration is that carbon dioxide is an essential nutrient for plant growth. In the absence of carbon dioxide, there are no vegetables or any other plants available. The question then becomes what is a sensible and reasonable course of action to follow?

Carbon dioxide is one of the so called green house gases considered by many people to be detrimental as far as global warming and changes in weather patterns are concerned. Those are debatable issues but, for the sake of this discussion, let's accept those end results. At the same time, let's ask whether if it is possible to do something to help this situation? Let me cite a few examples of what can be done and done with existing technology.

Yes, there are a few things that can be done to reduce the detrimental effects of carbon dioxide. First of all, it is essential that we all understand that carbon dioxide is an essential ingredient for plant growth. It is, therefore, not advisable to ban carbon dioxide entirely. Secondly, technology exists to convert carbon dioxide to useful products such as fertilizers and plastics. Thirdly, there is scientific and engineering work going on by many oil and gas companies to use carbon dioxide to "feed" a type of algae that can be used to produce biodiesel for use in transportation such as fuel for trucks and buses to deliver food and transport people all over this nation. Having said that you may ask: why is it that industry does not take advantage of these opportunities to convert a waste by-product into useful product? The answer is that they are taking advantage of that to some extent. But, we must also realize that it takes time and money to implement some of these solutions.

The oil industry is in many cases sponsoring research and development work to deal with this problem, but these companies do not have the financial wherewithal to solve all of the problems. It is something government can do and has done that in the past such as during World War II. The government can help by sponsoring academic and industrial research on a wider basis than a single oil company can and have a bigger impact as a result. Once it is realized that there is a potential to make money from waste products then the problem can be tackled and solved, but it takes time to reach a solution. That is the idea behind an innovation policy undertaken by government to tackle problems that impact our nation on a widespread basis thus creating new products and job opportunities for Americans.

In addition to creating new products and job opportunities, research sponsored by the US government has the potential of generating revenue for the government in terms of income taxes and royalty income from technology licensing. That's the preferred way of solving problems affecting our society; it is a much better solution that banning the use of the activity that produces the waste product. That's just one example.

In addition to the carbon dioxide problem, our country is facing many other problems relating to poverty, healthcare, education, food production, and many other issues that are afflicting not only Americans but the whole world. Here is a tremendous God sent opportunity to undertake a dedicated effort to eradicate these problems once and for all. Some people might say that is a very ambitious, idealistic, and unreachable goal; but, that is a topic where we can agree to disagree.

The author remembers a discussion that occurred several years before Americans astronauts landed on the moon. The discussion was with a couple of members of a religious group that knocked on neighborhood doors to convert home dwellers to their religious views. During that discussion, these people asked the author whether he thought man would ever reach the moon. My reply was a resounding yes. They were alarmed at my answer and indicated that it would never be possible for man to reach the moon. They took the position that if God had intended for man to go the moon He would have created a bridge to get there. My position, however, was that God gave us the intellect to develop the means to get to the moon and we used those God given talents to advance knowledge and improve the well being of all mankind. Needless to say, man went to the moon and that was quite an achievement. That was an indication that nothing would be impossible if we focus our attention on solving a problem or achieving a goal.

If going to the moon is possible then other things are also possible. The trick is to have the willingness, curiosity, educational background, and financial support to achieve the goal. Certainly, there are many Americans both native born and naturalized citizens who have the curiosity, willingness, educational background, and motivation to succeed in tackling a problem. The driver behind this motivation is not only to become financially independent but to satisfy our curiosity. In many cases, people get a sense of achievement that is, in their opinion, much more valuable than financial reward. It is said that Albert Einstein never realized how much money he was paid by the university that offered him a job; his wife had to negotiate his starting salary with the university.

In many cases, we have motivation and other attributes required to tackle a problem, but we lack financial support. It is possible to get such support from venture capitalists or from other sources; there are many examples of businesses that are now very successful that started in such a way. Another alternative is to secure the backing of the US government which is a big sponsor of blue sky research in connection with weapons development, space exploration, medical research, and many other activities that benefit the whole country. A colleague of mine was working on a project sponsored by the US government to convert chicken manure to fuel and animal feed. The point is everything is possible. Research and development work financed by either the private or public sector is an activity that needs to be encouraged and further expanded to create jobs and manufacturing activities to make new products available to consumers. In this manner, wealth is created for the private sector and the government in terms of new income streams from technology licensing royalties, sale of new products, and income taxes from employed workers and profitable corporations. This new source of income will be a starting point to continue financing innovation activities.

The US government demonstrated benefits of undertaking research and development efforts during WWII. It was a very effective means to develop new and more effective weapons systems to defeat our enemies. Obviously, initial results from this activity required development of other products to become functional. For example, new and more powerful airplane engines created a need for different types of aviation gasoline. As a result of R&D successes, the US became a world military, economic, and financial power. Now, it would be possible to regain the upper hand and defeat our present economic enemies using our intellectual power This can be done by developing new products and technologies that will ultimately leads us to the stars and to sustain our standard of living and create wealth for all Americans.

Government developed technology during the war years was

shared freely to enable production of large volumes of product required for the war effort. Now, the situation would be different. The US government would be in a position to undertake similar R&D programs but this time around it would license technology developed and impose conditions on where it can be used and to whom it could be licensed. That effort would results in a stream of income for the US government that would make it possible to continue sponsoring research efforts and, perhaps, put a dent on the national debt.

Benefits of having an innovation policy are many. It creates job opportunities for well educated people thus creating incentives for our children to pursue educational opportunities. It would motivate students to pursue academic excellence to work in an industrial setting, academic institution, or a national laboratory. This would challenge our educational system and force it to meet the expectations of our youngsters and nation. That, in and of itself, would be beneficial to prepare our workforce to compete effectively against foreign competitors in staffing highly technical jobs generated by research and development activities. The end result is to attract manufacturing activities back to the US.

There are other sides to the innovation policy that need to be included during implementation. The first one is to restructure the US Patent Office to enable it to examine inventions and grant patents in an expedited way rather than having to wait several years to determine whether or not a patent will be awarded.

The other side of the coin is government involvement in the protection of intellectual property. Protections include issuing strict warnings to countries whose citizens, corporate entities and government agencies engage in activities either directly or indirectly resulting in the theft of proprietary intellectual property. In the event such activities do not cease after issuance of this warning, the government would prosecute citizens and corporate entities and impose penalties on the offending country such tariffs on all products imported into the US. In other words, the penalties are meant to clearly show the offending country, its citizens and its corporate entities that the US will not tolerate theft of intellectual property.

CORPORATE POLICY

Corporate America is the backbone that strengthens the economic, financial, and military might of the United States. It is something that we all know and must protect. If we fail to meet this challenge we will be threatening our individual and national wellbeing. We all realize corporations have power to do many things benefiting mankind and those are the things that we want to encourage. At the same time, corporations are controlled by an elite group of individuals who may to act for their benefit regardless on the effect of employees and society as a whole. Corporations are not human beings but rather are only capable of acting through human beings – corporate executives. The corporate policy should focus on preventing activities that can be done by corporate executives for their own financial wellbeing without regard for the impact on or to the detriment of the rest of society.

Corporate executives hide behind a corporate veil to do things that they could not do and get away with as ordinary individuals. For example, executives can do a great deal of harm to a large number of people by merely deciding to fire everyone and relocating the company to a different country where workers can be and are abused. They have the power to raid the company's coffers and get huge bonuses to pay for living expenses and entertainment without anybody opposing such action; that is tantamount to legal robbery. Not only do they have the power but they also have the cooperation of willing accomplices to the detriment of shareholders, employees and customers; auditors are willing accomplices.

Furthermore, executives use the corporate entity to knowingly endanger the lives of people without having to face the consequences of such criminal activity. Consider the case of accidents in coal mines. In West Virginia, for example, several miners are killed after an explosion buried them alive in the mines. The mine owners are cited by regulatory agencies for repeated offenses prior to this tragic incident and do nothing to correct the situation. In fact, they hide additional incidences from federal and state inspectors. Then the accident happens, and the CEO of the mine company lies to the families of deceased miners by telling the relatives how concerned he and all other company executives have been about unsafe conditions and outline their attempts to remedy the situation. They also tell the relatives how sorry they are for their losses, but realize that is a risky job. Nothing happens to that CEO. He receives a bonus and an excellent retirement package; the deceased miners' families probably will have to sue to get anything from the mine owners. Now, these executives complain about lawyers' action in bringing suit against corporate wrongdoers and you begin to wonder on whose side you would be in a situation like that. I know where I would be. How can we continue to tolerate this situation? We have to and can do better

Financial pirates have taken over many corporations and are taking advantage of power available to them under the sun to enrich themselves without regards for the rights of shareholders, employees, customers, and society in general. Granted not all corporate executives behave similarly. There are still a whole bunch of executives who are honest, upright, ethical, and God fearing individuals who try to do their best for the company, shareholders, employees and customers; they are exceptional. If all companies were managed by ethical and decent executives there would be no need for this policy. Unfortunately, those people are the exception rather than the norm. It is, therefore, necessary to take action to eliminate abuses that are destroying our corporations and impacting our wellbeing.

We have experienced destruction of many companies and the elimination of many jobs to reward executives. A good example of that is the case that prevailed at GM and financial institutions. Strict action has to be taken to prevent abuses of power from continuing. Americans depend on Corporate America for their livelihood and the US depends on the corporate sector for its international economic, military, and financial strength; this is something that cannot be jeopardized. .

The purpose of this corporate policy is to do something to eliminate abuses of power by executives and to bring a sense of morality, ethics, and human decency to corporate behavior. And, in the process of achieving those goals, protect American corporations. Executives have a fiduciary duty under the law to act in a manner consistent with the best interest of shareholders. If they don't, then they may become liable to shareholders for damages resulting from violation of such responsibility. In theory, corporate executives do their best for the corporation and its owners. In reality, executives tend to think they own the corporation and can do whatever they want to satisfy their own needs and desires. Shareholders know that the deck is stacked against them and in favor of executives. Shareholders cannot do anything to eliminate abuses because executives control the board of directors and prescribe the manner in which change will take place in the corporate structure. It is now time to level the playing field. Corporate executives need to be held accountable for corporate actions. That is the primary motivation behind the development of a corporate policy.

Let's start by acknowledging state law controls corporate formation, requirements that must be met prior to incorporating, and how these entities will be allowed to operate. That is all fine and good. Federal law, however, should be the vehicle used to implement this corporate policy because many corporations are incorporated in one state and operate nationwide. The purpose of this policy is not to take away a right from or diminish the authority of individual states. It is rather an attempt to correct a very damaging situation that exists in every state of the union. It is an attempt to use US tax laws to get at wallets of executives and corporations so as to get their undivided attention and arrive at a solution to corporate abuses.

Some of these abuses include the power to grant executives excessive financial rewards in terms of bonuses, corporate compensation, and retirement packages. How many times you hear about a compensation package granted to an executive who has done nothing for the corporation except drive it into bankruptcy protection? Do you ever hear a situation where similar compensation or retirement packages are awarded to employees? How often do you hear about shareholders losing all of their investment in the corporation and executives lose nothing because they manage to sell their shares of stock just prior to the collapse of the company as done by executives at Enron? Is that fair? These abuses have to end.

Every once in a while, you read stories in local newspapers detailing executive's compensation packages. Those stories reveal a very interesting pattern. In good times, executives get raises that are out of this world and unbelievable. The same thing happens in bad times. There is never an economic crisis preventing executives from getting an annual raise. You never hear those executives, or for that matter the corporation itself, complain about excessive executive compensation; they always defend those obscene compensation packages in terms of the need to attract excellent leaders. If the term "excellent leaders" is meant to indicate leaders capable of driving the company into insolvency then I would hate to see what is meant by "poor leaders" or those considered inferior to lead. Now contrasts those stories to the situation when workers ask for a nickel an hour raise and have to fight the company tooth and nail to get that increase.

The other story is the one relating to retirement packages for executives that includes payment for everything including attendance to sporting events. The only thing excluded from these retirement packages are provisions to cover funeral expenses for retired executives; but that may be included in future packages. Have you not heard or read stories about companies that want to do away with retirement for workers because, they claim, those expenses are unbearable and unaffordable. What hypocrisy! Those are the inequities this corporate policy will cure.

The US Supreme Court granted corporations the right to contribute to political campaigns in the name of free speech. All that decision did was to legalize bribing of politicians by unscrupulous lobbyists. Do you think that decision improves commercial speech? Do you think your elected officials will prefer to talk to you or to his friendly financial contributor? That is the type of abuse we need to correct with this policy.

There are many other examples of executives engaging into an acquisition battle over a competing company. Once acquired, they do their best to strip the company of all valuable assets and fire the majority of workers. Then they learn the company cannot function so they sell whatever remains for pennies on the dollar. The reason for the acquisition is nothing more than a desire to eliminate a competitor. These acquisitions end up destroying companies and terminating many workers who depend on the acquired company for their livelihood and retirement. When that happens, their dreams evaporate. Executives of the acquired company, however, are rewarded by the acquiring company but workers end up losing everything they have worked hard to earn.

Merger and acquisition activity has to be looked at very carefully. There is nothing wrong when companies merge with one another so long as that merger is a long lasting marriage. It is offensive when a company secures financing at low interest rates to destroy a competitor; that should never be tolerated. What should be done to prevent that type of activity? First and foremost, the acquiring company would be unable to dispose of any assets for a period of no less than 3 years. Secondly, the acquiring company will have to offer jobs to acquired company's employees and keep them on the payroll for at least three years. Thirdly, no executives from either company executives would be entitled to special treatment or be rewarded for the merger. And, finally merger and acquisitions promoters will have to finance at least 50 percent of the cost of the acquisition from their own funds.

This corporate policy should be a vehicle used to achieve fairness in the corporate world and to protect corporations and employees of those corporations from greedy individuals. The vehicle to use in implementing this policy will be none other than the tax laws of the US. This is the same legal mechanism used in capturing well known criminals such as Al Capone. Here is how that level of fairness will be achieved.

Corporations granting excessive compensation or retirement packages to their executives that bear no resemblance or equity balance to wages and retirement packages granted to workers will be subject to a fairness tax. Corporations will have to pay a tax amounting to no less than 70 percent on all corporate profits regardless of where profits are generated. Similarly, executives receiving those benefits will be subject to a tax amounting to no less than 90 percent imposed on income plus their retirement benefits from that point on; that's an effective way to solve this problem because it impacts the wallets of both the corporation and its executives. Furthermore, the corporation will have to pay workers a handsome bonus to even the playing field. I doubt many corporations would ever consider abusing this policy.

In regards to the practice many executives follow when they abandon a sinking ship with a bag full of money, the remedy should be to immediately confiscate all of the executive's assets and put those assets under the jurisdiction of a competent court pending final adjudication of the case and payment of damages to shareholders or the corporation. We are familiar with reports detailing instances when executives have used corporate funds for the purpose of personal entertainment either for themselves or their relatives. How about using corporate jets to transport them and their relatives to sporting events in which their sons or daughters are active participants. That is an indication that many executives think they own the corporation. In those events, the policy would demand immediate dismissal from the company and reimbursing the corporation travel expenses.

Corporate America is too important to all of us to allow these abuses to continue unabated. We have to develop a solution to protect corporations from these unscrupulous executives and, at the same time, create undesirable consequences so that future corporate leaders will not be tempted to exhibit similar behavior.

REGULATORY OVERHAUL

The regulatory climate in the US is analogous to the situation prevailing in communist countries where the economy operates under the strict control of planners and bureaucrats unfamiliar with industrial operations. Results are disastrous. Any industry subject to such extreme degree of control is unable to operate efficiently or to satisfy variable consumer demand. Furthermore, companies operating in that strict environment are unable to develop and commercialize new technologies for the purpose of becoming more efficient and profitable, or to improve the quality of products. The accomplishment of all those controls and regulations is the destruction of industry and the collapse of their economies.

Soviet industry, or for that matter that of any other communist country, never achieved the lofty goals set by regulators. The population suffered tremendous hardships for years as a result of being denied essential necessities that industry could not or would not be able to produce. One thing that was never in short supply was rhetoric and exhortations to do more with less. Eventually, the whole bureaucratic control system collapsed. And, that was a blessing for the people of those countries. Look at the situation in China before and after the government began to allow industry to grow and develop along the lines of a capitalist system. Ask a Chinese if he or she would prefer to return to conditions existing prior to implementation of economic changes in China. It is true that China has changed slowly but it has achieved benefits that would have been unachievable under strict regulation and control.

US industry was totally unregulated until it became necessary to impose regulations to overcome abuses that led to the collapse of industry in the 1930s and culminated in the Great Depression. At that point, it became necessary to regulate industry to some extent in order to achieve worthy societal goals. Those regulations were necessary to save industry from its destruction. Since that time, regulators assumed that since a little regulation was beneficial and essential then a lot of regulation would be better. Consequently,

US industry began to be exposed to an ever growing number of regulations that would end up adversely impacting the company and eventually killing it.

Bureaucratic regulators, for example, decided automobile companies should produce electric vehicles; these bureaucrats mandated production of these vehicles. Consumers, on the hand, expressed a preference larger more comfortable SUVs that would consume more gasoline and be more expensive to operate. Now regulators issued mandate to force companies to produce electric vehicles or face heavy penalties for not meeting the standards. Keep in mind that these bureaucrats were not risking their money or were accountable to anyone; they just dictated edicts that industry was supposed to meet. What are companies to do?

Companies had two choices that were equally harmful to the company's financial interest and that of shareholders. It could elect to either produce electric cars and carry in inventory or refuse to make fuel efficient cars and face a stiff penalty. What gave unelected regulators such power? Where in the US Constitution was that power granted to these regulators? It would seem to me feasible to tell these regulators to take a hike. The sensible way would be to challenge all of these nonsensical mandates in the courts and in the market place. Henry David Thoreau is credited with paraphrasing the motto of the United States Magazine and Democratic Review in his essay on Civil Disobedience. He said:"That government is best which governs least." [133] That motto would be as applicable today as it was in the past particularly as we discussed the burdens imposed on industry by unaccountable regulatory agencies. President Obama recognized that regulatory agencies are strangling Corporate America and that something needed to be done about that to improve the economic climate and make it easier for industry to create job opportunities for Americans. That was a very positive change for President Obama and, hopefully, would lead to a change on how bureaucrats view industry. But the end result under President Obama was more regulation. It became was more rhetoric than positive action which explained why it took so long for the economy to recover from the Great 2009 Recession.

No one argues industry should be unregulated and allowed to operate completely without some controls. It is necessary to have some degree of regulation in place to prevent abuses such as the one we have witnessed in the financial institutions. Regulations are necessary, but they should be based on common sense rather than bias or prejudice or on the agendas of fanatics. There is no question we cannot totally eliminate risk. The question is how much risk is acceptable and how much we are willing to tolerate and pay to mitigate those risks? In short, regulations should be based on common sense and balanced approach to weigh benefits achieved by the regulation against economic harms caused by it. It has to be a realistic analysis based as much as possible on actual economic data.

We all would like to eliminate the threat of cancer from our midst, but we all know that is an impossible task. It is impossible because in some cases we do not totally understand what causes cancer and because some strains of cancer are the result of generic make-up. The best that can be done is to do research to learn more about the disease and to develop a strategy to mitigate its malignant effect. That strategy should be based on a cost benefit analysis that recognizes we cannot stop all human activity. What we can do is to protect ourselves by defining on a probabilistic base defining chances of contracting the disease and take steps to mitigate those chances without driving industry to bankruptcy.

Regulations are drawing the life out of Corporate America. If that continues, the US will end up losing its relevance in the world and corporate employees will lose their jobs thus creating a big social problem for the US. Consequently, all regulations should be carefully examined with the idea of getting rid of those that achieve no useful purpose. The best way to do that is to perform a cost and benefit analysis of each regulation. Those that show excessive cost and limited benefits should be repealed immediately. Those that show a balanced cost and benefit ratio should be further examined to verify that conclusion. Finally, those that show benefits should be retained and every year reexamined to determined continuing benefits.

TAX FAIRNESS POLICY

Tax laws in the US are used primarily to generate revenues for the government. Those laws are also used to achieve social policies politicians deem desirable. The tax code is so complicated that it becomes necessary to hire tax experts and lawyers to figure out the amount of tax due by citizens. There are many tricks or loopholes in the tax code that prevent fair results for individual taxpayers. Let's illustrate this point.

A taxpayer loses his job and collects unemployment benefits but the total income amount is insufficient expenses. As a result, he may have to withdraw funds from his retirement account such as an IRA or 401k plans. The point is that the taxpayer is liable for taxes due on his unemployment compensation benefits and on that that taxpayer may be penalized from drawing funds from his retirement account. GE, on the other hand, makes $15 billion profits around the world and pays absolutely no tax. Is that fair? Something is wrong with that picture.

This policy is an attempt to develop an easier tax code that everyone will be able to use to calculate taxes due to the federal government easily and quickly. There are no more loopholes to benefit the chosen few and punish the majority of taxpayers. That policy will be based on facts and will be fair to all taxpayers as required by law.

The US government collects about $1.6 trillion in income taxes annually. It also collects approximately $600 billion from other sources such as licenses, royalties, import duties, etc. The government annual revenue is, therefore, roughly $2.2 trillion. [134] It is evident that the government needs to continue collecting the $1.6 trillion in income tax and would still collects the $600 million in duties and so on.

Is there a way of generating this amount of money in a fair and equitable manner to all taxpayers – corporations and citizens alike? The answer is definitely yes, and here is how it can be achieved without raising tax rates. In fact, most taxes rates would decrease.

We must recognize everyone has to pay a fair share of taxes

as demanded by equality under law. The 2010 Gross Domestic Product (GDP) of the US is $14.5 trillion in terms of current dollars. As we all know, GDP is the value of all goods and services produced in the country. Consequently, if the government were to impose a 15 percent tax rate on all goods and services it would be able to generate in excess of $2.0 trillion annually. As GDP increases so would income tax revenue for the government. Notice a 15 percent tax rate is lower than tax rates most citizens are subject to pay at the end of the year. Secondly, the amount of revenues generated would exceed the amount presently collected by approximately $400 to $500 billion annually; that excess amount can and should be used to pay down the national debt. Thirdly, every taxpayer pays the same rate regardless of income earned by the taxpayer. That means that GE will have to pay 15 percent on that $15 billion of profits without any deduction.

There should, however, be some exceptions established to make the system more equitable. First of all, unemployment compensation benefits would be tax exempt. Secondly, the government would define the poverty level and everyone including corporations will liable for a 15 percent on all income above the poverty level; the poverty level would be adjusted on an annual basis. Thirdly, retirees like unemployed workers will not have to pay any tax on retirement benefits. Corporations and individuals would depreciate capital expenditures within three years or as soon as sufficient profits are generated to enable the deduction whatever occurs first. Fourthly, R&D expenditures would become an expense subject to immediate deduction from corporate income tax due. And, finally, the tax code will be simplified to enable every taxpayer to complete all tax forms without having to hire specialists.

Despite convincing historical evidence increasing taxes has a detrimental effect on any recovery from an economic crisis, the Obama Administration has floated the idea of raising taxes and continues to do so every chance it gets. Back in 1937, the rate of taxation increases from approximately 15 percent to 20 percent; that causes a reversal in the declining trend in the rate of unemployment and causes it to rise from 15 percent up to 20 percent.

Furthermore, historical evidence shows government revenues increased from 1934 through 1938 when the government spent significant sums of money on public projects (see Figure 12). When the rate of taxation increased in 1937, data show a reduction in government revenues. This effect can be seen by looking at data in Figures 12 and 13. The result of increasing rate of taxation was obviously contrary to the expectation behind the tax increase. In fact, this was not a fluke in the data. The explanation would be simply that the net effect of increasing tax rates is to reduce investments, thus preventing creation of new job opportunities and making it more difficult to earn and pay taxes. The same situation happens when taxes are raised on consumers, preventing them from purchasing goods and thus reducing demand for goods and services leading to job losses. Tax increases slow the recovery and cause job losses.

The effect of cutting taxes has been shown on several occasions to be generally beneficial to the economy and to the government. Figure 36 show increasing tendency in annual US Government revenues during the period 1940 to 2008.

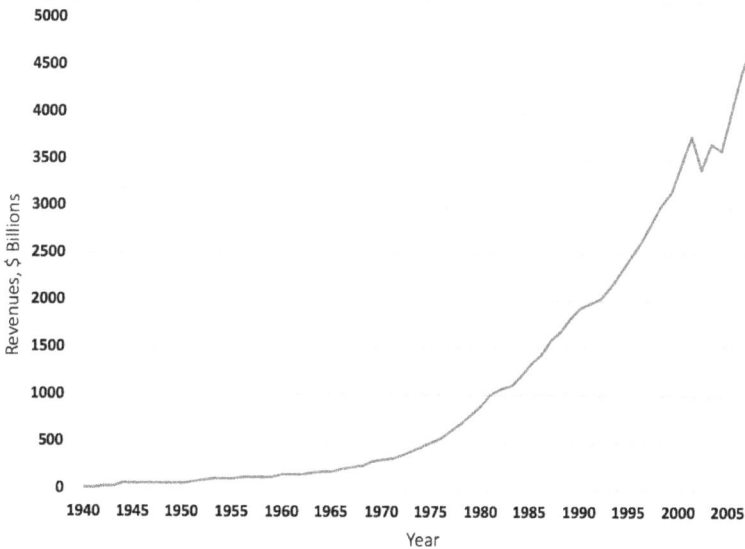

Figure 36. Federal Revenues [135]

Effective corporate tax rates are calculated from data found in reference 50. Results are plotted as shown in Figure 37. It is obvious US Government Revenues increase (See Figure 36) with decreasing tax rates (See Figure 37.)

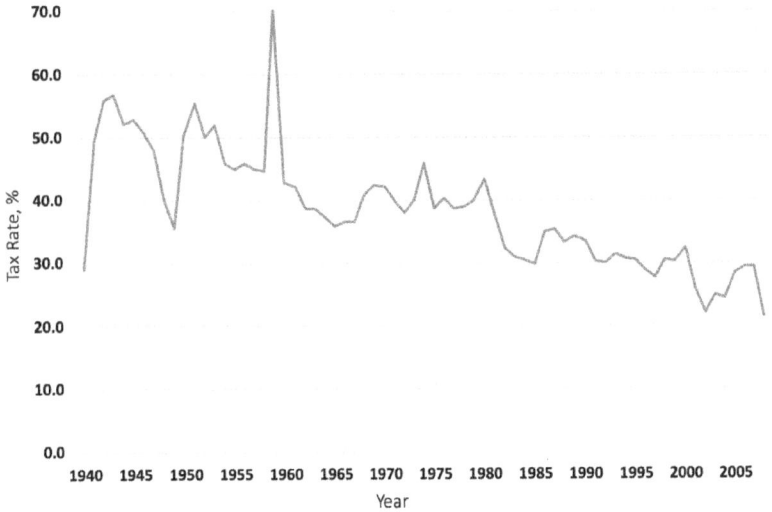

Figure 37. Effective Corporate Tax Rates [136]

EDUCATIONAL POLICY

The education of our young people is a prerequisite to enable our nation to continue its industrial development and growth. It is a requirement must be met to attract foreign industry. Since industry is so technically oriented, competencies in math and science are essential to be able to get a job in one of these industries.

Unfortunately, our secondary schools students are not particularly well grounded in math and science as compared to many foreign counterparts. In fact, many of our high-school graduates have to take remedial courses prior to starting their university studies. In Texas, approximately 50 percent of all high-school graduates have to take remedial courses before college. The cost of these remedial programs amounts to approximately $400 million a year. Texas is not the exception. This indicates an opportunity to do better in secondary schools and save money in the process. There is no need to complain about lack of opportunities to attend college. That problem can be solved by improving secondary-school education.

The point is that opportunities exist to better train our young children in order to better prepare them to compete with students from other parts of the world. It is also a necessity in order to provide the technically trained manpower required by our industrial sector. The federal government has the duty to ensure that all of our students are exposed to the same educational opportunities regardless of race, financial wellbeing, or state of residence. All of our students are equally important to our collective wellbeing, and not one of them can be neglected. All students should have the right to the best educational opportunities possible. That is not only good for students but also for our entire nation.

The federal government should ensure that all states meet identical criteria so all students are properly trained and able to compete against any student from any place in the world. That is a federal duty. It is also a duty to ensure adequate educational facilities are provided to ensure a learning environment for all children no matter where they live. In other words, the federal government has the duty to ensure that states provide sufficient financial resources and equal opportunities to all students.

Consequently, it is incumbent on the federal government to equalize educational opportunities, even if that results in expenditures of money to bring poor school districts to a level equal to that of richer districts. The US cannot neglect this very important duty for on education rests the future of this nation. The federal government has to be particularly vigilant to monitor progress in poor areas of the country.

Failure to provide adequate educational opportunities in poor areas of the country would lead to bad consequences. Number one, it would deny poor Americans their right to get themselves out of poverty. Those folks would turn to crime as a means of improving their economic lot. It would increase expenditures on crime fighting. It would increase incarceration costs. It would cause a lot of pain and suffering to the victims of crimes. Finally, it would be a great economic loss in losing the minds of those children who could potentially become future corporate and government leaders. It is time to eliminate poverty in our nation. Our nation cannot afford to waste the future of our children.

These policies recognize that is essential to have a multitude of tools available at our disposal to enable creation of jobs. In summary the energy policy focuses on ensuring availability of fuels to power our industry. The innovation policy ensures new products and technologies are developed and commercialized to keep our country at the leading edge of technology and to ensure that our manufacturing plants are competitive. The idea behind the corporate policy is to develop a climate where workers and management work together as an ethical and moral team to achieve results and improve the corporate world. The regulatory overhaul policy prevents regulations from strangling industry. The tax policy makes the tax code fair to all taxpayers. Finally, the educational policy focuses on providing well-educated workers to ensure America has qualified workers to man jobs created by a technically sophisticated industry. This set of policies is, in essence, how I propose to create job opportunities for Americans.

CHAPTER 9

DAWN OF A NEW ERA

History is an extremely important tool to evaluate outcomes and performance from economic and political situations under different input conditions and draw conclusions from those analyses. In other words, history is an ongoing process detailing inputs and reactions to those inputs. It is a vehicle allowing one to evaluate what is done right and also to view mistakes and consequences from those actions. In short, history details work done, how it is done, and the results obtained under each conditions in a given case or event. Companies are aware of the importance of preparing extensive reports at the end of all projects summarizing actions done at every phase of the project to understand what is done right, to define what goes wrong, how mistakes are overcome and the impact each step has on budget and schedule. This is done to prevent recurrence of the same mistake and to save money in doing so. This is an activity typically labeled known as a "Lessons Learned Exercise". In short, companies know this is a valuable and important exercise because of the lessons it can teach about every project history. These are lessons that can teach and disclose the good, the bad, and the ugly of every project; this information is extremely valuable. Edmund Burke, a famous Irish political philosopher, is known for a very famous quote. He is credited as the author of this quote: "Those who don't know history are destined to repeat it."

Think about that concept and the costs that can be avoided if mistakes made in a similar previous situation or event are not avoided. Let's look at some very specific cases to illustrate the importance of history. Assume, for example, a document is prepared listing in great detail events or causes leading up to World War II. Would it be worth avoiding the same mistakes and incurring the same costs? Would Japan be willing to repeat the attack on Pearl Harbor knowing how the US would respond? It is very likely the answer to both questions would be no under the same circumstances. Do you get the picture?

Mr. Burke's quote encourages us to study history to learn from mistakes made by others. Each past mistake and results arising from those situations are valuable lessons that can be applied when confronted with similar situations in our timeframe. In other words, every action and reaction to it tells a story detailing what to do, how to do it, when to do it, and likely outcome of those steps. It is analogous to a lab experiment where steps done to achieve a solution to a problem are monitored and outcomes from each action are noted. That in a nutshell is the goal behind the idea for learning history.

In terms of this book context, it would be easy to conclusively prove the validity of Mr. Burke's famous quote by focusing on topics covered in the book at different times by different people. In the 1930's, for example, President Roosevelt faces a very difficult economic crisis causing high levels of unemployment, and other difficulties that could potentially lead to civil unrest. President Roosevelt knows he has to tackle difficult issues arising out of the Great Depression of the 1930's.

The Roosevelt Administration does not have a playbook to follow where steps to implement are in an orderly fashion to achieve a solution. He comes up with some innovative policies to try but there is no assurance any of these ideas would be successful. Some actions prove successful and others are total failures. Fast-forward to the time President Obama is in charge and his administration has to deal with similar circumstances as faced by President Roosevelt during the Great Depression. President Obama is facing and must deal with issues presented by the Great Recession of the early 21st Century. How do these two presidents deal with similar issues arising from essentially similar situations? Can lessons learned from The "Great Depression" be successfully applied by President Obama to end the "Great Recession"? The answer is that more likely than not the same policies can successfully address and solve problems arising in this later crisis. President Obama proves to be a great orator but one who has not learned anything from history and, as a result, the recession last for a very long time.

You might recall, President Roosevelt starts his attack on the Great Depression with government spending on infrastructure. President Obama does the same thing. President Roosevelt, unlike President Obama, focuses these expenditures on parks and other public works projects to hire workers. The Obama Administration focuses its efforts on funding "Shovel Ready" projects but shovels are not easily found. In fact, it only finds printers to print sign on many roads to let people know the Obama Administration may be funding road repairs. The lessons President Obama should have learned is that infrastructure projects take a long time to start having, and that has an effect on unemployment, which he should have learned from results of the 1930 Crisis.

The great Depression comes to an end when World War II starts and the US becomes a major supplier of weapons and agricultural products. But, in reality, the underlying reason to learn is that manufacturing those weapons and war material is what impacts unemployment. In other words, it is the need to hire unemployed workers to work in manufacturing facilities producing weapons that reduces unemployment. In short, manufacturing becomes a key to reduce unemployment and generate funds for the government via income taxes on wages paid to manufacturing workers. President Obama cuts defense spending and spending on NASA. These two sources are significant contributors to manufacturing job creation and innovation leading to new jobs and products. In short, President Roosevelt increases defense spending and creates millions of manufacturing jobs. President Obama cuts defense spending and many manufacturing jobs are eliminated. On top of that, President Obama imposes job-killing regulations that further exacerbate the unemployment picture. As a result, many high paying manufacturing jobs are eliminated and manufacturing facilities are shut down or relocated to lower wage countries.

After President Obama leaves office at the conclusion of his term in 2016, President Trump comes into the picture in 2017 and changes course on President Obama's policies to more effectively deal with a continuing economic malaise relating to high unemployment, strangulation of industry by an out of control regulatory system, and many other problems. So it is incumbent on us to evaluate President Trump policies and determine how these policies differ from President Obama's policies and the effect on the resulting economic climate in the country.

You might recall President Roosevelt initially tackles the Great Depression economic crisis by spending on infrastructure work. This work while beneficial to get people back to work is not as effective as spending money on manufacturing activities such as it is demonstrated by increasing defense spending. The result of these defense expenditures is creation of high paying jobs in the manufacturing sector. A byproduct of these expenditures, is a move to relocate manufacturing facilities back to the US, to reopen and expand previously closed manufacturing facilities such as steel mills that are now required to supply steel to naval shipbuilders. These expenditures have a much faster impact on reducing unemployment and creating employment opportunities. President Trump recognizes that reality and increases defense spending. The result is an accelerating economic engine that is creating thousands and millions of jobs.

President Obama is not a fan of the hydrocarbon industry. In fact, it might be said he is main cheerleader behind elimination or banning of the hydrocarbon industry. Think about that. If there is no secured supply of hydrocarbons fuels and raw materials, what impact does that have on US industry? In the absence of hydrocarbons, US industry and society would face disastrous consequences. What would power our industry? Wind? Solar? Considering that supply of nuclear power generated electricity is limited and, for all practical purposes, unlikely to expand beyond present levels or decline slightly, what is there to drive industrial machinery and create jobs for our people?

President Obama is a signatory to the Paris Accord that limits or eliminates carbon dioxide emissions resulting from burning of hydrocarbon fuels. This accord forces the US to reduce carbon dioxide emissions over a short period of time while allowing China and India US to continue emitting at their present rates. The fallacy of this agreement is that it neglects to consider that carbon dioxide emissions generated in either China or India eventually migrate to the US forcing the US to deal with the problem. In other words, the agreement forces the US to pay to clean emissions generated by China, India and other countries. By the way, the US has been a very significant player in reducing these undesirable emission, so it seems the intent of the agreement is to punish the US. Obviously, China, India and those polluters think this is a heck of a great deal. You might want to go beyond rhetoric to get to the facts of his horrible agreement. This is evidence indicating President Obama is a globalist interested in destroying the US. In the opinion of the author, President Obama is the most divisive, inept and corrupt president ever elected in the US.

President Trump, on the other hand, is a president focusing his attention on the well being of he US. Under his leadership, the US has experienced a resurgence in the hydrocarbon industry and has become not only self sufficient in oil and gas but it has also become a major exporter of these commodities. That's a significant achievement that reduces our reliance on foreign supply and control of fuels but also provides a significant improvement to the US Balance of Trade. The US consumes approximately 20 million barrels a day representing a significant outlay of dollars to foreign countries. Banning US oil and gas production would have a significant financial impact on the US balance of trade. As a net oil exporter, however, the US balance of trade is impacted in a very positive way. The attack on hydrocarbons is not exclusively limited to oil and gas production. It also impacts coal production.

Coal production impacts not only the US economy but also the economies of several states including West Virginia, Kentucky and others. Americans in coal producing states depend on jobs in coalmines to support their families. And yet, several politicians are actively advocating these people be fired. The question that comes to mind is how are these people going to earn a living to support their families? There even crazier and more basically stupid politicians who claim the world would come to an end in 12 years which might provide a great excuse to get rid of coal miners to reduce their suffering. How disconnected are these inept corrupt politicians from reality? Perhaps, it would be a great idea to cut the supply of fuels to power the cars and air conditioners of these clowns and see how loud their complaints get.

It is fair to say President Trump's policies relating to taxes and regulations have provided capacity expansion incentives to Corporate America to expand manufacturing facilities and create new jobs. It is also fair to say reduction of personal income tax rates creates incentives for consumption expansion for products to further expand production capacity and create jobs. In short, President Trump's policies have revitalized the revival of Corporate America.

CHAPTER 10

EPILOGUE

I have written this book with one purpose in mind. My goal has been to raise a red flag warning Americans of future dangers I see for our country and our own individual wellbeing. I am very concerned about continuing tolerance to abuses of power and corruption in both business and governmental circles. I am worry about the future my children and grandchildren, who are now starting their journey to realization and fulfillment of their own American Dreams, would inherit. I am afraid they would be unable to enjoy the same opportunities I have enjoyed living in this great nation. I am not being selfish in my concerns because I share the same concerns for the children and grandchildren of all Americans.

I am afraid abuses of power and corruption have gone on for too long and it is something that has become endemic to our society. It is a cancer that continues to spread and, unless we as individuals stop that malignancy, it would lead to the collapse of our whole economic system. That would be a disastrous result for it would impact and destroy our corporate world and, in turn, destroy our nation; our dreams would not be spared from that destruction. We have already seen some impacts on Corporate America and on our political system. But, we have only seen the beginning of this upcoming catastrophe.

I came to this country as a young man from a communist country and, like many other immigrants before me, marveled at achievements made by uniting people with the common goal of reaching the American dream. I became aware of diversity of opinions and ideas existing and continuing to exist to this day. That diversity was the outcome of many ethnic groups coming together and sharing their life stories and backgrounds. I soon realized the American culture was a heterogeneous culture representing many points of view and causing the best point of view to emerge to the surface. That diversity added vitality and propelled our nation to reach unthinkable achievements. I saw a society rewarding people for achievements rather than laziness. I read about people who had become influential not by the color of their skin or ethnic heritage but rather by their actions and results of their actions. I heard some Americans who were criticizing foreign countries for human right abuses and I, at the same time, witnessed other Americans including Dr. Martin Luther King Jr. who were fighting for the rights of oppressed Americans. That, to me, represented the American character for we were willing to not only right abuses in foreign countries but also to undertake actions to get our own house in order. That, in my opinion, was the greatness of our country.

The American character is one rooted in hope and a desire to make a better future for our children and for their children. In other words, we are interested in challenging the status quo and making our nation a better place than what we as young individuals inherited from our parents. Now, after fifty years, I see a lack of hope and confidence in our people. I see the plight of unemployed parents struggling to get a job to earn necessary wages to support their families. I see politicians and corporate leaders turning their attention away from those who are suffering. I see politicians debating senseless ideas when they should be totally focused on addressing issues necessary to create jobs. There is no question in my mind jobs can be created by the government, but there is no will or leadership from our political leaders in Washington and Corporate America to solve the number one problem facing this nation – jobs creation. In short, part of the desperation I see is rooted in a dysfunctional government focusing exclusively on rewarding party loyalty over the needs and loyalty of constituents and country. It is indeed a sad situation, and yet I see potential in our country for greater things.

I would go to stores and find the majority products on shelves to be products made anywhere in the world but the US. And, that included many goods made by Corporate America in foreign countries. I would wonder how could it be possible to continue on this journey where we manufactured nothing or very little and were expected to consume products produced everywhere in the world. How could we afford that? How could we in the US, I asked myself, be expected to buy foreign made goods when we were unemployed? How could these manufacturers continue to expect us to purchase their goods? I knew for a fact that I could not afford to purchase anything unless I had a job enabling me to earn sufficient wages to purchase the goods that I either needed or wanted. I did not believe I was the exception. We needed jobs to continue earning enough money to acquire the things that we would need and demand.

Perhaps, I thought, we had become a nation accustomed to purchasing goods on credit thinking that we would never have to pay for those goods. It was easy to go to stores to purchase something and charged it to our credit card. That was instant satisfaction, but the day would come when we had to come up with the dollars to pay our debt to the credit card company. But, if we did not have a job where were we going to get the dollars to pay for goods we purchased and charged on our credit card. It was a simple concept that I failed to comprehend. Certainly, that was also true of the thinking of government officials and of bureaucrats running it. We all witnessed political gridlock and endless nonsense that kept this nation in a state of uncertainty leading to frustration and loss of hope. The same congress that engaged in authorizing expenditures on the government credit card also engaged in discussions to frustrate payment of those debts. The end result was loss of confidence in our government and its leadership.

We need jobs. If we do not have jobs, we would not be able to generate funds to pay our credit card purchases. In fact, our credit cards would be cancelled and we would be unable to charge our purchases as we have become so accustomed to do. Instead of instant satisfaction, we would have to make difficult choices and experience instant frustration. At that point, we are going to realize we must earn wages to allow us to consume the goods we need or we are going to do without them. It is as simple as that. The day is coming, if it has not already arrived, when we will have to come to terms with reality. If there are no jobs there is no consumer demand for products regardless of the amount of money held in Corporate America's coffer.

I refuse to believe Americans have become lazy or complacent or willing to tolerate economic adversity under any circumstance. At least, I would like to think that is not the case. If, however, that happens to be the case then we need to wake up and take charge of creating our own future for as it is now our future looks very cloudy indeed, and it is getting cloudier every day. We cannot survive as a nation relying on foreign producers to produce the majority of the goods we consume and expect our national standard of living to continue to improve on an annual basis. We cannot expect our nation's prosperity to increase if all we do is to consume and not produce. If we continue on our present path we would become a parasitic society in the sense of relying on others for our well being. And, indeed the others are sucking the blood out of all of us. That is not the American character as I understand it.

The American character is one that relies on independence and willingness to overcome adversity regardless of situation. American ingenuity and hard work have always been vehicles leading our country to a prosperous future. America and Americans must once again rely on hard work, high moral and ethical standards, ingenuity and fairness to create jobs for Americans. That is the only way to fuel the engine driving our own prosperity as a nation and as individuals.

We have experienced prosperity many times in our history and it has always been the result of hard work and not complacency. Nowadays, complacency has become an accepted part of life. We as individuals Americans must realize that our future depends on what we collectively do now in the present to make our future better. We must question reasons why manufacturers close plants here in the US, fire workers, relocate manufacturing activities outside the US, and bring goods manufactured in other countries back to the US to be sold to Americans who have seen their jobs disappear. Why is that situation happening? What can be done to stop that situation from occurring? How long can that situation be tolerated before action is taken? If that continues, the US would cease to exist as the greatest consumer market in the world, and it would also cease to exist as the greatest technological and military power in the world. But, the other side of the coin is that Corporate America would also cease to exist. Can we afford to see that happen? In short, we are all in this crisis together and we must join hands to save our individual and collective dreams. Now, you may begin to understand goals for writting this book.

Given that brief background, I have chosen to look at history to determine how our industrial and technological base evolved. This is an essential first step to gain a better understanding of how our country achieves its technological and productive might and its leadership status in the world. In other words, I ask what has made this nation so prosperous? It is only then that ideas emerge pointing out solutions to be implemented in order to turn any economic situation or crisis around and create a better economic climate for our collective benefit.

Since arriving in this country from a communist country in the early 1960's, I have observed dramatic transformations in US society. I have witnessed Corporate America become the envy of the world. I have seen the impact of a strong private sector on the standard of living of individual Americans. I have also observed, in my short history in this country, Corporate America become a shining beacon of light guiding our journey into a future that promises to be better for us than the past was for our parents. Now that shining beacon of light is becoming very dim and, if we don't do something about keeping it lit then the fire behind that beacon would be extinguished. What must we do to keep that beacon of light shining ever so brightly to continue guiding us on our journey into the future and, more importantly, to guide our children into a bright and prosperous future better than we have had in our generation.

I was interested in learning how industrial developments impacted our nation as a whole. In particular, I was interested in analyzing factors making the US a powerful industrial nation capable of supplying goods to satisfy the world's demand. I discovered that the greatness of the United States was the result of the American people and their character. It was the result of corporations, labor, and government working together as a team; that is the same idea that Japan and Germany used after WWII to turn their economies around and become prosperous. I also discovered the unselfish attitude of Americans regardless of social or economic status to be a powerful motivational driver for our nation's greatness and success.

The American character, in my opinion, has a moral fiber shaped by political and religious persecution as well as the result of economic adversity and successes. It is a rugged temperament ideally suited to address problems and overcome challenges in the face of adversity. It is a disposition fashioned by diversity of opinion. It is a character that recognizes that in unity there is strength. It is a character strengthened by a sense of right and wrong and reliance on the rule of law. I recognize that the strength of that American character is people from many ethnic groups coming together as one nation. It is in the blood of many people from all over the world that has been shed defending our beliefs and freedoms; it is the purity of our ideals; and it is the sky and stars above all of us in this great country. It is all of those elements in our common heritage that unite us and become the basis for the colors and symbols embedded in our national flag.

I have seen American workers, the US government, and Corporate America joining hands to meet challenges and solve problems for the benefit of all. I have seen that happening on several occasions. I have seen the result of that unity of purpose in the achievements made by our nation's institutions. I have witnessed our astronauts landing on the moon and the sense of pride and hope brought to our nation as a result of a challenge by an adversary threatening our very existence as a nation. I have seen students attempt to achieve to their fullest potential to enable them to pursue careers in NASA and to be able to continue exploring the universe. That is particularly true in the life story of NASA Astronaut Jose Hernandez.

Jose Hernandez, the son of Mexican migrant workers, was born in the US. His parents came to the US and had to work hard in agricultural fields and make difficult decisions to ensure a future for Jose. He had to overcome adversity in learning a new language at the age of twelve and get an education enabling him to become an engineer. His electrical engineering training and knowledge enables him to make significant contributions in the field of mammography to help early detection of breast tumors. His contribution to prevention and treatment of breast cancer is reason enough to question and negate the idea of denying educational privileges to Americans on account of their parent's immigration status; this is not a single exception.

As a result of working as a team and the availability of great educational opportunities, Corporate America became very strong. Corporate America was the engine driving economic activities making the US an economic powerhouse. People, however, were the sparks igniting fuel provided by ideas to get the economic engine moving. Everyone benefitted and, as a result, our standard of living became the highest in the world. Something happened in later years to transform that winning combination among people, private sector, and public sector. That transformational event over the past twenty to thirty years caused the present sense of frustration and hopelessness.

In the opinion of the author, the leading cause of that devastating transformation was the so called end of the "Cold War" after the collapse of the Soviet Union. At that point in time, it was believed our enemies had been defeated, but the reality was different. The only thing that had changed was the means used to exert power. In other words, during the Cold War period, it was believed that military power would be the deciding factor in achieving victory. All of the sudden military power became a secondary factor and economic and intellectual power assumed leading roles after the collapse of the Soviet Union. The US was an economic powerhouse and the Soviet Union was nothing more than a bankrupt nation with operating under a failing economic system. Consequently, the US government reduced military spending because it assumed the time had come to enjoy a peace dividend. This reduction in military spending had repercussions on the private sector.

The reduction in government expenditures directly impacted Corporate America. The reaction from Corporate America was forced to cut back on its own spending and that impacted its day to day activities. The day came for Corporate America to do whatever it needed to do to enjoy a peace dividend and cut expenses. Consequently, Corporate America switched operating focus from a culture of technological strength and achievement over to a reliance on financial gimmicks to improve profitability. As a result, Corporate America discontinued doing things that had proven so successful in the past to generate new products and improve operating efficiency. Industry began to lay off employees that had made Corporate America powerful. That started a trend that continued for many years and cost many thousands of corporate employees their jobs and livelihoods. The industrial focus was cost reduction no matter how achieved. Mass reduction of employees had the unintended consequence of turning many companies into functionally impaired entities. Terminated employees had to reduce their own expenditures and that became the basis for acquiring cheaper foreign made goods. That, in turn, led Corporate America to further cost reductions and to relocate manufacturing facilities. It became a devastating vicious cycle that eroded economic realities.

Executives figured they also deserve a peace dividend. They began to rely on financial gimmicks to inflate corporate profit margins and award themselves huge bonuses and ever increasing compensation packages bearing no relationship to corporate performance. In fact, many companies awarded obscene compensation packages and bonuses to executives that had driven their companies to bankruptcy. Given the fact corporate entities act through their executives, it became apparent corporate executives were the ones granting themselves those huge bonuses and compensation packages. In short, executives got a license to steal from corporate coffers and they would raid corporate coffers for their financial benefit. The situation could best be expressed by paraphrasing a very well known truism to the effect "that money corrupts and unhindered access to money corrupts absolutely".

Corporate leaders discovered corporate funds could also be used to buy political influence. That was necessary to create an operating climate encouraging government institutions to overlook abuses of corporate power. In the process of doing that, corruption became the means to get ahead. And, in so doing, corporate executives poisoned the economic climate and their companies began to suffer the consequences; many companies disappeared from the face of the earth such as for example Union Carbide and many financial institutions.

At the same time, politicians realized something had to be done for the people who had lost their jobs or for the failure to generate jobs. The answer was a welfare program that initially focused on helping needy families, but instead created a culture of dependency analogous to slavery. Politicians realized the welfare program could be their tickets to re-election; they expanded the program on a continuous basis year after year regardless of need. Abuse of the welfare system became endemic when people realized government was rewarding them for doing nothing. That dependency became the root cause of an ever increasing level of poverty; perhaps people also thought they were entitled to a peace dividend.

We need to turn that situation around. The government should help people in need without creating a dependency culture on an entitlement program. The government should help those in need to get back on their feet and, at the same time, create the incentives for needy people to become productive taxpayers. In other words, government should encourage and reward creation of wealth rather than promoting penalties for being wealthy and productive while encouraging laziness and condemning the poor to eternal poverty.

I am not opposed to having a welfare system that truly helps needy families. It is something that has to be done because every one of us is subject to fall in hard times needing a helping hand from government. That is what should be done and done in a way that truly provides incentives for people in need to get out of their misery and reach for the stars. Unfortunately, the welfare system fails to do that. Our government needs to take a long range view and pay welfare recipients to attend trade schools and colleges to gain the means of earning a decent salary. In that way, these citizens can become contributing taxpayers and have the opportunity to become wealthy. In short, the welfare system gives welfare recipients a dry fish to eat so they eat on a single day, but it fails to teach them how to fish so that they may be able to eat every day.

Unfortunately, social workers and the welfare system do not share that opinion. They see their mission as being one that expands the welfare system in order to ensure job security. In the process of doing that, social workers transform a system intended to help needy people to get back on their feet into a system that encourages dependency and leads to eternal poverty. One thing that should be kept in mind is that the system can be abused, and it has been abused. If you don't believe that then all you need to do is to create a system that financially rewards social workers for getting needy people out of the welfare system and poverty; the results would be very obvious. Our political leaders should create that latter Welfare system.

I witnessed the standard of living increased in the US during the 1960s. Then it reached a plateau and began to decline slowly but surely. It used to be the father, as head of the family, was the main wage earner. Then it became necessary for the mother to find a job outside of the home to provide for the family. This trend obviously had a significant impact on the family unit, but it was something that had to be done to survive and provide for our families. In short, this trend was an indication Americans was becoming poorer and poorer on a yearly basis. Statistics compiled over the past 20 years revealed the poverty rate had increased on a yearly basis and reached an alarming level early in the 21st Century. The number of Americans living in poverty at this time had risen to a level of 15.1 percent meaning 46.2 million of our citizens were living at or below the poverty level defined by annual earnings level of $22,113 or less for a family of four earns. [137] What was more disturbing was disclosure that 7 percent of people with jobs still fell below the poverty line and that children were most likely to be poor. That was a shocking revelation that could lead us to the conclusion this nation's future is in jeopardy.

I believe high poverty level is due to several factors coming together to achieve an undesirable result. First of all, Corporate America has done its best to break the sacred bond binding employees and employer. It has done that to cut costs in order to unrealistically inflate profit margins on which to justify granting ever increasing compensation packages to undeserving inept corporate executives; nothing has been done to reverse that situation. Is that a reflection of the value executives place on employees who were so influential in making Corporate America so successful and profitable? Secondly, relocation of production facilities to foreign countries has resulted in loss of many high paying jobs for Americans. Thirdly, the US regulatory system has eliminated many high paying jobs by enacting job killing regulations and imposing those regulations on Corporate America without doing cost and benefits analysis or evaluating impacts to determine if societal costs exceed benefits. Fourthly, politicians have failed to take effective action to get rid of uncertainty in the economic climate. One group of politicians is for spending and the other is for further cuts in government spending; that uncertainty prevents the private sector from planning and justifying future expansions. Finally, politicians at the state level have failed to improve the educational system so essential to provide a qualified work force and to attract business activity in their borders. In many cases, politicians have cut educational expenditures without taking into consideration the impact of this move on the quality of education or the impact this action would have on the future supply of qualified workers in their district, state, or nation. How can we expect a bright future when our corporate and political institutions are doing their best to dim it?

We need to encourage a major shift in the way our political and corporate leaders behave to cause a reversal in the trend leading the American people to poverty and eventually leading our corporate and governmental institutions to collapse. Neither our country nor our people can afford that. It is for that reason that I believe, a conversation is necessary to change our economic environment and provide a more solid foundation for our future and that of our nation and corporate entities. Our number one need is jobs for our people so that our nation may become wealthy again. More specifically, high paying jobs have to be created to reverse the poverty trend and to restore hope and optimism among our people.

We are facing a culture of greed that recognizes no boundary except what is financially beneficial to corporate and political leaders. It is a culture driving this country to the brink of ruin. Consequently, the only effective remedy to counteract that malignancy existing in corporate and political circles is to do things that financially and significantly impact corporate and political leaders. How can that be done? Consumers have the power of their consumer dollars and their votes to counteract corporate and political abuses, respectively. Government has the power to tax corporate compensation packages bearing no reasonable link to contributions made by executives or are excessive in comparison with salaries paid to other employees. At the same time, government has the power to impose punitive measures on corporations who contribute significant amounts of funds to political leaders and corrupts them; that has to stop if we ever expect to get rid of political corruption. It is only then that corporate and political leaders will realize Americans are unwilling to tolerate unethical and irresponsible behavior and force companies to generate executive compensation packages bearing a logical connection to their contributions to the entity and its profitability and end all political contributions which are basically bribes to politica leaders.

I remember the days when corporate executives and political leaders were held in high regards; they were role models for our children. Corporate leaders, in particular, adhered to high moral and ethical standards. Many politicians behaved ethically and acceptable manner even though there was always corruption in the political system. Now, it would appear about swindles and thievery taking place on a fairly routine basis leading one to wonder whether these individuals could really be trusted or emulated by our children. Corporate executives and political leaders once considered pillars of the community turned out to be nothing more than thieves and liars. If that represented a true picture of the character of individuals leading corporations and political institutions then we would realize our problem was much larger than we realized. Business would have to depend on creating relationship based on ethics, morality, and trust. If those attributes were lacking then our business climate would not be successful. Would you buy goods from thieves or liars? The majority of people would buy only from people they trust.

I remember the days when you would get on the nations' highways and see nothing but American cars. Nowadays, you see very few American branded automobiles and a lot of foreign branded automobiles on the road. This is an indication the country has undergone significant economic transformations. Granted many of those foreign branded cars are made in the US, which reinforces the continuing contributions of immigrants to this country. More importantly, why is it Corporate America leaders fail to see that a half empty glass is an opportunity to fill the glass as has been done by many foreign owned corporate executives such as those in the automobile industry?

I remember the days when Corporate America did most, if not all, of its research and development work in this country. Now, Corporate America is reduces research and development in this country and funds more activity in foreign countries. That's the cornerstone leading to relocation of manufacturing activities away from the US. Is that an indication our talent pool is too small, unqualified, or functionally unaffordable? If the pool of qualified investigators is too small then that may indicate young people see no benefit in pursuing careers in those fields of interest to Corporate America, young people are not sufficiently qualified, or that Corporate America prefers foreign talent either because it is cheaper or better qualified. These issues raise concerns about our future economic wellbeing and also about the quality of product from our educational system.

It is also apparent many developments and products coming out of research pipeline in this country are commercialized in foreign countries such as for example solar cell, cell phones, computers, and many other things. This indicates the US still has a qualified pool of talented people capable of developing creative solutions and developing new products. But, Corporate America still prefers to have those new products made in foreign locations thus risking the loss of new technology. It also risks losing the ability to scale up new technology and scientific developments from discovery to the commercialization stages. If Corporate America loses that ability then, for all practical purposes, the US would lose a powerful competitive advantage. This raises a very important challenge to claims by Corporate America that foreign actors are stealing its intellectual property. It seems Corporate America is giving away its intellectual property.

It is for those reasons the author believes it is necessary to focus attention on understanding issues preventing Corporate America from expanding economic activities in this country. It would then be possible to address those issues and implement solutions to lead to job creation for Americans in this country. There are many things that can be done to create jobs in this country.

It is necessary for the US to develop a realistic energy policy to ensure the US has access to energy sources required to power industrial activity. Energy is the cornerstone ensuring industrial activity and creating high paying jobs. The US is blessed with abundant reserves of hydrocarbons in terms of oil, gas, and coal that are necessary not only as fuels but also as essential raw materials for the production of foods, clothing, and medications. In short, these raw materials are essential for just about every product that we consume. An energy policy should encourage development of existing hydrocarbon resources as well as providing means to perfect alternate sources of energy. The end result of that policy would be energy independence as well as cost effective means of supplying raw materials. In addition, thousands of high paying jobs in many sectors of the economy would be created in the development of these sources of energy. A change in political leadership encouraging oil and gas exploration and production has caused the US to become energy independent and to be a net exporter of oil and gas.

An innovation policy is necessary to ensure US industry continues to work with government entities to develop new technologies and products in order to keep this country at the leading edge of scientific and engineering knowhow. There is no question government expenditures are essential to undertake basic research leading to new technologies and products not only for military applications but also useful for the development of products for the private sector. This also will result in the creation of thousands of jobs.

There is no question corporate abuses are increasing on a yearly basis and are having a detrimental impact on the private sector. These corporate abuses have to be eliminated by enactment and effective enforcement of existing laws and to establish a business climate based on morality, ethics, and trust. This would repair a corporate image that has been tarnished by inept executives and reestablishing trust and confidence among corporate suppliers, employees, and shareholders.

The regulatory system has to be overhauled to prevent unaccountable bureaucrats from strangling Corporate America and killing all incentive for job creation in this country. The regulatory system has to be made functional and capable of solving problems instead of punishing job creators. Regulatory agencies have to be disbanded or made accountable to the American people rather than being totally independent. It is possible to have beneficial effects from regulation without eliminating jobs. The time has come to act to make the private sector more efficient and creative rather than killing all incentive and strangling industry with unnecessary regulations. It has to be realized risk cannot be totally eliminated and that people's jobs have to be protected to the same extent as endangered species. In view of that, the regulatory system must focus on what is an acceptable level of risk. If these bureaucrats fail to do realistic societal costs and benefits analysis, they risk causing people to become endangered species.

The tax code is extremely burdensome and unfair; it has to be simplified and made fairer to all taxpayers. It is unthinkable that a corporation like GE makes $15 billion of profits and pays no income tax while unemployed workers have to pay income taxes on money received as unemployment compensation. It is hypocritical for President Obama to target oil companies while praising GE and seeking the advice of GE's CEO. Oil companies are paying their fair share of taxes and attempting to create jobs in this country only to be criticized on a continuous basis by President Obama.

Despite overwhelming evidence indicating raising taxes during an economic crisis would be disastrous to recovery from a recession, President Obama has indicated his intention to do exactly that in order to combat the Great Recession. The only reason for that is to get more power and to put more of our money at risk, and get more people on unemployment That also has the unwanted effect of destroying existing industry and forcing relocation to lower wage foreign nations at the expense of American workers. That rhetoric shows his intention to slow down the recovery and raises the level of unemployment at a time when he should be focused on reducing it and creating more jobs for American. He basically wants us as American citizens to become more dependent on government. This dependency undoubtedly leads to further federal control and to enslave citizenry to the will of inept and corrupt politicians. That same sentiment is shared by communist regimes, and you know how successful those regimes have been. President Obama is an inept corrupt politician favoring the destruction of our country so that other nations may become more powerful and relevant. Fortunately, President Trump has a more realistic vision of what our country and he is focused on making America great again.

Finally, it is important to realize that the most important asset a country has is its people. Consequently, it is essential to have a well educated people to become part of a highly qualified labor force to attract industry and create jobs. Yet, evidence indicates American students rank lower in terms of knowledge of science and math than foreign students. Significantly, the US spends quite a bit of money on education but gets poor results. Why is that? It is time to reevaluate our educational system and to recognize that qualified teachers are needed in the classroom. One way to attract qualified talent is to compensate teachers for the job they do and get rid of unnecessary overhead burdening the system and preventing achievement excellence in the classroom. It is time to emphasize academic activity rather than sports activities.

The economic crisis our nation faces during this recession in the 2009 – 2010 timeframe is one requiring innovative ideas and an overhaul of previous policies that have led us to the present state of affairs. There is no magic bullet to get this country back on the recovery road and to a better future for our children. We should all join together regardless of political affiliation to solve our common problems. It is time to stop all the political dickering in Washington DC and come up with solutions to create jobs. It is time for President Obama to quit being so divisive. President Obama and Congress should focus their attention and energy on job creation; that requires consideration of new ideas and not just a rerun of failed ones. It is time for President Obama to recognize raising taxes on millionaires does not solve our economic problems; millionaires leave the country and take their industry with the . The answer is to overhaul the tax system to make it equitable for everyone and not just GE.

Now that President Trump has taken power, we find a very upset group of democrats trying to overthrow a duly elected President of the United States. They are doing that by holding unnecessary investigations looking for reasons to impeach President Trump. In the last few months of his administration, President Obama does his level best to turn the IRS, FBI, Department of Justice and Intelligence Agencies against his political opponents to ensure democrats reap vengeance for losing the 2016 election. In that fashion, President Obama and his political allies hope to overthrow a duly elected President of the United States. Democrats are extremely upset because they have lost an election they would not have lost but for President Trump. There is a sad state of affairs existing in Washington, D.C.

Unlike Presidents Roosevelt, Truman, Kennedy, or Reagan, President Obama is not a leader. That lack of strong leadership raises the level of frustration of the citizenry and leads not only Americans but also the whole world to lose hope. Only those wanting to challenge US World leadership enjoy that lack of resolve and cross any red line drawn by President Obama. President Obama solves all problems by delivering a speech, drawing red lines with his crayons but there is no action or substance behind empty words. America deserves better and not just political demagoguery. President Obama keeps telling the American people we are in the horns of a dilemma. In my view, our country is indeed in the horn of a dilemma. There is a horn on the right and another horn on the left. But in between, there is a lot of bull. And, bull is not the answer. And that bull is coming from inept corrupt politicians who have never done a thing to earn a living except living at the expense of government. The answer is jobs and not bull! Luckily, President Trump is at the helm guiding the nation to new heights by eliminating all barriers imposed on Corporate America to prevent decisive action.

There are dark leadership clouds looming over our nation's horizon, and those clouds, if not blown away, would doom our future and destroy the American Dream in the hearts and minds of all Americans. Those dark clouds are rooted on anger and desperation.

The Democratic Party has undergone many very significant transformations over the past 30 to 40 years. In the past, most Democrats were centrists willing to work with opponents to achieve results. Now, most Democrats consider themselves "Socialist" Democrats with views mostly based on Communist views and ideology. And, the sad thing about this situation is that they fight among themselves to prove who can the most extreme leftist Democrat. These Socialist Democrats want to tear down our Constitution to ensure winning elections with minimum effort thereby releasing themselves of obligations to represent all Americans not just a few residing on both coasts. In other words, they would eliminate the Electoral College. They would change many Constitutionally protected rights such as right to own guns, impose restrictions on free speech, and due process under law, and many others. These Socialist Democrats would like to have every American depend on government handouts for everything and everything would be given free of charge. The question is who would pay for that? Since, these ideologues would confiscate all of our property and tax corporations and all of us to death. They fail to understand that what they are advocating is a perfect recipe for corporations to leave the country resulting in high unemployment. So what? They, like President Obama, believe the answer is that service jobs would be created. These low paying jobs at hamburger joins would enable Americans to supplement stipends provided by Government. The problem is, however, one of these Socialist Democrats advocates doing away with cows to prevent environmental contamination from gas released by these animals. There goes the hamburger joins. But the fortunate thing is that this same crazy Socialist Democrat predicts the world ends in 12 years. This is nothing more than Communist ideology. The question is how many countries under Communist rule have ever succeeded? Venezuela, Cuba, and North Korea are good examples of communist success. Is that what we want? I doubt it and pray these Communist in Democrats' attires are not successful. The American people have more sense than electing these clowns. They also want to have an unrestricted and uncontrolled immigration system. In short these Socialist Democrats want to destroy our country.

The most outlandish position held by all Socialist Democrats is their position on abortion; they willingly accept infanticide instead of providing birth control devices. Our country needs qualified people with common sense and not these political clowns to lead Corporate America and our political institutions.

REFERENCES

1. "Dow Chemical Co. has announced the dismissal of CEO Michael Parker and the appointment of William Stavropoulus" Industrial Paint and Powder, February 1, 2003.

2. "One Giant Chemical Company Agrees to Buy Another" HFN-The Weekly Newspaper for the Home Furnishing Network, July 6, 1998.

3. "Lyondell Petrochemical and ARCO Chemical Ratings put on S&P CreditWatch; Atlantic Richfield Affirmed" PR Newswire, June 18, 1998.

4. "Bayer buys Lyondell Polyols" Urethane Technology, December 1, 1999

5. "LyondellBasell's U.S. Operations file for bankruptcy" Houston Business Journal, January 7, 2009.

6. "Hathaway Closes Maine Factory, Last Major U.S. Shirt Plant" The New York Times, October 20, 2002.

7. "Put the Screws to Stanley Tools", opinion published by NY Daily News on May 5, 2002, (See: www.nydailynews.com/archives/opinions/2002/05/12).

8. "Chrysler Files to Seek Bankruptcy Protection" The New York Times, April 30, 2009.

9. "Chrysler to Make Fiat in Mexico" The Wall Street Journal, August 17, 2009.

10. "Toyota Boosts Alabama Plant" The Wall Street Journal, August 24, 2009.

11. " Why US Manufacturers need to Find Common Ground" Business Week, July 27, 2009, p.0.

12. "Union questions auto execs' pay packages", USATODAY.com, 10/10/2007 (www.usatoday.com).

13. "General Motors CEO Rick Wagoner's compensation valued at $14.9 million

14. Derived from Table 1 in US Department of Homeland Security, Office of Immigration Statistics, Yearbook of Immigration Statistics 2008. Available at

15. www.dhs.gov/ximgtn/statistics/publications/LPR08.shtm

16. Congressional Record April 19, 1999, Page E822.

17. Derived from Table 1 in US Department of Homeland Security

Office of Immigration Statistics, Yearbook of Immigration Statistics 2008Available online: www.dhs.gov/ximgtn/statistics/publications/LPR08.shtm.

18. Who Was Shut O?: Immigration Quotas, 1925–1927, http://historymatters.gmu.edu/d/5078/.

19. 22 Stat. 58

20. Catherine Lee, "Prostitutes and Picture Brides: Chinese and Japanese Immigration, Settlement, and American National Building, 1870-1920", Center for Comparative Immigration Studies, February 2003

21. 27 Stat. 25

22. 57 Stat. 600-1

23. 79 Stat. 911

24. Executive Order 589

25. Raymond L. Cohn, Illinois State University, Immigration to the United States, http://eh.net/encyclopedia/article/cohn.immigration.us.

26. 1913 OK CR 42, 8 Okl.Cr.686, 130 P.316

27. Mary Bellis, "The Cotton Gin and Eli Whitney," Background and Patent on the Cotton Mill, http://inventors.about.com/od/cstartinventions/a/cotton_gin_2.htm.

28. "Samuel Slater Biography (1768 – 1835)", www.madehow.com/inventorbios/19/Samuel-Slater.html.

29. "Francis Cabot Lowell", Albert Barnor and Lynn E. Browne, Federal Reserve Bank of Boston, July 2003, www.economicadventure.org.

30. Mary Bellis, "Elias Howe was the inventor of the first American-patented sewing machine", http://inventors.about.com/od/hstartinventors/a/Elias_Howe.htm

31. Mary Bellis, "Biography of Thomas Elias", http://inventors.about.com/od/estartinventors/a/Edison_Bio.htm.

32. Mary Bellis, "George Westinghouse-The History of Electricity" http://inventors.about.com/library/inventors/blwestinghouse.htm

33. J. Bradford DeLong, "Slouching Towards Utopia?: The Economic History of the Twentieth Century – XIII. The Roaring Twenties", University of California at Berkeley, February 1997.

34. http://www.j-bradford-delong.net/TCEH/Slouch_roaring13.html

35. "Duco ® Paint: 1923", DuPont Heritage, http://www2.dupont. com/Heritage/en_US/1923_dupont/1923_duco_indepth.html.

36. Ralph C. Epstein, "Industrial Profits in Prosperity and Depression 1919-1932", National Bureau of Economic Research Inc., Number 44, January 27, 1933.

37. "Historical Corporate Top Tax Rate and Bracket", www. taxpolicycenter.org/taxfacts.

38. http://www.usgovernmentrevenue.com/yearrev1920_0.html.

39. Daniel J. Mitchell, "The Historical Lessons of Lower Taxes" The Heritage Foundation, WebMemo #327, August 13, 2003, www. heritage.org.

40. Paul A. Gusmorino III, "Main Causes of the Great Depression." Gusmorino World (May 13, 1996). www.gusmorino.com/pag3/ greatdepression/index.html

41. Gene Smiley, "The US Economy in the 1920s", http://eh.net/ encyclopedia/article/Smiley.1920s.final.

42. "Great Depression Timeline", http://www.amatecon.com/gd/ gdtimeline.html

43. Robert VanGiezen and Albert A. Schwenk, "Compensation from before World War I through the Great Depression, Bureau of Labor Statistics, January 30, 2003. www.bls.gov/opub/cwc/ cm20030124ar03pl.htm.

44. Selected Equipment Production Figures World War II, http:// www.taphilo.com/history/WWII/Production-Figures-WWII. shtml

45. World War II aircraft production, http://en.wikipedia.org/wiki/ World_War_II_aircraft_production.

46. Military production during World War II, http://en.wikipedia. org/wiki/Military_production_during_World_War_II.

47. http://www.centennialofflight.gov/essay/Aerospace/WWII_ Industry/Aero7.htm.

48. US Private Sector Trade Union Market Share Loss Continues 40 Years Uninterrupted, http://www.demographia.com/lm-unn99. htm.

49. Richard E. Schumann, Compensation from World War II through the Great Society, http://www.bls.gov/opub/cwc/ cm20030124ar04p1.htm#author1.

50. G.T. Westbrook, A Salute to the WWII Pioneers in the Petroleum Refining & Chemical Industries, http://www.cems.umn.edu/

downloads/alumni/Tribute_To_C._Geankoplis_G_Westbrook. pdf.

51. The History of WWII Medicine, The Discovery of Penicillin, http://home.att.net/~steinert/wwii.htm

52. Labor Force Statistics from the Current Population Survey, http://data.bls.gov/PDQ/servlet/SurveyOutputServlet.

53. Bureau of Economic Analysis - National Economic Accounts, Table 1-12, National Income by Income Type, http://www.bea.gov/national/nipaweb/SelectTable.asp.

54. Marshall Plan, http://en.wikipedia.org/wiki/Marshall_Plan.

55. Occupation and Reconstruction of Japan, 1945-52, US Department of State, http://www.state.gov/r/pa/ho/time/cwr/91194.htm.

56. Thayer Watkins, The Physical and Institutional Reconstruction of Japan after World War II, http://www.sjsu.edu/faculty/watkins/japanrecov.htm.

57. Maciamo, Japan's postwar economic miracle (1950-1990), http://www.jref.com/society/japan_postwar_economic_miracle.shtml

58. Stanley K. Schultz, The 1950s: The Cold War and the Affluent Society http://us.history.wisc.edu/hist102/lectures/lecture24.html.

59. Glen E. Bugos, The History of the Aerospace Industry, http://eh.net/encyclopedia/article/bugos.aerospace.industry.history.

60. Measuring Worth, Six Ways to Compute the Relative Value of a U.S. Dollar Amount, 1774 to Present, http://www.measuringworth.com/uscompare/.

61. Martin Calhoun, U.S. Military Spending, 1945-1996, Center for Defense Information, http://www.cdi.org/Issues/milspend.html.

62. Strong Growth Predicted for Industrial R&D, Chemical & Engineering News, September 1, 1997, http://pubs.acs.org/cen/hotarticles/cenear/970901/industry.html.

63. Budget Information, http://www.nasa.gov/news/budget/index.html.

64. Stephen J. Dubner, Is Space Exploration Worth the Cost? A Freakonomics Quorum, http://freakonomics.blogs.nytimes.com/2008/01/11/is-space-exploration-worth-the-cost-a-freakonomics-quorum/.

65. Matt Apuzzo, Meltdown: Federal regulators rewarded despite failures, Business Section, Houston Chronicle, March 19, 2010.

66. James Graham, The Collapse of the Soviet Union, http://www.historyorb.com/russia/intro.shtml

67. US Natural Gas Well Head Prices, US Energy Information Administration, http://tonto.eia.doe.gov/dnav/ng/hist/n9190us3A.htm

68. Historical Crude Oil Prices, http://www.inflationdata.com/inflation/Inflation_Rate/Historical_Oil_Prices_Table.asp.

69. Loren Steffy, "Wouldn't you like to quit and make millions?", Houston Chronicle, Vol. 109, No. 99, January 20, 2010.

70. Mitch Ratcliffe, "Bad Idea Dept.: AT&T's Ed Whitacre to run General Motors" June 9, 2009, http://blogs.zdnet.com/Ratcliffe/?p=409.

71. Bruce Nussbaum, "Lessons from Home Depot's Bob Nardelli--Why command and control Is so bad", January 04, 2007, http://www.businessweek.com/innovate/NussbaumOnDesign/archives/2007/01/lessons_from_ho.html.

72. Portfolio's Worst American CEOs of All Time, http://www.cnbc.com/id/30502091?slide=5.

73. Brett Clanton, ConocoPhillips Chief zeros in on returns, Houston Chronicle, pg.D3, March 25, 2010.

74. Jessica Silver-Greenberg et al., "CEO Pay Drops, But…Cash is King" Business Week, pg 50, April 5, 2010.

75. Tara Kalwarski, "Top Innovators", page 76, Bloomberg Business Week, April 5, 2010.

76. Frank Green, "Ex-DuPont employee sentenced for espionage", March 19, 2010, Richmond Times Dispatch.

77. Alan Ohnsman et al, "The Humbling of Toyota", page 32, March 22 &29, 2010, Bloomberg Business Week.

78. Measuring Worth: Annual Inflation Rates in the US, http://www.measuringworth.com/inflation/.

79. http://www.federalreserve.gov/Releases/H15/data.htm

80. Unemployment Rate: Labor Force Statistics from the Current Population Survey, Bureau of Labor Statistics, ftp://ftp.bls.gov/pub/special.requests/lf/aat1.txt.

81. Dan Fost, Mergers a rite of passage in life of U.S. companies, December 19, 2004 http://w4.stern.nyu.edu/news/news.cfm?doc_id=3741.

82. Pfizer Scaling down for 2011, page 24, Bloomberg BusinessWeek, May 24-May 30, 2010

83. Leadership in a Complex Society, This is Dow Corporate Responsibility, http://www.dowethics.com/r/about/corp/newleader.htm.

84. U.S. Trade in Goods and Services - Balance of Payments (BOP) Basis, http://www.census.gov/foreign-trade/statistics/historical/gands.txt.

85. http://www.census.gov/foreign-trade/statistics/historical/petr.pdf.

86. Historical Crude Oil Prices, http://www.inflationdata.com/inflation/Inflation_Rate/Historical_Oil_Prices_Table.asp.

87. Top 10 Crooked CEOs, Time Magazine, http://www.time.com/time/specials/packages/article/0,28804,1903155_1903156_1903152,00.html.

88. Gasparino, Charles, "The Sellout", page 39, Harper Collins Publishers, 2009.

89. Stephen Bernard, "Stock market slumps as Goldman charged", Houston Chronicle, April 17, 2010.

90. Gregory Zuckerman, "Paulson Point Man on CDO Deal Emerges as Key Figure", The Wall Street Journal, April 19, 2010, http://finance.yahoo.com/retirement/article/109342/paulson-point-man-on-cdo-deal-emerges-as-key-figure?mod=retire&sec=topStories&pos=2&asset=&ccode

91. Louise Story et al., "SEC accuses Goldman of fraud in housing deal", Houston Chronicle, April 17, 2010.

92. "Divorce Decree in Cendant Case", Houston Chronicle, November 18, 2009.

93. Steve Eder et al., (Reuters), "Goldman's "Fabulous" Fab's conflicted love letters", April 26, 2010, http://finance.yahoo.com/news/Goldmans-Fabulous-Fabs-rb-932699120.html?x=0&sec=topStories&pos=6&asset=&ccode=.

94. Ken Bryson et al., "Co-resident Grandparents and Grandchildren", Current Population Reports, Special Studies, Census Bureau, May 1999, http://www.census.gov/prod/99pubs/p23-198.pdf.

95. Daniel Wagner, "Watchdog: SEC officials viewed porn as economy collapsed", Houston Chronicle, April 23, 2010.

96. Edward L. Barrett, "Constitutional Law—Cases and Materials", University Casebook Series, Fifth Edition, April 1977, Foundation Press, page 10.

97. Politicians and Elections in Influence & Lobbying, http://www.opensecrets.org/lobby/index.php

98. "U.S. child mortality rate slips to 42nd", Chicago Tribune, May 24, 2010, http://www.omaha.com/article/20100524/AP09/705249903

99. "Supreme Court Removes Limits on Corporate, Labor Donations to Campaigns", http://www.foxnews.com/politics/2010/01/21/supreme-court-sides-hillary-movie-filmmakers-campaign-money-dispute/.

100. J.O. Boyd, "The Court System Contrasted with the Bureau System", Iowa Bar Rev., 25, 28, 29 (1938-1939).

101. Paul Bedard, "Scientist: Carbon Dioxide Doesn't Cause Global Warming", October 7, 2009, http://www.usnews.com/news/blogs/washington-whispers/2009/10/07/scientist-carbon-dioxide-doesnt-cause-global-warming.

102. "Ronald Reagan Tear Down This Wall Speech", The History Place, Great Speeches Collection, http://www.historyplace.com/speeches/reagan-tear-down.htm.

103. Sam Dillon, "Study Compares States' Math and Science Scores with Other Countries'", November 14, 2007, http://www.nytimes.com/2007/11/14/education/14students.html.

104. How Does the United States Stack Up? International Comparisons of Academic Achievement, Alliance for Excellent Education Fact Sheet, March 2008, http://www.all4ed.org/files/IntlComp_FactSheet.pdf.

105. Education Statistics: Spending per Secondary School Student, http://www.nationmaster.com/graph/edu_spe_per_sec_sch_stu-spending-per-secondary-school-student

106. List of Countries by GDP, http://en.wikipedia.org/wiki/List_of_countries_by_GDP_(PPP)_per_capita.

107. Compared to other countries, US Flunks in Teacher Pay, Economic Policy Institute, April 1, 2008, http://www.epi.org/economic_snapshots/entry/webfeatures_snapshots_20080402/

108. National Voter Turnout in Federal Elections: 1960–2008; http://www.infoplease.com/ipa/A0781453.html.

109. Peter Coy, "The Wailing Wall", page 7, Bloomberg BusinessWeek, May 3-May 9, 2010.

110. Energy Imports, The World Bank, http://data.worldbank.org/indicator/EG.IMP.CONS.ZS.

111. About Coal, Clean-energy.US, http://www.clean-energy.us/facts/coal.htm.

112. Preston v. Bacon, 4 Conn. 480

113. Tom Doggett, Not Expanding Drilling May Cost US $2.4 trillion, http://www.reuters.com/article/idUSTRE61B2R520100216

114. Projected Costs of Generating Electricity, Executive Summary, International Energy Agency (IEA), http://www.iea.org/Textbase/npsum/ElecCostSUM.pdf.

115. S. Michael Hudson, Fall IUGREE Workshop, Nov. 1, 1999, http://www.eng.iastate.edu/iugreee/hudson/sld002.htm.

116. Government Revenues Downloads, http://www.usgovernmentrevenue.com/downloadmult_gr.php?year=1940_2008.

117. Projected Costs of Generating Electricity, Executive Summary, International Energy Agency (IEA), http://www.iea.org/Textbase/npsum/ElecCostSUM.pdf.

118. http://www.usgovernmentrevenue.com/yearrev1920_0.html

119. "U.S. child mortality rate slips to 42nd", Chicago Tribune, May 24, 2010, http://www.omaha.com/article/20100524/AP09/705249903

120. Politicians and Elections in Influence & Lobbying, http://www.opensecrets.org/lobby/index.php

121. Politicians and Elections in Influence & Lobbying, http://www.opensecrets.org/lobby/index.php

122. "Supreme Court Removes Limits on Corporate, Labor Donations to Campaigns", http://www.foxnews.com/politics/2010/01/21/supreme-court-sides-hillary-movie-filmmakers-campaign-money-dispute/.

123. "Supreme Court Removes Limits on Corporate, Labor Donations to Campaigns", http://www.foxnews.com/politics/2010/01/21/supreme-court-sides-hillary-movie-filmmakers-campaign-money-dispute/

124. J.O. Boyd, "The Court System Contrasted with the Bureau System", Iowa Bar Rev., 25, 28, 29 (1938-1939).

125. Paul Bedard, "Scientist: Carbon Dioxide Doesn't Cause Global Warming", October 7, 2009, http://www.usnews.com/news/blogs/washington-whispers/2009/10/07/scientist-carbon-dioxide-doesnt-cause-global-warming.

126. Obama Bars Toughened Smog Rules, Houston Chronicle, Sept 3, 2011.

127. 29 CFR Parts 1926.1053 et seq.

128. "Ronald Reagan Tear Down This Wall Speech", The History

Place, Great Speeches Collection, http://www.historyplace.com/speeches/reagan-tear-down.htm.

129. Nelson Mandela, www.brainyquote.com

130. Sam Dillon, "Study Compares States' Math and Science Scores with Other Countries'", November 14, 2007, http://www.nytimes.com/2007/11/14/education/14students.html.

131. How Does the United States Stack Up? International Comparisons of Academic Achievement, Alliance for Excellent Education Fact Sheet, March 2008, http://www.all4ed.org/files/IntlComp_FactSheet.pdf.

132. List of Countries by GDP, http://en.wikipedia.org/wiki/List_of_countries_by_GDP_(PPP)_per_capita

133. Compared to other countries, US Flunks in Teacher Pay, Economic Policy Institute, April 1, 2008, http://www.epi.org/economic_snapshots/entry/webfeatures_snapshots_20080402/

134. National Voter Turnout in Federal Elections: 1960–2008; http://www.infoplease.com/ipa/A0781453.html.

135. Peter Coy, "The Wailing Wall", page 7, Bloomberg BusinessWeek, May 3-May 9, 2010.

136. Quote / Counterquote – www.quotecounterquote.com/2010/06

137. US Government Revenue.com.

138. Government Revenues Downloads, http://www.usgovernmentrevenue.com/downloadmult_gr.php?year=1940_2008

139. Bureau of Economic Analysis - National Economic Accounts, Table 1-12, National Income by Income Type, http://www.bea.gov/national/nipaweb/SelectTable.asp.

140. Poverty level near 20 year high, Houston Chronicle, September 14, 2011